Lecture Notes in Artificial Intelligence 11097

Subseries of Lecture Notes in Computer Science

More information about this series at http://www.springer.com/series/1244

Andrey Ronzhin · Gerhard Rigoll
Roman Meshcheryakov (Eds.)

Interactive Collaborative Robotics

Third International Conference, ICR 2018
Leipzig, Germany, September 18–22, 2018
Proceedings

 Springer

Editors
Andrey Ronzhin 🆔
St. Petersburg Institute for Informatics
  and Automation of the Russian Academy
  of Sciences
St. Petersburg
Russia

Roman Meshcheryakov 🆔
Institute for Control Problem of the Russian
  Academy of Sciences
Moscow
Russia

Gerhard Rigoll 🆔
TU Munich
Munich
Germany

ISSN 0302-9743   ISSN 1611-3349 (electronic)
Lecture Notes in Artificial Intelligence
ISBN 978-3-319-99581-6   ISBN 978-3-319-99582-3 (eBook)
https://doi.org/10.1007/978-3-319-99582-3

Library of Congress Control Number: 2018952053

LNCS Sublibrary: SL7 – Artificial Intelligence

This Springer imprint is published by the registered company Springer Nature Switzerland AG
The registered company address is: Gewerbestrasse 11, 6330 Cham, Switzerland

Preface

The Third International Conference on Interactive Collaborative Robotics (ICR) was organized as a satellite event of the jubilee 20th International Conference on Speech and Computer (SPECOM) by St. Petersburg Institute for Informatics and Automation of the Russian Academy of Science (SPIIRAS, St. Petersburg, Russia), Technical University of Munich (TUM, Munich, Germany), and Tomsk State University of Control Systems and Radioelectronics (TUSUR, Tomsk, Russia).

Challenges of human–robot interaction, robot control, and behavior in social robotics and collaborative robotics as well as applied robotic and cyberphysical systems are mainly discussed during the conference.

ICR 2018 was hosted by the Leipzig University of Telecommunications (HfT Leipzig) in cooperation with SPIIRAS, TUM, and TUSUR. The conference was held during September 18–22, 2018, at HfT Leipzig, a private university of applied sciences funded by Deutsche Telekom and located in the middle of a popular student and nightlife district in the south of Leipzig, Germany.

During the conference, an invited talk on "Robot Learning Through Physical Interaction and Human Guidance" was given by Prof. Dongheui Lee (Technical University of Munich and Human-Centered Assistive Robotics Group at the German Aerospace Center, DLR, Germany).

This volume contains a collection of 30 accepted papers presented at the conference, which were thoroughly reviewed by members of the Program Committee consisting of more than 20 top specialists in the conference topic areas. Theoretical and more general contributions were presented in common (plenary) sessions. Problem-oriented sessions as well as panel discussions then brought together specialists in limited problem areas with the aim of exchanging knowledge and skills resulting from research projects of all kinds.

Last but not least, we would like to express our gratitude to the authors for providing their papers on time, to the members of the conference reviewing team and Program Committee for their careful reviews and paper selection, and to the editors for their hard work preparing this volume. Special thanks are due to the members of the local Organizing Committee for their tireless effort and enthusiasm during the conference organization. We hope that all attendees benefitted from the event and also enjoyed the social program prepared by the members of the Organizing Committee.

September 2018

Andrey Ronzhin
Gerhard Rigoll
Roman Meshcheryakov

Organization

The conference ICR 2018 was organized by the Leipzig University of Telecommunications, in cooperation with St. Petersburg Institute for Informatics and Automation of the Russian Academy of Science (SPIIRAS, St. Petersburg, Russia), Technical University of Munich (TUM, Munich, Germany), and Tomsk State University of Control Systems and Radioelectronics (TUSUR, Tomsk, Russia). The conference website is located at: http://specom.nw.ru/icr2018/.

Program Committee

Roman Meshcheryakov
(Co-chair), Russia
Gerhard Rigoll (Co-chair), Germany
Andrey Ronzhin (Co-chair), Russia
Christos Antonopoulos, Greece
Branislav Borovac, Serbia
Sara Chaychian, UK
Ivan Ermolov, Russia
Oliver Jokisch, Germany
Dimitrios Kalles, Greece
Igor Kalyaev, Russia
Alexey Kashevnik, Russia
Gerhard Kraetzschmar, Germany

Dongheui Lee, Germany
Iosif Mporas, UK
Vladmir Pavlovkiy, Russia
Viacheslav Pshikhopov, Russia
Mirko Rakovic, Serbia
Yulia Sandamirskaya, Switzerland
Jesus Savage, Mexico
Hooman Samani, Taiwan
Evgeny Shandarov, Russia
Lev Stankevich, Russia
Tilo Strutz, Germany
Sergey Yatsun, Russia

Organizing Committee

Oliver Jokisch (Chair)
Ingo Siegert
Tilo Strutz
Michael Maruschke
Gunnar Auth
Alexey Karpov

Andrey Ronzhin
Anton Saveliev
Alexander Denisov
Ekaterina Miroshnikova
Dmitry Ryumin
Natalia Kashina

Contents

Task and Spatial Planning by the Cognitive Agent with Human-Like Knowledge Representation

Ermek Aitygulov[1], Gleb Kiselev[2,3], and Aleksandr I. Panov[1,3(✉)]

[1] Moscow Institute of Physics and Technology, Moscow, Russia
aytygulov@phystech.edu, panov.ai@mipt.ru
[2] National Research University Higher School of Economics, Moscow, Russia
[3] Federal Research Center "Computer Science and Control" of the Russian Academy of Sciences, Moscow, Russia
kiselev@isa.ru

Abstract. The paper considers the task of simultaneous learning and planning actions for moving a cognitive agent in two-dimensional space. Planning is carried out by an agent who uses an anthropic way of knowledge representation that allows him to build transparent and understood planes, which is especially important in case of human-machine interaction. Learning actions to manipulate objects is carried out through reinforcement learning and demonstrates the possibilities of replenishing the agent's procedural knowledge. The presented approach was demonstrated in an experiment in the Gazebo simulation environment.

Keywords: Cognitive agent · Sign · Sign-based world model
Human-like knowledge representation · Behavior planning
Pseudo-physical logic · Reinforcement learning · Spatial planning
Task planning

1 Introduction

One of the main tasks researchers are facing with in the field of robotics and artificial intelligence is the task of ensuring the effective interaction of robots and people in collaborative scenarios, i.e. when a person and a machine perform joint actions in a shared environment. To solve this problem the questions arise of arranging the operation the robotic system in such a way that its actions are transparent, predictable and quickly interpretable by a person, in other words, it is necessary that the robot's behavior be human-like in cases of human-machine interaction becomes especially urgent. One of the directions of scientific research aimed at solving this issue is the direction for the development of cognitive agents, i.e. such intelligent agents who would learn and plan their actions using approaches based on cognitive models of human behavior [1,2].

© Springer Nature Switzerland AG 2018
A. Ronzhin et al. (Eds.): ICR 2018, LNAI 11097, pp. 1–12, 2018.
https://doi.org/10.1007/978-3-319-99582-3_1

In this paper, we consider the task of developing a cognitive agent that plans to move in space and actions to manipulate objects using the so-called sign-based world model [3–5]. This way of knowledge representation about the environment, the agent himself and other participants in joint activities is based on the psychological theories of Leontyev's activity [6] and Vygotsky's cultural-historical approach [7], which ensures his simple interpretation by human. In this paper, the agents world model is spatial procedural and declarative knowledge that use pseudo-physical logic [8], created with the use of psychological data on the human-like spatial reasoning. Spatial knowledge constructed by analyzing the map using egocentric coordinates allows maintaining the agent's autonomy regardless of the state of the "center", and various levels of map representation reduce the requirements for its computing resources.

The agent's actions planning, carried out within the world model, is also psychologically plausible. We leave out the details of the reactive functions [9, 10] and the algorithms for recognizing the objects of the surrounding space significant for the agent [11]. The presented in the paper algorithm of spatialMAP planning is hierarchical and abstracts from the details of the implementation of an action, solving the task of creating a sequence of abstract agent actions (moving, rotating, picking up an object), which will lead to the set goal. At each iteration of the plan execution, the planner can be restarted, which makes it possible to make a more detailed plan for implementing the abstract action.

The world model of a cognitive agent can be replenished through learning. In this paper, complex actions to move objects are constructed through reinforcement learning through the TRPO algorithm [12], which allows to optimize the strategies of choosing smaller actions with guaranteed monotonous improvement. The constructed functions, the control over which is transmitted every time after obtaining the appropriate prescription from the planning algorithm, allow to interact with different kinds of objects without classifying the methods of interactions and having only an abstract description of the required state at the end of the action. After the successful completion of the learning algorithm and the performance of the action, the action is saved as an experience and re-learning is no longer required.

The cognitive agent described in this paper is able to function in real environments, which is experimentally confirmed in simulations in Gazebo. Also, work is underway to implement experiments in real conditions with a robotic system that includes a platform allowing the movement of the agent, an arm similar to the one for the Turtlebot 2, as well as the camera, lidar and other sensors.

The paper is organized as follows. Part 2 presents the formulation of the problem of planning the movements of a cognitive agent, and briefly describes the algorithm for the operation of the cognitive agent. Part 3 provides an overview of modern methods of planning movements using pseudo-physical logics, as well as a comparison of reinforcement learning algorithms. Part 4 provides a detailed implementation of the planning and reinforcement learning algorithm. Part 5 contains a description of the experiments performed.

2   Problem Statement

The goal driven behavior of the cognitive agent is realized through an iterative procedure, which consists of 3 basic steps:

1. Agents learning.
2. Planning actions to achieve the target situation.
3. Plan implementation in the environment.

Agents learning is based on the reinforcement learning approach, for the implementation of which the algorithm TRPO is used. Learning takes place in a synthetic environment, which is a minimalistic model of the environment, containing only the information necessary for learning. Reinforcement learning is a machine learning tool that allows an agent to develop the desired behavior strategy based on the environmental response. This method uses a system of penalties and rewards for the actions of the agent, which allows you to take into account the experience of previous interactions. To describe the activity of a cognitive agent, a probability distribution $\pi(o|s)$ is used that characterizes the probability of an agent choosing an action o in a state s. Probability distribution π is called a strategy: $\pi(o|s) = P(o_t = o|s_t = s)$.

The agent, following the strategy, applies the actions and passes from the state to the state, receiving for it a reward r, which can be either positive or negative.

As an evaluation of the strategy, a value $\eta(\pi)$ is considered that is the mathematical expectation of the discounted remuneration for the whole session:

$$\eta(\pi) = E_\pi[\sum_{t=0}^{\infty} \gamma^t r(s_t)].$$

The TRPO algorithm described in this paper uses a surrogate function, the maximization of which, with the right choice of step, entails optimizing the value $\eta(\pi)$. Combining with the algorithm Natural policy gradient [13] greatly improves the work of the algorithm.

In the case of using as a goal situation for reinforcement learning some sub-goal in the overall task of planning, the result is a sequence of actions (strategy) to achieve this sub-goal. After the formation of such meta-actions for the sub-goals follows the process of planning actions. The plan P to achieve a set of facts G (the target state of a cognitive agent) is a sequence of pairs, where $a_0...a_N$ is the set of actions of the agent, and $\sum_0, ..., \sum_N$ a set of states such that $G \subseteq \sum_N$. The plan P describes the process of solving the planning problem.

The planning problem consists of a description of the initial situation S, the final situation F, and the planning domain $D = \langle T, R, \Pr, A \rangle$. The description of the situation S in the spatial planning case we are considering contains the initial coordinates of the objects on the agent map, the boundaries of the map, as well as a description of the agent's state (its direction and the state of the manipulator). The situation description F contains the final coordinates of the objects, the agent and the map constraints. Planning domain includes description of object types, description of roles R (abstract classes, for example "block?x", "direction-start", "region?y"), description of predicates and actions. Predicates express relationships between objects (predicate "ontable"), agent status ("manipulator empty", "agent direction") and spatial logic of the problem (predicates "close", "close", "far"). The predicates of spatial logic are interrelated in such a way that the predicate description for any distance, except for the "close" distance, consists of predicates of smaller distances to intermediate objects. Actions $\forall a \in A, a = \langle n, Cnd, Eff \rangle$ have the form, where n - the name of the action, Cnd - the facts describing the condition for the applicability of the action, but Eff - the facts that are actualized as a result of the application of the action.

The implementation of the plan is carried out in the Gazebo simulation environment, where a step-by-step execution of the plan takes place and the knowledge about the agent's capabilities obtained using the TRPO algorithm is used.

3   Related Works

The spatial representation of the planning task requires the cognitive agent to know the function of estimating distances, the possibility of representing and manipulating spatial quantities in its own world model. Most of the approaches that have been developed in this area can be divided into three areas: spatial-network approaches, approaches based on biologically plausible representation of the environment and approaches based on the psychological representation of knowledge.

Spatial-network approaches [14,15] do not require knowledge of the environment used by cognitive agents, but are among the most common approaches in robotics when using mobile non-intelligent systems. The description of their activities is reduced to the partition of the map of the area into cells and the transitions of agents through these cells. The advantage of these approaches over the others is the speed of building an action plan, as inadequacies can be distinguished inapplicability in real conditions with a previously unknown or partially known map of the environment.

The biological approach is typical for tasks that do not require the agent's conceptual general knowledge of the environment. In most cases, the agent is not intelligent, but is able to make simple deductive assumptions about changes in the environment. In [16], a model based on studies of rat's brain activity is described [17–19]. The model describes a hierarchical environment represented by maps of different scales. Planning of movement takes into account all possible goals of achieving the goal, which requires a large amount of resources for calculating possible changes in activity, taking into account the dynamics of environmental changes. This problem was partially addressed in [20,21], which led to the creation of the RatSLAM system, which allowed the agent to travel long distances in real terrain.

Within the framework of a psychologically plausible approach to the issue of agent action planning, problems associated with the incompleteness and inaccuracy of the description of the environment are considered. To solve the tasks set, a wide range of ways of representing the agent's knowledge is used, many of which allow approximating knowledge of the environment up to the level required for action planning. In [22,23], an approach is considered in which the spatial model is perceived by an artificial agent as a set of the most likely actions in the current position of the agent, which approximates the representation of the spatial relationships of the artificial agent to the representation that is used by human.

In this paper we describe an approach that takes into account the merits of the hierarchical representation of the map by the agent, the possible incompleteness of knowledge about the objects of the map and the dynamics of its change. Sign-based knowledge representation formalism allows an agent to cooperate with other cognitive agents [24] and create a plan consisting of actions based on the pseudo-physical logic of the spatial relationships of the location of objects on the map. The approach uses not only actions to move the agent, but also actions that manipulate the surrounding objects. For this, the capabilities of the reinforcement learning algorithm were used. The reinforcement learning algorithms can be conditionally divided into two groups: based on the choice of strategy by maximizing the value function and based on the search for an optimal strategy in the strategy space [29]. Examples of reinforcement learning algorithms based on utility maximization are the algorithms described in [25,26]. The algorithm of Q-learning [27] for the robotic system manipulator was applied, the reward depended on the distance from the part of the manipulator responsible for capture the target. The space of actions was discrete. An example of the application of the first approach in the continuum of action is the work [28]. To make a decision the agent trained according to the method from the first group compares the value of the utility function of each action, and in spite of the fact that this approach makes the algorithms flexible in application to various tasks, in some problems it is inefficient. Algorithms of the second group change the strategy directly without spending time on evaluating all actions. TRPO [12], used in this work, which allows to work in the continuum of action space, belongs to the second group and in the search for strategy changes parameters only in a certain neighborhood, therefore it converges along a smoother trajectory.

4 Synthesis of Behavior of Cognitive Agent

4.1 Human-Like Knowledge Representation

A sign representation of the agent's knowledge was proposed in [3,30]. The sign is a tuple of four components $s = \langle n, p, m, a \rangle$, where n - is the component of the name, p - the component of the image, m - the component of the significance, a - the component of the personal meaning. Signs can mediate both elementary objects and complex actions. The same semantic networks describe the components of the sign, whose nodes are special structures called causal matrices [5]. Causal matrices are structured sets of references to other signs and elementary features. Each of the sign components corresponds to a certain type of information, for example, the sign image component describes the process of object recognition and categorization. The significance component represents the agent's knowledge of the environment, and the component of the personal meaning describes the agent's preferences and the nature of his activity. The name component allows you to make a naming process, i.e. link the remaining components into a single logical structure.

The main task of the spatialMAP algorithm described in this paper is the synthesis of the plan for moving the agent with the sign-based world model on the map and the agent's implementation of the interaction with the objects that are located on it. In the agent's world model, the map is displayed using the signs of cells and regions [24], which are assigned to the agent in advance based on pseudo-physical logic. At the recognition stage, the agent divides it into 9 regions, the size of which depends only on the characteristics of the card itself, and associates them with the signs "Region-0" - "Region-8". Next, the agent looks at the region in which it is located. If no objects are present in the region, the agent connects the "Cell" and "Cell-4" signs with this area and builds around it a focus of attention that describes the current situation consisting of 9 cells. If there are any objects in the region, the agent recursively divides the region into 9 parts until a segment of the map containing only agent is formed. After this, the focus formation procedure described above is followed. Next, causal matrices are formed on a network of values for the "Location" and "Contain" signs (see Fig.1), which describe the location of all regions and cells relative to the cell with the agent, as well as the objects that are in them.

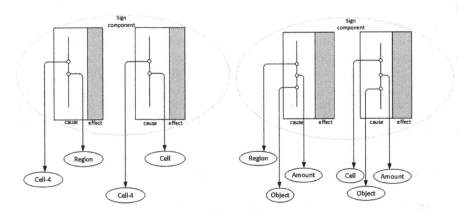

Fig. 1. Causal matrices of the the "Location" and "Contain" signs.

After this follows the process of formation of causal matrices of the initial and final situations and map that are required for the synthesis of the action plan (the process is shown in Algorithm 1). Matrices of situations consist of references to signs describing the relationship at the focus of attention of the agent, consisting of cells and the agent itself (its direction and the state of the manipulator). The map matrices describe the status of the task map on a more abstract level and contain references to the regions signs.

4.2   SpatialMAP Algorithm

The process of plan synthesis is implemented using the spatialMAP algorithm and allows you to build an action plan from the initial to the finish situations of the planning task. The input to the algorithm is given a description of the situations and the planning domain that is required to refine the predicates and actions applicable in the present task.

---

1 $T_{agent} := GROUND(map, struct)$
2 $Plan := MAP\_SEARCH(T_{agent})$
3 **Function** MAP_SEARCH($z_{sit-cur}, z_{sit-goal}, z_{map-cur}, z_{map-goal}, plan, i$):
4   **if** $i > i_{\max}$ **then**
5   **return** $\emptyset$
6   **end**
7      $z_{sit-cur}, z_{map-cur} = Z^a_{sit-start}, Z^a_{map-start}$
8      $z_{sit-goal}, z_{map-goal} = Z^a_{sit-goal}, Z^a_{map-goal}$
9      $Act_{chains} = getsitsigns\,(z_{sit-cur})$
10   **for** $chain$ in Act_{chains} **do**
11         $A_{signif}| = abstract\_actions\,(chain)$
12   **end**
13   **for** z_{signif} in A_{signif} **do**
14         $Ch| = generate\_actions\,(z_{signif})$
15         $A_{apl} = activity(Ch, z_{sit-cur})$
16   **end**
17     $A_{checked} = metacheck(A_{apl}, z_{sit-cur}, z_{sit-goal}, z_{map-cur}, z_{map-goal})$
18   **for** A in $A_{checked}$ **do**
19         $z_{sit-cur+1}, z_{map-cur+1} = Sit\,(z_{sit-cur}, z_{map-cur}, A)$
20         $plan.append(A, z_{sit-cur})$
21   **if** $z_{sit-goal} \in z_{sit-cur+1}$ and $z_{map-goal} \in z_{map-cur+1}$ **then**
22             $F_{plans}.append\,(plan)$
23   **end**
24   **else**
25             $Plans := MAP\_SEARCH$
                 $(z_{sit-cur+1}, z_{sit-goal}, z_{map-cur+1}, z_{map-goal}, plan, i+1)$
26   **end**
27   **end**

Algorithm 1. Process of plan synthesis by cognitive agent

The process of plan synthesis consists of two main stages: the stage of replenishing the agent's world model with new signs based on the planning and learning task (step 1) and the recursive search phase (steps 2–27). The recursive search phase begins with the comparison of the current recursion step with the maximum possible (steps 4–6), if the step is less than the maximum, then the matrices of the present and target situations and the map should be obtained (steps 7–8). Next, in step 9 chains of causal matrices of signs are formed, which enter the present planning situation (in the first step of the recursion, the matrix of the initial situation). In steps 10–12, a process is underway to search for matrices of abstract (not specified within the framework of the present task) actions. For each matrix of actions found, a process of its refinement takes place on the set of matrices of signs activated in this task (steps 13–14). At step 15, a process of selecting the appropriate actions in the present situation occurs. Then, at step 17, among all the remaining actions, those whose application will create the situation most similar to the target one are selected. After this, in steps 19–20 the plan is replenished with the selected action and a new situation is created from the effects of the action and the signs entering the present situation. In steps 21–23, the activation of the matrices of the target situation and the map by the agent is checked, if the matrices of the target situation and the cards were activated, then the algorithm ends, if not, then in step 25 a recursive call of the plan search function takes place with an increase in the number of iterations by 1. After the planning process is over, the shortest one is selected from all the plans that have been planned and the process of its execution begins. A plan is a list of tuples that consist of actions and states. Each state include coordinates, and direction of the agent after the action is performed.

$$Plan := [(a_1, S_1), (a_2, S_2), (a_3, S_3).$$

The plan is sent to the agent in the Gazebo environment sequentially, the agent after the execution of each of the actions returns the result of execution. If the result is positive, the next step is sent, otherwise there is replanning process.

The next step describes the process of generating personal meanings (actions), obtained with the reinforcement learning algorithm.

4.3   Learning of Sub-plans

To describe the agent's interaction with the environment, the Markov decision-making process (S, O, P, r, γ) is used, where S a set of states, O set of actions, $P : S \times O \times S \to [0, 1]$ transition probability distribution, reward function and γ discounting factor. In this paper, the action space is continual, so a multidimensional normal distribution $N(\mu, \sum)$ is used to determine the strategy π, where μ and $\sum$ are specified by the neural network. Thus, the strategy π is parametrized by the weights of the θ neural network, and all functions of π are functions of θ.

The function $\eta(\theta)$, which is the evaluation of the strategy π_θ, is replaced by the following surrogate function, which links the two strategies:

$$L_\theta(\widetilde{\theta}) = \eta(\theta) + E_{\pi_\theta} \frac{\pi_{\widetilde{\theta}}(o|s)}{\pi_\theta(o|s)} (Q_\theta(s, o) - V_\theta(s)),$$

where Q_θ and V_θ are the value functions of an action and a state and are defined as follows:

$$Q_\theta(\widetilde{s}_t, \widetilde{o}_t) = E_{\pi_\theta} (\sum_{l=0}^{\infty} \gamma^l r(s_{t+l}) | s_t = \widetilde{s}_t, o_t = \widetilde{o}_t),$$

$$V_\theta(\widetilde{s}_t) = E_{\pi_\theta}(\sum_{l=0}^{\infty} \gamma^l r(s_{t+l})|s_t = \widetilde{s}_t).$$

Optimization L_θ with $\widetilde{\theta}$ by restriction to the average Kullback-Leibler distance entails an increase in the initial function $\eta(\theta)$. To search the optimal direction problem, the natural policy gradient method is used, which uses linear approximation L and quadratic approximation $\overline{D}_{KL}$: for $\frac{1}{2}(\theta_{old} - \theta)^T K(\theta_{old})(\theta_{old} - \theta) \leq \delta$, where $K(\theta_{old}) = \Delta_\theta \overline{D}_{KL}^{\theta_{old}}$. Update rule:

$$\theta_{new} = \theta_{old} + \alpha K(\theta_{old})^{-1} \nabla_\theta L(\theta)|_{\theta=\theta_{old}}.$$

The value $K(\theta_{old})^{-1} \nabla_\theta L(\theta)|_{\theta=\theta_{old}}$ is the solution of the equation $K(\theta_{old})x = \nabla_\theta L(\theta)|_{\theta=\theta_{old}}$ with respect to x, the value α is selected by linear search for a maximum L with constraints $\overline{D}_{KL}^{\theta_{old}}(\theta_{old}, \theta) \leq \delta$.

5   Experiments in Simulator

As part of the demonstration of the procedure for synthesizing the behavior of a cognitive agent, an experiment was conducted to move the robotic agent Turtlebot 2 in Gazebo to the table where a small block was placed and the block was picked up by the agent's manipulator. The plan consisted of a list of actions, including "move", "rotate" and "pick-up" actions. The process was organized using a client-server architecture, where the client was a spatialMAP planner on a remote machine that sent a message using the services of the ROS operating system to the server. Messages are about the goal move point in case the "move" action was activated, about changing the direction of the agent when activating the action "rotate" and the activation of the "pick-up" action. When the "pick-up" action was activated, the script obtained using the TRPO algorithm started working. Agent's scheme of the environment is presented in Fig. 2.

To implement the TRPO algorithm, two environments were created: a synthetic learning environment and a framework for applying the algorithm to Gazebo. Two environments have the same space of states and actions. To describe the agent's interaction with them, an example of the manipulator's grip of an object on the table is given below.

Figure 3 shows the model of a manipulator in a synthetic environment in the two-dimensional case. Points 1–4 are joints of manipulators. The action is to change the angle in one of them (in 3D, rotation around the vertical axis is added). Point B - the target point at which the agent should move point 4.

The remuneration system works as follows: if, as a result of the action, the length of the vector $\overrightarrow{4B}$ has decreased, then the agent receives a reward in the amount $\left|\overrightarrow{4B}\right|$, if not changed, then it is fined 5, and if increased, is fined $2\left|\overrightarrow{4B}\right|$.

The state of the agent is a sequence $(\beta_1, \beta_2, \beta_3, \alpha_1, \alpha_2, \alpha_3, \overrightarrow{4B}, \overrightarrow{3B}, \overrightarrow{2B})$ (in 3D it is added α_4), where β_i are the angles in joints and α_i are the angles between the

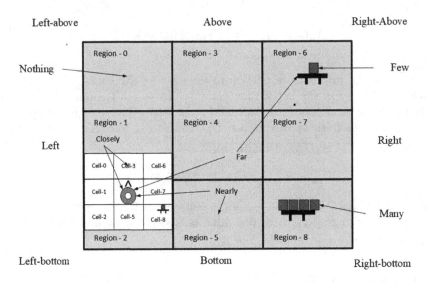

Fig. 2. Scheme of cognitive agent's spatial representations.

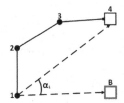

Fig. 3. Model manipulator in a synthetic environment.

following vectors: $\alpha_1 = (\overrightarrow{14}, \overrightarrow{1B})$, $\alpha_2 = (\overrightarrow{24}, \overrightarrow{2B})$, $\alpha_3 = (\overrightarrow{34}, \overrightarrow{3B})$. In such a state space, the inequality $\alpha_1 \leq 0$ means that the goal point B is below the vector $\overrightarrow{14}$ and it is necessary to make a turn in the joint 1 by the corresponding angle. This representation of the position of the manipulator relative to the goal point makes the strategy π less dependent on position B. Because the space of states and actions for the two media are identical, the neural network trained in a synthetic environment can be used in an environment interacting with Gazebo.

6   Conclusion

The paper presents an original approach to the synthesis of cognitive agent behavior, which is realized through the interaction of a reinforcement learning approach and a planning algorithm based on a psychologically plausible way of representing knowledge. A scheme of such interaction is proposed for robotic platforms with a manipulator, and an example of the work of this approach in the task of moving a platform in space and manipulating it with external objects is demonstrated. In future works, it is planned to disclose the interaction of centralized planning algorithms for agent coalitions and reinforcement learning methods, allowing the interaction of agents with the environment in real conditions.

Acknowledgments. The results concerning models of sign components and planning algorithms (Sects. 4.1 and 4.2) were obtained under the support of the Russian Science Foundation (project No. 16-11-00048), and the results on reinforcement learning for manipulator (Sects. 4.3 and 5) were obtained under the support of the Russian Foundation for Basic Research (project No. 17-29-07079).

References

1. Laird, J.E.: The Soar Cognitive Architecture. MIT Press, Cambridge (2012)
2. Sun, R., Hlie, S.: Psychologically realistic cognitive agents: taking human cognition seriously. J. Exp. Theor. Artif. Intell. **25**, 65–92 (2012)
3. Osipov, G.S., Panov, A.I., Chudova, N.V.: Behavior control as a function of consciousness. I. World model and goal setting. J. Comput. Syst. Sci. Int. **53**, 517–529 (2014)
4. Osipov, G.S., Panov, A.I., Chudova, N.V.: Behavior control as a function of consciousness. II. Synthesis of a behavior plan. J. Comput. Syst. Sci. Int. **54**, 882–896 (2015)
5. Panov, A.I.: Behavior planning of intelligent agent with sign world model. Biol. Inspired Cogn. Archit. **19**, 21–31 (2017)
6. Leontyev, A.N.: The Development of Mind. Erythros Press and Media, Kettering (2009)
7. Vygotsky, L.S.: Thought and Language. MIT Press, Cambridge (1986)
8. Pospelov, D.A., Osipov, G.S.: Knowledge in semiotic models. In: Proceedings of the Second Workshop on Applied Semiotics, Seventh International Conference on Artificial Intelligence and Information-Control Systems of Robots (AIICSR 1997), Bratislava, pp. 1–12 (1997)
9. Emelyanov, S., Makarov, D., Panov, A.I., Yakovlev, K.: Multilayer cognitive architecture for UAV control. Cogn. Syst. Res. **39**, 58–72 (2016)
10. Brooks, R.A.: Intelligence without representation. Artif. Intell. **47**, 139–159 (1991)
11. Siagian, C., Itti, L.: Biologically-inspired robotics vision Monte-Carlo localization in the outdoor environment. In: IEEE International Conference on Intelligent Robots and Systems, pp. 1723–1730 (2007)
12. Schulman, J., Levine, S., Moritz, P., Jordan, M., Abbeel, P.: Trust region policy optimization (2015)
13. Kakade, S.: A natural policy gradient (2002)
14. Daniel, K., Nash, A., Koenig, S., Felner, A.: Theta*: any-angle path planning on grids. J. Artif. Intell. Res. **39**, 533–579 (2010)
15. Palacios, J.C., Olayo, M.G., Cruz, G.J., Chvez, J.A.: Thin film composites of polyallylamine-silver. Superficies y Vacio (2012)
16. Erdem, U.M., Hasselmo, M.E.: A biologically inspired hierarchical goal directed navigation model. J. Physiol. Paris **108**(1), 28–37 (2014)
17. Morris, R.G.M., Garrud, P., Rawlins, J.N.P., O'Keefe, J.: Place navigation impaired in rats with hippocampal lesions. Nature **297**(5868), 681–683 (1982)

18. Steele, R.J., Morris, R.G.M.: Delay-dependent impairment of a matching-to- place task with chronic and intrahippocampal infusion of the NMDA-antagonist D-AP5. Hippocampus **9**(2), 118–136 (1999)
19. Steffenach, H.-A., Witter, M., Moser, M.-B., Moser, E.I.: Spatial memory in the rat requires the dorsolateral band of the entorhinal cortex. Neuron **45**(2), 301–313 (2005)
20. Milford, M., Wyeth, G.: Persistent navigation and mapping using a biologically inspired slam system. Int. J. Robot. Res. **29**(9), 1131–1153 (2010)
21. Milford, M., Schulz, R.: Principles of goal-directed spatial robot navigation in biomimetic models. Philos. Trans. R. Soc. B Biol. Sci. **369**(1655), 20130484–20130484 (2014)
22. Epstein, S.L., Aroor, A., Sklar, E.I., Parsons, S.: Navigation with learned spatial affordances, pp. 1–6 (2013)
23. Epstein, S.L., Aroor, A., Evanusa, M., Sklar, E.I., Parsons, S.: Spatial abstraction for autonomous robot navigation. Cogn. Process. **16**, 215–219 (2015)
24. Kiselev, G.A., Panov, A.I.: Sign-based approach to the task of role distribution in the coalition of cognitive agents. SPIIRAS Proc. **57**, 161–187 (2018)
25. Albers, A., Yan, W., Frietsch, M.: Application of reinforcement learning for a 2-DOF robot arm control, November 2009
26. Stephen, J., Edward, J.: 3D simulation for robot arm control with deep Q-learning (2016)
27. Watkins, C.J.C.H.: Learning from delayed rewards (1989)
28. Gu, S., Holly, E., Lillicrap, T., Levine, S.: Deep reinforcement learning for robotic manipulation with asynchronous off-policy update (2016)
29. Sutton, R.S., McAllester, D., Singh, S., Mansour, Y.: Policy gradient methods for reinforcement learning with function approximation (1999)
30. Osipov, G.S.: Sign-based representation and word model of actor. In: Yager, R., Sgurev, V., Hadjiski, M., and Jotsov, V. (eds.) 2016 IEEE 8th International Conference on Intelligent Systems (IS), pp. 22–26. IEEE (2016)

Path Finding for the Coalition of Co-operative Agents Acting in the Environment with Destructible Obstacles

Anton Andreychuk[1,2]([✉]) and Konstantin Yakovlev[1,3]

[1] Federal Research Center "Computer Science and Control"
of Russian Academy of Sciences, Moscow, Russia
andreychuk@mail.com, yakovlev@isa.ru
[2] Peoples' Friendship University of Russia (RUDN University), Moscow, Russia
[3] National Research University Higher School of Economics (NRU HSE),
Moscow, Russia

Abstract. The problem of planning a set of paths for the coalition of robots (agents) with different capabilities is considered in the paper. Some agents can modify the environment by destructing the obstacles thus allowing the other ones to shorten their paths to the goal. As a result the mutual solution of lower cost, e.g. time to completion, may be acquired. We suggest an original procedure to identify the obstacles for further removal that can be embedded into almost any heuristic search planner (we use Theta*) and evaluate it empirically. Results of the evaluation show that time-to-complete the mission can be decreased up to 9–12 % by utilizing the proposed technique.

Keywords: Path planning · Path finding · Grid · Coalition of agents
Co-operative agents · Co-operative path planning · Multi-agent systems

1 Introduction

Path planning for a point robot is usually considered in Artificial Intelligence and robotics as a task of finding a path on the graph whose nodes correspond to the positions the robot (agent) can occupy, and edges – possible transitions between them. Voronoi diagrams [8], visibility graphs [9], grids [19] are the most widespread graphs used for path finding, with grids being the most simple and easy-to-construct discretizations of the workspace. To find a path on a grid typically one of the algorithms from A* family is used. A* [5] is a heuristic search algorithm that searches in state-space comprised of the elements (nodes) corresponding to certain graph vertices (grid cells or corners). There exist various modifications of A* that are suitable for grid-based path finding. In this work we utilize so-called any-angle path finders that do not constrain agent's moves to cardinal and diagonal ones only but rather allow to move into arbitrary direction

© Springer Nature Switzerland AG 2018
A. Ronzhin et al. (Eds.): ICR 2018, LNAI 11097, pp. 13–22, 2018.
https://doi.org/10.1007/978-3-319-99582-3_2

as long as the endpoints of the move are tied to distinct grid elements. Among such algorithms Theta* [2], Field D* [3], Anya [4], etc., can be named.

Abovementioned algorithms can not be directly applied to multi-robot path planning which is gaining more and more attention nowadays due to numerous applications in transport [10], logistics [17], agriculture [14], military [7] and other domains, but they can be modified to become base blocks of multi-agent path finders such as CBS [13], M* [15], MAPP [1,16], AA-SIPP(m) [18], etc. Typically those planners consider the interaction between the robots only spatial-wise by taking into account possible collisions and avoiding them.

In this work we investigate the case when robots can interact and co-operate by performing not only move-or-wait actions but modify-the-environment actions as well. This is similar to integration of task and motion planning [6], but unlike other researchers in this field we do not concentrate on task planning with grasping the objects, which is a typical scenario, but rather on task planning with path finding. The approach we suggest can be of particular interest to solving so-called smart relocation tasks [11,12] when the mission can not be accomplished without the robots helping each other.

2 Problem Statement

Consider a coalition of heterogeneous robots that need to reach their respective goals in static, a-priory known environment, represented as a grid, composed of blocked and un-blocked cells. Without loss of generality we examine the case when only two heterogeneous robots, e.g. an UAV and a wheeled robot, are considered. The UAV can move directly to its goal, e.g. fly above all the obstacles, while the wheeled robot must circumnavigate them. An example of a modeled scenario is presented in Fig. 1.

The robots are different not only in the way they move, but they also may perform different set of actions. Wheeled robot can perform only move actions while UAV can destroy obstacles as well (at no cost). In order to do so it must first approach them. The problem now is to obtain coordinated mission completion plan composed of two sub-plans: one per each robot.The cost of the individual plan is the time needed to traverse the planned path, which is proportional to its length, so, without loss of generality the individual cost is the length of the path. Two metrics to measure the overall cost are considered, e.g. the flowtime (the sum of path lengths) and the makespan (maximum over path lenghts). We are interested in getting such solutions that have lower cost compared to the case when path planning is conducted independently by the robots. For the rest of the paper we assume that x- and y-coordinates of the start and goals location of two robots are equal, e.g. the UAV is hovering above the wheeled robot and its (x, y) goal location is the same. We will refer to the wheeled robot as to the first agent and to the UAV as to the second one.

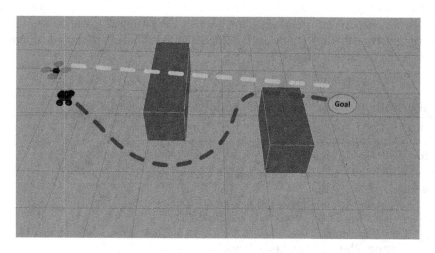

Fig. 1. Heterogeneous group of mobile robots in a grid-world. Locations of the robots are tied to the centers of un-blocked grid cells. Flying robot can move directly to the goal flying above the obstacles, while wheeled robot has to circumnavigate them.

3   Method

To decrease the cost of the initial non-cooperative solution one need to (a) identify the obstacles that force the second agent to deviate from the shortest possible, e.g. straight-line, path to its goal; (b) modify the original straight-line path of the second agent in such a way that it approaches each identified obstacle (thus destroying it); (c) re-plan a path for the first agent. Also a grid pre-processing is needed in order to assign the unique identifiers to all the obstacles in the environment. This is done trivially by traversing the grid cells one by one, and every time a blocked cell is found, all adjacent blocked ones are traversed and assigned with a unique identifier.

After finding and identifying all the obstacles on the grid, the trajectory for the first agent is planned using the modified heuristic search algorithm Theta*, which pseudocode is given in Algorithm 1. Besides finding the path the algorithm identifies obstacles whose removal can potentially shorten the length of such path. Detailed description of Theta* can be found in [2]. We reference the reader to this paper for details and now proceed with the description of the proposed modifications. One of such modifications is that an additional data structure, *obstacles*, is introduced (lines 3–4) that stores the number of times each obstacle was hit during the search. Main loop is similar to the original Theta*, e.g. on each step the most promising state is retrieved and its successors are generated. These successors correspond to moves from the current cells to the neighbouring grid ones. If the move is infeasible due to the target cell being blocked it is discarded (as in conventional heuristic search path planner), but we also count the number of such blocked cells in lines 11–13. Thus, when the algorithm terminates, one obtains not only the information about whether the path was found or not[1], but also the information about how many times the path-finder attempted to move through the particular obstacles.

Algorithm 1. Theta* with counting interfering obstacles

---

1   $parent(s_{start}) := s_{start};\ g(s_{start}) := 0;$
2   $OPEN := \{s_{start}\};\ CLOSED := \emptyset;$
3   **for** *each obstacle on grid as o* **do**
4      $obstacles(o) := 0;$
5   **while** $OPEN \neq \emptyset$ **do**
6      $s :=$ state with minimal f-value from $OPEN$;
7   remove s from $OPEN$ and add to $CLOSED$;
8   **if** $s = goal$ **then**
9   return obstacles and "path found";
10   **for** *each state in neighbours(s) as s'* **do**
11   **if** *s' is blocked* **then**
12          $obstacles(getObstacleAt(s'))$++;
13   continue;
14   **if** $s' \notin CLOSED$ **then**
15   **if** $s' \notin OPEN$ **then**
16            $g(s') := \infty;$
17   updateVertex(s, s');
18 return obstacles and "path not found";
19 **Function** *updateVertex(s, s')*
20   **if** *lineOfSight(parent(s), s')* **then**
21        $s := parent(s);$
22   **if** $g(s) + c(s, s') < g(s')$ **then**
23        $g(s') := g(s) + c(s, s');$
24        $f(s') := g(s') + h(s');$
25        $parent(s') := s;$
26   insert/update s' in $OPEN$;

Obviously, if the vertices (cells) of the obstacle o have never been considered during the search, e.g. $obstacles(o)$ is equal to 0, then this obstacle has no influence on robot's mission. If $obstacles(o) > 0$ then removing o might lead to a potentially shorter path. Thus, a simple criterion for removing an obstacle is suggested: $o = argmax_{o \in Obstacles}(obstacles(o))$, where $Obstacles$ stands for all obstacles on a grid. If it is possible to remove n obstacles, then n first ones with the largest values of $obstacles(o)$ are selected.

---

[1] The path itself can be reconstructed by iteratively tracing backpointers from goal vertex until start is reached.

After the obstacles are chosen, one needs to construct a trajectory for the second agent (flying robot), such that it passes through the vertices that are adjacent to the chosen obstacles. In case only one obstacle o is going to be removed, the shortest path for the second agent can be found as follows. The distances from each cell comprising the boundary of o to $start$ and $goal$ are calculated and such cell, c, is chosen that minimizes the distance $dist(start, c) + dist(c, goal)$, see Fig. 2b. This cell is used to form a path $[start, c, goal]$. If more than one obstacle is going to be removed, such an approach becomes computationally burdensome. Instead, we suggest another procedure that does not guarantee finding the shortest path, but works much faster.

Obviously, the shortest path from $start$ to $goal$ is the straight line segment connecting them $\langle start, goal \rangle$. Thus to minimize the length of the path that needs to pass through the vertices adjacent to the obstacles being removed, this path should be as close to this segment as possible. Therefore for each of the removing obstacles o we look for such vertex (residing at the boundary of o) that minimizes the distance to $\langle start, goal \rangle$ segment. After all, the sought path for the second agent is constructed by aligning these vertices in order of increasing distance from $start$.

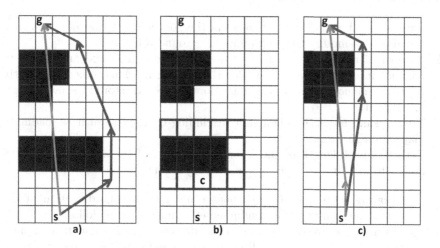

Fig. 2. Robots' paths before and after removing the obstacle. (a) initial paths for the ground robot and for the UAV (shown in blue and orange respectively) ; (b) boundary of the obstacle to be removed (shown in bold) and the cell c on this boundary that minimizes $dist(start, c) + dist(c, goal)$; (c) paths after removing the obstacle. (Color figure online)

An example of removing an obstacle and re-planning paths for both agents is presented in Fig. 2. As one can see the path for the flying robot (marked in orange) is almost un-affected, while the path for the ground robot (marked in blue) becomes significantly shorter, which means that time-to-complete the mission lowers down.

4   Experimental Evaluation

Described methods and algorithms were implemented in C++[2] and evaluated on a PC of the following configuration: OS - Windows 7, CPU - Intel Q8300 (2.5 GHz), RAM - 2 GB. Descriptions of the real-world urban areas were extracted from OpenStreetMaps and used as the input. 100 maps each being 1.2×1.2 km in size were transformed into 501×501 grids with blocked cells corresponding to buildings. Initially 200 instances per each grid were generated in such a way that the distance between the start and goal locations exceeded 960 m (400 cells). Then the instances for which the length of the trajectory found by the original Theta* algorithm differed from the straight-line distance by no more than 10% were discarded. Thus, a total of 1457 instances formed the resultant input.

To guide the search of the proposed modification of Theta* both un-weighted and weighted heurisic (Euclidean distance) was used, e.g. heuristic weight was set eiter to 1 (w = 1) or to 2 (w = 2). Using weighted heuristic makes the algorithm "greedy", i.e. more focused on the goal, as a result, it spends less time (and memory) to find a solution. The number of removed obstacles varied from 1 to 5. The following performance indicators were tracked:

(1) Path A – path length of the first agent (i.e., of the agent that does not have the ability to modify the environment – ground robot).
(2) Number of nodes – number of vertices that were processed and stored in memory in order to build path for the first agent. This indicator directly relates to memory consumption (the more vertices are stored the more memory is used).
(3) Time – runtime of the algorithm (excluding overheads, such as loading a map, saving a result, etc.).
(4) Path B – path length of the second agent (i.e., of the agent that has the ability to modify the environment – flying robot).

These indicators were tracked both before and after the modification of the environment. The results of the conducted experiments are as follows.

Figure 3 shows the average memory consumption after the first stage of planning (Stage 1), as well as after modifying the grid and removing the corresponding number of obstacles (Obs = 1, ..., Obs = 5). Left five columns correspond to the results obtained by the algorithm with un-weighted heuristic function (w = 1), while right 5 columns were gained with heuristic weight set to 2. One can note that removing obstacles leads to a notable reduction in the number of vertices processed by the path planning algorithm. If un-weighted heuristic is used (w = 1) than the memory consumption is reduced up to 30%, moreover if the weighted heuristic function is utilized (w = 2) – this consumption is reduced up to 65%.

---

[2] Source code is available at https://github.com/PathPlanning/AStar-JPS-ThetaStar/tree/destroy_obs_and_replan

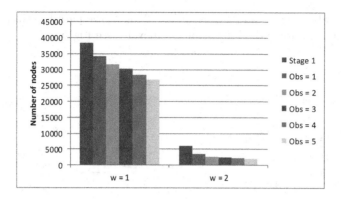

Fig. 3. Memory consumption (number of processed nodes) before and after removing the obstacles.

Similar claims can be done w.r.t. runtime—see Fig. 4 for details. This figure shows the average amount of time which the algorithm spends to find the trajectories for both agents. Similarly to memory consumption, the runtime decreases when the number of removed obstacles increases. For $w = 1$ the runtime is reduced up to 29.8%, and for $w = 2$—up to 71%.

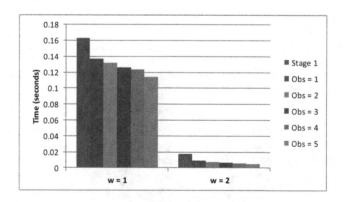

Fig. 4. Planning time before and after removing the obstacles.

To evaluate the quality of obtained solutions the following metrics were used:

- flowtime also known as sum-of-costs (SoC) – the sum of the lengths of individual trajectories;
- makespan – the maximum length of an individual trajectory.

Assuming that both agents move with identical speeds, the first metrics reflects the aggregate time-cost, associated with the mission; the second one shows when the last robot reaches its goal, so it can be seen as time to complete a mission.

Before analyzing SoC and makespan let's look at the path lengths (averages) of both agents before and after obstacle removal – see Fig. 5.

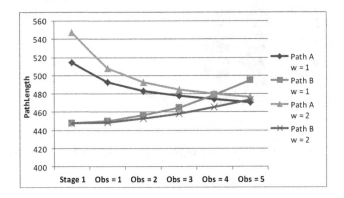

Fig. 5. Path lengths of both agents before and after removing the obstacles.

As can be seen, obstacle removal positively affects the path length of the first agent, but negatively affects the path length of the second one. So it's natural to assume that the number of removed obstacles should not be nor low nor high if one wants to reduce SoC and/or makespan.

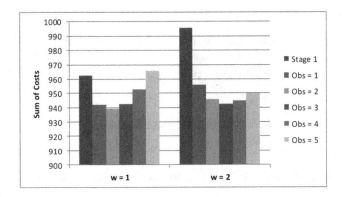

Fig. 6. Sum-of-costs before and after removing the obstacles.

Averaged SoC is depicted on Fig. 6. Analyzing this chart, one can claim that removing 2–3 obstacles leads to the best result, but percentage-wise the difference in SoC is not impressive (reduction by 3–5%). This might be due to the input data and we believe that for other environments, e.g. maze-like environments or the ones with spiral-shaped obstacles, the reduction might be more notable.

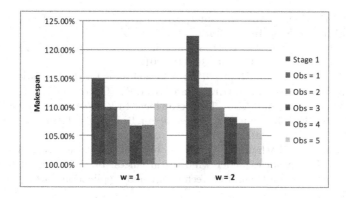

Fig. 7. Normalized makespan before and after removing the obstacles.

Average normalized values of makespan are shown on Fig. 7. We took the straight-line distance between the start and goal for 100%. As one can see, removing 3–4 obstacles (5, if weighted heuristics is used) leads to the best performance. Time to complete the mission (e.g. makespan) reduces by 9–12% is such cases, which is a notable reduction for numerous real-world applications.

5 Conclusion

We proposed an approach to plan a set of trajectories for the coalition of co-operative agents operating in the environment that can be modified by the actions of coalition members, e.g. some obstacles can be destroyed. The approach is based on the well-known heuristic search path planner, e.g. Theta*, as well as on a novel technique tailored to identify obstacles that obscure the path and thus should be potentially destroyed. Conducted experimental evaluation has shown that the suggested approach positively affects the solution quality, e.g. mission completion time (makespan) for the considered class of problems (navigation of ground and flying robots in urban environments).

Acknowledgments. This work was supported by the "RUDN University Program 5–100" (extracting data from OpenStreetMaps to conduct the experiments) and by the RSF project #16-11-00048 (developing path planning methods and evaluating them).

References

1. Andreychuk, A., Yakovlev, K.: Applying MAPP algorithm for cooperative path finding in urban environments. In: Ronzhin, A., Rigoll, G., Meshcheryakov, R. (eds.) ICR 2017. LNCS (LNAI), vol. 10459, pp. 1–10. Springer, Cham (2017). https://doi.org/10.1007/978-3-319-66471-2_1
2. Daniel, K., Nash, A., Koenig, S., Felner, A.: Theta*: any-angle path planning on grids. J. Artif. Intell. Res. **39**, 533–579 (2010)

3. Ferguson, D., Stentz, A.: Using interpolation to improve path planning: the field D* algorithm. J. Field Robot. **23**(2), 79–101 (2006)
4. Harabor, D., Grastien, A., Öz, D., Aksakalli, V.: Optimal any-angle pathfinding in practice. J. Artif. Intell. Res. **56**, 89–118 (2016)
5. Hart, P.E., Nilsson, N.J., Raphael, B.: A formal basis for the heuristic determination of minimum cost paths. IEEE Trans. Syst. Sci. Cybern. **4**(2), 100–107 (1968)
6. Kaelbling, L.P., Lozano-Pérez, T.: Hierarchical task and motion planning in the now. In: 2011 IEEE International Conference on Robotics and Automation (ICRA), pp. 1470–1477. IEEE (2011)
7. Khachumov, M., Khachumov, V.: The problem of target capturing by a group of unmanned flight vehicles under wind disturbances. In: 2017 Second Russia and Pacific Conference on Computer Technology and Applications (RPC), pp. 90–95. IEEE (2017)
8. Lavrenov, R., Matsuno, F., Magid, E.: Modified spline-based navigation: guaranteed safety for obstacle avoidance. In: Ronzhin, A., Rigoll, G., Meshcheryakov, R. (eds.) ICR 2017. LNCS (LNAI), vol. 10459, pp. 123–133. Springer, Cham (2017). https://doi.org/10.1007/978-3-319-66471-2_14
9. Lozano-Pérez, T., Wesley, M.A.: An algorithm for planning collision-free paths among polyhedral obstacles. Commun. ACM **22**(10), 560–570 (1979)
10. Morris, R., et al.: Planning, scheduling and monitoring for airport surface operations. In: AAAI Workshop: Planning for Hybrid Systems (2016)
11. Panov, A.I., Yakovlev, K.: Behavior and path planning for the coalition of cognitive robots in smart relocation tasks. In: Kim, J.-H., Karray, F., Jo, J., Sincak, P., Myung, H. (eds.) Robot Intelligence Technology and Applications 4. AISC, vol. 447, pp. 3–20. Springer, Cham (2017). https://doi.org/10.1007/978-3-319-31293-4_1
12. Panov, A.I., Yakovlev, K.S.: Psychologically inspired planning method for smart relocation task. Procedia Comput. Sci. **88**, 115–124 (2016)
13. Sharon, G., Stern, R., Felner, A., Sturtevant, N.R.: Conflict-based search for optimal multi-agent pathfinding. Artif. Intell. **219**, 40–66 (2015)
14. Vu, Q., Nguyen, V., Solenaya, O., Ronzhin, A.: Group control of heterogeneous robots and unmanned aerial vehicles in agriculture tasks. In: Ronzhin, A., Rigoll, G., Meshcheryakov, R. (eds.) ICR 2017. LNCS (LNAI), vol. 10459, pp. 260–267. Springer, Cham (2017). https://doi.org/10.1007/978-3-319-66471-2_28
15. Wagner, G., Choset, H.: M*: a complete multirobot path planning algorithm with performance bounds. In: 2011 IEEE/RSJ International Conference on Intelligent Robots and Systems (IROS), pp. 3260–3267. IEEE (2011)
16. Wang, K.H.C., Botea, A.: MAPP: a scalable multi-agent path planning algorithm with tractability and completeness guarantees. J. Artif. Intell. Res. **42**, 55–90 (2011)
17. Wurman, P.R., D'Andrea, R., Mountz, M.: Coordinating hundreds of cooperative, autonomous vehicles in warehouses. AI Mag. **29**(1), 9 (2008)
18. Yakovlev, K., Andreychuk, A.: Any-angle pathfinding for multiple agents based on SIPP algorithm. In: Proceedings of the 27th International Conference on Automated Planning and Scheduling (ICAPS 2017), pp. 586–594. AAAI Press (2017)
19. Yap, P.: Grid-based path-finding. In: Cohen, R., Spencer, B. (eds.) AI 2002. LNCS (LNAI), vol. 2338, pp. 44–55. Springer, Heidelberg (2002). https://doi.org/10.1007/3-540-47922-8_4

Sparse 3D Point-Cloud Map Upsampling and Noise Removal as a vSLAM Post-Processing Step: Experimental Evaluation

Andrey Bokovoy[1,2(✉)] and Konstantin Yakovlev[2,3]

[1] Peoples Friendship University of Russia (RUDN University), Moscow, Russia
1042160097@rudn.university
[2] Federal Research Center "Computer Science and Control"
of Russian Academy of Sciences, Moscow, Russia
{bokovoy,yakovlev}@isa.ru
[3] National Research University Higher School of Economics, Moscow, Russia
kyakovlev@hse.ru

Abstract. The monocular vision-based simultaneous localization and mapping (vSLAM) is one of the most challenging problem in mobile robotics and computer vision. In this work we study the post-processing techniques applied to sparse 3D point-cloud maps, obtained by feature-based vSLAM algorithms. Map post-processing is split into 2 major steps: (1) noise and outlier removal and (2) upsampling. We evaluate different combinations of known algorithms for outlier removing and upsampling on datasets of real indoor and outdoor environments and identify the most promising combination. We further use it to convert a point-cloud map, obtained by the real UAV performing indoor flight to 3D voxel grid (octo-map) potentially suitable for path planning.

Keywords: 3D · Point-cloud · Outlier removal · Upsampling
vSLAM · 3D path planning · Sparse map · Feature-based vSLAM

1 Introduction

Simultaneous localization and mapping (SLAM) is a well-known problem in mobile robotics, which is is considered for a variety of different applications [1,2] and platforms [3,4], with unmanned aerial or ground vehicles being the most widespread robots to use SLAM as part of the navigation loop [5–7]. There exists no universal SLAM method suitable for all robotic platforms and applications due to limitations these platforms/applications impose. Among the factors that influence SLAM the most one can name the following: available data (which in turn depends on the sensors type) and available computing capacities. One of the most challenging scenarios for SLAM is when only video-data, obtained from a single camera, is available and computational resources are limited. This is a

© Springer Nature Switzerland AG 2018
A. Ronzhin et al. (Eds.): ICR 2018, LNAI 11097, pp. 23–33, 2018.
https://doi.org/10.1007/978-3-319-99582-3_3

typical scenario for UAV navigation, and it leads to so-called monocular vision-based SLAM (vSLAM) [8]. vSLAM methods rely on the single-camera video-flow to construct (preferably in real-time) consistent 3D map of the unknown environment and can be classified into 2 major groups: indirect (or feature-based) and direct (dense and semi-dense) methods.

Indirect vSLAM algorithms utilize images' features [9] for mapping purposes. Thus the obtained map consists of the set of reconstructed image-features appropriately placed in 3D space. Since the amount of such features for every image is limited and is far less than image's size, the reconstructed map is likely to be sparse and contain large amount of free space (which is actually not free w.r.t obstacles) between the features. On the other hand, most of the feature-detectors utilized in vSLAM work fast (achieving real-time performance) and are invariant to image distortions, light, scale, rotation, etc., which makes them well-suited for real-world robotics applications

Direct methods, like LSD-SLAM [10,11] or D-TAM [12] use the entire images to reconstruct the map, leading to dense (or semi-dense) maps with large amount of environment details captured. These methods are sensitive to the input data, e.g. they can not handle well distortions, rolling shutter and other typical noise disturbances. They can not run in real-time (without GPU acceleration) as well. One should also mention direct vSLAM methods based on machine learning techniques (e.g. convolutional neural networks), see [13,14] for example, that have appeared recently. Unfortunately, they require significant computational resources and time to learn before application.

Obviously an ideal vSLAM method should combine the strengths of both approaches, e.g. it should construct detailed maps like direct algorithms do and be fast and robust like indirect ones are. In order to achieve such performance, we suggest to post-process sparse maps, produced by feature-based vSLAM algorithms in order to make them more detailed and suitable for solving further navigation tasks (like path planning [15–17], control [18] etc.). Such an approach potentially leads to producing detailed maps of the environment with no extra computing costs associated with running direct vSLAM methods.

In this work we study different post-processing techniques, e.g. outlier removal and upsampling, applied to 3D sparse point-cloud maps generated by state-of-the-art feature-based vSLAM algorithms. We evaluate different techniques on various datasets (indoor and outdoor) to find the best combination. We further use it to construct the octo-map of the indoor environment which was not the part of the training datasets.

2 Problem Statement

2.1 vSLAM Problem Definition

The vision-based simultaneous localization and mapping problem for monocular camera (monocular vSLAM) is defined as follows. Let the matrix $I_t \in \mathbb{R}^{m \times n}$

denote the image of $m \times n$ pixels, obtained by the robot at time step t^1. Thus the video-flow $\mathbf{I}_T$ is the sequence $\mathbf{I}_T = \{I_t \mid t \in [1, T]\}$, where T is the end-time.

Given $\mathbf{I}_T$, the localization task is to compute positions of the camera in the global coordinate frame: $\mathbf{X}_T = \{\mathbf{x}_t \mid \mathbf{x}_t = (x, y, z, \alpha, \beta, \gamma)\}$, where x, y, z are translation coordinates and α, β, γ are the orientation angles (e.g. pitch, roll and yaw).

Furthermore, for each I_t we need to find a set of image points $P_t = \{p_i \mid i \leqslant K \leqslant m \times n\}, P_t \in 2^{I_t}$, such that $P_t = f_{proj}(E, t)$, where $E = \{e_l \mid e_l \in \mathbb{R}^3\}$ is the environment and f_{proj} is the function, that projects 3D points from current observation (E, t) to the 2D image I_t as P_t.

Finally, the map $\mathbf{M}$ should be constructed using all the observations:

$$M_t = \{f_{proj}^{-1}(p_i) \mid i \leqslant m \times n, p_i \in P_t\}$$
$$\mathbf{M} = \bigcup_{t=1}^{T} M_t, \tag{1}$$
$$\mathbf{M} = \{m_i \mid m_i \in \mathbb{R}^3\}.$$

2.2 Map Post-Processing Problem Definition

Consider a filter that is function $filt : \mathbb{R}^3 \to 2^{\mathbb{R}^3}$ and a post-processed map, $\widehat{\mathbf{M}}$, that is constructed by sequentially applying the limited number of filters to the initial map: $\widehat{\mathbf{M}} = filt_1 \circ filt_2 \circ \ldots \circ filt_H(\mathbf{M})$.

We now want to find such combination of filters that enriches the map with additional points (the map becomes more dense) and at the same time keeps the model as close to the ground-truth as possible. Formally, $|\widehat{\mathbf{M}}|$ should be maximized and $Error(\widehat{\mathbf{M}}, E)$ should be minimized, where $Error(\widehat{\mathbf{M}}, E) = \frac{1}{|\widehat{\mathbf{M}}|} \sum_{r=1}^{|\widehat{\mathbf{M}}|} \|\widehat{m}_r - e_r\|$, $m_r \in \mathbf{M}$, $e_r = corr(m_r)$ – correspondence function between E and $\widehat{\mathbf{M}}$ (Euclidean distance, for example).

3   Evaluated Methods and Algorithms

We need to choose a suitable vSLAM method, which is able to produce maps that can be further used (possibly after the described post-processing phase) for various navigation tasks, with path planning being of the main interest. This method should be applicable to real-world robotic applications, e.g. it should be (i) fast (able to process at least 640×480 grayscale images at $30\,\text{Hz}$), (ii) able to work with distorted images, (iii) well studied and it's implementation should be available for the community. Based on the these criteria and taking into account the considerations specified in Sect. 1, ORB-SLAM2 [19] was chosen. We also took into account the evaluation results of [20].

The results of running ORB-SLAM2 on real data collected by the compact quadcopter, performing its flight in the indoor environment of our institute, are shown on Fig. 1.

---

[1] For the sake of simplicity we assume that the image is grayscale and pixels are real numbers.

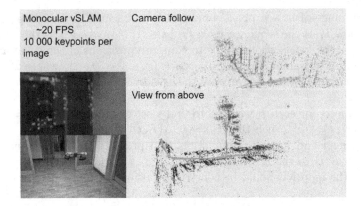

Fig. 1. ORB-SLAM2 output on real-world indoor flight performed by Parrot Bebop quadrotor. Video is available at https://www.youtube.com/watch?v=piuVq8f61gs

As one can see on Fig. 1, ORB-SLAM2 map is sparse and noisy. To make the output more suitable for further conversion to the octomap (3D grid) [21] we suggest applying 2 following steps: (i) outlier removal, (ii) upsampling.

3.1 Outlier Removal

There exists 2 general approaches to outlier removal for point-clouds: radius-based and statistical [22]. Radius-based methods filters the elements of the point-cloud based on the amount of neighbors they have. It iterates over input point-cloud once and retrieves the number of neighbors within the certain radius r. If this number is less than the predefined threshold b the point is considered an outlier.

Statistical approaches iterate throw the input point-cloud twice. During the first iteration average distance from each point to its nearest l neighbors is estimated. Consequently, the mean and standard deviation are computed for all the distances in order to determine a threshold. On the second iteration the points will be considered as outliers if their average neighbor distance is above this threshold. The main parameter of statistical methods is the standard deviation multiplier h that affects the final threshold.

3.2 Upsampling

Almost all upsampling filters for point-clouds are based on Moving Least Squares (MLS) [23] techniques. This techniques involve the projecting of the point-clouds into continues surface that minimizes a local least-square error. We choose the most common upsampling methods, such as Sample Local Plane, Random Uniform Density and Voxel Grid Dilation [24] for further evaluation. These methods are parameter-dependent and the parameters are: (i) upsampling radius (u_r), upsampling step size (u_{sz}) and maximum number of upsampling steps (u_s) for

Sample Local Plane, (ii) point density (d) for Random Uniform Density, (iii) dilation voxel size (s_{vs}) and dilation iterations (d_i) for Voxel Grid Dilation.

3.3   Map Scaling

For upsampling and oulier removal methods we need to find the best parameters at which this algorithms produce the most accurate and detailed maps. For this purposes, we need to compare the output of each method and their combinations with ground truth. Since ORB-SLAM2 produces the maps with unknown scaling, we need find corresponding points (Algorithm 1) and adjust the scaling of ORB-SLAM2's map and ground truth (Algorithm 2).

Algorithm 1. Corresponding points search.

---

1. Get $\mathbf{M}, \mathbf{X}_T, P_T = \{P_i\}, i \in [1, T]$ for ground-truth and $\widehat{\mathbf{M}'}, \mathbf{X}'_T$ for post-processed map.
2. Get $\mathbf{I}_T$ with corresponding ground-truth E_T
3. **for** each $I_i \in \mathbf{I}_T$
4.   **for** each pix $pix \in I_i$
5.   **if** $pix \in f_{proj}(E_i)$
6.   find the correspondence p' for pix in $\widehat{\mathbf{M}'}$ if exists
7.   add p' to P'_i
8.   **end if**
9.   **end for**
10.   **for** each $m_i \in \mathbf{M}$ with $m'_i \in \widehat{\mathbf{M}'}$ with correspondences P'_i
11.   Calculate per coordinate deviation: $D_i = m_i - \widehat{m'_i}$
12.   Add D_i to D
13.   **end for**
14. **end for**
15. **return** D

Algorithm 2. Map scaling.

---

1. Get an the resultant map $\widehat{\mathbf{M}'}$ with corresponding trajectory $\mathbf{X}'_T$
2. For ground truth map $\mathbf{M}$ and trajectory $\mathbf{X}_T$ adjust the x_1 pose to x'_1, x_T to x'_T and x_l with x'_l, where $l \in (1, T), l \in N$
3. Find the scale factor $s = (s_x, s_y, s_z)$ for each coordinate x, y, z using translation of the poses $\mathbf{X}'_T$
4. **return** $\widehat{\mathbf{M}} = \{s \circ m'_{pp_i}, i \in [1, K]\}$

---

4   Experimental Analysis and Results

Experimental evaluation consists of 2 main stages: **parameters adjustment** and **map quality estimation**. During the first stage we used limited amount of input data to adjust the parameters of outlier removal and upsampling filters. We also searched for best combination of the upsampler and the outlier removal. On the second step, we extrapolated the estimated parameters to a large variety of input data to estimate the quality of post-processed map. After all, we evaluated the suggested pipeline on the real-world scenario depicted in Fig. 1.

4.1   Tools

We used open-source realization of ORB-SLAM2[2], provided by its authors for sparse map construction and PointCloud Library (PCL) [25] with built-in implementations of upsampling and outlier removal algorithms for map enhancement. Experiments were run on the 3-PC cluster with each experiment executed in it's own processor's thread.

2 datasets were used: TUMindoor Dataset [26] and Malaga Dataset 2009 [27]. Malaga Dataset 2009 consists of 6 outdoor environments with ground-truth map, 6-DOF camera poses and corresponding video sequences. TUMidoor Dataset consists of the sequences, gathered inside of Technische Universitt Mnchen with ground-truth map and 6-DOF camera poses. The path length varies from 120 m to 1169 m. We split each initial sequence form the datasets into smaller sequences with a fixed path length of 10 m, thus 45 sequences from Malaga Dataset and 65 sequences from TUMindoor Dataset were used. The example of the provided environment is shown in Fig. 2.

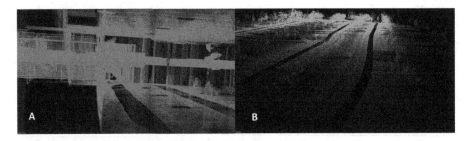

Fig. 2. Datasets, used for experimental evaluation. (a) TUMindoor Dataset (b) Malaga Dataset 2009

4.2   Parameters Adjustment

To adjust the parameters we used TUM RGBD-SLAM Dataset and Benchmark [28], particularity the "freiburg2_desk_validation" sequence.

---

[2] https://github.com/raulmur/ORB_SLAM2

Table 1. Map accuracy and processing time.

Algorithm	Parameters	Deviation in % (compared to ground-truth)	Time (s)	Map points
ORB-SLAM2	-	2.81	-	11 546
Radius filter	$b = 4$ $r = 8.9$	2.34	4	85 982
Statistical filter	$h = 1.8$	2.01	1.52	87 449
Sample Local Plane	$u_r = 1.12$ $u_s z = 0.58$ $u_s = 118$	1.98	3.2	90 178
Random Uniform Density	$d = 13$	2.13	4	89 965
Voxel Grid Dilation	$s_{vs} = 4.9$ $d_i = 3$	1.83	2.1	95 676

We varied each parameter described in Sect. 3 for each of the upsampling and outlier removal method. 25 000 of the parameters' combinations were evaluated in total. We estimated the runtime, resultant map size and map's accuracy compared to ground-truth. The results for best parameterizations are shown in Table 1. As one can see, the best performance is achieved by statistical outlier with $h = 1.8$ and by Voxel Grid Dilation with dilation voxel size set to 4.9 and dilation iterations set to 3.

4.3 Map Quality Estimation

We combined the statistical outlier filter with Voxel Grid Dilation upsampling algorithm to post-process the maps obtained by ORB-SLAM2 on all the available data: 110 data instances from both TUMidoor Dataset and Malaga Dataset. The results of the evaluation are shown in Fig. 3. As one can see, the suggested approach is able to produce more precise and dense maps, compared to original ORB-SLAM2.

Finally we tested the suggested pipeline on the video-data, captured form Bebop quadrotor performing indoor flight in our lab (video is available at https://www.youtube.com/watch?v=piuVq8f61gs) The visualization of the result is given on Fig. 4. Original map contains 8838 points, smoothed map has 6832 and upsampled map - 58416. As one can see, applying the suggested outlier removal and upsampling filters positively influence the quality of the resultant point-cloud map and, as a result, converted octo-map becomes more suitable for further usage (e.g. for path planning).

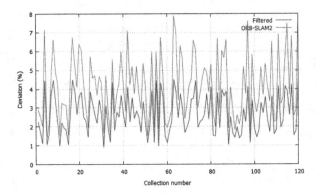

Fig. 3. Average deviation of the post-processed map and ORB-SLAM2's map from ground-truth. Less is better.

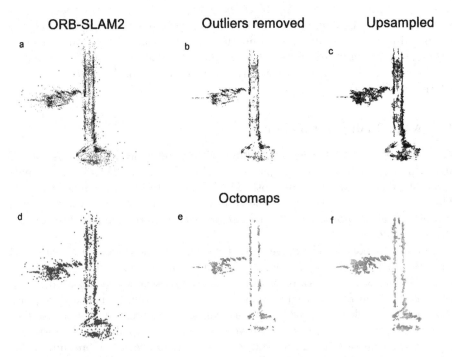

Fig. 4. (a) Original map, produced by ORB-SLAM2 (outliers are highlighted in red); (b) the map with outliers removed; (c) upsampled map. (d), (e), (f) – corresponding octrees (with the ceiling and the floor removed for better visualization).

5   Conclusion

We have considered the problem of enhancing the maps produced by monocular feature-based vSLAM (ORB-SLAM2). This problem naturally arises in various mobile robotics applications as typically the feature-based vSLAM maps are extremely sparse. We evaluated the post-processing pipeline that includes outlier removal and upsampling. Different combinations of known methods were evaluated and the best parameters for each method were identified. The best combination was then extensively tested on both well-known in the community indoor and outdoor collections of video-data and the video from real quadrotor captured in our lab. The results of such evaluation showed the increase of the accuracy and the density of the post-processed maps.

Acknowledgments. This work was partially supported by the "RUDN University Program 5-100" and by the RFBR project No. 17-29-07053.

References

1. Cadena, C., Carlone, L., Carrillo, H., Latif, Y., Scaramuzza, D., Neira, J., Reid, I., Leonard, J.: Past, present, and future of simultaneous localization and mapping: towards the robust-perception age. IEEE Trans. Robot. **32**(6), 1309–1332 (2016)
2. Balan, A., Flaks, J., Hodges, S., Isard, M., Williams, O., Barham, P., Izadi, S., Hiliges, O., Molyneaux, D., Kim, D., et al.: Distributed asynchronous localization and mapping for augmented reality, January 13 2015. US Patent 8,933,931
3. Li, R., Liu, J., Zhang, L., Hang, Y.: LIDAR/MEMS IMU integrated navigation (SLAM) method for a small UAV in indoor environments. In: 2014 DGON Inertial Sensors and Systems Symposium (ISS), pp. 1–15. IEEE (2014)
4. Leonard, J.J., Bahr, A.: Autonomous underwater vehicle navigation. In: Dhanak, M.R., Xiros, N.I. (eds.) Springer Handbook of Ocean Engineering, pp. 341–358. Springer, Cham (2016). https://doi.org/10.1007/978-3-319-16649-0_14
5. Caballero, F., Merino, L., Ferruz, J., Ollero, A.: Vision-based odometry and SLAM for medium and high altitude flying UAVs. J. Intell. Robot. Syst. **54**(1–3), 137–161 (2009)
6. Sazdovski, V., Silson, P.M.: Inertial navigation aided by vision-based simultaneous localization and mapping. IEEE Sens. J. **11**(8), 1646–1656 (2011)
7. Vu, Q., Nguyen, V., Solenaya, O., Ronzhin, A., Mehmet, H.: Algorithms for joint operation of service robotic platform and set of UAVs in agriculture tasks. In: 2017 5th IEEE Workshop on Advances in Information, Electronic and Electrical Engineering (AIEEE), pp. 1–6. IEEE (2017)
8. Buyval, A., Afanasyev, I., Magid, E.: Comparative analysis of ROS-based monocular SLAM methods for indoor navigation. In: Proceedings of the Ninth International Conference on Machine Vision (ICMV 2016), pp. 10341–10341 (2017). https://doi.org/10.1117/12.2268809
9. Rublee, E., Rabaud, V., Konolige, K., Bradski, G.: ORB: An efficient alternative to SIFT or SURF. In: 2011 IEEE international conference on Computer Vision (ICCV), pp. 2564–2571. IEEE (2011)
10. Engel, J., Schöps, T., Cremers, D.: LSD-SLAM: large-scale direct monocular SLAM. In: Fleet, D., Pajdla, T., Schiele, B., Tuytelaars, T. (eds.) ECCV 2014. LNCS, vol. 8690, pp. 834–849. Springer, Cham (2014). https://doi.org/10.1007/978-3-319-10605-2_54

11. Bokovoy, A., Yakovlev, K.: Enhancing semi-dense monocular vSLAM used for multi-rotor UAV navigation in indoor environment by fusing IMU data. In: The 2018 International Conference on Artificial Life and Robotics (ICAROB 2018), pp. 391–394. ALife Robotics Corporation Ltd. (2018)

12. Newcombe, R.A., Lovegrove, S.J., Davison, A.J.: DTAM: Dense tracking and mapping in real-time. In: 2011 IEEE International Conference on Computer Vision (ICCV), pp. 2320–2327. IEEE (2011)

13. Tateno, K., Tombari, F., Laina, I., Navab, N.: CNN-SLAM: Real-time dense monocular SLAM with learned depth prediction. arXiv preprint arXiv:1704.03489 (2017)

14. Makarov, I., Aliev, V., Gerasimova, O.: Semi-dense depth interpolation using deep convolutional neural networks. In: Proceedings of the 2017 ACM on Multimedia Conference, MM 2017, pp. 1407–1415. ACM, New York (2017)

15. Yakovlev, K., Baskin, E., Hramoin, I.: Grid-based angle-constrained path planning. In: Hölldobler, S., Krötzsch, M., Peñaloza, R., Rudolph, S. (eds.) KI 2015. LNCS (LNAI), vol. 9324, pp. 208–221. Springer, Cham (2015). https://doi.org/10.1007/978-3-319-24489-1_16

16. Magid, E., Tsubouchi, T., Koyanagi, E., Yoshida, T.: Building a search tree for a pilot system of a rescue search robot in a discretized random step environment. J. Robot. Mechatron. **23**(4), 567 (2011)

17. Makarov, I., Polyakov, P.: Smoothing voronoi-based path with minimized length and visibility using composite bezier curves. In: AIST (Supplement), pp. 191–202 (2016)

18. Buyval, A., Gabdulin, A., Mustafin, R., Shimchik, I.: Deriving overtaking strategy from nonlinear model predictive control for a race car. In: 2017 IEEE/RSJ International Conference on Intelligent Robots and Systems (IROS 2017), pp. 2623–2628, September 2017

19. Mur-Artal, R., Tardós, J.D.: ORB-SLAM2: An Open-Source SLAM System for Monocular, Stereo, and RGB-D Cameras. IEEE Trans. Robot. (2017)

20. Kitti vision benchmark suite. http://www.cvlibs.net/datasets/kitti/eval_odometry.php. Accessed 22 Aug 2018

21. Hornung, A., Wurm, K.M., Bennewitz, M., Stachniss, C., Burgard, W.: OctoMap: an efficient probabilistic 3d mapping framework based on octrees. Autonom. Robots **34**(3), 189–206 (2013)

22. Rusu, R.B., Marton, Z.C., Blodow, N., Dolha, M., Beetz, M.: Towards 3D point cloud based object maps for household environments. Robot. Autonom. Syst. **56**(11), 927–941 (2008)

23. Reuter, P., Joyot, P., Trunzler, J., Boubekeur, T., Schlick, C.: Surface reconstruction with enriched reproducing kernel particle approximation. In: Eurographics/IEEE VGTC Symposium Proceedings on Point-Based Graphics 2005, pp. 79–87. IEEE (2005)

24. Skinner, B., Vidal Calleja, T., Valls Miro, J., De Bruijn, F., Falque, R.: 3D point cloud upsampling for accurate reconstruction of dense 2.5 D thickness maps. In: Australasian Conference on Robotics and Automation (2014)

25. Rusu, R.B., Cousins, S.: 3D is here: Point cloud library (pcl). In: 2011 IEEE International Conference on Robotics and Automation (ICRA), pp. 1–4. IEEE (2011)

26. Huitl, R., Schroth, G., Hilsenbeck, S., Schweiger, F., Steinbach, E.: TUMindoor: an extensive image and point cloud dataset for visual indoor localization and mapping. In: 2012 19th IEEE International Conference on Image Processing (ICIP), pp. 1773–1776. IEEE (2012)

27. Blanco, J.L., Moreno, F.A., Gonzalez, J.: A collection of outdoor robotic datasets with centimeter-accuracy ground truth. Autonom. Robots **27**(4), 327 (2009)
28. Sturm, J., Engelhard, N., Endres, F., Burgard, W., Cremers, D.: A benchmark for the evaluation of RGB-D SLAM systems. In: 2012 IEEE/RSJ International Conference on Intelligent Robots and Systems (IROS), pp. 573–580. IEEE (2012)

Cloud Robotic Platform on Basis of Fog Computing Approach

Aleksandr Chueshev[1(✉)], Olga Melekhova[1(✉)],
and Roman Meshcheryakov[2(✉)]

[1] Teda Lab, Paris, France
{alex.chueshev, olga.melekhova}@tedalab.fr
[2] Tomsk State University of Control Systems and Radioelectronics,
Tomsk, Russia
meshcheryakov.roman@gmail.com

Abstract. This article describes the possibility of using the ideas of FOG computing as an additional layer between robotic devices and the cloud infrastructure. FOG layer, represented as a P2P network in combination with the containerized cloud infrastructure inspired by microservice patterns, provides the ability to process data based on its time-sensitivity and to increase overall benefits despite the fact of exponential growth of data. We consider that the solution of assignment problem obtained in terms of the platform is one of the keys to achieve the goal of data analysis close to devices.

Keywords: Robots · Cloud platforms · Manipulator · Computing
Control systems

1 Introduction

To begin with, cloud infrastructure refers to a virtual infrastructure that is delivered or accessed via a network or the Internet. This usually specifies the on-demand services or products being delivered through the model known as infrastructure as a service (IaaS), a basic delivery model of cloud computing [1–3]. At the same time it's critically important for real-time systems to process extremely time-sensitive information close to its sources especially due to the fact of exponential growth of data. In order to achieve this goal we additionally draw our attention to the concept of FOG computing [1, 2].

According to the previous statement our first step was to create a universal cloud platform for IoT, such as smart home automation system or smart energy solutions, with deep integration of mathematical distributed algorithms and to use it later as a separate computing level [4–7].

Adaptation of the developed cloud infrastructure for robotics connection via 5G including the concept of FOG computing and with the support of various mathematical and real-time stream processing is the next step of our work [3, 7].

In this paper we describe our platform with necessary benchmarks as a three-level model where the first level is represented by IoT and robotics infrastructure and the rest levels are FOG and Cloud computing respectively.

A. Ronzhin et al. (Eds.): ICR 2018, LNAI 11097, pp. 34–43, 2018.
https://doi.org/10.1007/978-3-319-99582-3_4

2 Cloud Computing Level

To start with complex description of the cloud computing level of our platform it should be noted that distributed architectures can be reduced to service-oriented architectures (SOA) in the case of applications separation into components and providing services to other components via communication protocols, typically over a network [4].

Moreover, there is another concept known as microservice architecture and according to Martin Fowler SOA is a superset of microservices, which can be described as services presented by independent processes communicating with each other using language-agnostic APIs. For communication between microservices the following technologies can be used:

- SOAP with WSDL;
- message brokers such as RabbitMQ, ActiveMQ paired, for example, with STOMP;
- REST, so on.

To achieve the necessary requirements for the cloud computing level the microservice architecture was chosen as the primary type of distributed architectures where the message broker Apache Kafka is the main tool for linking components together.

Such combination of microservices and message brokers is often called an event-driven architecture (EDA) and will be a good way to:

- isolate required logic and containerize microservices (for example, Docker container) with further auto deploy and load balancing;
- isolate development teams following Amazon "two pizza" rule;
- update and deploy independently all necessary microservices;
- specify the structure of the messages in the system using special JSON schemes registered in Apache Avro tool;
- connect either Apache Spark for cluster processing and Data Lake solutions to store data or other third-party platforms.

More than that, Apache Kafka demonstrates a great performance potential and allows us to use it as a central and one of the main components in the whole cloud infrastructure. The key of such behavior lies in the architecture originally developed by LinkedIn with the following features:

- based on distributed, replicated and fault-tolerant cluster paired with Zookeeper service and looked like a distributed filesystem dedicated to high-performance, low-latency commit log storage, replication, and propagation;
- persistent messaging with $O(1)$ disk structures;
- support hundreds of thousands of messages per second depending on the current configuration;
- two types of messaging: queuing and publish-subscribe;
- at-least-once delivery by default but exactly-once delivery for Kafka Streams and transactional producer/consumer processes.

With the help of Apache Kafka such patterns as CQRS or even Event-Sourcing can be natively implemented inside the cloud infrastructure using the described message broker. The most important things to be considered are the eventual consistency and distributed transactions among groups of microservices.

Another characteristic that should be described in this section is security [8–11]. One of the ways to implement the security layer is to create an isolated authentication microservice based on OAuth2.0 protocol but with the support of JSON web tokens (JWT) signed using RSA keys that will allow us to reduce the number of requests from simple microservices to auth one. At the same time it should be considered that information of JWT is only encoded but not encrypted. Generally it means that communication between microservices is built using non-trusted way secured by SSL or VPN, for example [12].

The final solution is created according to the current requirements with an understanding of request-reply pattern [13]. To sum up this section, there are 3 types of architectures depending on the specified IaaS and deployed with Ansible tool that allows us to create configuration models for automatic installations on various cloud providers. The designed cloud infrastructure can be deployed on Amazon, Google Cloud Platform, Microsoft Azure, VMware or OpenStack + MaaS solution to create a completely private cloud level. Moreover, the first type provides the possibility to run application clusters under Kubernetes with authentication (auth), service discovery and registry (SD).

The second type of architecture additionally allows users to use custom data lake based on HDFS and, additionally, Cassandra to store unstructured, semi-structured and structured data according to the database per service pattern secured by user permissions and ACL.

The third type of cloud infrastructure and the most complete gets the Apache Spark Cluster under the Mesos layer for parallel processing and analysis including stream processing. One of the main advantages of using Apache Spark is the possibility to install it on Hadoop environment, speed performance without mandatory classic Map-Reduce method and with built-in libraries (see Fig. 1):

- MLlib for distributed machine learning;
- GraphX for graph processing;
- Spark Streaming for steaming processing;
- SparkSQL for effective work with structured data in the term of BigData.

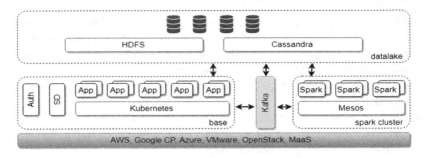

Fig. 1. Cloud Infrastructure type 3.

Described architecture schemes are represented in terms of Kubernetes and can be installed on various cloud providers by further improving open-source Kubespray project using our developed Ansible modules. This is a fairly flexible solution to solve possible problems especially using data pipelines for processing control but to handle the increasing amount of data (approaching 40% only in 2015) produced by devices physically close to IoT new extensions are required for the entire architecture.

At this point we assume that the analysis of data related to our system could be divided into 2 groups: "long-term" and "short-term" analysis, where the first one is submitted by Apache Spark cluster on the cloud level which is suitable for distributed high-performance processing and the second one is related to time-sensitive data and FOG computing represented by level between the cloud infrastructure and IoT devices or robotics.

We draw attention to the fact of widespread FOG computing usage in our solution due to its benefits and exponential growth of data.

3 FOG Computing Layer

Located between the Cloud computing and physical layers and represented by edge and physical devices or even group of virtualized resources as cloudlet FOG computing layer is related to completely time-sensitive data and aimed at data processing close to its sources. The main goal of using such layer is to reduce latency for "short-term" analysis and to route data to a higher level. Moreover it could help us to work in completely isolated networks using local infrastructure consisting of other devices and robotics as a computing unit. To do this we should formalize a way to determine the computational capabilities of the units described above for further task assignment according to this value. Imagine that there is a benefit b_{ij} of assigning task j for unit i where each task can be assigned only to one unit and the overall benefit $\sum b_{ij}$ for all assignments tends to a maximum.

One of the solutions for searching such assignments in accordance with the polynomial complexity was proposed by Dimitri Bertsekas in the form of holding an auction [4]. In order to solve the assignment problem formulated above but in decentralized networks we have used some other improvements that provide the same stable and optimum results [8]. According to these improvements each unit at the moment of time t can have incomplete knowledge of current assignments solved gradually and, technically, can be represented using state diagram.

4 Requirements for Robotic Systems

The complex architecture described above can be easily scaled for any purposes and spheres such as home automation, smart energy systems, company infrastructure and development infrastructure according to DevOps or even robotics systems. Of course, such cloud platform paired with FOG computing is especially interesting with the combination of IoT meaning robotics systems where Cloud computing level is a place of making deep and complex calculations like path planning, image recognition, clustering and creating the environment model, remote controlling and FOG computing level is a place for data processing in the terms of time-sensitivity and network isolation.

Among other things, 5G that should be scheduled for 2020 year paired with IPv6 propagation would be a new stage in the development of IoT and robotics systems development with communications in fault-tolerant and secure manners [14–17].

The modern complex robotics systems for industry may consist of several computational units to control various components including their connections to the cloud platform through 5G and full-duplex bi-directional communication (Web Sockets) under the protection of SSL and VPN. More than that, such robotics system can be presented as a local distributed architecture with the ability to virtualize resources and provide them to different computational processes according to the current real-time situation. In our opinion the implementation of this idea would improve the usage of the cloud level only as huge remote computational unit for global parallel processing and analysis, global storage for the data from different robotics sensors and as a reserve or a store of virtualized resources provided for the local architecture through the low latency communication (5G) in the case of high-loaded robotic processors.

Finally, it's important to note that such IoT systems as smart energy solutions often use cloud platform for different computations such as fingerprint detection of different electrical devices by creating specific transformations with frequency domain representation of the original signal for the further device detection locally on the special hub at home without unnecessary requests to cloud platform. The processed data is often called smart data. As a result the required information is more intelligent for the real-time process and can be used in the same manner in robotics systems but among other mathematical models [18–21].

5   Cloud Computing Test

To fully understand the capabilities of the chosen solution and the substitution conditions for the alternative, bandwidth measurements were measured, expressed through the delay time with respect to the p99-latency.

The experiment was conducted using the open-source tool Flotilla in comparison with the message queue RabbitMQ based on the AMPQ standard.

Selected message queues for measurements:

– RabbitMQ (v. 3.6.7);
– Apache Kafka (v. 0.9.0.x) is an implementation implemented within the framework of the platform.

Selected types of messages for measurements:

– 256B, 3.000 requests/s (768 KB/s);
– 1 KB, 3.000 requests/s (3 MB/s);
– 5 KB, 2,000 requests/s (10 MB/s);
– 1 KB, 20.000 requests/s (20.48 MB/s);
– 1 MB, 100 requests/s (100 MB/s).

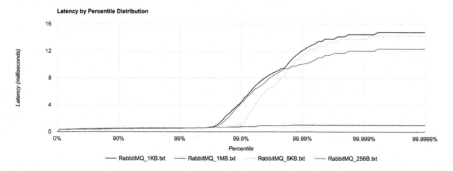

RabbitMQ, Latency, test 1

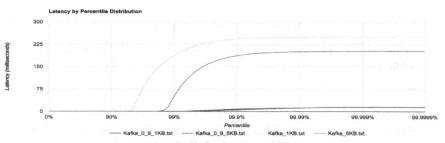

Apache Kafka, Latency, test 2

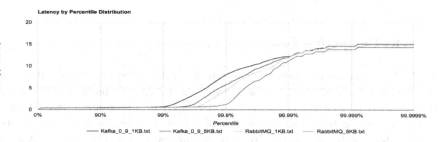

Apache Kafka, RabbitMQ, test 3

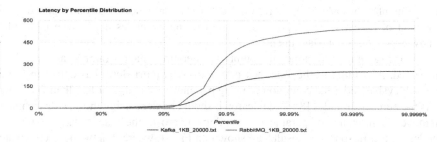

Apache Kafka, RabbitMQ, test 4

Fig. 2. Latencies for Apache Kafka and RabbitMQ in comparison.

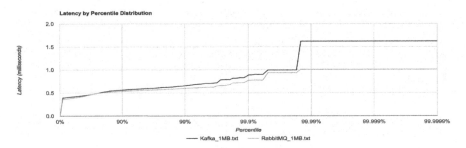

Apache Kafka, RabbitMQ, test 5

Fig. 2. (*continued*)

Selected types of units (nodes) for measurements:

- 2 m4.xlarge EC2 instance (2.4 GHz Intel Xeon Haswell, 16 GB RAM);
- Enabling enhanced networking.

Stages:

- execution of the request to publish the message in the queue;
- waiting for the response to the sent message (the size of the message with the request is equal to the size of the message with the response).

The results present on Fig. 2:

6 FOG Computing Test

To check the solution of assignment problem we have created a decentralized network of 25 independent nodes using Golang environment. The main problem is that among such parameters as ε and b_{ij} to control the speed of convergence and benefit of assigning task j to node i due to the fact of decentralization a new parameter called topology was additionally added. To prove this statement 2 networks were created with complete and random topologies respectively and the same values of benefits and ε (see Fig. 3). All the tests were performed for the system where the number of nodes is equal to the number of tasks and, moreover, such tests were successfully completed at the moment of time t when all tasks are assigned and all nodes don't have incomplete knowledge of current assignments.

At the same time to reduce the number of iterations such parameter as ε should be managed. According to the approach proposed by Dimitri Bertsekas optimum results are achievable under the condition of using parameter ε equal to or less than $1/n$, where n is the number of nodes [8]. Technically, it should be done using the ε-scale technic to remove the influence of parameter ε tending to zero in the case of large number of nodes. The corresponding results are shown on Fig. 4, where 2 networks were created with the same topology and overall benefit but using a different number of iterations for convergence.

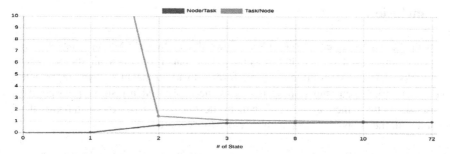

25 nodes, random topology, ε = 0.25, overall benefit is equal to 2310

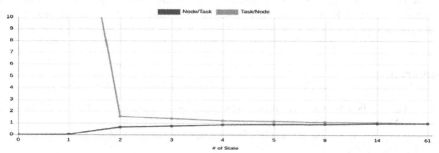

25 nodes, complete topology, ε = 0.25, overall benefit is equal to 2512

Fig. 3. Convergence. Test 1.

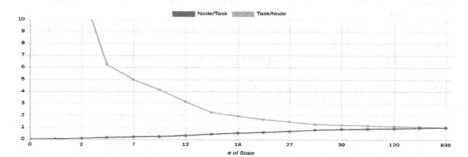

25 nodes, chain topology, ε = 0.25, overall benefit is equal to 2512

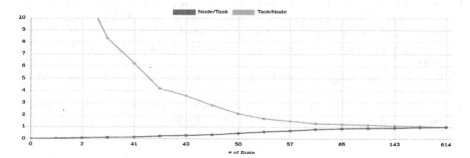

25 nodes, chain topology, ε = 0.85, overall benefit is equal to 2512

Fig. 4. Convergence. Test 2.

7 Conclusion

To sum up, there was presented a complex solution that includes two computing layers for data processing based on its time-sensitive. This paper provides all the necessary benchmarks, tests and description of the platform with additional FOG layer, represented as a P2P network in a combination with the containerized cloud infrastructure inspired by microservice pattern, increasing overall benefits despite the fact of exponential growth of data and with the support of data analysis close to its sources. [7, 19, 21].

Acknowledgements. The given paper is completed with the support of the Ministry of Education and Science of the Russian Federation within the limits of the project part of the state assignment of TUSUR in 2017 and 2019 (project 2.3583.2017) and science school (№ NSH-3070.2018.8).

References

1. Mung, C.: Fog networking: an overview on research opportunities. Princeton University (2015)
2. Fog Computing and the Internet of Things: Extend the cloud to where the things are. Cisco Whitepaper, 6 p (2015)
3. Francesco, P., et al.: Research on architecting microservices: trends, focus, and potential for industrial adoption. In: 2017 IEEE International Conference on Software Architecture (ICSA), pp. 21–30. IEEE (2017)
4. Bertsekas, D.P.: Auction algorithms for network flow problems. Comput. Optim. Appl. **1**(1), 7–66 (1992)
5. Osipov, Yu.M.: Modern problems of innovation: the manual. TUSUR, Tomsk, 140 p (2012). https://edu.tusur.ru/publications/1056
6. Zaharia, M., et al.: Spark: cluster computing with working sets. HotCloud 2010, vol. 10, 95 p (2010)
7. Data Age 2025: The Evolution of Data to Life-Critical. An IDC White Paper sponsored by Seagate, 25 p. April 2017
8. Zavlanos, M.M., Spesivtsev L., Pappas G.J.: A distributed auction algorithm for the assignment problem. In: 47th IEEE Conference on Decision and Control, CDC 2008, pp. 1212–1217 (2008)
9. Olfati-Saber, R., Murray, R.M.: Consensus problems in networks of agents with switching topology and time-delays. IEEE Trans. Autom. Control **49**(9), 1520–1533 (2004)
10. Smith, S.L., Bullo, F.: Target assignment for robotic networks: worst case and stochastic performance in dense environments. In: Proceedings of the 46th IEEE Conference on Decision and Control, New Orleans, LA, pp. 3585–3590 (2007)
11. Balinski, M.L.: Signature methods for the assignment problem. J. Oper. Res. **33**, 527–537 (1985)
12. Kuhn, H.W.: The Hungarian method for the assignment problem. Nav. Res. Logist. **2**(1–2), 83–97 (1955)
13. Bertsekas, D.P., Castanon, D.A.: Parallel synchronous and asynchronous implementations of the auction algorithm. Parallel Comput. **17**, 707–732 (1991)

14. Kostyuchenko, E., Gurakov, M., Krivonosov, E., Tomyshev, M., Mescheryakov, R., Hodashinskiy, I.: Integration of Bayesian classifier and perceptron for problem identification on dynamics signature using a genetic algorithm for the identification threshold selection. In: Cheng, L., Liu, Q., Ronzhin, A. (eds.) ISNN 2016. LNCS, vol. 9719, pp. 620–627. Springer, Cham (2016). https://doi.org/10.1007/978-3-319-40663-3_71

15. Khodashinsky, I.A., Meshcheryakov, R.V., Anfilofiev, A.E.: Identification of fuzzy classifiers based on weed optimization algorithm. In: Kravets, A., Shcherbakov, M., Kultsova, M., Shabalina, O. (eds.) CIT&DS 2015. CCIS, vol. 535, pp. 216–223. Springer, Cham (2015). https://doi.org/10.1007/978-3-319-23766-4_18

16. Khodashinsky, I.A., Zemtsov, N.N., Meshcheryakov, R.V.: Construction of fuzzy approximators based on the bacterial foraging method. Russ. Phys. J. **55**(3), 301–305 (2012)

17. Osipov, O.Yu., Osipov, Yu.M., Meshcheryakov, R.V.: Active driveline as an element of cyberphysical system. In: Proceedings of the Higher Educational Institutions (2016). Instrument **59**(11), 934–938

18. Vasiliev, A.V., Kondratyev, A.S., Gradovtsev, A.A., Dalyaev, IYu.: Research and development of design shape of a mobile robotic system for geological exploration on the moon's surface. SPIIRAS Proc. **45**(2), 141–156 (2016). https://doi.org/10.15622/sp.45.9

19. Kryuchkov, B.I., Karpov, A.A., Usov, V.M.: Promising approaches for the use of service robots in the domain of manned space exploration. SPIIRAS Proc. **32**(1), 125–151 (2014). https://doi.org/10.15622/sp.32.9

20. Motienko, A.I., Tarasov, A.G., Dorozhko, I.V., Basov, O.O.: Proactive control of robotic systems for rescue operations. SPIIRAS Proc. **46**(3), 169–189 (2016). https://doi.org/10.15622/sp.46.12

21. Ronzhin, A., Saveliev, A., Basov, O., Solyonyj, S.: Conceptual model of cyberphysical environment based on collaborative work of distributed means and mobile robots. In: Ronzhin, A., Rigoll, G., Meshcheryakov, R. (eds.) ICR 2016. LNCS (LNAI), vol. 9812, pp. 32–39. Springer, Cham (2016). https://doi.org/10.1007/978-3-319-43955-6_5

Toward More Expressive Speech Communication in Human-Robot Interaction

Vlado Delić[1(✉)], Branislav Borovac[1], Milan Gnjatović[1], Jovica Tasevski[1], Dragiša Mišković[1], Darko Pekar[2], and Milan Sečujski[1]

[1] University of Novi Sad Faculty of Technical Sciences, Novi Sad, Serbia
vlado.delic@uns.ac.rs
[2] AlfaNum – Speech Technologies, Novi Sad, Serbia

Abstract. It is well known that speech communication is a very important segment of human-robot interaction. The paper presents our experience from the project "Design of Robots as Assistive Technology for the Treatment of Children with Developmental Disorders", with focus on the development of more expressive dialogue systems based on automatic speech recognition (ASR) and text-to-speech synthesis (TTS) in South Slavic languages. The paper presents the most recent results of our research related to the development of expressive conversational human-robot interaction, specifically in the field of conversion of voice and style of synthesized speech based on a new generation of deep neural network (DNN) based speech synthesis algorithms, as well as the field of emotional speech recognition. The development of dialogue strategies is described in more details in the second part of the paper, as well as the experience in their clinical applications for treatment of children with cerebral palsy.

Keywords: Human-Robot interaction · Speech technology
Expressive communication · Dialogue systems

1 Introduction

Human-machine interaction is one of major challenges in the development of robots. Humanoid robots are usually capable of recognizing human speech with a certain degree of accuracy, as well as to synthesize human-like speech. The level of automatic speech recognition (ASR) and spoken language understanding (SLU) depends on many conditions: language, size of vocabulary, noise level, reverberation, microphone and its position, as well as speaking style. On the other hand, achieving a high level of naturalness and expressiveness of speech produced by TTS is also a great technological challenge, and it has been accomplished for still a relatively small number of languages, particularly those with large speaker bases and market potential. For these reasons, conversational human-robot interaction is still unavailable for a large majority of languages, and has reached various degrees of development.

Speech dialogue expressing emotions and attitudes is very important in human-robot communication and, in fact, more expressive robots have been proven to be preferable over more efficient ones [1]. Emotion based human-robot interaction can be considered from different points of view; apart from verbal communication, the use of non-verbal cues such

© Springer Nature Switzerland AG 2018
A. Ronzhin et al. (Eds.): ICR 2018, LNAI 11097, pp. 44–51, 2018.
https://doi.org/10.1007/978-3-319-99582-3_5

as mimics and body gestures can improve the understanding interlocutors' intentions [2]. More expressive verbal human-robot communication is considered in more details in this paper. Section 2 presents some research results in the development of emotional speech recognition and some new research results in the conversion of both voice and style of synthesized speech. The applications of speech technologies in the development of a humanoid robot and its dialogue system are described in more details in the Sect. 3, with focus on experience in applications of human-robot speech interaction tested in a hospital as assistive technology for the treatment of children with developmental disorders.

2   Development of ASR and TTS for More Expressive Speech Communication

Robot MARKO is able to speak in Serbian, based on ASR and TTS developed at the project "Development of Dialogue Systems for Serbian and Other South Slavic Languages". For the first time, these were small to medium size vocabulary ASR [3–5] and a concatenative TTS (a female voice) with intonation predicted by regression trees [6]. They provide from one side the recognition of speech commands in the domain of therapeutic work with children with developmental disorders, and from the other side synthesized speech that is comprehensible, reasonably natural-sounding, but always in a neutral speech style. In order to provide more expressive verbal communication, the activities on the project have included research on emotional speech recognition and synthesis of speech with emphasis on creating a framework which will allow easy incorporation of new speech styles/emotions and new speaker voices.

2.1   Emotional Speech Recognition

The research question of automatic emotional speech recognition integrates two issues: selection of an appropriate feature set and investigation of different classification techniques. Most speech emotion recognition systems were based on hidden Markov models (HMM) [7]. Recognising realistic emotions and affect in speech can be difficult, especially if emotions have a low level of arousal and valence [8].

Discrimination capability of the usually proposed feature set is compared with two feature sets (prosodic and spectral feature sets separately) in a five emotional states classification task (anger, joy, sadness, fear and neutral). Four different classifiers (linear Bayes classifier, perceptron rule, kNN classifier and multilayer perceptron) are trained and tested with observed three feature sets on the corpus of "Emotional and Attitude Expressive Speech" (GEES). A set of experiments with three feature sets: the prosodic, the spectral, and the combined one has been described in [9]. The linear Bayes, the perceptron rule and the kNN classifier were considered in all three experiments. The experimental results show that the highest recognition accuracy was obtained with the third feature set using the linear Bayes classifier.

Better recognition of emotional speech will provide more natural verbal human-machine communication. Based on recognized human emotions, a robot can correct the dialogue strategy. It should also be noted that a good dialogue strategy can sometimes be chosen solely on the basis of the decision whether the speaker emotion was identified as positive or negative.

2.2 Conversion of Voice and Speech Style

Recent technological development has enabled us to use deep neural networks (DNN) to model speech. A simple DNN-based TTS system is shown in Fig. 1. It consists of two neural networks, one predicting durations of phones, and the other predicting acoustic features. In our experiments all networks have 4 hidden layers with 1024 neurons, first three form a feed-forward network, while the output layer has neurons with long short-term memory (LSTM). The inputs are linguistic features extracted from annotated text. The acoustic features produced by the network are given to the vocoder from which the output speech signal is obtained. For producing intelligible and natural sounding speech, the model needs to be trained on several hours of speech, annotated phonetically and prosodically. While phonetic annotation is largely automatic, prosodic annotation requires significant human effort.

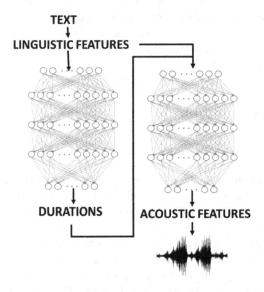

Fig. 1. Regular DNN based TTS.

In our recent research [10], we compared three different DNN-based methods for producing synthesized speech in multiple styles, originally proposed for modeling multiple speakers with a limited amount of data per speaker.

- **The method based on style code.** The idea is to have a database with one speaker, speaking in multiple styles. Besides standard linguistic feature inputs, another input is used, indicating the speech style. During training, this input is used to indicate the style of the speech data used, while in the synthesis phase, given a certain style code, the network will know which speech style to produce. The style is coded as one-hot vector.

- **Shared hidden layers.** This method is based on idea of having a separate output layer for each style, while sharing the hidden layers among different styles. In this way, all sections of the multi-style corpus are used to train the shared layers, but only a specific part of the corpus is used to train a certain output layer. In the synthesis stage, depending on which speaking style is to be produced, only a certain part of the entire model will be used.
- **Re-trained model.** The last model, maybe the most intuitive one, is based on re-training an already trained model. Namely, the idea is to train a model on a corpus of neutral speech in the regular way, and then to adapt it to a smaller speech corpus in a certain style. In such a case the number of models needed is equal to the number of styles to be produced.

Two listening tests (MOS and MUSHRA) with 20 amateur listeners, with neutral speech (3 h of training data) and angry, happy and sarcastic style of speech (5 min of training data per style) are conducted in [10]. It has been shown that intelligible and to some extent natural expressive speech can be produced by having only 5 min of speech in a certain style.

The approaches described above have originally been used for producing synthetic speech in different voices [11, 12]. However, in this case the amount of training material per speaker is higher, around 20 min. The ultimate aim of our research is to develop a framework able to produce synthetic speech in an arbitrary voice and speaking style, contributing to more expressive human-robot voice communication.

3   Evaluating the Robot Dialogue Behavior

The conversational human-like robot MARKO was developed as assistive tool for robot-supported therapy of children with cerebral palsy and similar movement disorders. One of the crucial functionalities of this robot is that it can engage in three-party natural language interaction with the child and the therapist [13–16, 18].

The dialogue behavior of the robot MARKO was experimentally evaluated in a therapeutic settings at the Clinic of Pediatric Rehabilitation in Novi Sad, Serbia (cf. Figure 2). The children who participated in this study were selected by qualified therapists. Their parents gave written permission for the children to participate, and, when possible, the children above age five gave assent. Due to the sensitivity of the research, all robot actions and speech acts were controlled by a human operator, under supervision of a therapist (cf. [18]).

The evaluation was performed in two phases. The aim of the first phase was to assess the children's receptivity to the robot MARKO at the first encounter. Thus, the experimental settings were not strictly therapeutic, but rather designed to engage a child in the interaction with the robot, and to motivate it to perform nonverbal actions on request. For example, MARKO says that it has lost a toy (i.e., confronting the child with a simple discourse), mimicking a sad facial expression (non-verbal expression of emotions can improve intention recognition, cf. [2]), and asks the child for help to find it. Twenty-nine children were involved in the first experimental phase (13 f, 16 m, avg. age 9.1, st. dev. 3.54). Twelve of them were healthy, and 17 were recruited from among patients

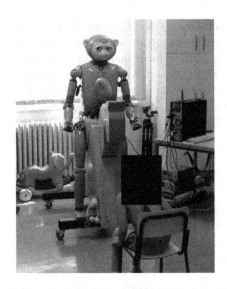

Fig. 2. The robot MARKO in the experimental setting.

with cerebral palsy and other movement disorders. In addition, the control group of patients not exposed to the robot contained 15 children (6 f, 9 m, avg. age 6.8, st. dev. 3.19). The first experimental phase validated that children positively respond to MARKO at first encounter, engage in interaction, and accept and perform given instructions. More detailed information on subjects, experimental settings, and produced corpus of child-robot interaction is given in [17, 18].

Table 1. Subjects.

ID	Age	Sex	Height [cm]	Width [kg]	Diagnosis	Mobility
s_1	15	F	159	46	hemiparesis, right sided weakness	can stand, can walk
s_2	14	F	164	50	hemiparesis, right arm disorder	can stand, can walk
s_3	9	F	129	27	paralysis cerebralis infantilis, vision problems	sitting, can stand, can walk a little with assistance
s_4	9	M	127	32	hemiparesis, left sided weakness, brain hemorrhage	can stand, can walk
s_5	15	F	150	50	paralysis cerebralis infantilis, spinal surgery	can stand, can walk
s_6	11	F	155	45	paralysis cerebralis infantilis (spastic diplegia), difficulty with speaking, vision problems, sensorimotor integration disorder	can stand, can walk
s_7	5	M	124	34	paralysis cerebralis infantilis	can stand, can walk with assistance

The second experimental phase was conducted as part of work reported in this paper. Seven children with cerebral palsy and similar movement disorders participated in this study (5 f, 2 m). The basic information on the children is given in Table 1.

The aim of this phase was to assess the children's longer-term motivation to undergo therapy in a therapeutic context. Therefore, compared to the first phase, the following aspects of the experimental settings were modified in the second phase:

(i) *Therapeutic settings.* The interaction was strictly focused on therapeutic exercises. The children were verbally instructed to perform ten Frenkel's exercises [19] selected by their respective therapists, including, but not limited to stretching in standing and sitting positions, walking along a line and between two parallel lines, lateral walking over obstacles, etc.

(ii) *Multiple sessions per child.* Each child was participating in a series of therapeutic sessions – one session per day, in a sequence of working days. Forty-four sessions were recorded. The average duration of a session was approximately 16 min, with a standard deviation of approximately 4 min. The additional information on the recorded sessions is given in Table 2.

Table 2. Sessions.

Subject ID	# Sessions	Average duration of session [s]	Standard deviation [s]
s_1	7	758	135
s_2	5	869	310
s_3	13	1104	286
s_4	4	949	237
s_5	3	933	22
s_6	7	1015	120
s_7	5	834	242
Total:	44	952	249

(iii) *Three-party interaction:* The interaction was evolving between the child, the therapist and the robot. For each child separately, in the first session, the therapist verbally instructed the child to perform exercises, while MARKO engaged in conversation either to encourage the child (e.g. by commending it), or to draw the child's attention to some aspects of the current exercise (e.g., warning the child to straighten the spine or knees, to drop the heel, etc.). From the second session, MARKO was taking the initiative in interaction from the therapist, following the dialogue strategy introduced in [18]. The robot was primarily instructing the child, while the role of the therapist was corrective.

A qualitative insight into the children's motivation to undergo robot-supported therapy was provided by their long-term therapists. The positive motivation was observed in all subjects. With respect to the level of motivation, the subjects can be classified in two groups. Subjects s_1, s_2 and s_7 were accepting the robot's instructions, and expressed steady-state motivation that was maintained but not increased through the sessions. In the remaining subjects, the motivation to undergo the therapy was established and then increased through the sessions. These subjects were not only accepting the robot's instructions, but also expressing higher engagement, e.g., they verbally interacted with MARKO, memorized the exercises, and tended to perform them in advance of the robot's instruction.

4   Conclusion

Experience in the development of a dialogue system for a humanoid robot is presented in the paper with focus on possible progress based on expressive speech recognition and synthesis. Speech technology development has evolved from small vocabulary HMM-based speech command recognition and neutral-style speech synthesized by concatenation, toward large vocabulary ASR including emotive speech and multi-style TTS – based on advantages of deep neural networks.

The reported dialogue system integrated with the robot MARKO has been tested in a clinical context. Although it includes the functionality of concatenative TTS, the children liked to participate in the dialogue and were motivated to repeat exercises that they otherwise find hard and boring (e.g., subject s_3 asked her parents to exercise on her own between sessions in order to be better during the next session with MARKO). According to the qualitative assessment provided by the involved therapists, introduction of emotions in human-robot interaction either by mimics or voice has contributed to the effects of dialogue. It is expected that a more expressive voice of the robot will further increase the positive effects, but real benefits will be assessed in future work.

Acknowledgments. Research was supported in part by the Ministry of Education, Science and Technological Development of Serbia (grants TR32035 and III44008).

References

1. Hamacher, A., Bianchi-Berthouze, N., Pipe, A.G., Eder, K.: Believing in BERT: using expressive communication to enhance trust and counteract operational error in physical Human-Robot Interaction. In: 25th IEEE International Symposium on Robot and Human Interactive Communication, 26–31 August 2016, 8 pages (2016). https://doi.org/10.1109/roman.2016.7745163
2. Berns, K., Zafar, Z.: Emotion based human-robot interaction. In: Ronzhin, A., Shishlakov, V. (eds.) 13th International Scientific-Technical Conference on Electromechanics and Robotics "Zavalishin's Readings", St. Petersburg, Russia, 18–21 April 2018, MATEC Web of Conferences, vol. 161, Article 01001, 7 pages (2018). https://doi.org/10.1051/matecconf/201816101001
3. Popović, B., et al.: A novel split-and-merge algorithm for hierarchical clustering of Gaussian mixture models. Appl. Intell. **37**(3), 377–389 (2012). https://doi.org/10.1007/s10489-011-0333-9

4. Popović, B., Ostrogonac, S., Pakoci, E., Jakovljević, N., Delić, V.: Deep Neural Network based continuous speech recognition for Serbian Using the Kaldi Toolkit. In: Ronzhin, A., Potapova, R., Fakotakis, N. (eds.) SPECOM 2015. LNCS (LNAI), vol. 9319, pp. 186–192. Springer, Cham (2015). https://doi.org/10.1007/978-3-319-23132-7_23

5. Pakoci, E., Popović, B., Pekar, D.: Language model optimization for a deep neural network based speech recognition system for Serbian. In: Karpov, A., Potapova, R., Mporas, I. (eds.) SPECOM 2017. LNCS (LNAI), vol. 10458, pp. 483–492. Springer, Cham (2017). https://doi.org/10.1007/978-3-319-66429-3_48

6. Sečujski, M., Pekar, D., Knežević, D., Svrkota V.: Prosody prediction in speech synthesis based on regression trees. In: Halupka-Rešetar, S., et al. (eds.) The 3rd International Conference of Syntax, Phonology and Language Analysis, pp. 224–236. Cambridge Scholar Publishing (2012)

7. Nwe, T., Foo, S., De Silva, L.: Speech emotion recognition using hidden Markov models. Speech. **41**, 603–623 (2003)

8. Schüller, B., Batliner, A., Steidl, S., Seppi, D.: Recognising realistic emotions and affect in speech: state of the art and lessons learnt from the first challenge. Speech Commun. **53**, 1062–1087 (2011)

9. Delić, V., Bojanić, M., Gnjatović, M., Sečujski, M., Jovičić, S.: Discrimination capability of prosodic and spectral features for emotional speech recognition. Elektronika ir Elektrotechnika **18**(9), 51–54 (2012). https://doi.org/10.5755/j01.eee.18.9.2806

10. Suzić, S., Delić, T., Jovanović, V., Sečujski, M., Pekar D., Delić, V.: A comparison of multi-style DNN-based TTS approaches using small datasets. In: 13th International Scientific-Technical Conference on Electromechanics and Robotics "Zavalishin's Readings", St. Petersburg, Russia, April 2018, MATEC Web Conference, vol. 161, 6 pages (2018). https://doi.org/10.1051/matecconf/201816103005

11. Fan, Y., Qian, Y., Soong, F. K., He, L.: Multi-speaker modeling and speaker adaptation for DNN-based TTS synthesis. In IEEE International Conference on Acoustics, Speech and Signal Processing (ICASSP), Brisbane, Australia, April 2015. https://doi.org/10.1109/icassp.2015.7178817

12. Hojo, N., Ijima, Y., Mizuno, H.: An investigation of DNN-based speech synthesis using speaker codes. In: Interspeech, San Francisco, USA. https://doi.org/10.21437/interspeech.2016-589

13. Gnjatović, M.: Therapist-centered design of a robot's dialogue behavior. Cogn. Comput. **6**(4), 775–788 (2014)

14. Gnjatović, M., Delić, V.: Cognitively-inspired representational approach to meaning in machine dialogue. Knowl. Based Syst. **71**, 25–33 (2014)

15. Gnjatović, M., Janev, M., Delić, V.: Focus tree: modeling attentional information in task-oriented human-machine interaction. Appl. Intell. **37**(3), 305–320 (2012)

16. Mišković, D., Gnjatović, M., Štrbac, P., Trenkić, B., Jakovljević, N., Delić, V.: Hybrid methodological approach to context-dependent speech recognition. Int. J. Adv. Robot. Syst. **14**(1), 12 (2017)

17. Gnjatović, M., et al.: Pilot corpus of child-robot interaction in therapeutic settings. In: Proceedings of the 8th IEEE International Conference on Cognitive Infocom. (CogInfoCom), Debrecen, Hungary, pp. 253–257 (2017)

18. Tasevski, J., Gnjatović, M., Borovac, B.: Assessing the Children's Receptivity to the Robot MARKO. Acta Polytechnica Hungarica, Special Issue on Cognitive Infocommunications (in press)

19. Zwecker, M., Zeilig, G., Ohry, A.: Professor Heinrich Sebastian Frenkel: a forgotten founder of rehabilitation medicine. Spinal Cord **42**, 55–56 (2004)

The Dynamic Model of Operator-Exoskeleton Interaction

Valery Gradetsky, Ivan Ermolov, Maxim Knyazkov, Eugeny Semenov,
and Artem Sukhanov[✉]

Ishlinsky Institute for Problems in Mechanics RAS, Pr. Vernadskogo 101-1, Moscow, Russia
sukhanov-artyom@yandex.ru

Abstract. Improving efficiency and productivity is an important factor in the development of robotic devices that can solve many human problems. Complex and monotonous actions that require precision and accuracy when moving large objects or performing technological processes can be carried out by redistributing part of the load on the robotic system. An example of such a system is an exoskeleton device. Active exoskeletons are referred to robotic human-machine systems. The interaction of operator and exoskeleton determines the quality of the functioning of such systems.

Practical purpose of research and development of active exoskeleton device for the human limbs is the reallocation of labor-intensive, monotonous activities on mechatronic system of exoskeleton.

This paper discusses the dynamic model of interaction between exoskeleton system and operator.

Keywords: Exoskeleton · Human-machine device · Mathematical simulation
Interaction · Dynamics · Lagrange equation

1 Introduction

For the organization of feedback in the control system of the exoskeleton information-measuring modules different types of sensors are essential. They allow monitoring the state of the system, obtaining information about the external environment and manipulated objects. In our work we consider three types of data levels involved in processing in control system of the exoskeleton.

The strategic level of the exoskeleton requires information about the planned movements of the operator, based on his current actions. The tactical level uses information about manipulated objects and the state of the environment. The executive level uses information about drives, the state of the brake elements and the state of limit switches.

2 The Interaction Problem

In exoskeleton systems, position sensors, strain gauges, muscle activity sensors, as well as inertial sensors are most often used as information-measuring systems [1].

© Springer Nature Switzerland AG 2018
A. Ronzhin et al. (Eds.): ICR 2018, LNAI 11097, pp. 52–59, 2018.
https://doi.org/10.1007/978-3-319-99582-3_6

In direct contact with the target object Fig. 1(a) the operator evaluates the current position of $Q_t(t)$ of the object in space, determines its orientation $W_t(t)$. The operator plans the movement of his arm for the implementation of pre-designed manipulations with the object (Q_{t+1}, W_{t+1}), acting on the object with force F and receiving tactile information about the reaction of the object R.

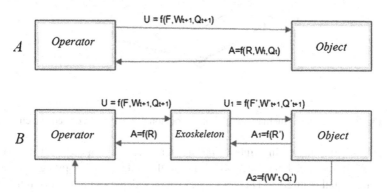

Fig. 1. Direct human interaction with the object (a) and interaction via an exoskeleton device (b).

Thus, the information about the desired position and orientation of the object at the next time (Q_{t+1}, W_{t+1}) is involved in the direct communication channel "Operator-Object" and the necessary force F is applied to perform the intended manipulations.

In the absence of knowledge about the mass of the object, a person is guided by his experience and evaluates this parameter during direct contact with the object, moving it in space and receiving tactile information about the reaction forces R.

Using the exoskeleton device (Fig. 1b) there may be no direct contact between the human arm and the object. In this case, the operator receives all the information about the forces and torques, interacting with the elements of the exoskeleton links (F, Q_{t+1}, W_{t+1}).

The control system of the exoskeleton, guided by its algorithms, interprets the human movement in the necessary movement of the links in the form of vector (F', Q'_{t+1}, W'_{t+1}). Thus control over position of object in space is assigned to the visual system of the person receiving information about the current position of the object (Q_t, W_t). The force applied to the object F' will depend on the settings of the control system.

$$F' = K_F F, \tag{1}$$

The scaling factor K_F in Eq. (1) of the applied force is dictated by the application field of the exoskeleton device. Depending on the application and the tasks to be solved, the scaling factor K_F can be linear or nonlinear. The nonlinear law of changing K_F is used in the tremor compensation of the operator's hands.

Feedback from the exoskeleton in addition to visual channel may be carried out by the resistive torques in motors located in joints of the exoskeleton device. An example of kinematics of such design is shown in Fig. 2.

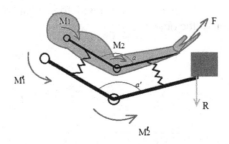

Fig. 2. Schematic kinematic model of interaction within the described system.

When changing angles in joints of the master device, the motors on the copying device create torques $M'1$ and $M'2$, which rotate the links of the copying device until the angle a' is equal to angle a. The velocity of rotation depends on the misalignment of angles a and a'.

However, the implementation of this scheme in practice shows the necessity of taking into account the kinematic characteristics of the exoskeleton links and operator's arm links, as the diagram describes the system with affine similarity of the kinematics of the links [2, 3].

With affine similarity of the master device (human arm) and coping device (exoskeleton), the position error of the exoskeleton will be k times greater than the positioning error of the operator's arm, where k is the coefficient of affine similarity [4].

The control system for the proposed exoskeleton device is based on bioelectric potentials processing. Figure 3 shows the relations between the elements of the proposed system.

It uses the information about muscular activity to form the rotation speed of exoskeleton drives. The exoskeleton's servo drive system is based on the feedback technique of acquiring information from the actuators and passing it to the control system via the HMI. Here is the functional model of the exoskeleton control system. The operator's nervous system sends signals for muscles' tension. EMG-sensors obtain data from human muscles and send signal to the preamplifier and band pass filter. Then data goes to the analog input of the microcontroller for processing. The amplified, rectified, and smoothed signal is recorded for analysis. The controller forms control signal for drive system and it performs action based on algorithms. Visual and tactile data is obtained by operator while control.

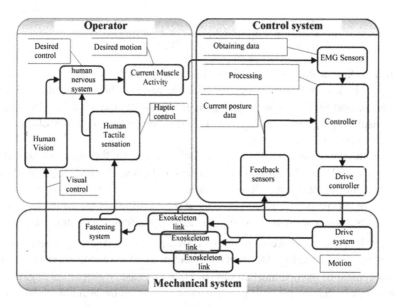

Fig. 3. Generalized model of Operator-Exoskeleton interaction.

3   The Arm Model

The dynamic model of the arm exoskeleton should take into account not only the geometric parameters of the design under consideration, but also the mass distribution of the exoskeleton links and their interaction with the operator [5]. The system Operator-Exoskeleton may be considered as a complex system consisting of two interacting and interdependent subsystems.

To simplify calculations let us consider the movement of the human arm in the exoskeleton in the sagittal plane. The operator's arm in this case may be represented as a system of two rigid bodies connected by rotary joints. The movement of the links of this subsystem is described by the Lagrange equation:

$$\frac{d}{dt}\left(\frac{\partial T_a}{\partial \dot{q}_{i.a}}\right) - \frac{\partial T_a}{\partial q_{i.a}} = M_{i.a} - \frac{\partial W_a}{\partial q_{i.a}}, \tag{2}$$

where T_a is the kinetic energy of the arm, W_a is the potential energy of the arm, $q_{i.a}$ are joint coordinates associated with the operator's arm, $M_{i.a}$ – torques corresponding to the their coordinates $q_{i.a}$. The kinetic energy of the considered arm can be found as the sum of the kinetic energies of its components: $T_a = \sum_{i=1}^{n} T_{i.a}$, where n is the number of considered links.

For an exoskeleton system that performs the operator-defined movement, the mathematical description should be similar. Considering that each link of the operator's arm is referred to its own link of the exoskeleton system, it can be noted that the movement of the links of this subsystem is described as follows:

$$\frac{d}{dt}\left(\frac{\partial T_e}{\partial \dot{q}_{i.e}}\right) - \frac{\partial T_e}{\partial q_{i.e}} = M_{i.e} - \frac{\partial W_e}{\partial q_{ie}} - M_{i.ext}, \tag{3}$$

Here T_e is kinetic energy of the exoskeleton, W_e is potential energy of the exoskeleton, $q_{i.e}$ ere joint coordinates associated with the parts of the system of exoskeleton, $M_{i.e}$ – generalized forces (torques) acting on an exoskeleton system, $M_{i.ext}$ is vector of external disturbing torques resulting from the interaction of links of the exoskeleton with the objects of the external environment.

In free movement in relation to the exoskeleton system, the vector of generalized forces (torques) $M_{i.a}$ will be formed by the efforts of the operator and will depend on the activity of its muscular system. However, taking into account the delay in the formation of the control action, the vector of generalized forces (torques) $M_{i.e}$ of the exoskeleton system will be formed with delay, which can lead to position misalignment of the operator's arm links and exoskeleton links. Thus $|q_{i.e}(t) - q_{i.a}(t)| \le \epsilon_i$, where ϵ_i is the maximum position deviation. Attachment devices of the exoskeleton impose restrictions on the movement of the operator's limbs [6, 7]. In this case, if there is such gap $\varepsilon_i > 0$, while $\varepsilon_i < \epsilon_i$, which is the possible constructive deviation of the arm link of the operator from the corresponding link of the exoskeleton, than in the Eqs. (1) and (2) vectors $M_{i.a}$ and $M_{i.e}$ will contain the interaction reactions of the arm and the exoskeleton links. In this case, the movement of the arm will be subject to a one-way constraint. For the exoskeleton device, this constraint turns to a disturbing effect [8].

Thus, the mathematical description of the movement of the exoskeleton-human system will be determined as follows:

$$\begin{cases} \frac{d}{dt}\left(\frac{\partial T_a}{\partial \dot{q}_{i.a}}\right) - \frac{\partial T_a}{\partial q_{i.a}} + \frac{\partial W_a}{\partial q_{i.a}} = M_{i.a} + R_i l_{i.a} \\ \frac{d}{dt}\left(\frac{\partial T_e}{\partial \dot{q}_{i.e}}\right) - \frac{\partial T_e}{\partial q_{i.e}} + \frac{\partial W_e}{\partial q_{ie}} = M_{i.e} - M_{i.ext} - R_i l_{i.e} \\ R_i = \begin{cases} 0, & if |q_{i.e}(t) - q_{i.a}(t)| \le \varepsilon_i \\ -k_i(q_{i.e}(t) - q_{i.a}(t) - \varepsilon_i), & if q_{i.e}(t) - q_{i.a}(t) > \varepsilon_i \\ k_i(q_{i.e}(t) - q_{i.a}(t) + \varepsilon_i), & if q_{i.e}(t) - q_{i.a}(t) < -\varepsilon_i \end{cases} \end{cases} \tag{4}$$

where k_i is a proportional factor, $l_{i.a}$ is arm for the force in the i-th joint of the operator's arm, $l_{i.e}$ is arm for the force in the i-th joint of the exoskeleton.

It should be noted that within a particular designed gap ε_i the operator's hand can be moved freely setting the movement of the links of the exoskeleton by the force of muscles. When the arm contacts with the link of the exoskeleton the not-holding joint appears, generating reactive efforts, making changes in the dynamics of the nominal system and in the dynamics of the desired motion of the exoskeleton.

4   The Experimental Investigation

In the Laboratory of Robotics and Mechatronics of the Ishlinsky Institute for Problems in Mechanics RAS a physical model of arm exoskeleton was made for experimental investigation (Fig. 4).

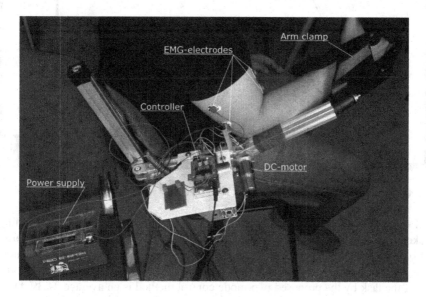

Fig. 4. The designed exoskeleton arm prototype.

It is based on DC-motor and controlled via PWM signal. Perceptive sensors reveal the value of muscle activity and transmit it for processing into the controller, where this signal is filtered and normalized. Based on the power of current muscular activity control algorithms make decision to move exoskeleton's link in the desired direction with certain velocity.

The controller sets the required speed of movement. Depending on the result of the algorithm, the current position of links is stabilized or the movement of links of the exoskeleton device performes. At the same time, the current readings of the angular encoder and the speed of the relative movement of the links are monitored by the control system, as well as by the operator, whose nervous system perceives the tactile data from the arm clamp of the exoskeleton and carries out visual perception of the current action for further planning.

Theoretical studies have been confirmed experimentally (Fig. 5). As a result of the experiments, the biopotential data of the operator muscle groups in the performance of various actions were obtained.

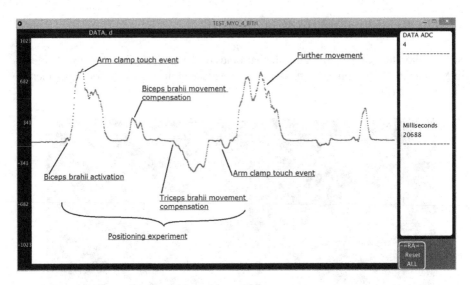

Fig. 5. Biceps brachii and Triceps brachii activity with exoskeleton device.

A series of control algorithm tests was carried out to determine the efficiency of the exoskeleton when performing the task of positioning the exoskeleton link in different control modes. In the experimental studies, the time spent on the operation to achieve the target position was measured. The control system tests have shown that the performance of the task by the proposed two-mode control method is on average 24.3% faster than single-mode control based on the proportional dependence of torque on the activity of the operator's biopotentials.

5 Conclusion

To implement the desired movement of the exoskeleton links it is necessary to process information coming from various sources (operator, reactive forces from the objects). Processing that data is essential for generation of control signal for the exoskeleton system.

A human, as a part of the "Operator-Exoskeleton" system, forms the desired impact on the objects in the environment and receives information about them. The operator has its own subsystems such as tactile sensing, visual sensing, and planner.

Control of the desired actions as well as evaluation of the object properties processed through the visual channel. Tactile sensing allows operator to evaluate the reaction forces when interacting with objects in the environment. In the presence of exoskeleton device operating between human and the environment, it is necessary to understand that the integration of such a link into the information channel between human and the object leads to complex problems of that interaction. One of these problems is evaluation of reaction forces between human arm and the robotic device.

Acknowledgments. This study was partly supported by FASO Russia (Project No. AAAA-A17-117021310384-9).

This study was partly supported by the Program №.29 "Advanced Topics of Robotic Systems" (Project No. AAAA-A17-117121120021-9) of the Presidium of the Russian Academy of Sciences.

References

1. Zhechev, M.M.: Equations of motion for singular systems of massed and massless bodies. J. Multibody Dynamics **221**(K4), 591–597 (2007)
2. Pons, J.L.: Upper-limb robotic rehabilitation exoskeleton: tremor suppression. In: Kommu, S.S. (ed.) Rehabilitation Robotics, 648 p. Itech Education and Publishing, Vienna (2007)
3. Bergamasco, M.: An arm exoskeleton system for teleoperation and virtual environment applications. In: IEEE International Conference on Robotics and Automation, pp. 1449–1454 (1994)
4. Burdea, G.C.: Force and Touch Feedback for Virtual Reality. Wiley, New York, 368 p. (1996)
5. Park, H.S.: Developing a multi-joint upper limb exoskeleton robot for diagnosis, therapy and outcome evaluation in neurorehabilitation. IEEE Trans. Neural Syst. Rehabil. Eng. **21**(3), 490–499 (2013)
6. Thompson, R.L.: Integration of visual and haptic feedback for teleoperation. Ph.D. thesis, Trinity College Department of Engineering Science University of Oxford, 153 p. (2001)
7. Kazerooni, H.: Extenders: a case study for human-robot interaction via the transfer of power and information signals. In: Plenary Speaker at the 2nd IEEE International Workshop on Robot and Human Communication, Tokyo, Japan (1993)
8. Ishida, T.: Movement analysis of power-assistive machinery with high strength-amplification. In: Proceedings of SICE Annual Conference, pp. 2022–2025 (2010)

The Influence of Various Factors
on the Control of the Exoskeleton

Valery Gradetsky, Ivan Ermolov, Maxim Knyazkov, Eugeny Semenov,
and Artem Sukhanov[✉]

Ishlinsky Institute for Problems in Mechanics RAS, Pr. Vernadskogo 101-1, Moscow, Russia
sukhanov-artyom@yandex.ru

Abstract. The operator is an important component of the Operator-Exoskeleton system. He is a source of signals and he controls the result of the actuators motion. The main source that drives the links of the human skeleton is the force of muscle contraction. The amplitude and frequency of the control signal is formed by the central nervous system. The work of muscles due to physiological processes leads to movement of human limbs. Biomechanics deals with the problems and tasks of the human motor system, as well as the tasks of optimization of operator's limbs movement, evaluation of the effectiveness of the application of forces for a better achievement of the goal. This paper discusses the influence of various factors on the control of the exoskeleton.

Keywords: Exoskeleton · Human-machine device · Mathematical simulation
Interaction · EMG sensors · Biopotentials

1 Introduction

For limb movements, the central nervous system sends impulses, stimulating the membranes of motor units of myofibrils. This excitation leads to the dissociation of ions of the near-cell space inside the myofibrils and the interaction of actin and myosin proteins, which leads to contraction of this cell. Each impulse of the operator's central nervous system exceeding a certain amplitude threshold reduces a separate thread of myofibrils collected in a bundle of fibers. The effort and the amount of reduction depend on the elasticity of muscle fibers and their viscosity, as well as the speed of biochemical processes.

2 The Operator's Muscle Model

This effect was mathematically described by many researchers [1], but the most reliable is the Hodgkin-Huxley model. Failures of combining the Hodgkin-Huxley model and the Hill model [2] are explained by the inability to give an accurate answer to the question about the number of motor units and the neurons that excite them in a single muscle by its external features without invasive examination.

© Springer Nature Switzerland AG 2018
A. Ronzhin et al. (Eds.): ICR 2018, LNAI 11097, pp. 60–69, 2018.
https://doi.org/10.1007/978-3-319-99582-3_7

The velocity of muscle contraction on the Hill model with maximum force should be equal to zero. In the absence of load on a muscle the contraction speed should be maximal.

$$V_a = \frac{b\left(F_{max} - F_{des}\right)}{F_{des} + a}.$$

(1)

Here, b is the empirical nonlinear variable with dimension of speed, a is an empirical non-linear variable with dimension of force. Variable b increases numerically with increasing temperature. It is shown that when the environment is heated by 10°, the numerical value of b increases by 2–2.5 times [3–5]. A numerical variable of a is 25–40% of the value of the maximum force of isometric contraction. This variable in the calculation models is called the optimal reduction effort. It characterizes the maximum power developed by the muscle when it creates the current strength. This parameter can vary for different types of muscles and reach 60% of the maximum force for a person. In the estimated models, this parameter is equal to $0{,}31 \, F_{max}$. F_{des} is the desired force.

The existing models of muscle contraction represent static calculations, which allow determining the desired force by the known parameters of muscle-length and contraction speed. In these computational models researchers are trying to find the ratio of the current length of the muscle, the rate of contraction and the actual force. The force developed by the muscle is expressed by the following way:

$$F_{des}(t) = f_{FV}\left(V_a\right) f_{Fl}\left(l_a\right) a(t) F_{max}.$$

(2)

Here $f_{FV}\left(V_a\right)$ is functional dependence of contraction force from speed of muscle contraction, $f_{Fl}\left(l_a\right)$ is dependence of contraction force from the current length of the muscle. Mathematical models of these dependencies were obtained by the authors of these articles [6]. The activation level a(t) is the value determined by the ratio of the force $F_{des}(t)$, to maximum possible force, developed under the current parameters of the length $l_a(t)$ and the reduction rate $V_a(t)$.

$$a(t) = \frac{F_{des}(t)}{F_{max}\left(l_a(t), V_a(t)\right)}.$$

(3)

The value of the activation level is formed by the human brain on the basis of the planned action and the current tactile and visual information from the feedback channels. We model the brain of an operator as the task scheduler which tries to establish the desired force on the object (forming the force on the muscle $F_{des}(t)$) based on the amount of mismatch to the desired length of the muscle $l_{des}(t)$ and the actual length of the muscle $l_a(t)$. On the basis of this, we assume that the formation of the desired force is described by the proportional control law:

$$F_{des}(t) = K_f\left(l_{des}(t) - l_a(t)\right).$$

(4)

Here K_f is stiffness.

Each muscle, as an element of the biomechanical system, has a number of current parameters: the current non-zero length $l_a(t)$, the current contraction rate $V_a(t)$ and the current developed contraction force. In addition to the current parameters of the muscle there are boundary conditions. They are include the maximum muscle extension length l_{max}, the minimum muscle length l_{min}, the neutral length in the passive state l_0, as well as the maximum possible force that the muscle can develop for the current length and contraction speed $F_{max}(l_a(t), V_a(t))$.

In this paper we consider a certain type of muscle – skeletal muscle. Each skeletal muscle in the human body is composed of motor units. Each motor unit is externally excited cell, surrounded by a solution of potassium and sodium ions. Motor units are connected together in the thread, and the threads themselves are assembled into bundles. Nerve impulses generated by the human brain come to bundles of motor units via neurons. This changes the electric potential of cell membranes.

When the polarity changes positively charged sodium ions penetrate into the cytoplasm of the motor unit cells. This starts the process of contraction of these cells. In this case, the membrane of the cells of motor units can be in two states – excited or not excited. This effect in physiology is known as the law of "all or nothing", so the interaction of the neuron and the membrane can be modeled by the PWM element, the duty cycle of which per unit time will show the frequency of occurrence of the action potential in the muscle cell. This duty cycle will be determined by the activation level parameter $a(t)$ (Fig. 1).

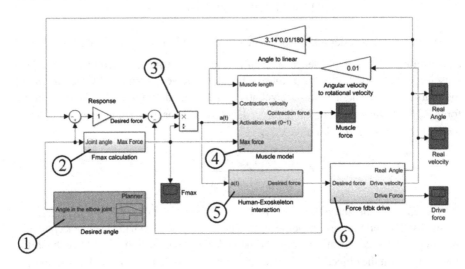

Fig. 1. Interaction model of the Operator-Exoskeleton system.

Figure 1 shows the scheme of interaction between the operator and the exoskeleton on the example of biceps brachii work. It reflects the links between the various elements. The task scheduler {1} can be considered as the master device in this scheme. The scheduler is equivalent to the target task, represented in a graphical form. In this case, the desired law of motion is represented in the form of a linear change of the generalized coordinate from 0° corresponding to the situation of lowered down of the operator's arm to 135°, which corresponds to the arm bent in the elbow joint.

The desired position of the arm corresponds to the maximum possible developing force that can be applied by the operator. To get this parameter, the control system must be calibrated to the individual characteristics of the operator, determining the maximum isometric load and evaluating the resulting angle. The chart of maximum force change from the angle is shown in Fig. 2.

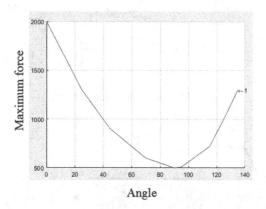

Fig. 2. The chart of isometric force application.

The data of this chart is needed for the control system to determine the maximum effort that the operator can develop for the current position of his limbs. Such database can be created for any skeletal muscle involved in the movement control of the exoskeleton. In the Fig. 1, this database is marked as {2}.

In this study we used the model of muscle contraction (Fig. 1 {4}), which is described in papers [7–10] and modified for obtaining the contraction force depending on the parameter of the maximum force (Fig. 3).

The activation level a(t) is calculated based on the expression (6) (Fig. 1 {3}), which is an important information parameter for the muscle contraction model. This parameter is also a source of information for the biopotential sensor (EMG sensor). Sending impulses, the brain generates tension in muscle. Operator-Exoskeleton interaction block (Fig. 1 {5}) is a link between the duty cycle of the operator's nervous system impulses and the motor control system of the exoskeleton (Fig. 1 {6}). In this block (Fig. 4) the time delay of the reaction of the synapse, the excitation of the muscle fiber, as well as the reaction of calcium exchange in the cells of the muscle were taken into account [11, 12].

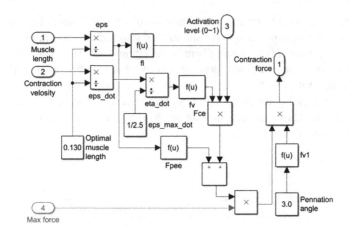

Fig. 3. Modified muscle model [7–9].

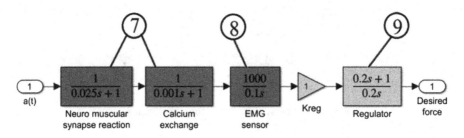

Fig. 4. Operator-Exoskeleton interaction block.

Here the control of the exoskeleton starts to form (Fig. 4). Delay in processing the signal of nerve impulses for the synapse and the process of calcium ion exchange in cells formed as aperiodic links {7}.

The transfer function of the biopotential sensor corresponds to the integrating unit with a sufficient gain ratio, which corresponds to the actual amplification of the EMG sensor {8}. The real integrating link has a transfer function $W_{ir} = \dfrac{K_I}{T_I s^2 + s}$. Unlike the linear transient characteristic of an ideal integrator, the transient characteristic of such an integrator should be curvilinear.

Block {9} is a PI controller that generates a control signal to the actuator input of the exoskeleton. It has customizable settings for integration time, the T_{reg} and transfer coefficient K_{reg}.

The actuator of the exoskeleton Fig. 1{6} is a multi-circuit electromechanical system, closed via force. In addition to force feedback, this system provides speed and current feedback Fig. 5.

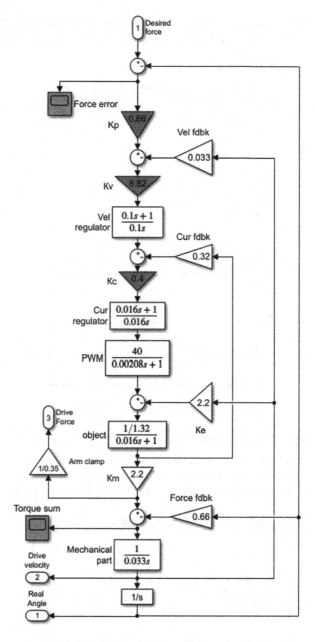

Fig. 5. Exoskeleton's drive with force feedback.

The mechanical part of this drive uses the total moment of inertia of the operator's arm and the exoskeleton link with the fastening clamp. This system was considered in more detail earlier [13, 14].

The change of the coefficients T_{reg} and K_{reg} inside the control block leads to a change in the dynamics of the system of Operator-Exoskeleton. For example, reducing the time T_{reg} leads to the overshoot (Fig. 6).

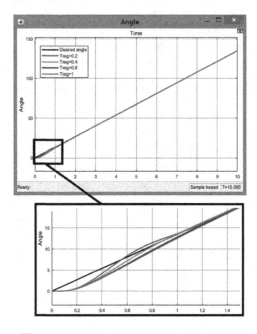

Fig. 6. Angular coordinate in the elbow joint.

As it can be noticed from the chart (Fig. 6), the best result was achieved at $T_{reg} = 0.4$ s. At this value, the hit in the 5% accuracy tube was obtained with the lowest transition time. In further experiments, this value of the regulator parameter was used.

Dynamics of change of speed of rotation of a link is shown in Fig. 7.

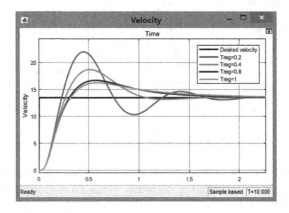

Fig. 7. Drive's velocity chart.

A significant decrease of the parameter T_{reg} leads to loss of stability of the system, which is associated with the reaction of the operator, reflected in the muscle model. Increasing the time T_{reg} significantly increases the duration of the position and speed transient processes for the drive of the exoskeleton.

The gain coefficient in the regulator is also of great importance in the synthesis of the control formation. The results of the experiment are shown in Fig. 8.

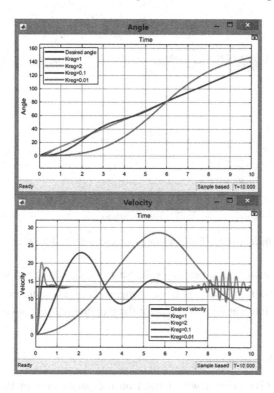

Fig. 8. The influence of K_{reg} variation on the behavior of the drive system.

The Fig. 8 shows that the reducing of the coefficient K_{reg} leads to a significant increase of transient parameters of the angle and velocity. Further increase of this parameter, however, leads to the appearance of beats, expressed in increasing of the velocity amplitude. This is due to the fact that the reaction of the operator to the velocity changing of the exoskeleton's links does not have enough time. The operator continues to move his arm even after drive compensation of misalignments on the position. That leads to mistiming of actions of the operator and the exoskeleton and desynchronizes movement.

Experiments have shown that these beats appear when $K_{reg} > 1$.

The experiments also showed the effect of changing the gain coefficient of the EMG sensor on the dynamics of the exoskeleton movement (Fig. 9).

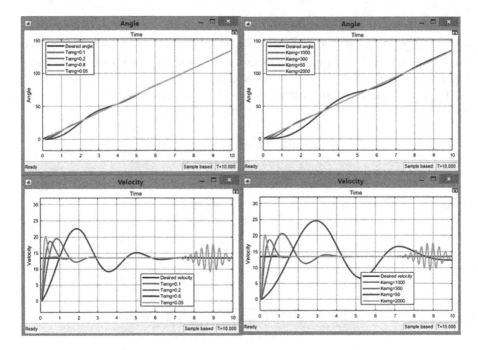

Fig. 9. The Influence of the EMG sensor parameters on the dynamics of the system.

Increasing parameter K_{EMG} decreases the time of transients process of velocity and angle, but also results in beats, as does changing K_{reg}. The similar situation can be obtained when the integration time T_{EMG} for the biopotential sensor changes.

3   Conclusion

The exoskeleton drive control will depend on the parameters of the controller and biopotential sensor. The choice of the parameters of these elements will significantly affect the dynamics of the exoskeleton. In this paper, we have proposed the interaction model of the exoskeleton system with the operator modeled via biceps brachii action. The study simulated the effect of system parameters variations on the dynamics of the Operator-Exoskeleton system. The results of modeling were presented.

Acknowledgments. This study was partly supported by FASO Russia (Project No. AAAA-A17-117021310384-9).

This study was partly supported by the Program №.29 "Advanced Topics of Robotic Systems" (AAAA-A17-117121120021-9) of the Presidium of the Russian Academy of Sciences.

References

1. Novoselov, V.S.: On mathematical models of molecular contraction of skeletal muscles. Vestnik SPbGU. Ser. **10**(3), 88–96 (2016). (In Rus.)
2. Gasser, H.S., Hill, A.V.: The dynamics of muscle contraction. Proc. Roy. Soc. London Ser. B **96**, 398–437 (1924)
3. Hill, A.: Physiology of muscular activity, labor and sports: manual of physiology. Mech. Muscle Contraction (1969)
4. Abbott, V.S., Wilkie, D.R.: The relation between velocity of shortening and the tension-length curve of skeletal muscle. J. Physiol. **120**, 214–223 (1953)
5. Wilkie, D.R.: The mechanical properties of muscle. Br. Med. Bull. **12**, 177–182 (1956)
6. Haeufle, D.F.B., Grimmer, S., Seyfarth, A.: The role of intrinsic muscle properties for stable hopping—stability is achieved by the force–velocity relation. Bioinspir. Biomim. **5**(1), 016004 (2010). https://doi.org/10.1088/1748-3182/5/1/016004
7. Sancho-Bru, J.L., et al.: Towards a realistic and self-contained biomechanical model of the hand. In: Theoretical Biomechanics, pp. 212–240 (2011)
8. Zajac, F.E., Gordon, M.E.: Determining muscle's force and action in multi-articular movement. Exerc. Sport Sci. Rev. **17**, 187–230 (1989)
9. Zajac, F.E.: Muscle and tendon: properties, models, scaling, and application to biomechanics and motor control. CRC Crit. Rev. Biomed. Eng. **17**, 359–411 (1989)
10. http://youngmok.com/hill-type-muscle-model-with-matlab-code/
11. Vladimir, R.: Neuromodulation: Action Potential Modeling. Master of Science Thesis in Biomedical Engineering, 130 p. (2014)
12. Andersson, S.: Active Muscle Control in Human Body Model Simulations, Master's Thesis in Automotive Engineering, CHALMERS, Applied Mechanics, Master's Thesis, 62, 64 p. (2013)
13. Gradetsky, V., Ermolov, I., Knyazkov, M., Sukhanov, A.: Generalized approach to bilateral control for EMG driven exoskeleton. In: 12-th International Scientific-Technical Conference on Electromechanics and Robotics "Zavalishin's Readings", vol. 113 (2017)
14. Ermolov, I.L., Sukhanov, A.N., Knyaz'kov, M.M., Kryukova, A.A., Kryuchkov, B.I., Usov, V.M.: A sensory control and orientation system of an exoskeleton. In: Proceedings of Saint Petersburg International Conference on Integrated Navigation Systems, vol. 22, pp. 181–185 (2015)

Sign Language Numeral Gestures Recognition Using Convolutional Neural Network

Ivan Gruber[1,2(✉)], Dmitry Ryumin[3], Marek Hrúz[1,2], and Alexey Karpov[3]

[1] Faculty of Applied Sciences, Department of Cybernetics,
UWB, Pilsen, Czech Republic
grubiv@kky.zcu.cz
[2] Faculty of Applied Sciences, NTIS, UWB, Pilsen, Czech Republic
mhruz@ntis.zcu.cz
[3] SPIIRAS, St. Petersburg, Russia
dl_03.03.1991@mail.ru, karpov@iias.spb.su

Abstract. This paper presents usage of convolutional neural network for classification of sign language numeral gestures. For requirements of this research, we created a new dataset of these gestures. The dataset was recorded via Kinect v2 device and it consists of recordings of 18 different people. Only depth data-stream was used in our research. For a classification task, there was utilized classic VGG16 architecture and its results were compared with chosen baseline method and other tested architectures. Our experiment on classification showed the great potential of neural networks for this task. We reached recognition accuracy 86.45%, which is by more than 34% better result than chosen baseline method.

Keywords: Sign language · Image recognition · Classification
Neural network · Assistive robot · Computer vision

1 Introduction

The task of increasing the level of automation and robotization in all spheres of human activity is one of the keys in the modern information society. In this connection, scientists and leaders of developed countries, as well as developing countries, in cooperation with world scientific centers and companies pay attention to technologies for an effective, natural and universal interaction of a person with computers and robots.

Currently, interactive information systems are used in the areas of social services, medicine, education, robotics, the military industry, community service centers, to interact with people in various situations. In addition, robotic assistants are finding more and more widespread which are simple and intuitive in use. Compared to industrial robots that are only able to repeat predetermined tasks, robot-assistants are aimed at interacting with people in the performance

A. Ronzhin et al. (Eds.): ICR 2018, LNAI 11097, pp. 70–77, 2018.
https://doi.org/10.1007/978-3-319-99582-3_8

of tasks. In this case, many classical interfaces are not enough. Instead, more intuitive and natural approaches for human interfaces are needed (speech [2], gestural [3], multimodal [1,4–6], etc.). For example, gestures can transmit simple commands to a robot that will carry unambiguous meaning and are effective at some distance from the robot and in noisy conditions when speech is ineffective.

It is also known that deaf people have limited capabilities when communicating with the hearing. Therefore, there is necessity to develop recognition of sign language technologies for deaf people. In addition to large world companies, national research centers are also working in this direction. Scientists from the American Institute of Robotics at Carnegie Mellon University are working on a system that can analyze the language of the body and gestures up to the point of the fingers [7]. A number of researchers rightly point out that serious differences in the semantic-syntactic structure of written and sign languages do not yet allow an unambiguous translation of the sign languages. Therefore, there are currently no fully automatic sign language translation systems. To create a complete model, it is necessary to make a semantic analysis of written phrases, and this is still possible only at a superficial level because of imperfections in text analysis algorithms and knowledge bases.

At present, Microsoft provides a tool in the form of a sensor-rangefinder Kinect for the development of systems with the possibility of recognizing the sign language [8,9], which allows us to obtain a three-dimensional video stream of information in the form of a depth map or a three-dimensional cloud of points. MS Kinect 2.0 provides simultaneous detection and automatic tracking of up to 6 people at the distance of 1.2–3.5 meters from the sensor. In the software, a virtual model of human's body is presented as a 3D skeleton of 25 points.

The paper is organized as follows: in Sect. 2 we introduce used dataset; in Sect. 3 we presented used processing methods and discuss software implementation details; in Sect. 4 we describe the experiment and show obtained results; and finally in Sect. 5 we draw a conclusion and outline our future research.

2   Dataset

In this paper, we use our own dataset of numeral hand gestures. We recorded 10 gestures of a hand performing numbers from American Sign Language. These gestures are, to some extent, universal and many other sign languages use them. We recorded 18 people performing the gestures with 5 repetitions using a commercial depth sensor Kinect v2. For the purpose of this research, we use only the depth data-stream. Each repetition of a gesture consists of a movement of the hand into the performing space, where the hand stops and a static gesture representing a number from zero to nine is shown. To obtain only the frames with the gesturing static hand we implemented our own semi-automatic labeling algorithm. Since Kinect provides us with a skeletal model of a human it is easy to follow the movement of the hand by tracking a joint representing the palm of the hand. Some time synchronization is needed but the position of the joints changes linearly between consecutive frames and thus the proper position of the palm joint in the time of depth map acquisition is easily interpolated. The palm joint location is considered as a center of a 3D box containing the hand. Since Kinect uses orthographic projection in the depth axis the depth of the 3D box is always constant and has been chosen to be 200 mm. However, the xy-axes use projective transformation and thus the size of the 3D box in this image plane has to be adapted according to the depth of the palm joint. We use the same size of the box in both the x and y axis computed using the formula:

$$M = \frac{\alpha \cdot \text{depth}_{\text{max}}}{\text{depth}}, \tag{1}$$

where M is the size of the box in pixels, $\text{depth}_{\text{max}}$ is the maximal depth of the capturing device (in our case 8000), depth is the measured depth in the palm joint location, and α is a scale coefficient, which we experimentally chose equal 15. All the 3D boxes are resized to 96×96 pixels and the depth in the box is normalized from 0 to 1. These resulting hand depth images are manually labeled as either one of the numeral gestures or as a non-informative gesture simply named background. Furthermore, if the performer used his/her left hand for gesturing the resulting hand depth image was flipped.

Next, the hand depth images were augmented to help with the training of the neural network. We used random translation and planar rotation to obtain the final dataset. Each hand image was translated four times by a randomly selected 2D vector representing the planar translation. The numbers were drawn from a uniform distribution in an interval $[-12; 12]$ px. The rotation was performed three times by a randomly selected angle from the interval $\pm 20°$. In total, the dataset consists of 130843 depth images of hands. Some examples of the dataset are shown in Fig. 1.

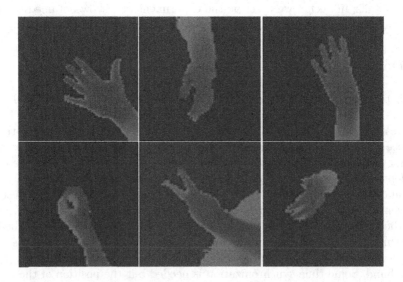

Fig. 1. Example of the dataset. From top left to the bottom right: gesture for no. 5, background, no. 4, no. 0, no. 2, and background again.

3   Methods

Due to the neural networks improvements since 2012 [10], most hand-crafted feature descriptors in image classification, if enough data available, become inferior in comparison with machine-learned ones. In this paper we tested two approaches on the task of numeral gesture classification.

First, we calculated Histogram of Gradients (HoGs) [11] for all the data. Each HoG's cell had 16×16 pixels and each block had 3×3 cells. With this settings we obtained feature vector with dimension of 1152 for each image.

These HoGs were used to train standard Support Vector Machine (SVM) [12] classifier with RBF kernel. This setup is used as our baseline method.

Second, we trained convolutional neural network with modified VGG16 architecture [13]. This architecture belongs to the golden standard among neural network architectures used for image classification, especially for tasks with a lower amount of training data. The exact network configuration we used is shown in Table 1.

Table 1. Modified VGG16 architecture.

Layer	Properties	Activation fcn
Conv1a	3×3, stride 1, filters 64	ReLU
Conv1b	3×3, stride 1, filters 64	ReLU
Max pool	2×2, stride 2	
Conv2a	3×3, stride 1, filters 128	ReLU
Conv2b	3×3, stride 1, filters 128	ReLU
Max pool	2×2, stride 2	
Conv3a	3×3, stride 1, filters 256	ReLU
Conv3b	3×3, stride 1, filters 256	ReLU
Max pool	2×2, stride 2	
Conv4a	3×3, stride 1, filters 512	ReLU
Conv4b	3×3, stride 1, filters 512	ReLU
Max pool	2×2, stride 2	
Conv5a	3×3, stride 1, filters 512	ReLU
Conv5b	3×3, stride 1, filters 512	ReLU
Max pool	2×2, stride 2	
Fully-connected1	1024D	ReLU
Dropout	dropout rate 0.5	
Fully-connected2	11D	SoftMax

4   Experiments and Results

In our experiment, we evaluate the performance of methods on the classification task of numeral gestures, i.e. we want to classify the input image into one of 11 classes (10 numerals and background).

Due to the amount of data, we use cross-validation with 10 different cross-validation settings. For each of them, our dataset was split into two subsets - train set, and test set, where each test set contained data from 4 speakers and train set rest of them.

As a benchmark method SVM classifier trained on HoGs with dimension of 1152 was used. The average recognition accuracy among all the cross-validation settings was 52.31% ± 3.51% on the test data.

Table 2. Comparison of the recognition accuracy results from individual cross-validations (CVs).

CV split	Accuracy, %
No. 1	83.37
No. 2	83.72
No. 3	92.04
No. 4	87.01
No. 5	88.11
No. 6	83.74
No. 7	88.85
No. 8	84.80
No. 9	84.16
No. 10	88.73

For neural network architecture, we come out from VGG16 architecture, however, we cut one of the fully-connected layers entirely and the second one was resized from 4096 to 1024, i.e. this layer provides feature vector with size 1024, which is comparable with the dimension of used HoG descriptor.

The neural network was trained with 20 epochs with mini-batch size 64 and with initial learning rate = 10^{-3}. The learning rate was decreased after 10 epoch to 10^{-4}. For updating network parameters standard SGD optimization with momentum = 0.9 and weight decay = 5×10^{-4} was used. As a loss function, standard Softmax loss was used. Neural network was implemented in Python using Keras deep learning library [14]. The average recognition accuracy among all the cross-validation setting was 86.45% ± 2.93%, which is by more than 34% better than used baseline method. The results from the individual cross-validations can be found in Table 2.

The results show us, that not each cross-validation is equally difficult. This phenomenon is probably caused by the different ability of each speaker to perform numeral gestures properly. Further, it can be caused by inconsistency during labeling among our annotators. You can see some examples of misclassification in Fig. 2.

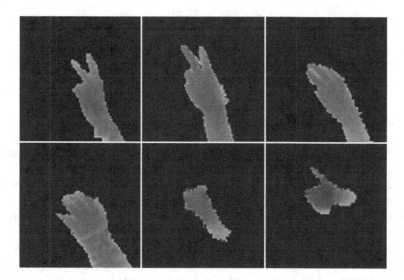

Fig. 2. Examples of misclassification. From the top row left to right: classified as 3 instead 2, classified as 7 instead 2, classified as background instead 3. Bottom row: classified as background instead 5, classified as background instead 6, classified as background instead 7. Last two are examples of wrong labels in our dataset.

We also tested some other neural network architectures during our initial experiments. All of them were tested only on cross-validation split number 1 with the same training settings as our modified VGG16. For comprehensive comparison see Table 3. CNN3 × 32 is a simple architecture with three convolutional layers, whereas each of them has 32 filters with kernel size 3 × 3, and two fully-connected layers (one with size 1024 and the last one with size 11 as a classification layer). CNN3 × 32b is almost the same architecture, however, the number of filters of the second convolution is doubled and the third one is quadrupled. CNN3 + 5 + 7 has three convolutions and 2 fully-connected layers again, however, each convolution has different size of the kernel (3, 5, and 7 respectively). All of the convolutional layers have 32 kernels again. Last tested architecture CNN3 + 5 + 7b utilizes the same approach as CNN3 × 32b, e.g. the number of kernels in convolutions is appropriately increased.

Overall, the experiment shows the superiority of the approach utilizing a neural network and machine-learned features over the classic HoG+SVM approach. Moreover, we reached very promising results, which show us a great potential of neural networks for gesture and sign language recognition.

Table 3. Comparison of baseline method, modified VGG16 and other tested architectures in terms of recognition accuracy.

Method	Accuracy, %
HoG+SVM	50.12
VGG16_1024	**83.72**
CNN3 × 32	71.23
CNN3 × 32b	73.18
CNN3 + 5 + 7	74.42
CNN3 + 5 + 7b	75.11

5   Conclusion and Future Work

Sign language recognition and gesture recognition is very demanded task in the modern world. We believe it is essential for next generation of robotic assistants, as well as an assistive tool for deaf people. In this paper, we show the great potential of the usage of neural networks for this task. Moreover, we reach very promising recognition results on our own dataset of sign language numeral gestures. We believe that with some minor modification of our neural network architecture, with more augmentations, and with bigger training set, we can reach flawless results.

In our future research, we would like to extend our dataset with recordings from more speakers. Additionally, we would like to add some other important sign language gestures.

Acknowledgments. This work is financially supported by the Ministry of Education and Science of the Russian Federation, agreement No. 14.616.21.0095 (reference RFMEFI61618X0095) and the Ministry of Education of the Czech Republic, project No. LTARF18017. The work has been also supported by the grant of the University of West Bohemia, project No. SGS-2016-039. Moreover, access to computing and storage facilities owned by parties and projects contributing to the National Grid Infrastructure MetaCentrum provided under the programme "Projects of Large Research, Development, and Innovations Infrastructures" (CESNET LM2015042), is greatly appreciated.

References

1. Ivanko, D.V., Karpov, A.A.: An analysis of perspectives for using high-speed cameras in processing dynamic video information. SPIIRAS Proc. **44**(1), 98–113 (2016). https://doi.org/10.15622/sp.44.7
2. Karpov, A., Kipyatkova, I., Zelezny, M.: Automatic technologies for processing spoken sign languages. Procedia Comput. Sci. **81**, 201–207 (2016)
3. Ryumin, D., Karpov, A.A.: Towards automatic recognition of sign language gestures using kinect 2.0. In: Antona, M., Stephanidis, C. (eds.) UAHCI 2017. LNCS, vol. 10278, pp. 89–101. Springer, Cham (2017). https://doi.org/10.1007/978-3-319-58703-5_7

4. Karpov, A., Krnoul, Z., Zelezny, M., Ronzhin, A.: Multimodal synthesizer for Russian and Czech sign languages and audio-visual speech. In: Stephanidis, C., Antona, M. (eds.) UAHCI 2013. LNCS, vol. 8009, pp. 520–529. Springer, Heidelberg (2013). https://doi.org/10.1007/978-3-642-39188-0_56

5. Karpov, A., Ronzhin, A.: A universal assistive technology with multimodal input and multimedia output interfaces. In: Stephanidis, C., Antona, M. (eds.) UAHCI 2014. LNCS, vol. 8513, pp. 369–378. Springer, Cham (2014). https://doi.org/10.1007/978-3-319-07437-5_35

6. Ivanko, D., et al.: Using a high-speed video camera for robust audio-visual speech recognition in acoustically noisy conditions. In: Karpov, A., Potapova, R., Mporas, I. (eds.) SPECOM 2017. LNCS (LNAI), vol. 10458, pp. 757–766. Springer, Cham (2017). https://doi.org/10.1007/978-3-319-66429-3_76

7. Cao, Z., Simon, T., Wei, S.-E., Sheikh, Y.: Realtime multi-Person 2D pose estimation using part affinity fields. In: CVPR (2017)

8. Shibata, H., Nishimura, H., Tanaka, H.: Basic investigation for improvement of sign language recognition using classification scheme. In: Yamamoto, S. (ed.) HIMI 2016. LNCS, vol. 9734, pp. 563–574. Springer, Cham (2016). https://doi.org/10.1007/978-3-319-40349-6_55

9. Guo, X., Yang, T.: Gesture recognition based on HMM-FNN model using a Kinect. J. Multimodal User Interfaces 11, 1–7 (2016)

10. Krizhevsky, A., Sutskever, I., Hinton, G.E.: Imagenet classification with deep convolutional neural networks. In: Proceedings of Advances in Neural Information Processing, pp. 1106–1114 (2012)

11. Dalal, N., Triggs, B.: Histograms of oriented gradients for human detection. In: Proceedings of the 2005 IEEE Computer Society Conference on Computer Vision and Pattern Recognition (CVPR 2005), pp. 886–893 (2005)

12. Hearst, M.A.: Support vector machines. IEEE Intell. Syst. 13, 18–28 (1998)

13. Simonyan, K., Zisserman, A.: Very Deep Convolutional Networks for Large-Scale Image Recognition. CoRR (2014)

14. Chollet, F.: Keras (2015). https://keras.io

Consensus-Based Localization of Devices with Unknown Transmitting Power

Nurbanu Güzey$^{(\boxtimes)}$ and Hacı Mehmet Güzey

Elektrik-Elektronik Mühendisliği, Erzurum Teknik Üniversitesi,
Ömer Nasuhi Bilmen Mahallesi, Yakutiye Cd. No: 53, 25050 Erzurum, Turkey
{nurbanu.guzey,mehmet.guzey}@erzurum.edu.tr

Abstract. A novel localization scheme, based on RSSI is demonstrated in this manuscript. Previous methods require fingerprinting which is not suitable to locate sources in different environments or they need to know the transmitted power from the source as well as antenna and channel characteristics to apply the propagation loss formula. However, the proposed method of this paper only compares the received powers by antennas on a linear array and applying a control algorithm to ensure the formation, then find the location of the source device. The new control algorithm is driven by using the differences of received signal powers.

Keywords: Localization · Unknown transmitting power · Consensus

1 Introduction

Localization of electronic devices has a great importance in commercial life and also in defence and surveillance applications. To locate an electronic device various techniques have been developed through years. The first and basic one is localization with Received Signal Strength Indicator (RSSI) [1]. In this method, when the transmitted power is known, with fading formula of transmitted signal, location of the device can be found. However, the transmit power of a signal varies device to device and other physical factors such as; battery of device effects the transmitted power. Therefore, relying on transmit power will not give a precise location. To overcome this, developing a fingerprint map appeared especially in indoor localization [2]. But this method will be practical in a steady media. To use in different environments, fingerprinting is required each time which will not be efficient.

The other technique is utilizing antenna arrays and using Time-of-Arrival (TOA) differences of antennas in the array [3]. This technique needs a very accurate synchronization. Another usage of antenna arrays is Angle of Arrival (AOA) method [4]. İnstead of arrival time, arrival angle to each antenna is used for localization. The accuracy of AOA method relies on the number of the antenna and position of the source where if the source is in the end points of the array, accuracy of the localization decreases.

The proposed method in this paper also uses antenna array in different way: to provide formation. A mobile linear antenna array which is separated by a reference point (middle point of the array) moves with a control algorithm to ensure left and right

© Springer Nature Switzerland AG 2018
A. Ronzhin et al. (Eds.): ICR 2018, LNAI 11097, pp. 78–84, 2018.
https://doi.org/10.1007/978-3-319-99582-3_9

sided antennas have the same received power. When both sides have the same received power, consensus is provided. With this information, the position on x (or y) axis is calculated. After finding the position in one axis, the other position is calculated with geometry and propagation loss formula. Introduced technique in the manuscript does not require either the transmitted power from device or a very precise synchronization among antennas and source to be located. It compares the received power of antennas among a linear array.

An efficient control algorithm is also developed in this work. Firstly, received power error is obtained by using the differences cumulative received signal powers from the right and left hand sided antennas. Then, the power error is utilized to assign desired locations for each antenna separately. When the left hand side and right hand side antennas receive the same cumulative signal power, power error converges to zero. Desired location of each antenna becomes their current location and the control signal goes to zero.

2 Methodology

Assume there are N sensors/antennas located on a line as providing a linear array. S is the electronic source which we want to locate. The array is mobile and source is stable. The localization procedure in this manuscript depends on the received signal power by the array. Middle point of the array will be the reference. When right hand-side and left hand-side antennas receive the same cumulative power value, formation is satisfied and middle antenna comes to same position with the source in one axis (array and source come across). If received power by right and left sided antennas are different, the array tends to move towards to make both powers equal. For example, if the total received power by the right hand side is larger than the left side, control mechanism moves the array to right until both side receives equal cumulative power. The procedure is summarized in Fig. 1.

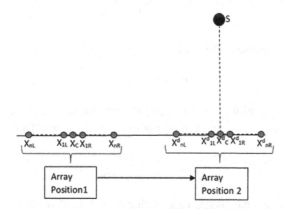

Fig. 1. Array shifts to right due to different cumulative received power.

Assumption 1: It is assumed that a control algorithm drives the antennas to the left or right on x axis until left hand side and right hand side antenna groups receive the equal cumulative signal power.

In this work, regulation controller is developed for a group of $2n + 1$ point-mass robots given by:

$$\dot{x}_i = v_i;$$
$$\dot{v}_i = u_i,$$

(1)

where x_i and is the ith robot's coordinate in the x plane for $i = 1, 2, \ldots, 2n + 1$, v_i is the velocity in the x direction, for the ith robot, and u_i is the control input controlling the velocity of the ith robot in the x direction.

The dynamics can be expressed in a compact form as:

$$\dot{X}_i = A_i X_i + B_i u_i,$$

(2)

where $A_i = \begin{bmatrix} 0 & 1 \\ 0 & 0 \end{bmatrix}$, $B_i = \begin{bmatrix} 0 \\ 1 \end{bmatrix}$, $X_i = \begin{bmatrix} x_i \\ v_i \end{bmatrix}$, and u_i represents the internal dynamics, input transformation vector, system states and control input, respectively. The controllers, u_i, is going to be utilized to bring the system to the desired x position while making the velocity v_i zero.

3   Problem Formulation and Controller Design

In order to bring the antennas to Array Position 2 from Array Position 1 as given in Fig. 1, first define the received power of each antenna as P_i. The total signal power of the antennas on the right and left hand side can be defined respectively as:

$$P_R = \sum_{i=1}^{n} P_{iR}, P_L = \sum_{i=1}^{n} P_{iL}.$$

Define the error between the total powers as^

$$e_p = P_L - P_R.$$

(3)

Objective of the controller of each agent, u_i, will be making sure $e_p \to 0$ as $t \to \infty$.

Controller design: Based on the power error in (3), each antenna defines its desired location as:

$$x_i^d(t) = x_i(t) - e_p k_P,$$

(4)

with $k_P > 0$ is a design parameter. Then, define the regulation error of each antenna as $e_r = x_i - x_i^d$. Controller of each system is given as:

$$u_i = -k_1 e_r - k_2 v_i \tag{5}$$

with $k_1, k_2 > 0$ are the design parameters.

Theorem: Given the controller (5) mentioned in Assumption 1, then the location of the source is given as:

$$(x_s, y_s) = (x_C(T), y_C(T) + d_0),$$

with T is the time when the power error goes to zero,

$$d_0 = \frac{l}{\sqrt{1 - \frac{P_0}{P_n}}}, \tag{6}$$

where d_0 is the distance between the middle of the antenna and source. P_0 and P_n is the received signal power of the 0th and n^{th} antennas, respectively, l is array length in one side (distance between the 0th and n^{th} antennas).

Proof: Free space propagation model defines the power received by an antenna as follows

$$P_r = P_t G_t G_r \frac{1}{(4\pi)^2} \frac{1}{d^2}, \tag{7}$$

where P_t is the transmitted power, G_t, G_r are gain of transmitter and receiver antennas respectively and λ is the wavelength of the signal. D is the distance between transmitter and receiver antenna. With this formula received powers by the center and the nth antennas will be

$$P_0 = P_t K \frac{1}{d_0^2}, P_n = P_t K \frac{1}{d_n^2} \tag{8}$$

respectively where $K = \frac{G_t G_r \lambda^2}{(4\pi)^2}$. From the Pythagorean's theorem, observe in Fig. 2 and obtain

$$d_n^2 = d_0^2 + l^2. \tag{9}$$

Using (8) and (9), the distance between the middle antenna and the source is found as:

$$d_0 = \frac{l}{\sqrt{1 - \frac{P_0}{P_n}}}. \tag{10}$$

If it is assumed that the array can move on x axis and the coordinate of the middle antenna is (x_0, y_0), the coordinate of the source will be $(x_0, y_0 + d_0)$.

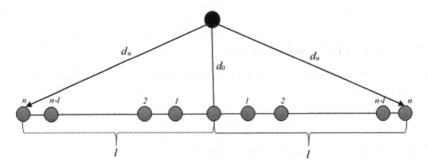

Fig. 2. The position of antennas with zero power error, e_p.

4 Simulation Results

In order to verify our theoretical claims, an array of antennas consists of identical and omnidirectional four antennas are utilized in this section. Initial x positions of four antennas are chosen as:

$$x(0) = [x_{L2}(0) \quad x_{L1}(0) \quad x_{R1}(0) \quad x_{R2}(0)]^T = [-10 \quad -20 \quad -30 \quad -40]^T.$$

The location of the source is selected as $(x_s, y_s) = (150, 200)$. The controller gains and the desired location calculation gain is chosen as $k_1 = 0.4$, $k_2 = 0.1$, $k_p = 1.1$. The power error is calculated based on the path loss formula (7) and the formula of the power error (3). The controller algorithm (5) along with the novel desired locations of each antenna (4) was applied to move each antenna *separately*. As it is illustrated in Fig. 3, the controller was able to bring the antennas around the x location of the source

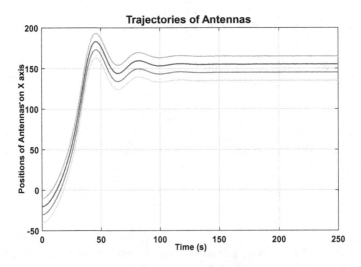

Fig. 3. Trajectories of all four antennas on x axis till the power error converges to zero.

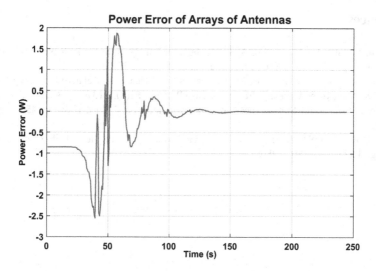

Fig. 4. Received cumulative power error between right hand side and left hand side antennas.

$x_s = 150$ from their initial locations. The oscillation between the 50th and 100th can be removed by choosing smaller controller gains k_1, k_2 and the smaller gain in the desired position selection k_p. Drawback of choosing smaller gains will be the longer convergence time. Figure 4 shows that the power error converges to zero around 130th second.

5   Conclusions and Future Works

A new localization technique based on formation control is demonstrated in the manuscript. A control algorithm was developed to move the linear antenna array in order to make both sided antennas receive equal power based on the middle point of the array. Therefore, the array and source comes across and position of source in one axis is found. The other coordinate is found with propagation formula. In this paper, source is assumed to be stable, our next work will be to introduce a localization and tracking method when the source is also mobile. The dynamics of the moving target can be approximate by using two layer Neural Networks. Additionally, applying this novel consensus based localization and tracking method to unmanned systems such as quadrotors will be one of our future works.

Acknowledgments. This work is supported by the Scientific and Technological Research Council of Turkey (TUBİTAK) (Project № 217138, Project name: Harmonic).

References

1. Salman, N., Ghogho, M., Kemp, A.H.: On the joint estimation of the RSS-based location and path-loss exponent. IEEE Wirel. Commun. Lett. **1**(1), 34–37 (2012)
2. Patwari, N., Hero, A.O., Perkins, M., Correal, N.S., O'Dea, R.J.: Relative location estimation in wireless sensor networks. IEEE Trans. Sig. Process. **51**(8), 2137–2148 (2003)
3. Peterson, B.B., et al.: Spread spectrum indoor geolocation. J. Inst. Navigat. **45**(2), 97–102 (1998)
4. Schmidt, R.: Multiple emitter location and signal parameter estimation. IEEE Trans. Antennas Propag. **34**(3), 276–280 (1986)

Modelling Characteristics of Human-Robot Interaction in an Exoskeleton System with Elastic Elements

Sergey Jatsun ⓘ, Sergei Savin$^{(\boxtimes)}$ ⓘ, and Andrey Yatsun ⓘ

Southwest State University, Kursk 305040, Russia
teormeh@inbox.ru, savinswsu@mail.ru

Abstract. In the paper, problem of modelling the human robot interactions in an exoskeleton system is investigated. In particular, a the case of a lower limb exoskeleton is considered. The interaction is supported by a special connector device featuring elastic elements and pressure sensors, allowing measuring the relative position of the human body and the mechanism links. An algorithm for calculating the position of the human body using the feedback from the pressure sensor is presented. Simulation results taking into account the noise and quantization of the sensor output showed validity of the proposed algorithm. Further simulations allowed to analyze the behavior of the control system in the case of harmonic inputs over a range of different frequencies.

Keywords: Human-robot interaction · Control · Exoskeletons
Pressure sensors

1 Introduction

Robotic systems designed for collaborative work with humans have been a focus of research for last decades. Especial interest has been placed on assistive and rehabilitation devices, such as exoskeletons. Such robots not only allow to improve the life quality for the patients, but also can be used to make the work of medical personnel easier, simplifying operations related to exercise, patients transportation and others [1–4].

Successful development of exoskeletons and similar technology depends on solving a number of control problems. These include guaranty of vertical stability of the device when it performs motion [4–9], planning footsteps that can be safely executed [10, 11], tuning controllers [12–15], designing algorithms for processing sensor information [16] and deriving methods for determining human intentions and integration of these to the control loop. Solutions for some of these problems have been proposed. However, the problem of introducing the human into the control loop of an exoskeleton remains open.

There are a number of works on using EMG in order connect human and the exoskeleton [17–19]. Alternative approaches can include use of pressure sensors [20]. In this paper we consider an alternative approach, based on use of elastic connector elements between the human operator and the exoskeleton links. The elastic properties of these connectors can be used to measure the relative motions between the human and the

© Springer Nature Switzerland AG 2018
A. Ronzhin et al. (Eds.): ICR 2018, LNAI 11097, pp. 85–94, 2018.
https://doi.org/10.1007/978-3-319-99582-3_10

robot's links. There are previous works that considered introducing elastic elements into the exoskeleton structure, focusing on minimizing the energy consumption [21–25]. However, the possibility of using the properties of these elements in the control loop have not been studied yet.

2 Description of the Sensory Connector

In this section, we introduce the model of the sensory connector device. The device can be installed at each link of an exoskeleton. Figure 1 illustrates the places where the sensory connector device can be installed.

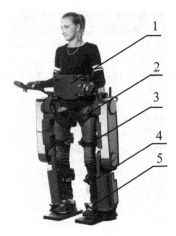

Fig. 1. General view of ExoLite exoskeleton with a user with fixed using connector pads; 1 – pads for torso connectors, 2 and 3 – pads for hip connectors, 4 – pad for shin connector, 5 – pad for foot connector.

The pads shown in Fig. 1 are typical for a range of exoskeleton devices, as they are used to fixate the patient on the device, to make wearing the exoskeleton for long durations of time more comfortable, and to minimize the risks of traumatic events related to human body coming into contact with moving mechanical parts. Therefore, installation of sensory connectors should be simple for a range of exoskeleton models and would not require significant changes in their designs.

Connectors can be modelled as a system of rigid and elastic elements, equipped with pressure sensors. The scheme of the sensory connector is shown in Fig. 2.

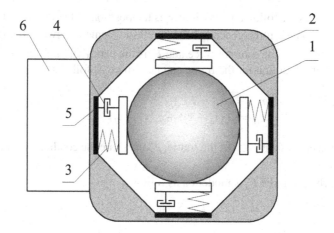

Fig. 2. The scheme of the sensory connector device; 1 – the cross section of the human limb fixed in the connector, 2 – frame of the sensory connector, 3, 4 – spring and damper between the fixator and the connector frame, 5 – pressure sensors, 6 – the exoskeleton's link to which the connector is attached.

One of the features of this system is that it allows inferring the movements of the human body relative to the exoskeleton links, using the pressure sensor feedback. The positions and velocities of the exoskeleton links in turn are measured by its sensor system (including encoders and MEMS gyroscopes). This allows to estimate the absolute position and velocity of the human body, which can be used to organized the human-driven control.

3 Model Description

Let us consider the motion of the frame of the connector relative to the human body part (from here on we refer to it as "leg") in a one-dimensional case. As it was shown in Fig. 2, the two are connected via elastic elements and dampers. The frame is actuated, where are the leg's motion can be arbitrary. Figure 3 shows a simplified model of the integration between the leg and the frame.

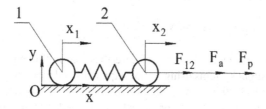

Fig. 3. The diagram of the integration between the leg and the frame; 1 – leg, 2 – the connector frame.

The Fig. 3 uses the following notation: x_1 is the position of the leg, x_2 is the position of the frame, F_{12} is the force generated by the elastic element between the leg and the connector frame, F_a is the actuator force and F_p is the perturbation force.

The equation of motion for the frame can be written as follows:

$$\begin{cases} m_2\ddot{x}_2 = F_{12} + F_a + F_p \\ F_{12} = \mu_e(\dot{x}_1 - \dot{x}_2) + c_e(x_1 - x_2) \end{cases},$$ (1)

where m_2 is the equivalent mass of the frame, μ_e and c_e are the coefficients of the spring-damper system.

The perturbation force F_p is modelled as follows:

$$F_p = -\mu_p\dot{x}_2 - k_p\text{sign}(\dot{x}_2),$$ (2)

where μ_p and k_p are constant coefficients, which in the simulation are taken as random numbers with normal distribution, parametrized by the means $\mu_{p,mean}$, $k_{p,mean}$ and standard deviations $\sigma_{p,\mu}$, $\sigma_{p,k}$.

The actuator equation have the following form:

$$\begin{cases} L_a\dfrac{dI}{dt} + R_aI + C_e\eta\dot{x}_2 = u \\ F_a = C_\tau\eta I \end{cases},$$ (3)

where L_a is the inductance of the motor coils, R_a is the resistance, C_e and C_τ are the motor constants, η is the actuator gear ration, I is the current and u is the voltage supplied to the motor.

4   Control System Design

In this work we consider a feedback control system that minimizes the difference between x_1 and x_2. This can be achieved with a proportional-derivative controller. There are examples of using this type of controller with exoskeletons described in [15, 26]. For the system described here this controller takes the following form:

where $e = x_1 - x_2$ is the control error,

$$u = K_d\dot{e} + K_pe,$$ (4)

K_d and K_p are controller gains. Paper [14] describes tuning this type of controller for multi-input multi-output systems using Sobol sequences and work [27] compares global optimization methods for this task.

In order to compute the control error the value of x_1 needs to be measured. This value can be calculated using the force sensor data, measuring the value of the force F_{12}. Let us consider the case when the force F_{12} is measured by a sensor with additive white noise and a quantized output. The model for such sensor is shown below:

$$F_{12}^m = \xi \bmod (F_{12} + \rho, \ \xi), \tag{5}$$

where ξ is the accuracy of the sensor, ρ is the additive noise and F_{12}^m is the measured value of the force F_{12}.

There are two alternative approaches to using the feedback from the force sensor to compute x_1. First approach requires an assumption that the value of μ_e is sufficiently low. Then it is possible to produce the following estimate of x_1:

$$x_1^m = F_{12}^m / c_e + x_2, \tag{6}$$

where x_1^m is the estimation of x_1.

The second approach does not require the assumption about the value of μ_e, but it requires the value of x_1 measured on the previous iteration of the algorithm (denoted as $x_1^m(t - \Delta t)$) to be known:

$$\begin{bmatrix} x_1^m(t) \\ \dot{x}_1^m(t) \end{bmatrix} = \begin{bmatrix} c_e & \mu_e \\ 1 & -\Delta t \end{bmatrix}^{-1} \begin{bmatrix} F_{12}^m + c_e x_2 + \mu_e \dot{x}_2 \\ x_1^m(t - \Delta t) \end{bmatrix}, \tag{7}$$

Unlike the first method, this approach requires information about velocity $\dot{x}_2$ and its accuracy is affected by the error in the initial value estimation for x_1.

5   Simulation Results

In this section, we present the simulation results for the system described previously. The simulation was carried out for the following parameters of the model: $m_2 = 1\,\text{kg}$, $\mu_e = 1\,\text{Ns/m}$, $c_e = 100\,\text{N/m}$, $L_a = 0.1\,\text{H}$, $R_a = 1\,\text{Om}$, $C_e = 0.01\,\text{Vs/m}$, $C_\tau = 0.01\,\text{N/A}$, $\eta = 50$, $K_d = 100$, $K_p = 1000$, $\xi = 1\,\text{N}$, $\rho \in [-0.5\ 0.5]\,\text{N}$. Motion of the leg is modeled as $x_1(t) = 0.05 \sin(10t)$.

Figure 4 shows the time functions for $x_1(t)$ and $x_2(t)$ obtained for the case, when formula (6) was used to calculate x_1^m. The first derivative of that value was obtained through finite differences.

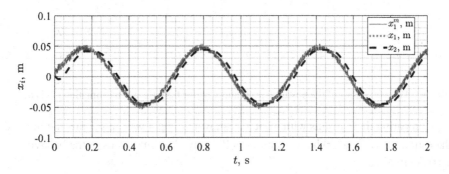

Fig. 4. Time functions of the positions $x_1(t)$ and $x_2(t)$.

Figure 4 shows that the estimation x_1^m becomes slightly more accurate after the transient process is over, however it does not converge to the actual value $x_1(t)$ and remains noisy. The value of $x_2(t)$ demonstrates phase lag and lesser amplitude compared to $x_1(t)$.

Figure 5 shows the work of the force sensor, the feedback from which is used to calculate x_1^m.

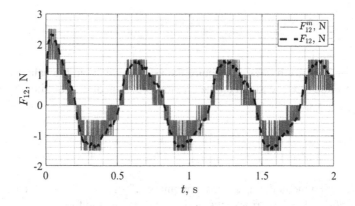

Fig. 5. Time functions of the measured and real values of $F_{12}(t)$.

We can see that the sensor introduces noticeable measurement errors, which in turn affects the quality of estimation for $x_1^m(t)$.

Figure 6 shows time functions for $x_1(t)$ and $x_2(t)$ from the same experiment done with the estimation function (7). For this and following experiments we introduce initial estimation error for $x_1^m(t)$: $x_1(0) - x_1^m(0) = 0.02$ M.

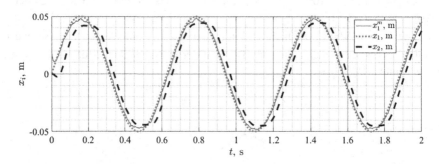

Fig. 6. Time functions of the positions $x_1(t)$ and $x_2(t)$ for the case when estimation (7) is used.

Comparing these results with what was shown in Fig. 4 we can see that the jitter of the estimated value $x_1^m(t)$ has lessened significantly. The alterations in the behavior of $x_2(t)$ are minimal.

To analyze the influence the parameters of the control input and the controller settings have on the behavior of the control system we can look at its frequency response. Figure 7 shows how the amplitude ratio of the input and the output signals change with the frequency of the control input. The graph was plotted for different values of proportional gain of the controller: $K_p = 100,\ 200$ and 500.

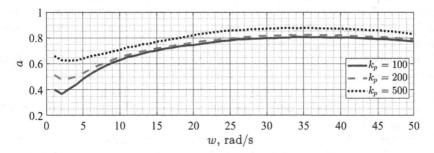

Fig. 7. Amplitude ratio of the input and the output signals for the control system plotted versus the frequency of the control input.

As we can see, there is a weak maximum in the amplitude ratio achieved at the control input frequencies at 33–35 rad/s. Change in the proportional controller gain scales the graphs without shifting this peak.

Figure 8 shows how the phase difference between the input and the output signals changes with the frequency of the control input. The phase was calculated using the algorithm [28]. The graph was plotted for the same three values of the proportional controller gain.

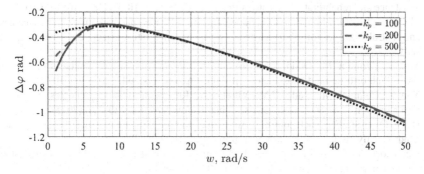

Fig. 8. Phase difference between the input and the output signals for the control system plotted versus the frequency of the control input.

We can notice that the phase lag (in absolute values) increases with the frequency and shows a minimum at 2–3 rad/s. The increase in the phase difference might be significant for the user of the device, as it affects the responsiveness of the system. The effect of both lag and amplitude errors on the perceived comfort of using exoskeletons needs to be investigated further.

6 Conslusions

In this paper, the problem controlling a human-robot system have been considered. The design of the connector element outfitted with pressure sensors have been presented. It was proposed to use the pressure sensor in order to estimate the relative position of the human body part and the robot link. This information can then be used in the feedback control loop. The simulations were conducted with a nonlinear pressure sensor module which included additive white noise and quantization of the output signal. PD controller was used for stabilization and tracking.

Two methods for retrieving the positional information from the pressure sensor data has been proposed, their comparison was shown in simulation. The result suggested that both methods are viable, however they require different assumptions. It was shown that the proposed control system design can demonstrate lag and magnitude errors when tracking periodic signal.

The future work includes integrating the proposed sensor data processing methods into the full scale control system of the robot and combining it with other sensor processing algorithms.

Acknowledgements. The reported study was funded by RFBR according to the research project 18-08-00773 A.

References

1. Lu, R., Li, Z., Su, C.Y., Xue, A.: Development and learning control of a human limb with a rehabilitation exoskeleton. IEEE Trans. Ind. Electron. **61**(7), 3776–3785 (2014)
2. Huo, W., Mohammed, S., Moreno, J.C., Amirat, Y.: Lower limb wearable robots for assistance and rehabilitation: a state of the art. IEEE Syst. J. **10**(3), 1068–1081 (2016)
3. Meng, W., Liu, Q., Zhou, Z., Ai, Q., Sheng, B., Xie, S.S.: Recent development of mechanisms and control strategies for robot-assisted lower limb rehabilitation. Mechatronics **31**, 132–145 (2015)
4. Yan, T., Cempini, M., Oddo, C.M., Vitiello, N.: Review of assistive strategies in powered lower-limb orthoses and exoskeletons. Robotics Auton. Syst. **64**, 120–136 (2015)
5. Yan, T., Cempini, M., Oddo, C.M., Vitiello, N.: Review of assistive strategies in powered lower-limb orthoses and exoskeletons. Robot. Auton. Syst. **64**, 120–136 (2015)
6. Harib, O., et al.: Feedback control of an exoskeleton for paraplegics: toward robustly stable hands-free dynamic walking. arXiv preprint arXiv:1802.08322 (2018)
7. Panovko, G.Y., Savin, S.I., Yatsun, S.F., Yatsun, A.S.: Simulation of exoskeleton sit-to-stand movement. J. Mach. Manuf. Reliab. **45**(3), 206–210 (2016)
8. Jatsun, S., Savin, S., Yatsun, A.: Motion control algorithm for a lower limb exoskeleton based on iterative LQR and ZMP method for trajectory generation. In: Husty, M., Hofbaur, M. (eds.) MESROB 2016. MMS, vol. 48, pp. 305–317. Springer, Cham (2018). https://doi.org/10.1007/978-3-319-59972-4_22
9. Jatsun, S., Savin, S., Yatsun, A.: A control strategy for a lower limb exoskeleton with a toe joint. In: Ronzhin, A., Rigoll, G., Meshcheryakov, R. (eds.) ICR 2016. LNCS (LNAI), vol. 9812, pp. 1–8. Springer, Cham (2016). https://doi.org/10.1007/978-3-319-43955-6_1

10. Jatsun, S., Savin, S., Yatsun, A.: Walking pattern generation method for an exoskeleton moving on uneven terrain. In: Proceedings of the 20th International Conference on Climbing and Walking Robots and Support Technologies for Mobile Machines (CLAWAR 2017) (2017)

11. Jatsun, S., Savin, S., Yatsun, A.: Footstep planner algorithm for a lower limb exoskeleton climbing stairs. In: Ronzhin, A., Rigoll, G., Meshcheryakov, R. (eds.) ICR 2017. LNCS (LNAI), vol. 10459, pp. 75–82. Springer, Cham (2017). https://doi.org/10.1007/978-3-319-66471-2_9

12. Liu, L.K., et al.: Interactive torque controller with electromyography intention prediction implemented on exoskeleton robot NTUH-II. In: 2017 IEEE International Conference on Robotics and Biomimetics (ROBIO), pp. 1485–1490. IEEE (2017)

13. Aguirre-Ollinger, G., Nagarajan, U., Goswami, A.: An admittance shaping controller for exoskeleton assistance of the lower extremities. Auton. Robots **40**(4), 701–728 (2016)

14. Jatsun, S., Savin, S., Yatsun, A.: Parameter optimization for exoskeleton control system using sobol sequences. In: Parenti-Castelli, V., Schiehlen, W. (eds.) ROMANSY 21-Robot Design, Dynamics and Control, pp. 361–368. Springer, Cham (2016). https://doi.org/10.1007/978-3-319-33714-2_40

15. Jatsun, S., Savin, S., Yatsun, A.: Comparative analysis of iterative LQR and adaptive PD controllers for a lower limb exoskeleton. In: 2016 IEEE International Conference on Cyber Technology in Automation, Control, and Intelligent Systems (CYBER), pp. 239–244. IEEE (2016)

16. Tamez-Duque, J., et al.: Real-time strap pressure sensor system for powered exoskeletons. Sensors **15**(2), 4550–4563 (2015)

17. Leonardis, D., et al.: An EMG-controlled robotic hand exoskeleton for bilateral rehabilitation. IEEE Trans. Haptics **8**(2), 140–151 (2015)

18. Peternel, L., Noda, T., Petrič, T., Ude, A., Morimoto, J., Babič, J.: Adaptive control of exoskeleton robots for periodic assistive behaviours based on EMG feedback minimisation. PLoS ONE **11**(2), e0148942 (2016)

19. Siu, H.C., Arenas, A.M., Sun, T., Stirling, L.A.: Implementation of a surface electromyography-based upper extremity exoskeleton controller using learning from demonstration. Sensors **18**(2), 467 (2018)

20. Jatsun, S., Yatsun, A., Savin, S., Postolnyi, A.: Approach to motion control of an exoskeleton in "verticalization-to-walking" regime utilizing pressure sensors. In: 2016 IEEE International Conference on Cyber Technology in Automation, Control, and Intelligent Systems (CYBER), pp. 452–456. IEEE (2016)

21. Walsh, C.J., et al.: Development of a lightweight, underactuated exoskeleton for load-carrying augmentation. In: Proceedings 2006 IEEE International Conference on Robotics and Automation, ICRA 2006, pp. 3485–3491. IEEE (2006)

22. Walsh, C.J., Endo, K., Herr, H.: A quasi-passive leg exoskeleton for load-carrying augmentation. Int. J. Humanoid Robot. **4**(3), 487–506 (2007)

23. Jatsun, S., Savin, S., Yatsun, A.: Improvement of energy consumption for a lower limb exoskeleton through verticalization time optimization. In: 2016 24th Mediterranean Conference on Control and Automation (MED), pp. 322–326. IEEE (2016)

24. Jatsun, S., Savin, S., Yatsun, A., Postolnyi, A.: Control system parameter optimization for lower limb exoskeleton with integrated elastic elements. In: Advances in Cooperative robotics. Proceeding of the 19th International Conference on CLAWAR 2016, pp. 797–805 (2016)

25. Wiggin, M.B., Sawicki, G.S., Collins, S.H.: An exoskeleton using controlled energy storage and release to aid ankle propulsion. In: 2011 IEEE International Conference on Rehabilitation Robotics (ICORR), pp. 1–5. IEEE (2011)
26. Jatsun, S., Savin, S., Lushnikov, B., Yatsun, A.: Algorithm for motion control of an exoskeleton during verticalization. In: ITM Web of Conferences, vol. 6, pp. 1–6. EDP Sciences (2016)
27. Jatsun, S., Savin, S., Yatsun, A.: Comparative analysis of global optimization-based controller tuning methods for an exoskeleton performing push recovery. In: 2016 20th International Conference on System Theory, Control and Computing (ICSTCC), pp. 107–112. IEEE (2016)
28. Sedlacek, M., Krumpholc, M.: Digital measurement of phase difference – a comparative study of DSP algorithms. Metrol. Meas. Syst. 12(4), 427–448 (2005)

Safety-Related Risks and Opportunities of Key Design-Aspects for Industrial Human-Robot Collaboration

Lukas Kaiser[✉][ID], Andreas Schlotzhauer[ID], and Mathias Brandstötter[ID]

JOANNEUM RESEARCH ROBOTICS - Institute for Robotics and Mechatronics - Mechatronic Systems Group, Klagenfurt, Austria
{Lukas.Kaiser,Andreas.Schlotzhauer,Mathias.Brandstoetter}@joanneum.at

Abstract. For several years, sensitive robots are used in industry and in some cases perform collaborative tasks directly with humans on shared workplaces. At first glance, this type of human-machine interaction is associated with high risks. However, additional devices, advanced functionalities and risk mitigation activities can ensure that such collaborative scenarios are safe for humans. The essential aspects are the collaborative operation methods, workspace layout, end effectors, human machine interfaces and ergonomics. In this work we shed light on these important aspects of human-robot collaboration and discuss its facets. By adequately reducing and communicate potential indiscernible risks a robot is made trustworthy for a human being.

Keywords: Industrial human-robot collaboration · Safety
Collaborative robots

1 Introduction

Advanced Human-Robot Collaboration (HRC) is one of the key technologies to enable the current 4th industrial revolution, often called Industry 4.0 [6]. The strength of HRC lies in the flexibility and fast reconfiguration of the used collaborative robots. This flexibility is necessary in order to achieve small batch sizes as desired by Industry 4.0. Nevertheless, these new robots and the new technology associated with them not only present opportunities but also new risks.

Different aspects of collaborative robot applications, especially the contact between a human and a robot, are well studied. [5] describes possible injuries during collisions between humans and robots; [16] is about the detection of and reaction to contact situations and [17] describes a strategy to avoid the contact altogether. The system requirements from the operators point of view are addressed in [22]. Also the overall safety of such an application is discussed in [4,18]. In this paper we focus not only on the risks, but also on opportunities of different technologies, while giving an overview of different practical approaches to develop and integrate a safe industrial HRC application. The key aspects, we focus on, are the collaborative operation methods, workspace layout, end effector, human machine interface and ergonomics.

© Springer Nature Switzerland AG 2018
A. Ronzhin et al. (Eds.): ICR 2018, LNAI 11097, pp. 95–104, 2018.
https://doi.org/10.1007/978-3-319-99582-3_11

1.1 Norms and Standards

The relevant international standards regarding industrial collaborative robots are the ISO 10218 [8,9] and the Technical Specification ISO/TS 15066 [13]. While the field of collaborative robotics evolves fast, the available standards lack of guidance for the implementation of industrial mobile robots and also lack an effective method to verify the biomechanical loads for an operator during a collision with a robot in the field. For mobile robots in industrial environments an ISO draft [12] exists and the sub-committee R15.08 "Mobile Robot Safety" of the US RIA is currently working on a new standard. A method to verify the biomechanical load is described in [2], but it neither covers the transient contact nor considers the shape of the struck body part. An overview of relevant documents can be seen in Fig. 1.

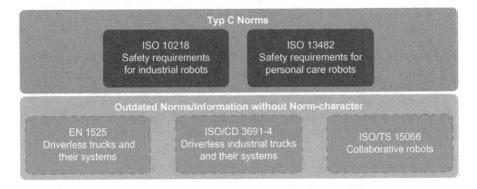

Fig. 1. Relevant norms and standards for HRC

1.2 Classification of HRC

Collaborative operation is defined in [10] as the *"state in which purposely designed robots [...] work in direct cooperation with a human within a defined workspace"*. This definition is rather general in the aspect of the degree of interaction. Therefore, we classify the HRC in 4 degrees of interaction, *"the 4 Cs"*, as shown in Fig. 2. The extent of interaction increases from Fig. 2(a) to (d), where *enCapsualtion* means no interaction at all and *Collaboration* allows the human and the robot to work simultaneously on the same workpiece.

2 Key Design-Aspects

In the following, design-aspects are presented, which are relevant for a safe industrial HRC application. Not only the risks of those aspects are presented, but also related opportunities to increase safety and add additional value for the operator.

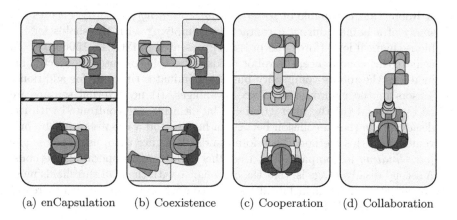

(a) enCapsulation   (b) Coexistence   (c) Cooperation   (d) Collaboration

Fig. 2. The 4 Cs: 4 degrees of interaction between a human and a robot

2.1   Collaborative Operation Methods

A collaborative robot can often solve a certain task in several ways. In the ISO/TS 15066 [13] and ISO 10218-2 [9], four collaborative operation methods (see Fig. 3) are defined, which can be applied to an HRC application.

(a) An application protected by a *safety-rated monitored stop* (Fig. 3(a)) is the most conservative collaborative operation method, because the interaction between human and robot happens when the robot stands still. The chance of hazardous situations is low compared to the other operation methods, but the possible benefits of collaboration are low as well.

(b) The *hand guiding* operation (Fig. 3(b)) can be safe, even though a direct contact between human and robot is necessary, because the robot acts passively. The interaction by hand guiding is intuitive and easy to learn. To increase the operators comfort during hand guiding, a compliant control strategy can be used. While this operation method is highly collaborative, the human attention and input is always necessary.

(c) During *speed and separation monitoring* (Fig. 3(c)) the robot keeps a safe distance to surrounding objects and humans at all times. Sensors provide the necessary information to adjust the distance dynamically, which can be placed directly on the robot. Alternatively, sensors can be mounted in the environment, monitoring fixed zones around the robot. Speed and separation monitoring prevents the contact between the robot and humans entirely, reduces downtime and thereby balances safety and productivity. Crucial design parameters are (i) the type of sensors, (ii) the sensor resolution (which determines the minimum object size, that can be detected) as well as (iii) the maximum reach and stopping time of the robot. The drawback of more advanced versions of such systems is their high complexity and the associated high computational demand.

(d) A Robot that is capable of *power and force limiting* (Fig. 3(d)) ensures the safety of a human during a contact, by complying with thresholds for the biomechanical load (force and pressure) presented in ISO/TS 15066 [13]. To achieve this compliance, the robot needs to be able to sense a contact. This increases the robots complexity but also eliminates the need for additional sensors in the environment. Two advantages, (i) no external sensors are necessary and (ii) the interaction can be intuitive, are confronted with the disadvantage that a collision between a human and a robot can not be prevented with this method. Therefore the risk is higher when using *power and force limiting* in comparison to the other collaborative operation methods. A second disadvantage is, that the compliance with the load thresholds must be validated in the field for all possible contact situations, which increases the integration effort.

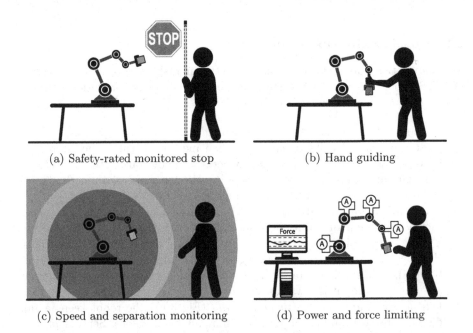

(a) Safety-rated monitored stop   (b) Hand guiding

(c) Speed and separation monitoring   (d) Power and force limiting

Fig. 3. Collaborative operations according to ISO/TS 15066 [13]

2.2 Workspace Layout

The workspace layout design relates not only to the safety of the whole application, but also to the efficiency and the ergonomics (see Sect. 2.5) of an application. Many ergonomic problems arises from the layout design and can be solved by altering it slightly. In general a bigger workspace increases the number of probable hazardous situations, but also enables a greater variety of applications. Constrains are given by (i) the task (ii) the implemented collaborative operation methods and (iii) the capabilities of the used robot. Additionally the layout is influenced by the individual ergonomic requirements of possible operators. While in classical robot applications, the workspaces of humans and robots are strictly separated (see Fig. 4(a)), a collaborative workspace is needed in HRC applications. The collaborative workspace can be just an overlap (see Fig. 4(b)) of the two workspaces, the entirety of one becomes the collaborative workspace (see Fig. 4(c)) or all three are equal (see Fig. 4(d)).

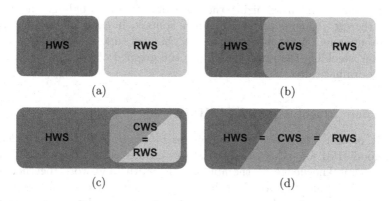

Fig. 4. Possible Workspace Layouts (H...Human, R...Robot, C...Collaborative, WS...Workspace)

Serious hazards that arises from the layout and geometry of the workplace are shear edges or pinch points, especially between the robot and its surroundings. Furthermore the operator can be indirectly at risk because of poor lightning conditions or constrained visibility of important areas.

To overcome these problems, the possible positions and movements of the robot should be considered. For stationary robots, the position of the robot base is crucial, and for mobile robots the possible working range respectively. In mobile applications, the workspace should exclude untrained personnel and hazardous objects. In stationary applications, the distance between the robots base and the collaborative workspace should be maximized, to reduce obstructive shadows around the workpiece and to prevent the robot from blocking the view of the operator. At the same time the movements of the robot should be as limited as possible to reduce the danger of an unwanted collision and to make the robot behavior more predictable.

2.3 End Effector

The end effector, typically a gripper, is usually the physical interface of a robot to its environment during normal operation and is therefore from great interest for the design of an HRC application. The gripper should in the best case, ensure a safe grip, flexible usage and needs to be safe for the human. To ensure safe gripping, form-fit should be preferred to force-fit, as form-fit is not prone to loosing the grip during higher acceleration, and also still grips the object after loss of energy. Another hazardous situation, the clamping of human body parts between the fingers of the gripper, can be prevented by minimizing the clearance to the gripped object or by monitoring the gripping force. There are specialized gripping solutions, which can improve the safety in some cases. For example soft grippers, suction cups and electromagnetic grippers. In general an inherent safe design is preferable. Most mentionable thereby is a lightweight construction, to reduce the mass; and maximizing the radii of corners, to enlarge the surface area and thereby reducing pressure during a contact. In cases where the gripper-design is inherent unsafe and can not be changed, due to limitations of the application, shielding the gripper and also the gripped object [21] can increase the safety dramatically.

2.4   Human Machine Interface (HMI)

The HMI, or user interface is the *"means for information and action exchange"* [10]. A good HMI for industrial applications ensures, that operator and robot share the same knowledge on the applications status and work together in an intuitive and productive way. With increasing complexity of a robot system, a good HMI becomes crucial. To ensure a safe application, also the security risks of the applied technology should be considered, especially the confidentiality, availability and integrity of the transferred information.

The communication between humans and robots is possible in both directions, from human to robot and from robot to human respectively. Different technologies are available to implement the HMI, depending on the addressed sensory stimulus and whether the action/information originates from the human or the robot. Table 1 categorizes possible interaction technologies according to the mentioned dependencies.

Augmented Reality (AR) and Projections. AR, as an interface technology, can evoke or reduce risks. A common AR-device, the smartglasses, can be used to highlight dangerous areas or guide the operator to prevent a faulty operation. At the same time the operators field of view is limited and the situation awareness could decrease. The use of virtual reality devices results in motion sickness for some users [15]. Although this issue seams to be less likely to occur in AR, it can decrease the usability and acceptance.

Projections are another technology to enrich the real world and can be used to display graphics in the collaborative workspace [20]. The displayed information can be used to show the robots next actions or to highlight risks in order to prevent contact situations between the human and the robot. In contrast to smartglasses, the operator is not constrained by additional gear, but the projections are limited to certain areas.

Table 1. Classification of HMIs

		Input originates from....	
		Robot	Human
Sensory stimulus	Visual	Gestures, Signal lamp, Display, Projections (Projector, AR-Glasses)	Gestures, Gaze
	Acoustic	Speech, Sounds	Speech, Sounds
	Haptic	Contact, Haptic device	Contact, Haptic device, Joystick, Keyboard/Mouse, Touchscreen

Data Representation. An important aspect in the interaction design is the representation of data, especial but not limited to Graphical User Interfaces (GUIs). In todays applications a lot of data accumulates, which can be used to monitor and control the application. With this increasing amount of data, processing it becomes crucial, as the operator simply cannot monitor every parameter at all times. Instead only meaningful information should be provided incidental to the operator [19]. According to [1] information should be *event-based*, *future-oriented* and *structured*.

(a) If providing information *event-based*, the user is only disturbed, when the information is relevant to the actual context. An example is to display the reason for a safety stop, right after it occurs or the information that a monitored parameter leaves its usual range.
(b) The information provided, should be *future-oriented*, so the operator has the chance to prepare for upcoming events and plan his/her actions accordingly. A future-oriented information would be the trend of a parameter or the remaining lifespan of a component.
(c) To quickly find a specific information or value, the collected data should be *structured*. This can be achieved by classifying the data in a searchable hierarchical structure or by visually separating and grouping the data.

2.5 Ergonomics

The ergonomics of an industrial HRC application is crucial for the operator. Even if the application is harmless, its success depends also on the acceptance by the operator.

According to [3], there is a connection between the operators stress level and his/her situation awareness. This situation awareness can be influenced by stressors of physical (e.g. noise, lighting conditions, boredom) or psychological (e.g. fear, uncertainty, consequences of events) nature. A reduced situation awareness leads to an increased probability of hazardous situations. In [14], hazards related to manual manipulation of heavy objects are addressed; general ergonomical hazards are listed in [11].

The following design errors in industrial robot applications in relation to ergonomics should be taken into account:

- misleading communication between human and robot, especially due to
  - unsuitable designed control- or programming-pendant,
  - poorly marked control elements or
  - unsuitable designed loading/unloading post;
- unsuitable localized lightning conditions or
- unsuitable height of the work surface, control elements or loading/unloading post.

If an existing workstation is upgraded with a robot, ergonomics is particularly important, since the existing design was usually not planned with a robot in mind and the temptation is great to leave the workstation design as it is in order to reduce effort.

These failures could lead to invalid programming or control inputs by the operator, which again lead to hazardous situations. Repeated and unintentional contact situations between the operator and the robot are also more likely, which increases the strain and fatigue of the operator. If safety devices disturb or annoy the operator, the risk of manipulation of these safety devices is high. In order to avoid such hazards, the workplace design should meet the requirements of the operators and their individual physical characteristics and habits. Future operators should be involved in the planning process from the outset in order to prevent the bypassing of safety devices [7].

By mitigating the presented ergonomically hazards, not only a reduction or elimination of the hazards can be achieved but they can even be turned into opportunities to create a welcoming environment for the user, where he/she likes to work and is at ease.

3   Conclusion

Right now robots enter more fields of applications beside industrial ones (e.g. households, elderly care, agriculture) and the number of people, interacting with robots, increases. The ease of use of robots and therefore their interfaces is quite important, as not all operators have a technical background and are able to understand the technology, especially children and the elderly.

In industrial applications, the high degree of freedom enables serial manipulators to extensive and complex sequences of movement, which are not always predictable for humans and may not be intuitive. In combination with the close human interaction, this can result in hazardous situations. To combat that, an appropriate communication interface between man and machine (HMI) is essential. A good interface can reduce the induced stress, which ensures good health of the operator in the long run. Another factor for the need of a good interface, is the high complexity of collaborative robots in combination with the demand for ease of use.

Certainly, robots will change our workplaces and homes, but design-factors like the interaction between humans and robots will decide, whether it is a good or a bad place to work and live. Additional factors like the workspace-layout, end-effector design or the collaborative operation methods will not only affect the acceptance of such systems but also the safety of the operators. Guidelines for those factors, in form of norms, are already available, at least for stationary applications. Norms for mobile robots, on the other hand, are still in their draft phase. Which means more thought has to go into the development of such systems.

Only when all the conditions that were stated in this work are met, the way will be paved for trustworthy robots.

Acknowledgment. The results incorporated in this paper were gained within the scope of the project "HRC-Safety for employees" commissioned by the Allgemeine Unfallversicherungsanstalt (AUVA).

References

1. Christoffersen, K., Woods, D.D.: How to make automated systems team players. In: Advances in Human Performance and Cognitive Engineering Research, Chap. 1, vol. 2, pp. 1–12. Emerald Group Publishing Limited (2002)
2. DGUV: Collaborative robot systems - Design of systems with "Power and Force Limiting Function" function. Technical report FB HM-080 Issue 08/2017, Deutsche Gesetzliche Unfallversicherung (2017)
3. Endsley, M.: Toward a theory of situation awareness in dynamic systems. Hum. Factors J. Hum. Factors Ergonomics Soc. **37**, 32–64 (1995)
4. Guiochet, J., Machin, M., Waeselynck, H.: Safety-critical advanced robots: a survey. Robot. Auton. Syst. **94**, 43–52 (2017)
5. Haddadin, S., Albu-Schäffer, A., Hirzinger, G.: Soft-tissue injury in robotics. In: Proceedings of the 2010 IEEE International Conference on Robotics and Automation (2010)
6. Hirsch-Kreinsen, H.: Digitization of industrial work: development paths and prospects. J. Labour Market Res. **49**, 1–14 (2016)
7. HVBG: Bypassing of protective devices on machinery. Technical report, Hauptverband der gewerblichen Berufsgenossenschaften (2006)
8. ISO: 10218–1:2011–07 Robots and robotic devices - Safety requirements for industrial robots - Part 1: Robots. Standard, International Organization for Standardization (2012)
9. ISO: 10218–2:2011–07 Robots and robotic devices - Safety requirements for industrial robots - Part 2: Robot systems and integration. Standard, International Organization for Standardization (2012)
10. ISO: 8373:2012–03 Robots and robotic devices - Vocabulary. Standard, International Organization for Standardization (2012)
11. ISO: 12100:2010–11 Safety of machinery - General principles for design - Risk assessment and risk reduction. Standard, International Organization for Standardization (2013)

12. ISO: CD 3691-4 Industrial trucks - Safety requirements and verification - Part 4: Driverless industrial trucks and their systems. Draft standard, International Organization for Standardization (2016)
13. ISO: TS 15066:2016 Robots and robotic devices - Collaborative robots. Technical specification, International Organization for Standardization (2016)
14. IVSS: Leitfaden für die Gefährdungsbeurteilung in Klein- und Mittelbetrieben - Manuelle Lastenhandhabung - Heben, Halten, Tragen, Ziehen, Schieben - Ermittlung und Bewertung von Gefährdungen; Festlegen von Manahmen. Technical report, Internationale Vereinigung für Soziale Sicherheit (2010)
15. Joseph, J., LaViola, J.: A discussion of cybersickness in virtual environments. ACM SIGCHI Bull. **32**, 47–56 (2000)
16. Kuehn, J., Haddadin, S.: An artificial robot nervous system to teach robots how to feel pain and reflexively react to potentially damaging contacts. IEEE Robot. Autom. Lett. **2**(1), 72–79 (2017)
17. Lacevic, B., Rocco, P.: Kinetostatic danger field - a novel safety assessment for human-robot interaction. In: 2010 IEEE/RSJ, International Conference on Intelligent Robots and Systems (IROS), Taipei, Taiwan, pp. 2169–2174 (2010)
18. Michalos, G., Makris, S., Tsarouchi, P., Guasch, T., Kontovrakis, D., Chryssolouris, G.: Design considerations for safe human-robot collaborative workplaces. Procedia CIRP **37**, 248–253 (2015)
19. Peissner, M., Hipp, C.: Potenziale der Mensch-Technik Interaktion für die effiziente und vernetzte Produktion von Morgen. Technical report, Fraunhofer IAO (2013)
20. Vogel, C., Walter, C., Elkmann, N.: Safeguarding and supporting future human-robot cooperative manufacturing processes by a projection- and camera-based technology. In: 27th International Conference on Flexible Automation and Intelligent Manufacturing. FAIM 2017, Modena, Italy, pp. 39–46 (2017)
21. Werner, J.K., Salimian, A.C., Bollinger, R.S., Gordon, R.P., Swenson, K.A.: Safety device for a mechanical motion device, 3 May 2015. https://patents.google.com/patent/EP3265275A1/en, US20160257005A1
22. Wurhofer, D., Meneweger, T., Fuchsberger, V., Tscheligi, M.: Reflections on operators and maintenance engineers experiences of smart factories. In: Proceedings of the 2018 ACM Conference on Supporting Groupwork, pp. 284–296 (2018)

Improvements in 3D Hand Pose Estimation Using Synthetic Data

Jakub Kanis[1([⊠])], Dmitry Ryumin[1,2], and Zdeněk Krňoul[1]

[1] Faculty of Applied Sciences, NTIS - New Technologies for the Information Society, University of West Bohemia, Univerzitní 8, 306 14 Pilsen, Czech Republic
{jkanis,zdkrnoul}@ntis.zcu.cz, dl_03.03.1991@mail.ru
[2] St. Petersburg Institute for Informatics and Automation of the Russian Academy of Sciences, SPIIRAS, St. Petersburg, Russian Federation

Abstract. The neural networks currently outperform earlier approaches to the hand pose estimation. However, to achieve the superior results a large amount of the appropriate training data is desperately needed. But the acquisition of the real hand pose data is a time and resources consuming process. One of the possible solutions uses the synthetic training data. We introduce a method to generate synthetic depth images of the hand closely matching the real images. We extend the approach of the previous works to the modeling of the depth image data using the 3D scan of the subject's hand and the hand pose prior given by the real data distribution. We found out that combining them with the real training data can result in a better performance.

Keywords: Hand pose estimation · Synthetic data · Sign language

1 Introduction

Hand gestures play a very important role in human communication and it is only natural to extend this into human-machine interaction. The problem of the hand pose estimation in real-time from visual data is being addressed in many fields - robotics [1], medicine, automotive, virtual/augmented reality [10], gesture and sign language processing [20]. The human hand has a large number of degrees of freedom with frequent self-occlusions of fingers and the hand pose estimation leads to nonlinear regression. Despite this, there is a huge demand for such technologies that would perform well with consumer quality sensors. The case of the hand pose estimation from depth data has two main challenges: how to obtain precise ground-truth data and how to recover the hand pose.

We formulate a problem of upper body pose estimation of one gesturing person with a non-invasive and commonly used capturing device. This setup is suitable for sign language recognition. The recorded gestures can be also used for sign language synthesis. Preservation of intelligibility during transferring the hand pose to a 3D model (e.g. signing avatar) is a crucial factor. Machine learning

© Springer Nature Switzerland AG 2018
A. Ronzhin et al. (Eds.): ICR 2018, LNAI 11097, pp. 105–115, 2018.
https://doi.org/10.1007/978-3-319-99582-3_12

methods and neural networks currently outperform earlier approaches to detection and tracking of the hand pose. In this scenario the hand pose learning is either supervised [3,4] or semi-supervised [14,18]. The problem of training deep convolutional neural networks (DNN) is data acquisition that is crucial to the overall success. It naturally consists in a relatively easy collection of real training samples (depth images). However, for the supervised training techniques proper annotation is often semi-automatic or fully manual and thus time-consuming and manual labor demanding that limits the task just for the particular domain at the expense of its robustness. But a large volume of training data can determine a precise and robust predictor [19]. The synthetic training data could easily circumvent this problem. The challenging task is an integration of the synthetic data into the training process to model the wider range of the training samples and to enhance the prediction robustness from the relatively smaller real data annotations.

This work contributes to the understanding of the effect of the synthetic data in the task of the hand pose estimation. We are extending the modeling of the synthetic data presented in the previous work [9] by introducing the modeling of the hand pose prior and compare the performance of the several training sets.

2   Related Works

Supervised learning techniques need the proper objective data - ground truth annotation of depth maps. Hand pose annotation is most often given by positions of hand joints' centers and/or positions of fingertips in training depth maps. It is created either by time-consuming full manual annotation or often semi-automatically [7,11]. Unfortunately, the depth map does not provide the exact third coordinate (z-axis) due to the ambiguity between the hand surface (skin) projected to the depth pixels and the correct 3D positions of the anatomical joint centers. By contrast, semi-automatic approaches provide the joint centers by interactive searching for the best match of a personalized 3D hand model in the depth images which pose is often initialized and/or post-processed by the annotator. Nevertheless, for both types of annotation, fingers' self-occlusion is common during hand articulation and causes missing information [9]. For example in [12], up to 20% disagreement between annotators has been observed. Thus, such annotation process is inaccurate, mainly when only one depth map is available to annotators. Current automatic annotation approaches rely on an additional source(s) of hand pose measurements independently on the depth map. Such approaches provide more accurate annotation and are less time-consuming and include information not explicitly captured in the depth map.

Synthetic data have from the definition a precise and error-less annotation and furthermore, it is possible to obtain unlimited amount of the training data from any reference view, any depth map resolution with any background, and any skin color [5,9,10]. The main issue is then the choice of the distribution of the synthetic samples which simulate the real features of the scene, the natural movements of the hand, and the intrinsic and extrinsic parameters of the sensing device. The depth map is created by rendering the 3D animated model of the hand. The prior of the shape and movement can be given manually, which is demanding and does not fully respond to the reality. A technique that combines a synthetic shape model with natural movements obtained by a measurement provides better synthetic depth maps [5].

3   Methods

We consider the hand pose estimation from the depth map as a machine learning task of the training on the ground-truth data. For this purpose, the ground-truth data of the hand pose are provided by a 3D skeletal model of the hand. The skeletal model describes selected bones of the hand and the hand pose is given by their rotations, commonly used in 3D computer graphics.

Our 3D skeletal model is composed of 17 joints of the right hand and includes the one forearm, one wrist, and 5×3 finger bones. In this assumption, the palm is a rigid object and its flex is not modeled. Since the forearm joint is integrated into the 3D skeletal model, we can model and generate depth data of the forearm. The root of the hand skeleton is defined in the elbow joint and has 6 DoFs (Degree of Freedom, 3 rotations and 3 translations), next there are 3 DoFs for the wrist and the thumb ball joint, proximal phalanges have 2 DoFs and the other phalanges have just 1 DoF.

3.1   Annotation of Hand Pose Real Data

Unlike other current methods, we acquire the real depth data and their ground-truth hand pose data simultaneously by a depth sensor and by a VICON motion capture system. This approach is similar to acquisition approach of the dataset BigHand [19] where the ground-truth data are also collected independently on the depth maps however by using a couple of electromagnetic sensors.

We used standard passive retro-reflective markers that are attached to the hand, see Fig. 1 left; 5 markers are spherical with a radius of 14 and 6.5 mm and 15 are hemispherical with a radius of 4 mm. The markers on the fingers are in the middle of the dorsal side of the phalanges. The markers are tracked by 8 VICON MX cameras with 2 Mpix resolutions and 120 fps. The acquired recordings need

Fig. 1. Left: Marker setup (omitting elbow marker). Middle: 3D model of the subject's hand. Right: Generic hand model [17].

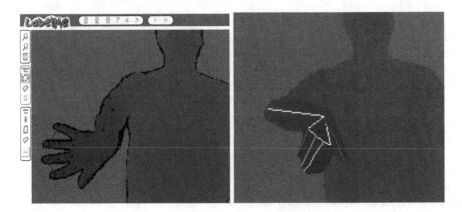

Fig. 2. Left: Using on-line annotation tool (http://labelme2.csail.mit.edu/Release3.0/index.ht to collect calibration frames. Right: Projection of the 3D VICON skeleton to the depth image.

to manually clean and label positions of the markers in 3D and fill gaps in the 3D marker trajectories caused by its occlusion in the VICON cameras, present mainly for fingers. The hand poses are automatically solved using the skeletal model that is extended about joint/marker constraints and pre-calibrated on the subjects' hand.

Most of the current body or hand pose estimation methods are based on the direct prediction of the 3D joint positions [2,5,8]. We used the forward kinematic to transform the solved hand poses given by the angular data to the 3D joint positions and assume the only subset of 15 joints for our learning task. The joint positions that are natively defined in the VICON coordinate frame, are projected to the depth images as a new 3D vector of $(u_x, u_y, depth_z)$ locations, see Fig. 2 right. For this purpose, we identified the position of the depth sensor in the VICON coordinate system. The extrinsic camera parameters of the depth sensor are identified by the Perspective-n-Point algorithm. We use several calibration frames from the depth sensor capturing the hand and label image coordinates of the projected markers, see Fig. 2 left. The intrinsic depth camera parameters are generally known.

3.2 Data Acquisition

We use a common depth sensor based on ToF (Time of Flight) technology - Kinect v2. The recording rate is 30 fps and the image resolution is 512 × 424 pixels. The sensor is positioned in 3rd person's point of view approximately 1.2 m in front of performer's hand. The sensor captures the whole upper body (see Fig. 3). Synchronization of the VICON mocap system is made by time stamps of the depth maps and a synchronization gesture performing at the beginning of every capturing. The synchronization error is under a millisecond.

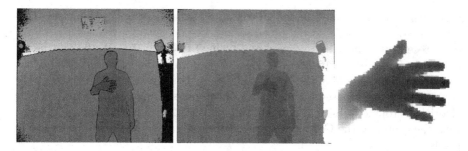

Fig. 3. Left: Input depth image, Middle: Depth image after depth hole filling, Right: Result of the hand tracking.

To collect the artificial synthetic data, we use the Blender software[1]. We set intrinsic and extrinsic camera parameters to be the same as the real depth sensor and the hand model rendering to the Z-buffer. Moreover, we employ the ARTEC 3D scanner[2] to get the 3D surface of the subject's hand in the rest pose, see Fig. 1 middle. The 3D polygonal surface naturally corresponds to the topology of the pre-calibrated skeleton model. It enables rendering of the depth map to be close as possible to the real depth data. On the other hand, we adapt our hand skeleton to the polygonal surface of the different realistic hand model [17] such that we got an instance of the generic hand model, see Fig. 1 right. In general, there are no synchronization errors for the synthetic data because the depth image directly matches the given hand pose. In this stage, we do not model any noise or shadows which are an effect of the ToF capture technology.

3.3   Data Post-processing

The ToF technology does not measure the depth of the highly reflective surfaces (like used retro-reflective markers) and produces missing data (holes) in the real depth maps. The image holes (mostly zero pixels) are actually better than the faulty (no zero) depth data because it can be easily detected. The smaller mocap markers (4 mm) are projected onto the holes with a size of ≈3 pixels only. We automatically fix the real depth maps via our method based on the nearest neighbor grid data interpolation. In addition, this process removes the unmeasured pixels which arose due to the noise or hand contour shadows, see Fig. 3 middle. This data interpolation modifies the real depth data to be as close as possible to the artificial data which are in principle generated without the unmeasured pixels.

The localization of the hand ensures an area of the depth map, rescaled onto input shape of the CNN, which is independent on the distance of the hand from the sensor. The hand localization comes from either the ground-truth or can be provided by a detector. Generally, the hand localization precedes the hand

---

[1] www.blender.org.
[2] www.artec3d.com.

pose estimation and can influence the results of the hand pose estimation. This different stage is mostly solved by either random decision forests (RDF) [15] or, more recently, a specially designed and trained CNNs [5,16]. We fix this factor in our method and assume the hand localization from the ground-truth, i.e. our results are independent of the localization stage. For this purpose, we employ the cropping algorithm based on the center of the mass (CoM) of the hand [8]. The algorithm crops depth hand data by the 3D box (250 mm × 250 mm × 250 mm) with the center in the CoM and rescales all depth maps to the uniforms size in pixels.

3.4 Pose Estimator

The annotated ground-truth 3D joint positions are also transformed into the coordinate frame of the CoM. For example, the dataset [13] incorporates the CoM as the first joint position in the annotated hand joints set. For our data, the forward kinematics does not provide this "joint", therefore we approximate it as the mean location extracted from the ground-truth positions of the little and index phalanges and wrist joint.

We assume the pose estimator defined as: $\hat{Y} = f(D_{crop})$, where $\hat{Y}$ is the estimated hand pose $Y = \{y_i\}, i = 1 \ldots N$, y_i are the 3D joint positions (x, y, z), $f(D_{crop})$ is the per-frame predictor and D_{crop} is the hand area in the depth map, see Sect. 3.3. The depth map D is obtained either by the real depth sensor or artificially. The pose estimator $f(D_{crop})$ is in the form of the CNN.

4   Experiments

The real training data (*real*) was created by the process described in previous Sect. 3. The training set contains 4361 depth images of the right hand from one capturing session. There was one subject, who performed 10 different hand poses used in sign languages (depicted in Fig. 4) in different rotations and positions relative to the depth sensor. The synthetic data were created by modeling the

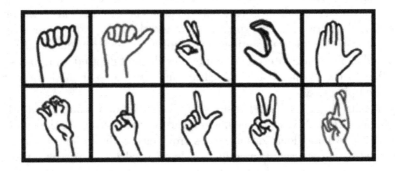

Fig. 4. Hand poses used for creating the training data.

same 10 hand poses by the 3D model of the subject's hand (Fig. 1 middle) or by the generic realistic hand model and rendering corresponding depth images (Fig. 1 right). There are three sets of the synthetic training data, all of the size of 4500 depth images. The first one *prior* set was obtained by the random sampling of the wrist and the forearm rotations from the real data distribution, the second *range* set by the random sampling of these rotations from the given ranges (wrist: $[-15°, 15°]_x$, $[-30°, 30°]_y$, $[-30°, 30°]_z$, forearm: $[-45°, 45°]_x$, $[-60°, 60°]_y$, $[-45°, 45°]_z$). The last *generic* set is the same as the *range* set, but the depth images were rendered by the generic hand model. The development data are composed of 1255 frames of the calibrating take ROM (Range Of Movements) and the frames with arbitrary free hand pose/movement. The test data consist of 634 frames of another take with arbitrary free hand pose/movement.

We used the Deepprior++[3] framework (with necessary modifications) to perform all experiments. The hand detection in depth maps was performed by the algorithm described in Sect. 3.3. The detected hand region is resized to the size of 128×128 pixels. To be able to use this framework with our data, we converted its annotation to the format of the ICVL dataset[4]. All training frames were augmented using the Deepprior++ default methods (adjusting already cropped image such that a moving CoM normalization is simulated; rotating hand virtually in the image plane by a given angle) and randomly shuffled to remove any time correlation between consecutive frames.

In our experiments, we compared results for the prediction of joint positions trained from the real data with the prediction trained from the synthetic ones. In all cases we used a standard CNN with the topology described in [8] (Fig. 1, type (d)). For our purposes, we experimentally found out that this topology is superior to the later one based on ResNet (Residual Network) architecture [6]. For optimization, we used gradient descent algorithm ADAM on batches of size 128, with the standard hyper-parameters and the learning rate of 0.0001, which was progressively adjusted with a number of training epochs, and train for 100 epochs.

Table 1 summarizes the results for the different training sets. For the comparison, we are using the average Euclidean distance between ground truth and the predicted joint 3D locations, which was established as a standard measure for this problem. We can see that the usage of the subject's hand model instead the generic one for the data rendering improves the prediction accuracy (cf. development: 23.6×22.8; test: 25.3×24.9). Next, adding the random sampling of the wrist and the forearm rotations based on the prior distribution given by the real data brings even bigger improvement, especially in the case of the test data (cf. 22.8×21.5; 24.9×18.7). Moreover the *prior* results are quite close to the *oracle* score (cf. 21.5×19.9; 18.7×18.1). The training set for the *oracle* score was created by re-synthesize the *real* training set one to one using the 3D scan of the subject's hand and the ground-truth joint rotations. Still of course, even

---

[3] https://github.com/moberweger/deep-prior-pp.
[4] https://labicvl.github.io/hand.html.

Table 1. Results for the different training sets on the development and the test data.

Method	Develop [mm]	Test [mm]
Real	**12.9**	**12.5**
Prior	21.5	18.7
Range	22.8	24.9
Generic	23.6	25.3
Oracle	19.9	18.1
Real + Prior	12.3	12.1
Real + Range	12.4	12.1
Real + Generic	12.8	12.2
Real + Prior_42	**11.5**	**11.3**

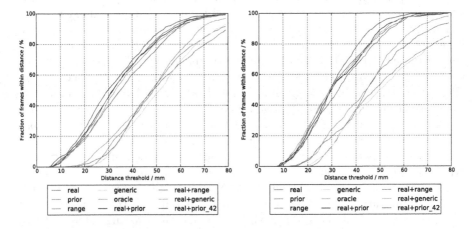

Fig. 5. Max joint distance error, left: development data, right: test data.

the best synthetic-only *prior* result significantly lacks behind the *real* data result (cf. 21.5×12.9; 18.7×12.5).

Nevertheless, we can combine the real and the synthetic data to get better results, as we did in the second part of Table 1. Among the three previous synthetic sets the best result is achieved by the combination *real + prior* set, but in the case of the test data all three combination sets perform almost equally.

The best result (*real + prior_42*) we got by adding the data synthesized from the prior distribution of the real data rotations and 42 additional missing hand poses used in the Czech Sign Language[5] captured by the VICON system. To obtain these poses we captured and processed only 42 additional mocap frames, one for each pose, and the resulting training data contains 23 261 depth frames in total. Using these data improves the results by 1.2 mm (cf. 12.5×11.3) absolutely or 10% relatively. Figure 5 shows the fraction of frames where all joints

---

[5] There are 52 basic hand poses in the Czech Sign Language in total.

of a frame are within a maximum distance from the ground truth. We can see that *real + prior_42* performs best again. Figure 6 then shows some qualitative comparisons.

Fig. 6. Hand pose estimation: line 1 = oracle, line 2 = prior, line 3 = real, line 4 = real + prior_42 (blue = ground-truth, red = prediction). (Color figure online)

5 Conclusion

We explored the contribution of the synthetic depth images for the training a convolutional deep neural network in the task of the 3D hand pose prediction. We introduced a method to generate synthetic depth images of the hand closely matching the real images. We extended the approach of the previous works to the modeling of the depth image data using the 3D scan of the subject's hand and the hand pose prior given by the real data distribution. We found out that combining them with the real data for the training can result in a better estimation performance. Creation of the large synthetic training sets can be done easily and significantly extend ranges of the real data usage as well as, the real data needed to be captured and annotated only on a smaller subset of the training data.

Acknowledgments. This work is financially supported by the Ministry of Education and Science of the Russian Federation, agreement No. 14.616.21.0095 (reference RFMEFI61618-X0095) and the European Regional Development Fund under the project AI&Reasoning (reg. no. CZ.02.1.01/0.0/0.0/15 003/0000466). This work was supported by the Ministry of Education of the Czech Republic, project No. LTARF18017. Access to computing and storage facilities owned by parties and projects contributing to the National Grid Infrastructure MetaCentrum provided under the programme "Projects of Large Research, Development, and Innovations Infrastructures" (CESNET LM2015042), is greatly appreciated.

References

1. Feix, T., Romero, J., Ek, C.H., Schmiedmayer, H.B., Kragic, D.: A metric for comparing the anthropomorphic motion capability of artificial hands. IEEE Trans. Robot. **29**(1), 82–93 (2013)
2. Ge, L., Liang, H., Yuan, J., Thalmann, D.: 3D convolutional neural networks for efficient and robust hand pose estimation from single depth images. In: The IEEE Conference on Computer Vision and Pattern Recognition (CVPR), July 2017
3. Ge, Y., Liang, H., Yuan, J., Thalmann, D.: Robust 3D hand pose estimation in single depth images: from single-view CNN to multi-view CNNs. In: Proceedings of CVPR 2016, June 2016
4. Ivanko, D., Karpov, A.: An analysis of perspectives for using high-speed cameras in processing dynamic video information. SPIIRAS Proc. **44**(1), 98–113 (2016). https://doi.org/10.15622/sp.44.7
5. Mueller, F., Mehta, D., Sotnychenko, O., Sridhar, S., Casas, D., Theobalt, C.: Real-time hand tracking under occlusion from an egocentric RGB-D sensor. In: The IEEE International Conference on Computer Vision (ICCV), October 2017
6. Oberweger, M., Lepetit, V.: Deepprior++: Improving fast and accurate 3D hand pose estimation. In: ICCV Workshops 2017, Venice, Italy, 22–29 October 2017 (2017)
7. Oberweger, M., Riegler, G., Wohlhart, P., Lepetit, V.: Efficiently creating 3D training data for fine hand pose estimation. In: The IEEE Conference on Computer Vision and Pattern Recognition (CVPR), June 2016
8. Oberweger, M., Wohlhart, P., Lepetit, V.: Hands deep in deep learning for hand pose estimation. In: CVWW, February 2015
9. Sharp, T., Keskin, C., et al.: Accurate, robust, and flexible real-time hand tracking, pp. 3633–3642. ACM, April 2015
10. Sinha, A., Choi, C., Ramani, K.: Deephand: robust hand pose estimation by completing a matrix imputed with deep features. In: The IEEE Conference on Computer Vision and Pattern Recognition (CVPR), June 2016
11. Sun, X., Wei, Y., Liang, S., Tang, X., Sun, J.: Cascaded hand pose regression. In: CVPR 2015, June 2015
12. Supancic, J.S., Rogez, G., Yang, Y., Shotton, J., Ramanan, D.: Depth-based hand pose estimation: data, methods, and challenges. In: The IEEE International Conference on Computer Vision (ICCV), December 2015
13. Tang, D., Jin Chang, H., Tejani, A., Kim, T.K.: Latent regression forest: structured estimation of 3D articulated hand posture. In: The IEEE Conference on Computer Vision and Pattern Recognition (CVPR), June 2014
14. Tang, D., Yu, T.H., Kim, T.K.: Real-time articulated hand pose estimation using semi-supervised transductive regression forests. In: ICCV 2013. IEEE Computer Society, Washington (2013)
15. Tompson, J., Stein, M., Lecun, Y., Perlin, K.: Real-time continuous pose recovery of human hands using convolutional networks. ACM Trans. Graph. **33**(5), 169:1–169:10 (2014)
16. Vodopivec, T., Lepetit, V., Peer, P.: Fine hand segmentation using convolutional neural networks. CoRR (2016)
17. Šarić, M.: Libhand: A library for hand articulation (2011). http://www.libhand.org/, version 0.9
18. Wan, C., Probst, T., Van Gool, L., Yao, A.: Crossing nets: combining GANs and VAEs with a shared latent space for hand pose estimation. In: The IEEE Conference on Computer Vision and Pattern Recognition (CVPR), July 2017

19. Yuan, S., Ye, Q., Stenger, B., Jain, S., Kim, T.K.: Bighand2.2m benchmark: hand pose data set and state of the art analysis. In: CVPR, July 2017
20. Zimmermann, C., Brox, T.: Learning to estimate 3D hand pose from single RGB images. In: ICCV 2017 (2017)

Ontology-Based Human-Robot Interaction: An Approach and Case Study on Adaptive Remote Control Interface

Alexey Kashevnik[1]([⊠]), Darya Kalyazina[2], Vladimir Parfenov[2],
Anton Shabaev[3], Olesya Baraniuc[2], Igor Lashkov[2],
and Maksim Khegai[2]

[1] SPIIRAS, St. Petersburg, Russia
`alexey@iias.spb.su`
[2] ITMO University, St. Petersburg, Russia
`darya.kalyazina@mail.ru`, `parfenov@mail.ifmo.ru`,
`ob@itc.vuztc.ru`, `igor-lashkov@ya.ru`,
`maksimkhegai@gmail.com`
[3] Petrozavodsk State University (PetrSU), Petrozavodsk, Russia
`ashabaev@petrsu.ru`

Abstract. The paper presents an approach to human-robot interaction in socio-cyberphysical systems. The paper propose a socio-cyberphysical system ontology that is aimed at describing the knowledge of the system resources. Humans are interacted with robots using personal smartphones. Every robot and mobile application for smartphone are designed based on the ontology that allows to support their semantic interoperability in socio-cyberphysical system. A case study considered in the paper is aimed at controlling the robots by group of humans. Group of robot consists of several robot types. Every type of robot has competencies that are described in the robot competency profile. Human experts also have own competencies that are described in the human profile. To control a robot a human should be available and have an appropriate competency for such type of robot. The paper describes the developed prototype for Android-based smartphone. The prototype implements the proposed approach and based on the developed ontology and Smart-M3 information sharing platform.

Keywords: Semantic interoperability · Ontology · Socio-cyberphysical system
Competency

1 Introduction

The research in the area of human-robot interaction becomes more and more popular last years [1–3]. The are a lot of interfaces have been developed for such communication. The systems that joins together human, robots, and information resources are the socio-cyberphysical systems. This systems tightly integrate socio, physical, and information spaces based on interactions between these spaces in real time. Human and robots are exchange information with each other in information space while their physical interaction occurs in physical space. Community of humans is the socio space.

© Springer Nature Switzerland AG 2018
A. Ronzhin et al. (Eds.): ICR 2018, LNAI 11097, pp. 116–125, 2018.
https://doi.org/10.1007/978-3-319-99582-3_13

The aim of this paper is to develop ontology-based human-robot interaction approach and show it applicability for the case study on robot control by humans. The approach is based on smart space technology [4, 5] that is aimed at seamless integration of different devices by developing ubiquitous computing environments, where different services can share information with each other, make different computations and interact for joint tasks solving. The interaction between robots and humans is implemented in Smart-M3 information sharing platform. This technology allows to organize ontology-based information and knowledge sharing for various participants based on publication subscription mechanism. The proposed adaptive remote control interface is more universal and useful than radio control devices since smartphone screen allows to show only functions that are related to the human preferences, current situation, and robot capabilities.

2 Related Work

There are several papers have been considered that describe research and development of the control interfaces. An adaptive remote control interface should be able to take into account human preferences, context situation, and robot capabilities as soon as offer a real-time feedback.

The most popular approach to control interface development is the application of directional arrows [6]. Up, down arrows are responsible for the throttle commands (move forward, backwards), and the leftward and rightward arrows to control the robot steering. This approach is the easiest to learn for the humans due to its intuitiveness. However, it has some drawbacks. For example, it may be problematic to make turns and maneuvers quickly while the robot moves along a complex trajectory since it is required for human switch between buttons frequently.

Another approach to the control interface development is virtual joystick utilization [7]. In compare with the previous one the approach supports the large amount of possible wheel steering angles that allows to control by the robot more precisely. The movement direction control includes only one human's hand and leaves more freedom for simultaneous manipulation of several functions, in contrast to the previous solution.

A virtual steering wheel approach is used by the Artificial Intelligence Group at Freie Universität Berlin in the iDrive application [8]. The approach is often used to simulate the car driving, which is quite evident. In other cases, this method is not successful due to the non-intuition and redundancy set of possible rotation angles, which is why the rotation of icon to the extreme values takes much time.

Utilization of such elements as the vertical and horizontal sliders is also one of the possible approach to the control interface development [9]. Users have to press and hold the button and move it along the slider to select a value from the continuous range. The horizontal and vertical sliders are used to control the steering and throttle commands respectively. By moving the button along the slider, users can control the speed and direction of the robot. As part of a safety feature, the sliders will return to the neutral position which is the centre when the user lifts their finger off the screen. This approach is rarely used because of its non-intuitive for this action.

Controlling by a built-in smartphone accelerometer is one of the most technologically advanced approaches [10]. Accelerometer measures the parameters of smartphone motion along three axes. This measuring is not enough for the robot control since only three axes can be decomposed into a translational motion or only a rotational motion. For the robot control a six measurement axes are required. The main link in the motion recognition system is the gyroscope, which is traditionally used to determine the absolute speed of rotation.

Utilization of voice for robot control [11] has advantages and disadvantages. One of the essential components of the spoken interface is microphone that records both control commands and noise. So the remote control interface developer should be careful about the irrelevant instruction for a specific environment. The approach is the most convenient in situations where the operator's hands are busy. On the contrary, it requires complex filtering and recognition mechanism and depends on the level of noise.

The authors of the paper [12] used Nintendo Wii Remote Controller (Wiimote), commercial-off-the-shelf (COTS) input device which allows for a variety of input schemes. The controller includes the traditional joystick and accelerometer for gestural control. The Wiimote communicates wirelessly using the BlueTooth communication protocol and open-source libraries allow access to the Wiimote from a PC.

Authors of the paper [13] present the cognitive user interface that enables a user-adaptive scenario in human-machine interactions based on semantic modelling. The interface prototype is able to communicate with users via speech and gesture recognition, speech synthesis and a touch display.

Authors of the paper [14] present non-invasive brain-computer interface for mobile robot control. The interface performs electroencephalographic signal decoding, which includes several steps: filtering, artefact detection, feature extraction, and classification.

Based on the presented analysis it is possible to conclude that each of the approaches considered has its pros and cons. The usage of directional pad is the most intuitive for the user, but difficult to use in a situation that requires the simultaneous use of a high number of functions. On the other side, the most modern approach using an accelerometer and a gyroscope can be utilized only for a limited set of functionality. It can also be deduced that for complex robotic systems with a large number of functions it is hard to use one specific approach. In such systems, a combined approach to developing a management interface is used.

3   An Approach to Human-Robot Interaction in Socio-Cyberphysical Systems

The general scheme of the developed in the paper adaptive remote control interface is shown in Fig. 1. The displayed at the interface items for the robot control are generated based on the following information: human preferences, context constraints, and robot capabilities. Human preferences characterize the human: how he/she would like to get information, what interfaces he/she would like to use for the robot control and etc. The context constraints characterize the current situation. E.g., if the robot meets an obstacle in physical space and it can be overcome automatically the interface shows a button for a human "Overcome obstacle". The robot capabilities describes all functions that the robot can perform. The robot considered in the paper consists of different units. In this case every unit has a set of drives or sensors and can perform a set of commands that is shown by controls in the interface.

During the human-robot interaction the design of the current robot remains static and does not require a change in the user interface, while the displayed controls can be dynamically changed depending on the robot context and human preferences. The simplest example is the various kinds of obstacles that arise before it. If there is an obstacle in front of the robot that cannot be overcome the "move forward" function is blocked.

The Fig. 2 shows the reference model of the human-robot interaction system. The main task of interaction is to determine user preferences, robot capabilities, and context situation; generate the items for remote control interface; transfer control commands to the robot; and shows feedback on the user interface. One or more humans and one or more robots can participate in the scenario. Several humans can control a robot or a

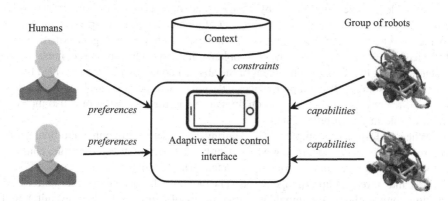

Fig. 1. Adaptive remote control interface.

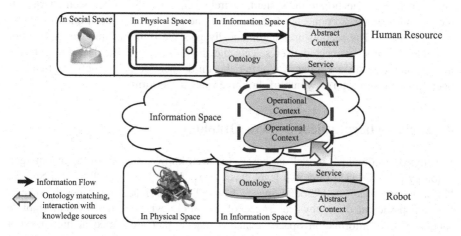

Fig. 2. Reference model of the human-robot interaction system.

human can control several robots simultaneously. An adaptive remote control interface can be installed to any computer supported network connection.

For interaction between humans and robots in socio-cyberphysical system the semantic interoperability and information & knowledge sharing between humans and robots has to be supported. Humans are operated in social space, robots are operated in physical space, and their interaction is implemented in information space. One of the possible approach to problem domain modelling is ontology management. The socio-cyberphysical system ontology has been developed and interaction of humans and robots is implemented based on this ontology. For current situation modelling and reducing the search space of potential coalition members the utilization of context management technology is proposed. Context is defined as any information that can be used to characterize the situation of an entity. An entity is a person, place or object that is considered relevant to the interaction between a user and an application, including the user and application themselves. Context is suggested to be modeled at two levels: abstract and operational.

These levels are represented by abstract and operational contexts, respectively. Abstract context is an ontology-based model of a potential coalition participant related to the current task. Abstract context is build based on integrating information and knowledge relevant to the current problem situation. Operational context is an instantiation of the domain constituent of the abstract context with data provided by the contextual resources. Human preferences determine the type of controls and command modes. Preferences are also depend on human role in the scenario group also includes the user role in the current scenario.

When performing a complex task requiring multiuser robot control the final set of control elements is divided among users according to their roles. For example, consider the scenario of overcoming a complex obstacle. The functionality of the robot can be divided into three groups of operations: (1) moving (throttle commands and wheel rotation commands), (2) manipulation (commands of lifting and lowering units), and complex actions (require participation of experts). Groups are shared between humans on the following principle: the first operator automatically gets access to all possible operation after connection to the system. Thereby he/she fulfils all the specified roles. If the second operator is connected to the system, the first one can select one of the two control groups. The second user automatically gets the rights of another group. For example, the first connected user selects the driver role, and the last one gets the manipulator role. In a similar way, after the third operator connection the first two operators choose by turns which of the three roles to perform.

4   Socio-Cyberphysical System Ontology

Developed ontological model is based on well-known suggested upper merged ontology (SUMO) [15] three top-level classes have been proposed: "Physical Space", "Information Space", and "Social Space". Class "Physical Space" describes the objects that are participated in physical space of the socio-cyberphysical system (mobile robots). Class "Information Space" contains objects that are aimed at human-robot interaction support. Class "Social Space" includes information about humans.

Consider the part of the ontology related to the class "Physical Space" in more details (see Fig. 3). The class contains a description of the physical objects and includes the following subclasses: "Collection", "Device", and "Environment". Class "Collection" defines a complex device that consists of several elementary devices defined in the class "Device" (e.g., robot is a collection that consists of the following devices: motor, wheels, sensors, and etc.). Class "Device" consists of following subclasses: "Connect_Interface", "Battery", "Hull", "Motor", "Sensor", "Switch", "Whell". Class "Connect_Interface" describes types of connection that can be used to implement interaction between devices. The subclass of the class "Connect_Interface" is "Wirelessinterface". The class defines the wireless interface that is used to device connection and includes the following subclasses: "Bluetooth" and "WiFi". Class "Bluetooth" determines the information exchange between devices by means of Bluetooth technology. Class "WiFi" allows organizing the information exchange with utilization of Wi-Fi technology. Class "Motor" describes the motors that can be used to a device collection operation. Class "Sensor" describes sensors used for device collection operation. Subclasses of class "Sensor" represent the following different types of sensors: class "DistanceSensor" describes the type of sensor that measures the distance, class "HeatSensor" describes the type of sensor for measuring temperature, class "LightSensor" describes the type of sensor for measuring the light condition. Class «TouchSensor»˙ describes the type of sensor for touching determination. Class "Wheel" describes the wheels that can be used by the device collection. Class "Battery" defines the power supplies installed on the devices. Class "Switch" describes the type of switches that can be used by device collection. Class "Environment" defines the area scenarios execution.

Class "Information Space" consists of following subclasses: "CompetenceProfile", "Configuration", "Context", "Policy", "Interaction", "Process", "Agent", "Human_profile", "Resource", and "Resource_profile". Class "CompetenceProfile" defines competences of device collection. The class consists of subclass "History" that stores all information related to performed tasks. Class "Agent" describes the program agent that participates in a scenario and control a device collection. Class "Configuration" contains a description of a collection components that should be considered in the information space. Class "Context" contains information about the current situation in physical space. The class consists of the following subclasses: "ResourceContext" that describes the current situation of a device collection and "EnvironmentContext" that describes current situation in the area where scenario should be executed. Class "EnvironmentContext" is divided into subclasses "Spatial" and "Temporal". Class "Spatial" includes subclass "Location" that defines location of the area where scenario should be executed. Class "Temporal" includes subclass "Time" that describes the time intervals associated with the execution of a scenario. Class "Human_profile" describes human information, preferences, and competencies. The class includes subclass "Competency". Class "Competency" defines main characteristics, which characterize an expert and consists of the following subclasses: "Knowledge", "Skills", and "Proficiency_level". Class "Knowledge" contains all knowledge related to the certain human which have been formalized. Class "Skills" describes all information about skills the human has. Class "Proficiency_level" includes information about humans's qualification related to every knowledge or skill.

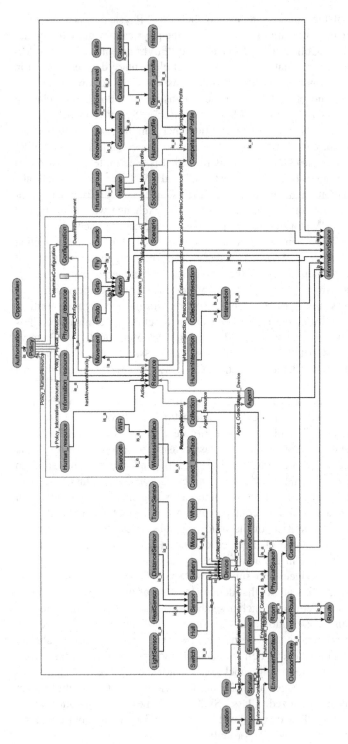

Fig. 3. Socio-cyberphysical system ontology.

Class "Interaction" describes types of interaction "HumanInteraction" and "CollectionInteraction" for solving tasks together. Class "HumanInteraction" defines information related to human and robot interaction and class "CollectionInteraction" describes information related to interaction of robots. Class "Policy" defines rights of the resources. Class "Scenario" contains information about scenarios which can be executed by the resources. The class contains subclass "Action" that describes actions performed by a resource. The class consists of the following subclasses: "Movement", "Photo", "Grip", "Fly", and "Check". Class "Movement" includes information related to resource movement. It consists of class «Route» that contains the following subclasses: class "IndoorRoute", and class "OutdoorRoute". Relationship of other classes can be seen in Fig. 3.

Class "Social Space" consists of class "Human", which includes information about people who can participate in the execution of scenarios. Class "Human" includes subclass "Human_group". Class "Human_group" determines a group formed by various characteristics: profession, skills and requirements.

5 Case Study

The presented case study is aimed at robot control by humans using the developed adaptive remote control interface. The interface has been developed for Android-based smartphone. The development process is implemented in Android Studio IDE. For the Smart-M3 platform deployment the DD-WRT-Based wireless router has been used. After the successful connection to Smart-M3 platform the application queries the following information in smart space: *("robot1", "blockAmount", "null")*. The triplet is aimed as query information about configuration of the robot *1*. If the response is not empty the interface starts to receive the information about blocks one by one by sends the following query triplets: *("block_i", "hasPart", "null")*, where *i* runs from *0* to the *blockAmout-1*. Then the interface initialize the following subscription for the manipulating robot monitoring: *("null", "event", "null");* and the following subscription for *("null", "task", "null"])* to determine a task when it appears in smart space. When the event or task is appeared in smart space the robot gets notification. The examples of the templates are the RDF triples that robots are generated based on the socio-cyberphysical system ontology.

The screenshots in the Fig. 4 displays the example of the main interface functions. At the standby state, the interface displays only the appearance of the current robot. All functions of the robot are hidden. Depending on the current task and the human preferences the appropriate list of functions is showed to the human. The user touches are displayed as white circles in the screenshots. On the first screenshot the "move front" function is displayed. If the human choose this function the appropriate information is published to the smart space and all robot modules understands that it is needed to move front and robots starts the movement. If the human needs to start the movement of a particular axle drive he/she should press to the wheel icon. The human (or group of humans) has an ability to interact with several functional elements at the same time and to submit several functions simultaneously.

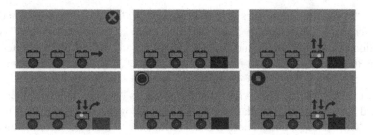

Fig. 4. Prototype screenshots: adaptive remote control interface.

When the "move front" function is activated the stop icon is shown on display. If the human activates the "stop" function the robot completes execution of all functions and stops completely. If an obstacle is detected, the robot publishes the corresponding triplet to the smart space. Then a human is notified about this event by displaying an obstacle icon. If the obstacle is analyzed and the appropriate algorithm is found to overcome it automatically the obstacle icon becomes green. If not the obstacle icon becomes red. In this case the human can control the robot to overcome the obstacle in manual mode and train the system.

6   Conclusion

The paper presents ontology-based human-robot interaction approach and its implementation for adaptive remote control interface. The ontology of the socio-cyberphysical system has been presented. Based on this ontology humans interact with robots.

The case study shows the example of the obstacle overcoming task by the multi-module robot. Robots implement the task and human has to take robot control in case of impossibility to overcome obstacle automatically. The developed interface for Android-based smartphone has been proposed and described. It has been evaluated on Samsung (Galaxy S4 mini), Asus (Zenfone 2), ZTE (Blade X3), and Xiaomi (Mi5) devices. Display size was ranged from 4.3 to 5.5 in. Application interface has drawn correctly and accurately regardless of the screen size and resolution through the vector icons usage.

Acknowledgements. The work has been partially financially supported by grants #16-29-04349, 16-07-00462 of Russian Foundation for Basic Research, by Russian State Research #0073-2018-0002, and by ITMO University (Project #617038).

References

1. Lemaignan, S., Warnier, M., Sisbot, E., Clodic, A., Alami, R.: Artificial cognition for social human–robot interaction: an implementation. Artif. Intell. **247**, 45–69 (2017)
2. Kryuchkov, B., Syrkin, L., Usov, V., Ivanko, D., Ivanko, D.: Using augmentative and alternative communication for human-robot interaction during maintaining habitability of a lunar base. In: Ronzhin, A., Rigoll, G., Meshcheryakov, R. (eds.) ICR 2017. LNCS (LNAI), vol. 10459, pp. 95–104. Springer, Cham (2017). https://doi.org/10.1007/978-3-319-66471-2_11
3. Andreev, V., Pletenev, P.: Method of information interaction for distributed control systems of robots with modular architecture. SPIIRAS Proc. **2**(57), 134–160 (2018)
4. Korzun, D., Kashevnik, A.: Balandin S.: Novel Design and the Applications of Smart-M3 Platform in the Internet of Things: Emerging Research and Opportunities, p. 150 (2017)
5. Mikhailov, S., Kashevnik, A.: Smart-M3-based smart space creation using a DD-WRTbased device. SPIIRAS Proc. **3**(52), 180–203 (2017)
6. Luo, Y., Liu, J., Gao, Y., Lu, Z.: Smartphone-controlled robot snake for urban search and rescue. In: Zhang, X., Liu, H., Chen, Z., Wang, N. (eds.) ICIRA 2014. LNCS (LNAI), vol. 8917, pp. 352–363. Springer, Cham (2014). https://doi.org/10.1007/978-3-319-13966-1_35
7. Seo, Y., Jung, H., Lee, C., Yang, T.: Remote data acquisition and touch-based control of a mobile robot using a smart phone. Comm. Comp. Inf. Sc. **265**, 219–226 (2011)
8. Wang, M., Ganjineh, T., Gohring, D.: Reuschenbach: A.: iDriver - human machine interface for autonomous cars. In: 2011 Eighth International Conference on Information Technology: New Generations (ITNG), Las Vegas, NV, pp. 435–440 (2011)
9. Chua, C., Foo, F., Lee, L.: Interactive methods of tele-operating a single unmanned ground vehicle on a small screen interface. In: Proceedings of the 6th International Conference on Human-Robot Interaction (HRI 2011), p. 121. ACM Press, New York (2011)
10. Chen, G., King, S.A., Scherger, M.: Robot remote control using bluetooth and a smartphone augmented system. In: Yang, D. (ed.) Informatics in Control, Automation and Robotics. Lecture Notes in Electrical Engineering, vol. 133, pp. 453–463. Springer, Heidelberg (2011). https://doi.org/10.1007/978-3-642-25992-0_63
11. Abdullahi, Z., Muhammad, N., Kazaure, J., Amuda, F.: Mobile robot voice recognition in control movements. Int. J. Comput. Sci. Electron. Eng. (IJCSEE) **3**(1), 11–16 (2015)
12. Varcholik, P., Barber, D., Nicholson, D.: Interactions and training with unmanned systems and the nintendo wiimote. In: Interservice/Industry Training, Simulation, and Education Conference (I/ITSEC), Orlando, Florida, USA, no. 8255 (2008)
13. Jokisch, O., Huber, M.: Advances in the development of a cognitive user interface. In: 13th International Scientific-Technical Conference on Electromechanics and Robotics "Zavalishin's Readings", vol. 161, 6 p. (2018)
14. Gundelakh, F., Stankevich, L., Sonkin, K.: Mobile robot control based on noninvasive brain-computer interface using hierarchical classifier of imagined motor commands. In: 13th International Scientific-Technical Conference on Electromechanics and Robotics "Zavalishin's Readings", vol. 161, 5 p. (2018)
15. IEEE Robotics and Automation Society. IEEE Standard Ontologies for Robotics and Automation (2015)

A Decentralized Data Replication Approach for the Reconfigurable Robotic Information and Control Systems

Eduard Menik[1] and Anna Klimenko[2(✉)]

[1] Southern Scientific Center of the Russian Academy of Science,
41 Chekhov street, Rostov-on-Don 344006, Russia
[2] Scientific Research Institute of Multiprocessor Computer Systems of Southern
Federal University, 2 Chekhov street, GSP-284, Taganrog 347928, Russia
Anna_klimenko@mail.ru

Abstract. This paper continues our previous studies on the reconfigurable robotic information and control system dependability. We consider the approach to the configuration forming optimization problem solving. This approach presupposes the criteria number reducing by the additional software functions implementation. These functions include tasks context data replication to the computational units, where those tasks can be launched after the reconfiguration procedure. Within the current paper some generic approaches to the context data storage element interaction are presented. The first approach is centralized and based on the principles of Viewstamped replication protocol, the second one is fully decentralized. Both of the approaches are discussed and estimated in terms of the communication environment workload, the conclusion is made, as well as some outlines of the future work.

Keywords: Information and control system · Reconfiguration
Reliability · Data replication

1 Introduction

The dependability of the robotic information and control systems is a question of a highest priority nowadays. A huge number of industries uses autonomous robots, collaborative robots, mechatronic production complexes: it is extremely important, for example, for activities where the man is not supposed to be (hazardous industries) or where the maintenance and reparation of the system is hardly possible. Obviously, the robotics in such areas should be reliable, fault-tolerant and, as a consequence, reconfigurable.

A good examples of reconfigurable robotic systems are the well-known modular robots, which begin with CEBOT [1] and continue their evolution with M-TRAN, ATRON, TRANSMOTE [2–4]. Another example is the collaborative flying drones [5], which are to solve one problem, e.g., landscape photographing. In case of drone failure, the others can distribute its tasks among the community. The same relates to the communities of modular robots.

© Springer Nature Switzerland AG 2018
A. Ronzhin et al. (Eds.): ICR 2018, LNAI 11097, pp. 126–136, 2018.
https://doi.org/10.1007/978-3-319-99582-3_14

Within this paper we consider the system dependability from the reliability and fault-tolerance point of view.

Reliability can be defined as the probability that a system will produce correct outputs up to some given time t [6]. According to [7], fault-tolerance is a means to achieve dependability and can be implemented by the complex of particular procedures, e.g. error detection (concurrent or preemptive), recovery (error handling, fault handling). Fault handling includes such procedures as diagnosis, fault isolation, reconfiguration and reinitialization, and in the current paper the reconfiguration procedure will be considered.

A fault-tolerance is provided by system reconfiguration and its implementation depends on the system reservation method. Nowadays there are some studies on the reliable ICS development [5, 8], but the overwhelming majority of them considers the structural reservation method with the structural redundancy usage. On the other hand, there are research papers considering the performance redundancy as an alternative for the structural reserve [9–12]. The performance redundancy usage can improve the reliability of the system as well as cost and weight characteristics, but needs more complicated reconfiguration procedure because of the need to distribute tasks among the operational nodes. Here the "configuration" term is of a high importance: configuration in the current paper is assumed as monitoring and control tasks (MCT) distribution among the set of computational units (CUs). The configurations designed affect the CU reliability [11, 12]. So, the way to distribute the MCTs among the CUs affects the overall system reliability too.

Configuration forming problem was considered precisely in our papers [11]. This optimization problem is multicriteria with constraints, so, the better configurations quality in terms of reliability criterion, the higher system overall reliability. To improve the configuration quality the "criterion delegating approach" (CDA) was developed and presented in [12]. The key idea is to reduce the number of criteria for the optimization problem and so to improve the configurations quality. Yet the task of the criterion eliminated must be implemented by other facilities, for example, by some additional software.

The paper [12] contains the detailed description of CDA with simulation results, which show that combining the CDA and the hybrid search via simulated annealing allowed to improve the quality of configurations significantly. Yet in the previous papers the mechanisms of system element interaction in order to implement the CDA was not considered in details. So, the current paper presents the general models of CDA implementation: centralized and the decentralized. Further sections of this paper contain:

- a brief description of CDA;
- basic models of the context data replication;
- selected simulation results;
- conclusion and future work outlines.

2 Criterion Delegating Approach

The model of configuration forming problem was presented and described in details in [12]. To recall the problem in general, the objective functions of configuration forming problem are presented below:

$$
\begin{aligned}
F_1 &= \sum_{i=1}^{N} (a_i - a_i') \rightarrow MIN \\
F_2 &= |A| - |A'| \rightarrow MIN, \\
F_3 &= \sum_{k=1}^{K} u_{kj}' - \sum_{l=1}^{L} u_{lq}' \rightarrow MIN, \ \forall j, q
\end{aligned}
\tag{1}
$$

where F_1 is the number of MCTs, which are relocated from the operable CUs, F_2 – the number of non-critical MCTs to be removed from the system, and F_3 is the workload dispersion on the CUs after the reconfiguration procedure, a_i is the tuple $<j, u_{ij}, t_i>$, which describes the link between MCT i and CU j. Here u_{ij} is the CU resources utilization percentage. A determines the configuration before the recovery, and A' – the configuration after the recovery, assuming $A = \{a_i\}$. The need to minimize the MCTs removing from the operable CUs has the quite obvious cause: all context data will be lost. Of course, this criterion restricts the configuration forming process.

Yet the important assumption was made in previous work: if we reduce the number of objective functions, we can solve the optimization problem with reduced objective function number and get a result of a better quality in terms of reliability.

It must be mentioned, that we don't consider the case of multicriteria optimization problem transformation into a one-criterion one by forming the constraints of the remaining criteria. The key idea of the CDA is to reduce the number of objective functions, while the desired aim (in our case – not to loose any context data) can be reached by some additional software.

In previous work some simulations were made, and we got a solution for the configuration forming problem in two ways: like a three criteria optimization problem solving and like a two criteria one. The quality of the results was evaluated from the workload point of view due to its importance for the CU reliability function. Finally, the elimination of the tasks relocation criterion allowed to obtain the configurations of a better quality in terms of CU workload [14].

The current paper presents the generic models of the system elements interaction to obtain the distributed context data storage. The following sections of this paper present the detailed models of the distributed data storage implementation, including communicational environment workload estimation.

3 Models of Multiagent Information and Control System Decentralized Data Storage Approaches

To obtain the possibility to relocate MCTs from the operable CU and not to lose task context data, the distributed and decentralized data storage must be implemented.

Before the presentation of the data storage models, some important assumptions about the MCTs are to be made. Let's assume the MCT as a determined state machine, so as each state can be described by the values of input data and the ones of internal variables. The simplified scheme of such presentation is shown in Fig. 1.

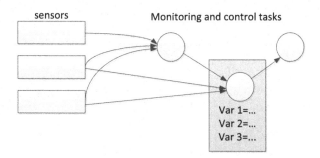

Fig. 1. A generic MCT state description presentation.

Assuming this, we can determine the portions of input data and internal variables as a kind of transactional data, which is generated periodically by portions. Each portion is a result of the following: input data received from sensors and/or another MCTs and internal variable values.

Also we assume that transitions between states are instantenious, and each state generates a data portion for replication and further storage. Previously [12] we presupposed the following draft model of the data storage:

1. There is an active MCT, which sends the portions of context data to inactive MCT copies;
2. In case of reconfiguration inactive MCT is activated by the CU agent.
3. It consumes the up-to-date context data and distributes the following context to the inactive copies of itself.
4. Such model of the distributed data storage as is presented in Fig. 2.

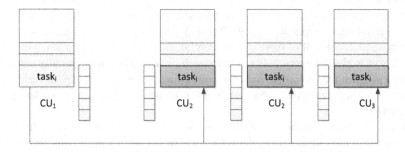

Fig. 2. A draft model of the distributed data storage.

The model described above allows to eliminate the objective of the active task relocation number minimization, yet it does not handle the case of task$_i$ failure. As is seen, if the active task fails (yet the CU does not), the context data distribution is stopped, and if there is a CU failure after that, the system will not recover properly.

The obvious solution of this problem is a redundancy in terms of active MCTs, as is shown in Fig. 3.

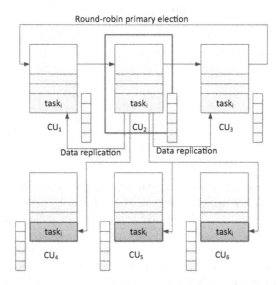

Fig. 3. Centralized approach model based on Viewstamped replication protocol principles.

Here we presuppose that active MCT$_i$ is launched on the $2f + 1$ CUs, where f – is the number of failures to be handled. Besides, we presuppose the fair behavior of the MCTs without the byzantine one. The system is asynchronous, and every replica of the MCT$_i$ receives input data from sensors in the same order but, may be, not in the same time moments. Also we assume that the running MCT can not consume the new context data. The general aim is to reach the data consensus in case of reconfiguration.

In order to implement this the most used replication protocols were analyzed: Paxos, Viewstamped replication, Raft, Zab [15–19]. The main conclusion was made about those protocols: all of them use the centralized scheme of replication. The leader (or primary) is elected every ballot (view/epoch), and, except the particular cases, the leader establishes the up-to-date data. The discipline of the election can be various, for example, Viewstamped replication uses simple round-robin discipline dependent on the view number.

In our particular case the active copies of the MCTs have to elect the leader, which would replicate its context data to those CUs where this MCT can be launched after the reconfiguration. It must be mentioned, that the relations between active MCTs and their replicas can be determined as a passive replication [15]. Context data is presupposed to be stored in chain-like structure of the fixed size with FIFO discipline.

So, the simplified model of data storage elements interaction was developed on the basis of the Viewstamped replication.

Within this interactional model, every data portion is "stamped" with <view_number, package_number> , where view_number is the number of view (epoch) and initially is 0, and the package_number is the number of context data portion generated by active task. The data chains are supposed to be identical if <view_number, package_number> of the first chain are equal to the <view_number, package_number> of the second chain.

Leader election

1. The leader is elected by round-robin discipline like it is done in Viewstamped Replication protocol.
2. Once the leader has been elected, the replicas send it their data storage content.
3. The leader chooses the data storage with a MAX(view_number, package_number) as up-to-date and sends this data store to other active MCT replicas. The choice of MAX(view_number, package_number) is expedient due to possible failures of active task replicas as is used in ViewStamped Replication.

Operational state

1. Only leader sends its context data to passive replicas
2. Followers just collect their own context data, marking it with <view_number, package_number>.

View change

1. view_number++;
2. Leader election

Task failure and recovery

1. If the leader is inoperable, the view change is initialized;
2. If the follower is inoperable, it can be restored by the operation system software. After recovery a follower can request the context data from leader to update its data storage, or it can be done on the *View_change*.

Reconfiguration

1. The passive task replica is active now and consumes all context data from its store.
2. According to the configuration list the communication between the replicated tasks is established
3. View change.
4. Go to the Operational state.

The model based on the Viewstamped replication protocol has the strong advantage, reducing the communication environment workload on the operational stage, as well as the space needed for data storage. Yet if the primary fails, the change view procedure must be initialized. Besides, change view procedure seems to be slow due to the context data storages exchange and distribution.

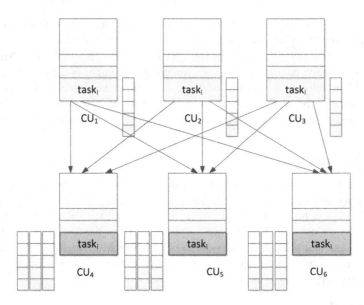

Fig. 4. Decentralized approach model.

So, we decided to avert the centralized interaction and developed the fully decentralized model of a context data storage (Fig. 4).

In the model proposed there is no primary at all, all active tasks are identical. The "stamp" is changed: instead of "view_number" (there are no views), the "replica_id" is used. So, each data portion is marked with <replica_id, package_number>.

The operational stage begins from the reconfiguration: each task sends its context data to each inactive replica. Then, if any of the replicas fail, nothing happens to data storages of inactive tasks. So, there will be just two stages: operational stage and recovery stage after the reconfiguration.

Operational state

1. Active MCTs send their context data, marked with <replica_id, package_number>, to the inactive MCT replicas.
2. Inactive task replicas collect context data (it can be done also by the agent of the CU).

Reconfiguration

1. New active task replica takes the context data from the storage with max (package_number). There can be several data portions with the same package_number, but identified by the <replica_id, package_number>.
2. According to the configuration list the communication between the replicated tasks is established.
3. Active task replica selects the context data by random selection from the set of data portions.
4. Go to the operational state.

So, it is seen that the fully decentralized model is much simpler, yet generates more communication environment workload.

To compare decentralized data replication approach with the centralized one more precisely the network workload estimation models were developed. We estimated the network workload during the reconfiguration and on the operational state, combining the general agents' functions and replication.

Firstly, in both cases, the CU agents establish the connection between the CUs within the decentralized ICS. Assuming V_p as a data volume for agents' information exchange, the data volume transferred through the network is as follows:

$$V_a = V_p(n+k)(n+k-1); \tag{2}$$

where V_p is the volume of heartbeat message, n is the number of active MCT replicas, k is the number of passive MCT replicas.

The estimation of reconfiguration network workload for the centralized approach is as follows:

$$N_{rc} = V_p(n+k)(n+k-1) + (n-1)V_{ds} + (n-1)V_{dl}; \tag{3}$$

where V_{ds} is the volume of active MCT data storage (assuming that they have almost the same volumes);

V_{dl} is the volume of the leader elected data storage which is to be distribute among the other active MCT replicas.

For the decentralized replication model the network workload can be estimated as follows:

$$N_{rd=}V_p(n+k)(n+k-1), \tag{4}$$

because of no leader election and data storages' transferring at all.

At the same time, the operational states of the centralized and decentralized models are described as follows:

$$N_{oc} = V_p(n+k)(n+k-1) + V_{cd} * k; \tag{5}$$

where V_{cd} is a volume of context data to be replicated.

$$N_{od} = V_p(n+k)(n+k-1) + n * k * V_{cd}. \tag{6}$$

4 Simulation Results

Firstly, the network workload was estimated for the reconfiguration procedure.

It is seen in Fig. 5 that with relatively small volume of heartbeat messages, the centralized approach generates the weighty network workload. The explanation of such result is quite obvious: every reconfiguration includes the "view change" procedure, which contains the leader election stage. As the leader election is related to the

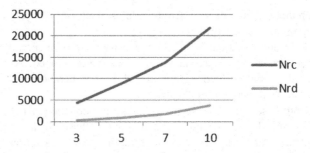

Fig. 5. The network workload of the reconfiguration stage of the centralized (Nrc) and decentralized (Nrd) approaches.

intensive data exchange between the leader and replicas, the reconfiguration procedure of the centralized model generates relatively high network workload.

At the same time, the decentralized approach is much better in terms of the network workload: there is no leader election, and if the reconfiguration is done, the new active replica just gets the context data from its storage and continues to perform.

Yet, for the operational stage the results were as follows in Fig. 6.

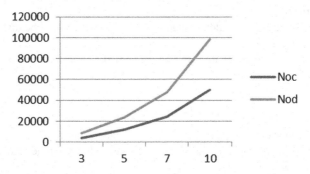

Fig. 6. The network workload for the operational state for the centralized (Noc) and decentralized (Nod) approaches.

It is seen that the network workload of the centralized approach is much better than the network workload of the decentralized one: the amount of replicated data depends on the active replicas number and the number of CUs, where the MCT can be launched in case of reconfiguration, while centralized scheme presupposes the data transmissions from one (leader) CU.

Such simulation results make us to consider the important issue, which is presented in the conclusion section.

5 Conclusion and Future Work

In the current paper the decentralized data replication approach for the reconfigurable robotic information and control systems is under consideration. The data replication models within the CDA were developed, compared and estimated. The general results of the research are the following:

- the centralized data replication approach is stable, reliable and ideally suited for the operational stage of the ICS, but consumes redundant resources and time through the reconfiguration procedure;
- the decentralized data replication approach is stable too, and fast when the reconfiguration occurs, but consumes resources on the operational stage of the system;

As the reconfiguration time is extremely important for real-time systems, the decentralized approach seems to be preferable. Yet there is an important question, which outlines our future work: organizing the additional context data exchange on the operational stage, there is a problem to keep all bonuses of the CDA. In other words, the new optimization problem must be formalized and solved: which parameters of the information exchange must be chosen not to worsen the reliability function of the system, which is obtained due to the CDA implementation.

Acknowledgements. The paper has been prepared within the GZ SSC RAS N GR project 01201354238 and RFBR projects 18-29-03229 and 18-05-80092.

References

1. Fukuda, T., et al.: Cellular robotics system - self-organization of the intelligent robotic system, Technical Paper – Society of Manufacturing Engineers (1994). http://www.scopus. com/inward/record.url?eid=2-s2.0–0028697546&partnerID=40&md5=73964e31549c04381 b635c130808565d
2. Brandt, D., Christensen, D.J., Lund, H.H.: ATRON robots: versatility from self-reconfigurable modules. In: Proceedings of the 2007 IEEE International Conference on Mechatronics and Automation, ICMA 2007, pp. 26–32 (2007). https://doi.org/10.1109/icma. 2007.4303511
3. Murata, S., et al.: M-TRAN: Self-reconfigurable modular robotic system. IEEE/ASME Trans. Mechatron. **7**(4), 431–441 (2002). https://doi.org/10.1109/TMECH.2002.806220
4. Qiao, G., et al.: Design of transmote: A modular self-reconfigurable robot with versatile transformation capabilities. In: IEEE International Conference on Robotics and Biomimetics, ROBIO 2012 - Conference Digest, pp. 1331–1336 (2012). https://doi.org/10.1109/ROBIO. 2012.6491153
5. Inaltekin, H., Gorlatova, M., Mung, C.: Virtualized control over fog: interplay between reliability and latency, CoRR, vol. abs/1712.0 (2017)
6. Crestani, D., Godary-Dejean, K.: Fault tolerance in control architectures for mobile robots: fantasy or reality? In: 7th National Conference on Control Architectures of Robots (2012). http://hal.archives-ouvertes.fr/docs/00/80/43/70/PDF/2012_CAR_FTRobotic-FantasyOr Reality.pdf

7. Avizienis, A., Laprie, J.C., Randell, B.: Fundamental concepts of dependability. Technical report Seriesuniversity of Newcastle Upon Tyne Computing Science, vol. 1145, pp. 7–12 (2001). https://doi.org/10.1.1.24.6074

8. Carlson, J., Murphy, R.R.: How UGVs physically fail in the field. IEEE Trans. Rob. **21**(3), 423–437 (2005). https://doi.org/10.1109/TRO.2004.838027

9. Melnik, E., Korovin, I., Klimenko, A.: Improving dependability of reconfigurable robotic control system. In: Ronzhin, A., Rigoll, G., Meshcheryakov, R. (eds.) ICR 2017. LNCS (LNAI), vol. 10459, pp. 144–152. Springer, Cham (2017). https://doi.org/10.1007/978-3-319-66471-2_16

10. Melnik, E.V., Klimenko, A.B., Schaefer, G., Korovin, I.S.: A novel approach to fault tolerant information and control system design. In: 5th International Conference on Informatics, Electronics and Vision, ICIEV (2016). https://doi.org/10.1109/ICIEV.2016.7760182

11. Korovin, I., Melnik, E., Klimenko, A.: A recovery method for the robotic decentralized control system with performance redundancy. In: Ronzhin, A., Rigoll, G., Meshcheryakov, R. (eds.) ICR 2016. LNCS (LNAI), vol. 9812, pp. 9–17. Springer, Cham (2016). https://doi.org/10.1007/978-3-319-43955-6_2

12. Melnik, E., Klimenko, A., Korobkin, V.: Reconfigurable distributed information and control system multiagent management approach. In: Advances in Intelligent Systems and Computing, vol. 680 (2018). https://doi.org/10.1007/978-3-319-68324-9_10

13. Klimenko, A.B., Klimenko, V.V., Melnik, E.V.: The parallel simulated annealing-based reconfiguration speedup algorithm for the real time distributed control system fault-tolerance providing. In: Proceedings of 9th International Conference on Application of Information and Communication Technologies, AICT (2015). https://doi.org/10.1109/ICAICT.2015.7338562

14. Strogonov, A.: Dolgovechnost Integralnih schem I proizvodstvenniye metody ee prognozirovaniya. ChipNews **6**, 44–49 (2002)

15. Liskov, B.: From Viewstamped replication to byzantine fault tolerance. In: Charron-Bost, B., Pedone, F., Schiper, A. (eds.) Replication. LNCS, vol. 5959, pp. 121–149. Springer, Heidelberg (2010). https://doi.org/10.1007/978-3-642-11294-2_7

16. Kirsch, J., Amir, Y.: Paxos for system builders. In: Proceedings of the 2nd Workshop on Large-Scale Distributed Systems and Middleware, LADIS 2008, p. 1 (2008). https://doi.org/10.1145/1529974.1529979

17. Liskov, B., Cowling, J.: Viewstamped replication revisited. In: IEICE Transactions on Information and Systems, (MIT-CSAIL-TR-2012-021), pp. 1–14 (2012) http://18.7.29.232/handle/1721.1/71763

18. Van Renesse, R., Schiper, N., Schneider, F.B.: Vive La Différence: Paxos vs. Viewstamped Replication vs. Zab. IEEE Trans. Dependable Secure Comput. **12**(4), 472–484 (2015). https://doi.org/10.1109/TDSC.2014.2355848

19. Junqueira, F.P., Reed, B.C., Serafini, M.: Zab: High-performance broadcast for primary-backup systems. In: Proceedings of the International Conference on Dependable Systems and Networks, pp. 245–256 (2011). https://doi.org/10.1109/DSN.2011.5958223

The Model of Autonomous Unmanned Underwater Vehicles Interaction for Collaborative Missions

Igor Kozhemyakin, Ivan Putintsev, Vladimir Ryzhov,
Nikolay Semenov, and Mikhail Chemodanov$^{(\boxtimes)}$

Saint-Petersburg Marine Technical University, Saint-Petersburg, Russia
chemodanov@smtu.ru

Abstract. Results of the work carried out by Saint-Petersburg State Marine Technical University in the framework of the project, connected with complex researches in maintenance of creation of a multi-agent sensory-communication network based on marine robotic platforms (MRP), are presented. In the context of the mentioned works, creation and testing of communication protocol for µAUVs with hydroacoustic modems is proposed. The article describes steps of protocol creation: from mission planning to modem control and modeling with digital imitation model testing (Solving the task of monitoring the seabed area). Within the framework of the concept of a "budget", limited serial product, functional systems/modules of µAUV are worked out, taking into account the availability of equipment and components (concerning required technical characteristics and their cost). For the selected external appearance and design dimensions of the device, the simulation of hydrodynamic, signal power and energy characteristics were performed. Within the framework of the project, a software and hardware architecture of the information system of the vehicle was developed, as well as a model of interaction between the µAUV, the wave glider and control center. The work results in proposal and testing of µAUVs communication through the water. Simulation results of implementing mission by a group of developed µAUVs can be modeled by ground robots with some software limitations. Based on the results, ways for further work on the subjects are being determined.

Keywords: Marine multi-agent sensory-communication network
Communication protocol · OSI · Contract Net Protocol
Marine robotic platform · Micro autonomous underwater vehicle
Group missions

1 Introduction

Development of autonomous unmanned underwater vehicles (AUUV), that is underwater robots, represents one of the most dynamically developing areas of elaboration of foreign naval technologies, universities and commercial firms. World leaders in the development of the AUUVs are the United States, Great Britain, Canada, France, Germany and Japan. The number of devices created abroad has exceeded 9000 [1].

© Springer Nature Switzerland AG 2018
A. Ronzhin et al. (Eds.): ICR 2018, LNAI 11097, pp. 137–147, 2018.
https://doi.org/10.1007/978-3-319-99582-3_15

The main difference of AUUVs from terrestrial robots and UAVs is large movement resistance, ability to move in 3D, hang (in contrast to UAVs) and a strong limitation of the communication speed, range and positioning.

Functionally, all AUUVs contain mission control system, information system, motion control system, sensor system, mechanical and power system, communication system and payload (Fig. 1) [2].

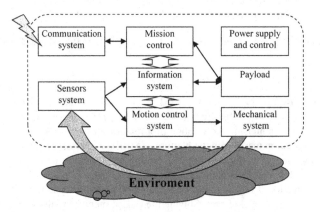

Fig. 1. Functional diagram of AUU.

It was shown in the researches [3–7] that this problem is most effectively solved by decentralized distributed network-centric systems of group control. Let us consider the system of network interaction of AUUV group and the ways of its modeling and prototyping.

The model of interaction of any autonomous robots, including AUUV, can be described by the 7-level model of the OSI network interaction, depicted in Table 1 [8].

Table 1. Levels of network interaction in OSI model.

Application layer	Mission control, arbitration, voting, task planning
Presentation layer	Presentation of agent data for communication purposes (task list, voting, arbitration, task distribution)
Session layer	Forming of communication session, choosing of a subscriber, communication route planning
Transport layer	Data communication protocol between the agents
Network layer	Logical addressing, routing, message delivery confirmation. Protocols ICMP, SS7
Data link layer	Package formation, check sum, physical adressing. Protocols x.25, ARP, DSS
Physical layer	Hydroacoustic modem, OFDM, …

The exchange protocol between agents must perform the following functions [9]:

1. Access to the network (Physical and Data link layers of the OSI model). A hydroacoustic modem is used for the physical layer and X.25 - for the link layer. These protocols allow to generate messages as addressed ones (for one subscriber), and as broadcasted or multicast (for all available).
2. Network (batch level). The basic protocols are ICMP, IP, SS7. If a message from one agent to another cannot be transmitted directly due to the signal propagation features and to a long distance, other agents located between these two subscribers may pass it along the chain.
3. Application layers (Application, Presentation, Session, Transport layers) are responsible for the group application of network agents and mission planning and control.

Currently, autonomous agent communication languages, including group AUUV, continue to evolve actively, new algorithms and methods, methods for resolving conflicts in a group are emerging to increase the effectiveness of this group. Since compatibility is the defining agent characteristic, in the development of MAS, standardized communication is of great importance [8, 9]. The main objects for standardization are: agent architecture, agent interaction languages, agent interaction protocols, agent knowledge, agent programming languages. When developing its own multi-agent network of underwater and surface robots, the Contract Net Protocol (CNP) [9] developed by FIPA was chosen, with modification in which abstract tenders were replaced by virtual money relations.

Exchange between agents at the application level involves the distribution of tasks among agents, resolving conflicts when sharing resources, informing about the task status change and so on. These messages are high-level and universal. Communication languages at the application level can be identical for underwater robots, terrestrial or flying.

But for the correct modeling of entire network interaction system, it is necessary to provide a correct simulation of the network formation level and of the network access level. If network access level is determined by parameters of the hydroacoustic modem (hydroacoustic modem is the most long-range data transporter for wireless communication under water), level of network formation depends strongly on the features and limitations of this hydroacoustic modem.

A time delay in implementation of the exchange protocol significantly depends on speed of delivery of the message to the addressee and receiving confirmation. So, when using a radio communication, delays for sending a message to a destination located at a distance of 1.5 km will be 5 µs, but using a hydroacoustic communication channel it will be 1 s. In the protocol shown in Fig. 2, at least 3 transmissions are required to start the work by the private trader, that is, if the delay for transmitting one message is 1 s, the total delay will be 3 s. And this is only for the information exchange between two agents. Therefore, when exchanging messages between AUUVs under water, it is necessary to minimize the number of requests and responses to obtain an efficient solution.

In the case where the message is impossible to deliver directly from the sender to the recipient, it is necessary to support resending of the request by agents that are not recipients, but are available for reception from the sender. This protocol should also minimize the number of messages to save time.

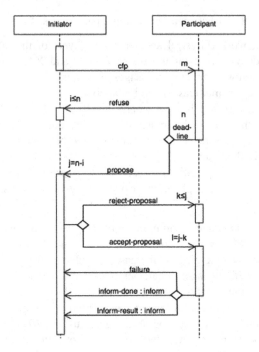

Fig. 2. Exchange protocol Contract Net Protocol.

2 Routing

Nowadays, there are no strict specifications for a handover implementation ("seamless" movement of correspondent agents between the transmitter and the receiver) [8–10]. However, to provide such a transition, special procedures for scanning the ether and joining ("association") are provided. The implementation of handover in networks can be carried out in various ways, for example, based on the Radius protocol or under control of an intelligent wireless controller, that organizes a "tunnel" when the client moves to the service area of a neighboring access point. The 802.11k specification describes procedures that allow an agent to select an access point (intermediate agent) to which one should connect to create the current connection (Fig. 3). Figure 3 shows the possible lines of communication between agents.

Considering traffic between agents within a session as a function of the amount of data transmitted $S^D(t)$, session on the time interval $[T_b; T_e]$, $T_e > T_b$ could be described by the vector

$$S^D = [S_1^D, S_2^D, S_3^D, \ldots, S_M^D],$$

breaking the interval of observation $t \in [T_b, T_e]$ into M incrementing segments.

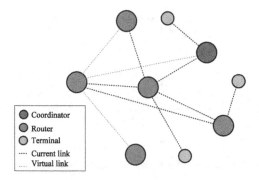

Fig. 3. An example of a self-organizing agent network structure.

Moreover, the elements of the S^D vector are such that,

$$S_i^D = \genfrac{}{}{0pt}{}{t = T_b + (i+1)\Delta t}{t = T_b + i\Delta t} \, | \, \sum_{K=1}^{K_i} S_{i,k}^D,$$
$$i = 0, 1, \ldots, (M-1),$$

that is, each element of S_i^D represents the sum of the sizes of $S_{i,k}^D$ (or quantity) of packets transmitted within this session in the i-th time interval Δt. The vector S^D itself is a histogram of traffic on the time axis, and the smaller the interval Δt, the closer this histogram to the real function $S^D(t)$.

When it is necessary to send messages through correspondents (when it is not possible to directly transmit the message from the source to the receiver), the problem of optimal routing appears, that is, the formation of the transmission path, which requires minimal time and energy resources.

The mechanism of the "logical distance" allows the source and the nodes located on the request path to select the minimum "logical distance" of the route from the source to its destination as shown in Figs. 4 and 5.

In Fig. 4 it is seen that the broadcast request from I to A cannot be delivered, since I is bounded by the communication distance. Therefore, the request must be retransmitted through intermediary agents. An example of finding the optimal route is shown in Fig. 5. Agents 2 and 4 can send a message to agent A, but the logical distance from agent 4 to A is less (signal strength is greater). Therefore, this route is preferable.

The described basic algorithm is efficient and versatile, can work in dynamic conditions for automatic re-routing, and therefore it is recommended to use it to find the relay route.

For example, for the purpose of site surveys, each indexed site is a profit. Resources for the survey - direct costs. Simple work on time and loss of resources when moving through already surveyed areas - fines. To bring all the parameters to a uniform dimension, it is convenient to recalculate them into conditional energy units:

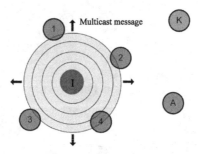

Fig. 4. An example of a broadcast request in an agent network.

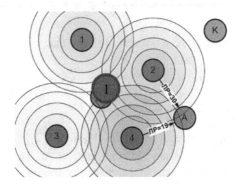

Fig. 5. Finding the optimal route for relaying

$$U = k \cdot \sum_{i=1}^{N} X_1 - \sum_{i=1}^{M} P_i - \sum_{k=1}^{M} Z_k,$$

where U is the budget of the agent, k is the incentive factor for the work performed, X_i is the work done on the sites, P_i is the additional costs for the inspection of the sites, Z_k – fines.

To simulate the interaction of AUUV in a group, it is necessary to determine which parameters will have a communication channel, namely hydroacoustic communication. From the general communication theory (Shannon's theorem) [8], it is known that the limiting communication rate between two subscribers is limited by the bandwidth of the frequencies used and the signal-to-noise ratio as:

$$C = B \log_2 \left(1 + \frac{S}{N}\right),$$

where C – bandwidth of the channel, bit/s; B – bandwidth of the channel, Hz; S – total signal strength over the bandwidth, W or V^2; N is the total noise power over the bandwidth, W or V^2.

Unfortunately, in hydroacoustic low frequencies can be hardly emitted by small antennas, and high frequencies are rapidly decayed, so frequencies of tens of kilohertz are used to transmit information at distances in units of kilometers (range of small, autonomous robots), and the bandwidth is not more than an octave. The structure of the dependence of the maximum communication distance on the frequency of the communication system operation is shown in Fig. 6.

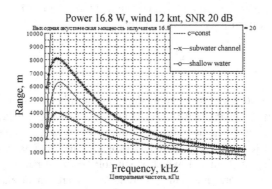

Fig. 6. Dependence of maximum communication distance from operating frequency.

Since in the marine environment supply multipath propagation of the signal as a result of salinity heterogeneity, density and temperature instability, the superposition of all possible rays comes to the receiver, which can be summed up both in phase and in the opposite phase, that is, by subtraction. This causes fading in the communication channel. The impulse response of such a channel with fading looks like

$$h(t) = \sum_{m=0}^{L-1} h_m e^{j\Phi_m} \delta(t - \tau_m),$$

where h_m has a Rayleigh distribution and F_m has a uniform distribution.

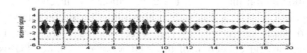

Fig. 7. An example of a fading multipath signal on a receiver.

An example of a signal with fading is shown in Fig. 7:
The following equation is used to calculate the power at each rectifier:

$$Q(n) = \frac{e^{-\frac{nT_c}{T_d}}}{\sum\limits_{n=0}^{L-1} e^{-\frac{nT_c}{T_d}}},$$

where T_d is the damping constant, which is assumed to be 1 ms. The standard deviation of noise sources for each track has the form:

$$\sigma_n = \sqrt{\frac{Q(n)}{2}}, n = 0, 1, \ldots, L - 1.$$

Many communication channels are modeled as multi-beam channels with Rayleigh fading, having a pulse characteristic $h(k; l)$ and representing a delay line with taps, where the k-th coefficient is a Gaussian random process with a variable time l. In [3], a stationary uncorrelated scattering model is proposed to facilitate the description of channels with fading. This model, which is suitable for most radio channels, suggests that signal constituents arriving with different delays are uncorrelated and that the correlation properties of the channel are stationary. The autocorrelation function taking into account these assumptions has the form:

$$E[h(k_1, l_1)h^*(k_2, l_2)] = \delta(k_1 - k_2)R(k_1; l_1 - l_2).$$

Without loss of generality it is assumed that the greatest value of the profile of the trajectory is observed at $k = 0$, i.e. in addition, the received signal is subject to a complex-valued additive white Gaussian noise with a spectral density of power N_0.

In addition to fading in the channel, the signal is also distorted by noise. The noise dispersion depends on the E_b/N_0 ratio, the encoding rate C, and the spectrum efficiency. The noise dispersion has the form

$$\sigma_n^2 = \frac{1}{2n} \frac{1}{C} \left(\frac{E_b/N_0}{10} \right).$$

where n is the modulation intensity of the digital modulation scheme used.

The development of AUUV interaction algorithms for group interaction is a very complicated and costly operation [13–15], since the procedure for launching, controlling the operation and collection of the AUUV group requires the use of a large number of participants, the accompanying vessel and the need to debug possible errors with the risk of losing costly devices. Numerical simulation on a computer may not cover all possible situations that agents fall into [15]; therefore, it is necessary to use a simple, reliable and inexpensive way to debug algorithms for network interaction of mobile robots. In this way, it is the use of terrestrial mobile robots that perform a mission similar to AUUV group, for example, to search for objects of a given shape and color on a specific territory [11]. Such robots are equipped with an autonomous positioning system and information transmission with software server delays and bit errors to simulate hydroacoustic communication channel [12].

An example of a mission performed by terrestrial robots in the process of modeling the AUUVs group is shown in Fig. 8. Robots of different types ("R" - repeaters, "S" - searchers) must go from the base ("B") to the search area, agree with each other on the trajectory of the movement so that it does not interfere with each other to effectively examine the territory, find the object sought and call the robot "Y" from the base (destroyer).

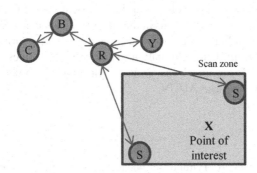

Fig. 8. An example of a team of interacting mission robots.

3 Conclusion

Thus, for modeling the interaction of AUUV in the group, it is necessary to implement by software all seven levels of network interaction OSI. But if the levels 2..7 are logical and are easily simulated on both computer models and on any movable robots, then level 1 (physical level of interaction) has a number of features and limitations that need to be taken into account in order to model the hydro acoustic interaction itself:

1. Distribution delays associated with low rate of transmission.
2. Limit on the maximum communication range determined by the absorption and scattering of the acoustic signal at the modem operating frequency, as well as the presence of interference.
3. Random fading effects as a consequence of multipath propagation.
4. Bit error messages transmitted as a result of interference.

For example, if the range of the modem is 1..2 km, the depth is 50 m, the soil is dense stony, the temperature is 6..8°, salinity 12‰, then the following parameters can be used in the model:

1. The propagation delay depends only on the distance and speed of sound in water at a given temperature and salinity: $t = r/c$, where r is the distance, c is the sound velocity ($\sim$1480 m/s).
2. Random fading effects in hydroacoustic are introduced as an anomaly coefficient, which can take values from 0 to 2..3 by the Relay distribution with $\sigma = 1.0$.

3. Bit errors are simulated by randomly replacing a certain number of bits in the transmitted packet, and the number of bits is set by the BER parameter, calculated from the signal-to-noise ratio in current conditions: $N = BER * len$, where N is the number of bits to be spoiled, BER is the intensity of the errors taken from Fig. 3, len is the packet length in bits. Then the range over the distance is determined by the distance at which the intensity of the bit errors during the transmission becomes unacceptable, for example, more than 10^{-1}.

Thus, it is possible to obtain a model of information transfer between underwater small-sized robots, close by parameters to the real conditions, and to use it in the development of interaction protocols taking into account all the main constraints that affect the operation of acoustic modems in the aquatic environment. And the algorithms of the interaction of a robot group can be debugged on mobile surface robots that are easier to trace, read from them information, which are many times more reliable and cheaper than AUUV's designed for group application, in order to then use the debugged algorithms on these AUUV.

References

1. Kiselev, L., Medvedev, A.: Patrol of sea boundaries by a group of autonomous underwater robots. In: Perspective Systems and Tasks of Management. Materials of the XIII All-Russia Scientific-Practical Conference, pp. 168–173 (2018)
2. Kozhemyakin, I., Rozhdestvensky, K., Ryzhov, V., Semenov, N., Chemodanov, M.: Educational marine robotics in SMTU. In: Ronzhin, A., Rigoll, G., Meshcheryakov, R. (eds.) ICR 2016. LNCS (LNAI), vol. 9812, pp. 79–88. Springer, Cham (2016). https://doi.org/10.1007/978-3-319-43955-6_11
3. Zanin, V., et al.: Open-source modular µAUV for cooperative missions. In: Ronzhin, A., Rigoll, G., Meshcheryakov, R. (eds.) ICR 2017. LNCS (LNAI), vol. 10459, pp. 275–285. Springer, Cham (2017). https://doi.org/10.1007/978-3-319-66471-2_30
4. Kozhemyakin, I., et al.: Development of an autonomous group management system for heterogeneous surface and underwater unmanned vehicles. In: Proceedings of the 7th All-Russian Scientific and Technical Conference «Technical Problems of Development of the World Oceans», Vladivostok, pp. 63–72 (2017). (in Rus.)
5. Gorodetsky, V.I., Karsayev, O.V., Samoylov, V.V., Serebryakov, S.V.: Tools for open network agents. Izvestiya RAN. Theory Control Syst. 3, 106–124 (2008). (in Rus.)
6. Wittich, V.A., Skobelev, P.O.: The method of conjugate interactions for managing resource allocation in real time. Autometry 45(2), 78–80 (2009)
7. Skobelev, P.O.: Multiagent technologies in industrial applications: to the 20th anniversary of the foundation of the Samara Scientific School of multi-agent systems. In: Mechatronics, Automation, Control, no. 12 (2010). (in Rus.)
8. Fink, L.M.: The theory of the transmission of discrete messages, 2nd edn. Publishing House "Soviet Radio", 728 p. (1970)
9. Foundation for Intelligent Physical Agents. FIPA 2001: Specification: agent communication language. http://www.fipa.org. Accessed 28 June 2018
10. Maggio, M., Bini, E., Chasparis, G.C., Årzén, K.-E.: A game-theoretic resource manager for RT applications. In: Proceedings of the 25th Euromicro Conference on Real-Time Systems, Paris, France (2013)

11. Inzartsev, A., Pavin, A., Eliseenko, G., Panin, M.: Algorithms for monitoring the water area with the help of a group of specialized autonomous underwater robots. In: Perspective Systems and Tasks of Management. Materials of the XIII All-Russia Scientific and Practical Conference, pp. 140–148 (2018). (in Rus.)
12. Chopra, et al.: Research directions in agent communication. TIST **5**, 1–26 (2010)
13. Vervoort, J.H.A.M.: Modeling and control of an unmanned underwater vehicle. Master traineeship report, University of Canterbury, Christchurch, New Zealand, 109 p. (2008)
14. Das, B., Subudhi, B., Pati, B.B.: Cooperative formation control of autonomous underwater vehicles: an overview. Int. J. Autom. Comput. **13**(3), 199–225 (2016)
15. Martynova, L.A., Mashoshin, A.I., Pashkevich, I.V., Sokolov, A.I.: Control system is the most complicated part of autonomous unmanned underwater vehicles. Marine electronics **4**(54), 27–33 (2015). (in Rus.)

Cognitive Components of Human Activity in the Process of Monitoring a Heterogeneous Group of Autonomous Mobile Robots on the Lunar Surface

Boris Kryuchkov[1], Vitaliy Usov[1], Denis Ivanko[2,3],
and Ildar Kagirov[2(✉)]

[1] Yu. Gagarin Research & Training Cosmonauts Center,
Star City, Moscow Region, Russia
{b.kryuchkov,v.usov}@gctc.ru
[2] St. Petersburg Institute for Informatics and Automation of the Russian
Academy of Sciences (SPIIRAS), St. Petersburg, Russia
denis.ivanko@corp.ifmo.ru, ankhu@mail.ru
[3] ITMO University, St. Petersburg, Russia

Abstract. The article examines the peculiarities of cognitive activity of a Human Operator (HO) to remote monitoring a heterogeneous group of Autonomous (unmanned) Mobile Robots (AMR) in aspects of ensuring security of their collaborative operations. As an example of such a group, one of the possible solutions for the use of AMRs in lunar missions is considered: monitoring of a group of AMRs on the lunar surface by a cosmonaut, located over a long distance in a lunar base. In the "Human-Machine System" the cognitive approach to manage tasks is considered as a main principle of the distribution of functions. Current tasks assigned to the AMR are assumed by HO as separate cognitive units. In evaluating the current situation, this approach allows to use the following knowledge: (1) the available options for decision-making; (2) the conditions for the implementation of particular task in the required chain of tasks; (3) the parameters of activity of all members of the group, (4) the amount of data about the environment and the current situation. To build coordinated actions, that meet the requirements for collisions prevention, it is necessary to use a single semantic basis for designing Human-Robot Interaction (HRI) and special tools for information support of HO. This paper discusses a few of possible solutions.

Keywords: Human Operator (HO)
Allocation of functions in "Human-Machine Systems"
Heterogeneous group of autonomous mobile robots (AMRs)
Coordinated operation in groups · Human activity's cognitive components

© Springer Nature Switzerland AG 2018
A. Ronzhin et al. (Eds.): ICR 2018, LNAI 11097, pp. 148–158, 2018.
https://doi.org/10.1007/978-3-319-99582-3_16

1   Introduction

The use of groups of mobile Unmanned Vehicles (UVs) is in the focus of attention of many researchers and corresponds to the global trend of increasing of use UVs both in specially prepared conditions (e.g. highway vehicles), and in difficult conditions, that require self-organization groups of robots [7].

The greatest difficulties are encountered in solving the problems of self-organization of heterogeneous groups of robots, because their tactical and technical characteristics may vary over a wide range of values: in the types of their activity, functionality, on – Board equipment, etc., and, in addition, from a tactical point of view they may differ in a structure of the interconnection to ensure environmental safety. Today, there are a number of studies, that discuss the problem of the collision avoidance control in scenarios involving the activity of AMR of heterogeneous forms [2, 8, 17–20].

In these works the formalized models are combined with elements of heuristic approach, and set a role of HO as an active element for inclusion in management of a heterogeneous group, because HO in the role of "Manager – Observer" can dynamically form the risk criteria and explicitly set limits on the activity of both the whole group and separately considered robots in related areas of their functioning.

Further, taking into account the formerly proposed design solutions for the lunar missions, the potential application of a heterogeneous group of AMRs in joint work on the lunar surface as part of the lunar mission will be discussed. One of the possible approaches to organize the functioning of AMR may base on the use of cognitive capabilities of a person, who perceives each of the tasks for AMR as a separate cognitive component of decision-making [6, 11]. This approach, based on the principles of "Task-based Guidance" [21], can be used in the development of the domain ontology and in the construction of a computer model of a current situation.

In this regard, the requirements to be applied to the on-Board equipment of the AMR and to the software environment that allows maintaining situation awareness of HO are considered [5].

In the visual display (indication) of the current situation at the workplace of the cosmonaut, who remotely monitors the operation of the group (as an observer-dispatcher) a special role can be played by the induced reality technology, which is currently being applied for modeling and visualization in virtual environments [26]. Heuristic techniques, which HO can use to perform monitoring to reduce the collisions risks in the group by apply limits and standing orders on the tasks of AMR, are also of interest.

2   The Usage of Autonomous Mobile Robots During the Crew's on-Planet Activity on Lunar Surface Outside the Stationary Lunar Base

Currently, much attention is being paid to the prospects of human exploration of the Moon and planets and to the peculiarities of activities in extreme conditions [1, 3, 4, 14, 16].

The expected types of activity of cosmonauts (in accordance with cosmonaut's crew functional duties), when performing lunar missions during on-planet activities in the proposed design solutions, are the following [13, 22]:

- the solution of target tasks (implementation of a program of scientific research and experiments; development of new space technologies, extraction and processing of lunar resources);
- the participation in the construction of space infrastructure (on the lunar surface);
- the work with the delivered equipment (unloading and loading operations, delivered and removed cargo inventory tracking, transportation on the lunar surface);
- the control of on-planet robotic systems, including anthropomorphic types;
- ensuring the safety of on-planet activity;
- providing medical assistance to the injured cosmonaut in case of a medical emergency or incident, that led to loss of efficiency, including the failure of protective equipment, life support systems and others.

In a series of works it is noted that mobile robotics systems capable of performing transport, scientific and a number of other tasks on the lunar surface will play a special role in lunar missions. It is assumed that the first stages will be carried out with the help of automatic-only vehicles, and then with the use of automatic and manned moon-rovers. However, further steps to do a systematic and deep study of the Moon can be carried out only with the participation of cosmonauts, supported by the robots designed to work in hazardous and extreme conditions.

According to the works [1, 14], the "industrial" stage of the Moon exploration should be preceded by studies on its surface using a network of stationary and self-propelled scientific stations.

For example, thematic geological survey and preliminary geological exploration, according to [22] are an important and necessary stage of the Moon exploration.

At this stage, it is expected not only to collect extensive scientific information about the Moon itself, but also to gather the necessary information for placement of the long-term or periodically visited lunar base, which is a first step towards the deployment of the primary industrial infrastructure.

In general, it can be assumed that various modifications of autonomous mobile robots with different functionality will be tested with the development of robotics. The crew will be safe located in a stationary lunar base and primarily ensure the safety of work and remote monitoring of groups of robots. Thus, there is a new direction of cosmonauts activity associated with monitoring the activity of AMR, which can be considered as a kind of dispatching functions, supplemented by operational planning and analysis of prerequisites for incidents related to potential conflicts and problems of joint operation of groups of robots [11].

3   Distribution of Functions During Remote Monitoring of the Activity of a Group of Robots by Cosmonauts

The problem of distribution of functions in Human-machine Interactions is one of the key in ensuring the safety of complicated technical systems. At the same time, this problem has not been sufficiently studied and highlighted in the literature with regard to space robotics, especially for the use of groups of robots under the control of the crew in lunar missions. The undeniable progress in the field of increasing the autonomy of mobile robots and their adaptive capabilities to extreme environments does not remove questions about the control of their activity on the part of a human, when joint participation of the crew and robots in extravehicular on-planet activity is planned. Unlike a robot, which is assigned for narrow and particular tasks, a human has the ability to understand these tasks at the mission level, that is, to understand the current situation in general [11]. To do that he must know how: (1) plan the execution of tasks taking into account the possible collisions in the conflict of "interests", (2) monitor the activity of a group of robots, (3) get data about their exact location and free movement limits in designated zones, (4) identify the risk of collision when moving in the intersecting routes of mobile robots, (5) use communication equipment to control the tasks, and (6) anticipate the actions, performed by robots, that can affect the performance of tasks by group members, etc.

At present, it is not possible to achieve full automation that would realize certain cognitive functions inherent in adaptive human behavior in problem situations.

Thus, the problem is transferred to the plane of division of functions at the level of planning and execution of tasks in flight operations, and the role of "Supervisor" in a complex system of monitoring the activity of a heterogeneous group of agents is assigned to a human. For fulfilling these demands it is necessary to provide mechanisms for setting regulations for AMR's activity and control of compliance with these regulations by HO. In fact, this means the need to build a unified information base on the monitoring area in which the group operates (in the form of electronic maps), using the tools of localizing all participants at specific time periods. In addition HO needs the development of means of introducing restrictions on robots mobility in order to separate traffic routes over space-time parameters, etc. To some extent, in this case, we can talk about the need to use information tools similar to those used in the activities of dispatchers, which found its justification in [12, 15, 23].

However, the most significant issues of HRI design are related to the use of a single semantic space for design the Dialogue for Human Robot Interaction during monitoring a group's activity, and to the use of a virtual environment, that simulates real-time events for full control of the situation by HO and for its constant "inclusion" in the situation on the basis of visual representations, which is covered by the concept of situation awareness.

4 Tools for Visualization the Current Situation, Focused on the Cognitive Components of HO Activity During the Monitoring of the AMR Group

In order to create the conditions for the actualization of the cognitive capabilities of the HO, it is necessary to design the information support. In particular to supplement the traditional types of information about the parameters of AMR movement in the way that contribute to the constant involvement of a HO in the situation, his full situation awareness and the rapid detection of signs indicative of a risk of contingency and collisions of AMR. As noted in [15, 23], the basic principle of building an information display system for HO, performing the functions of Manager – Supervisor of the group of active agents is the use of multimode displays that allow representing visual images with different semantic content.

One of the widely used forms of displaying information about objects in a controlled territorial zone is a multilayered electronic map, layers of which represent various characteristics of the territory, including: (1) the nature of the terrain and the designation of natural obstacles to the movement of mobile vehicles, (2) the location of stationary artificial objects that can serve as landmarks for navigation of active agents and the coordinates of which are used to adjust the dynamically measured parameters; (3) coordinate grid for more precise visual control of the mutual position of mobile objects; (4) designations assigned to different routes of vehicles in accordance with the provided scenarios, etc.

Management of the AMR group, taking into account the composition of tasks, may require the introduction of new visualization elements that facilitate the actualization of cognitive functions during the monitoring of the AMR group for trouble-free interaction. For this purpose it is offered to enter differentiation and indication (marking) of the working zones connected with accomplishment of concrete tasks by these or those types of robotic complexes. This makes it possible to clearly identify the zone of manifestation of AMR activity, and during the active operation of the robot to monitor the penetration of other robots into this zone. Practically, this means the visualization of regions according to the principle of association tasks, that they are executed in specific periods. In addition to this information layer of the electronic map, a data frame may be provided for HO, which shows a time chart of the AMR loading with specific tasks in a particular area of the controlled territory. On this basis HO can control adjacent zones of activity of AMR, and if necessary allocate space-apart or "to compartmentalize" in time this activity for minimization collisions risks. These heuristic methods of planning and control should be at the disposal of the HO within its competence, and the event display system should show how these or those events relate to the time and place of manifestation.

Another version of the visual representation is associated with the necessity to build a picture of events in the egocentric coordinate system associated with a particular AMR. In fact, created conditions for monitoring the situation are based on the information that is available from on-Board means of the concrete AMR, including the measurement of its location relative to landmarks and boundaries of the permissible area of active movement, the detection of moving objects near the control zone and others. This type of display corresponds to a circular overview indicator, in the center of which there is a label corresponding to the position of the concrete AMR, from which it is possible to count the distance to other mobile objects.

The most difficult option for HO is monitoring, associated with the passage of a particular AMR through the set of zones allocated for the tasks of other members of the AMR group. In this case, it may be necessary to provide management functions to the AMR itself (as a "Leader"), and at the same time on the part of the HO, it is necessary to ensure the passage of the transition team to the subordination of the AMR – the "Leader" of those AMR, whose areas of responsibility intersect when passing the route. Visual indication of this type of scenario can be performed using the "External Observer" technology, and for this it is possible to apply modeling and visualization of the virtual environment of the AMR – "Leader" [15].

In other words, different scenarios of interaction between robots among themselves may require initialization of different cognitive components of the activity of HO.

5   Software and Information Environment for Information Support the Human in Remote Monitoring the Group of AMRs

To provide situation awareness of HO in remote monitoring the group of AMR, we need to provide software and informational tools to keep up to date the information required to manage tasks for a group of AMR and monitoring of progress. The main goal facing the HO is to achieve a coherent, conflict-free functioning of the heterogeneous group of AMR. The general structure can be described as follows.

The first component is a distributed hardware – software complex for the collection of raw data from the AMR, implemented: (1) as part of on-Board devices that are equipped with AMR for navigation in the environment; (2) in the telemetry and communication system for data exchange and for accumulation of all available information at the workplace.

As the second component, it is possible to identify the tools that should be available to HO for integration and visualization information in an understandable form of the entire set of data that is promptly received through AMR's communication channels and delivered to the workplace of the HO.

The purpose of the third component is to support the management mechanism of the group by setting objectives of the AMR in the framework of the formed ontology. As part of this component is implemented HRI, which allows to build a visual image corresponding to the mental representations of the person about how to interact with AMR, so that their activity meets the principles of accident-free and conflict prevention.

Possible principles and methods of construction of the environment that meets the goals of modeling such a complex technical system are discussed in a number of papers [9, 10, 19].

In [10] questions of construction of interaction of humans and robots and improvement of situation awareness of HO on the basis of agent-oriented approach of the mixed team of AMR and group of cosmonauts in protective equipment on the surface of the moon in the controlled territorial area are considered.

In [19] for a similar situation of construction of HRI it is offered to use ontology to provide semantic interoperability of robots and humans at their interaction.

An example of building HRI in monitoring a group of AMRs is shown in Fig. 1. According to the proposed approach, ontologies store knowledge about the tasks that need to be performed, as well as knowledge about the functionality of robots and the current situation. This knowledge determines the tasks that based on the current state of the active agents. Ontologies are published in the intellectual space, allowing active agents to carry out indirect interaction on the basis of operational information about the current situation. To do this, all active agents generate and publish tasks when additional resources are needed to complete them.

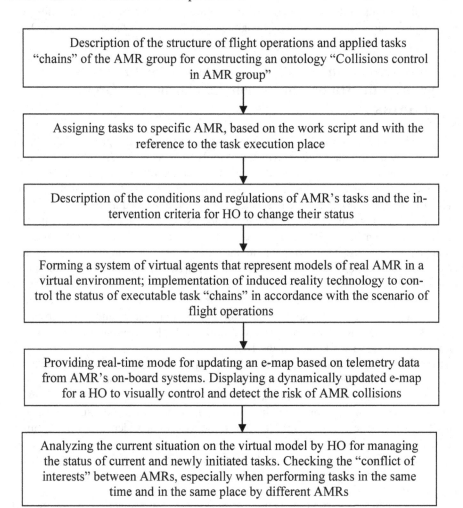

Fig. 1. Building HRI in monitoring a group of AMRs.

As mentioned above, the realization of human cognitive capabilities in such a slow information environment is possible with the fulfillment of certain prerequisites and agreements.

The main proposal is that when the system "team of cosmonauts – group of robots" is projected, it is assumed that the degree of autonomy of robots allows them not only to perform fairly complex assign actions, but also to independently navigate the obstacle area and to adapt dynamically changing environmental conditions.

In the literature on the problem of constructing a Dialog of Humans and Robots as a HRI form [24, 25], this range of methodological problems is considered from the standpoint of finding ways to interact on a single semantic basis (for example, in the form of ontology), available for expression in human categories of space and time in relation to the object of the external environment.

In this work, as one of possible solutions, we propose to consider the agent-oriented building of HRI, in which "virtual proxy agents" on behalf of the real intelligent agents, operating in a real environment, can act both as sources and as consumers of information transmitted between the participants of team interaction. This approach develops, to some extent, the ideas of induced virtual reality. It is aimed at replacing existing active agents with their virtual analogues (with which HO interacts, using the visual representation of the interactive virtual environment), which are able to collect, process, summarize, purposefully deliver and display the agreed source data to the recipient on the basis of a common understanding and a single semantic interpretation of the current situation.

In other words, in addition to the actual active agents, the "virtual agents" or proxy agents that are shown on the HO's display can support the course of such interaction, organize it, and provide situation awareness to the participants of the dialogue. This is based on the knowledge of the natural limitations for each real agent to collect information about the environment; participate in the solution of specific tasks and the preparation of a common task; the necessary and available resources, etc. A key feature of remote control of a group of robots and the tasks of monitoring the situation is that humans and robots, interacting in a mixed team, coordinate their actions through a dialogue about their current capabilities, immediate goals and effectiveness of solving previous problems.

6 Conclusions

The paper deals with the peculiarities of the use of AMR in manned lunar exploration programs. According to the available design solutions, the success of the flights will largely depend on the ability of specialized robotic systems to work on the lunar surface and perform many different tasks.

At the same time, unlike the researches devoted to the application of homogeneous groups of ARM in terrestrial conditions, under review the new issues have to be included that concern the variant of the heterogeneous group of AMR, when a cosmonaut, located at a long distance in the lunar base, has to conduct monitoring of the activity of AMR.

In the course of a specific operation HO should perform the following functions:

(1) analyze the functioning of the AMR as a part of the complex organizational and technical system and make decisions based on a priory data on flight operations, e-maps of lunar surface regions, various AMR task chains and their resources;

(2) promptly and timely receive the data on the successfully completed tasks from all members of the group, the location of all members of the group and other data (e.g. environmental data).

Human-Robot Interaction (HRI) is generally the object of interdisciplinary research, since the ARM group should perform an increasing number of functions in lunar expeditions. Cosmonauts in addition to the implementation of narrow operator tasks (manual control and emergency intervention), should additionally be able to plan the work of a group of robots and ensure their safe joint work. This requirement created new problems to HRI that can be solved using the "Human – Robot" Form of the Dialogue with a semantic context.

Assessing the prospects for the further development of this approach, we can state the need to pay attention to the design of complex activities related to cognitive tasks to assess complex tactical situations arising from planetary activities, when the support of a cosmonaut by ground teams will be severely limited, in contrast to the current practice of flying orbital space stations. These issues are closely related to the prospects for developing an "Electronic Adviser" for a cosmonaut, designed to develop a plan of further action for each of the following cycles of the group's activities. This work should be carried out by the cosmonaut a priory, with a special emphasis on finding a possible way out of conflict situations and failures of robotics products.

Acknowledgments. This research is financially supported by the Russian Foundation for Basic Research (project No. 18-37-00306), as well as by the state research No. 0073-2018-0002.

References

1. Bartlett, P., Wettergreen, D., Whittaker, W.L.: Design of the scarab rover for mobility and drilling in the lunar cold traps. In: Proceedings of the 9-th International Symposium on Artificial Intelligence, Robotics and Automation in Space (iSAIRAS) (2008). http://repository.cmu.edu/robotics/1104/. Accessed 02 Apr 2018

2. Beloglazov, D.A., et al.: Group control of moving objects in uncertain environments. FIZMATLIT, Moscow (2015). Edited by V.H. Psychopov, 305 p. (In Russian)

3. Bodkin, D.K., Escalera, P., Bocam, K.J.: A human lunar surface base and infrastructure solution. In: Space, p. 7336 (2006). https://doi.org/10.2514/6.2006-7336

4. Chertok, B.E., et al.: Cosmonautics of the XXI century. Under the editorship of Academician of RAS. B.E.M.: Publishing House "RTSoft" (2010). 864 p. (In Russian)

5. Endsley, M.R.: Situation awareness global assessment technique (SAGAT). In: Aerospace and Electronics Conference, pp. 789–795 (1988)

6. Falzon, P., et al.: Cognitive Ergonomics: Understanding, Learning, and Designing Human-Computer Interaction. Academic Press, London (2015). Edit by Pierre Falzon, 261 p

7. Gaiduk, A., Kapustyan, S., Shapovalov, I.: Self-organization in groups of intelligent robots. In: Kim, J.-H., Yang, W., Jo, J., Sincak, P., Myung, H. (eds.) Robot Intelligence Technology and Applications 3. AISC, vol. 345, pp. 171–181. Springer, Cham (2015). https://doi.org/10.1007/978-3-319-16841-8_17

8. Huang, J., Farritor, S.M., Qadi, A., Goddard, S.: Localization and follow-the-leader control of a heterogeneous group of mobile robots. IEEE/ASME Trans. Mechatron. **11**(2), 205–215 (2006). https://doi.org/10.1109/TMECH.2006.871100

9. Karpov, A., Ronzhin, A.: Information enquiry kiosk with multimodal user interface. Pattern Recogn. Image Anal. **19**(3), 546–558 (2009)

10. Karpov, A.A., Kryuchkov, B.I., Ronzhin, A.L., Usov, V.M.: Design of human-robot interaction as a part of a single team of cosmonauts and autonomous mobile robots on the surface of the moon. Extreme Robot. **1**(1), 71–81 (2016). (In Russian)

11. Kryuchkov, B.I., Usov, V.M.: The human-centered approach to the organization of joint activities of cosmonauts and an anthropomorphic robot-assistant on manned spacecrafts. Manned Space Flights **3**(5), 42–57 (2012). (In Russian)

12. Kryuchkov, B.I., Usov, V.M., Chertopolokhov, V.A., Ronzhin, A.L., Karpov, A.A.: Simulation of the Cosmonaut-Robot system interface on the lunar surface based on methods of machine vision and computer graphics. Int. Arch. Photogramm. Remote Sens. Spat. Inf. Sci. **XLII-2/W4**, 129–133 (2017). https://doi.org/10.5194/isprs-archives-xlii-2-w4-129-2017

13. Kryuchkov, B.I., Usov, V.M., Yaropolov, V.I., et al.: About the features of professional activities of cosmonauts during the implementation of the lunar missions. Manned Space Flight **2**(19), 35–57 (2016). (In Russian)

14. Legostaev, P.V., Lopota, V.A.: The Moon - A Step to the Technology of Development of the Solar System. RSC Energia, Moscow (2011). Edited by Legostaev P.V., Lopota V.A., 584 p. (In Russian)

15. Mikhailyuk, M.V., Kryuchkov, B.I., Usov, V.M.: The types of interface for remote interaction of cosmonauts with Autonomous mobile robots during extravehicular activity on the lunar surface. Pilot. Flights Space **4**(22), 41–53 (2017). (In Russian)

16. Moroz, V.I., Huntress, V.T., Shevelev, I.L.: Planetnye ekspeditsii XX veka [Planetary expeditions of the XX century]. Space Res. **40**(5), 451–481 (2002). (In Russian)

17. Mylvaganam, T., Sassano, M.: Autonomous collision avoidance for wheeled mobile robots using a differential game approach. Eur. J. Control **40**, 53–61 (2018). https://doi.org/10.1016/j.ejcon.2017.11.005

18. Nasir, A.K., Hsino, A., Hartmann, K., Chen, C., Roth, H.: Heterogeneous capability multi-robots cooperative framework. In: Proceedings of the 1st IFAC Conference on Embedded Systems, Computational Intelligence and Telematics in Control – CESCIT, Würzburg, Germany, pp. 157–162 (2012) https://doi.org/10.3182/20120403-3-DE-3010.00088

19. Petrov, M.P., Kashevnik, A.M.: Ontolo-oriented approach to the indirect interaction between users and robots to work together to solve problems. Sci. Bull. NSU **1**(66), 133–146 (2017). https://doi.org/10.17212/1814-1196-2017-1-133-146. (In Russian)

20. Sunkara, V.R.: Cooperative collision advance and formation control for objects with heterogenic shapes. IFAC PapersOnLine **50-1**, 10128–10135 (2017). https://doi.org/10.1016/j.ifacol.2017.08.1793

21. Uhrmann, J., Schulte A.: Task-based guidance of multiple UAV using cognitive automation. In: COGNITIVE 2011: The Third International Conference on Advanced Cognitive Technologies and Applications, pp. 47–52 (2011)

22. Vasil'ev, A.V., Kondratyev, A.S., Gradovtsev, A.A., Galaev, I.Y.: Research and development of design of the shape mobile robot system for carrying out geological exploration on the Moon's surface. Proc. SPIIRAS **45**, 141–156 (2016). (In Russian)

23. Vorona, A.A., Syrkin, L.D., Kryuchkov, B.I., Usov, V.M.: Visual representation of a group of Autonomous mobile robots on the surface of the Moon to a cosmonaut to prevent their collisions. Manned Space Flights **3**(20), 41–57 (2016). (In Russian)
24. Yusupov, R.M., Kryuchkov, B.I., Karpov, A.A., Ronzhin, A.L., Usov, V.M.: The use of multimodal interfaces on a manned space complex to maintain the communication of cosmonauts with a mobile robot-assistant of a crew. Manned Space Flights **3**, 23–34 (2013). (In Russian)
25. Yushchenko, A.S.: Dialog control robots using grid models Integra models and soft computing in charge intelligence: Sat. Tr. Int. Sci. **1**, 97–108 (2009). (In Russian)
26. Zakirov E.A., Malev M.V.: Creation of software architecture of heterogeneous control system for a group of mobile robots. http://nauka-rastudent.ru/35/3717. Accessed 06 Apr 2014

About One Approach to Robot Control System Simulation

Eugene Larkin[1], Alexey Bogomolov[1], Aleksandr Privalov[2(✉)],
and Maksim Antonov[1]

[1] Tula State University, Tula 300012, Russia
elarkin@mail.ru
[2] Tula State Pedagogical University, Tula 300026, Russia
privalov.61@mail.ru

Abstract. Mobile robot onboard equipment functioning is considered. It is shown, that abstract analogue of one equipment unit operation is an ordinary semi-Markov process. This abstraction is insufficient for analytical modeling the mobile robot as a whole, so to simulate synchronized onboard equipment functioning, it is necessary to use more complicated abstraction based on integration of ordinary processes to so-called M-parallel semi-Markov process. For definition of such abstraction notification "functional states" as combinations of structural states is introduced. Method of definition of semi-Markov matrix parameters, such as time of residence in functional states and probabilities of switches from current functional states to neighboring functional states is proposed. Theoretical result is confirmed by modeling of homogeneous system, every unit of which may resident in "on" of "off" state.

Keywords: Mobile robot · Cyclic algorithm · Structural state
Functional state · semi-Markov process

1 Introduction

Mobile robot, as object under control, is a complex system that includes a number of equipment units, each of which is controlled by digital controller and operates in accordance with its own algorithm [1, 2]. The units operation leads to realization of a robot corporative aim, so for proper control one should to know state of equipment as a whole at any time [3, 4]. Operation of separate unit one would to simulate with use of semi-Markov process theory [5, 6] due to next features of control algorithms [5–7]:

- control algorithm is a cyclic one, and is divided onto operators, so after the reaching by algorithm the "end" operator, it immediately returns to the "begin" operator;
- every operator, is linked with the physical states of proper unit under digital control;
- all operators of cyclic algorithm are actual, i.e. from every operator there is at least one way to any other operators, and there is at least one way, which leads to every operator from any other operators;
- time of operator interpretation is a random one, switches from current operator into neighboring operators are a stochastic one.

© Springer Nature Switzerland AG 2018
A. Ronzhin et al. (Eds.): ICR 2018, LNAI 11097, pp. 159–169, 2018.
https://doi.org/10.1007/978-3-319-99582-3_17

States of semi-Markov process are abstract analogue of algorithm operators, and linked with them states of proper onboard unit. When investigate number of units, united by common aim, knowledge of state of separate semi-Markov process is insufficient for definition state of mobile robot as a whole, so there should be worked out special approach to description of such control process, which permits to define so called functional state of onboard equipment, i.e. state of all units at current time. Semi-Markov models of parallel process are not of widely used, and their creation is rather complicated scientific problem. This fact explains importance and relevance of investigations in this domain.

2 *M*-Parallel semi-Markov Process

M-parallel semi-Markov process may be defined as co-joint of M ordinary independent semi-Markov processes:

$$\mu = \bigcup_{m=1}^{M} \mu_m;$$ (1)

$$\mu_m \cap \mu_k = \begin{pmatrix} \emptyset, \text{ when } m \neq k; \\ \mu_m \text{ otherwise}; \end{pmatrix}$$

$$\mu_m = \{A_m, \boldsymbol{h}_m(t)\},$$ (2)

where μ_m – is an ordinary semi-Markov process [8–10]; $A_m = \{a_{1(m)}, \dots, a_{j(m)}, \dots, a_{J(m)}\}$ – is set of states; $\boldsymbol{h}_m(t) = \left[h_{j(m),n(m)}(t)\right] = \boldsymbol{p}_m \otimes \boldsymbol{f}_m(t)$ – is the semi-Markov matrix of size $J(m) \times J(m)$; $\boldsymbol{p}_m = \int_0^\infty \boldsymbol{h}_m(t)dt = \left[p_{j(m),n(m)}\right]$ – is the stochastic matrix of size $J(m) \times J(m)$; $\boldsymbol{f}_m(t) = \left[\frac{h_{j(m),n(m)}(t)}{p_{j(m),n(m)}(t)}\right] = \left[f_{j(m),n(m)}(t)\right]$ – is the matrix of pure time densities.

Structure of the process (1) is shown on the Fig. 1a.

Processes (2) belong to the category of ergodic semi-Markov processes and its structures are represented with full oriented graph with loops. All other structures may be obtained from structure (2) by means of deleting some nodes and/or arrows from graph. Processes μ_m, $1 \leq m \leq M$, operate simultaneously in all units of parallel system, and for proper control the system as a whole it is necessary to build up the model of complex semi-Markov process.

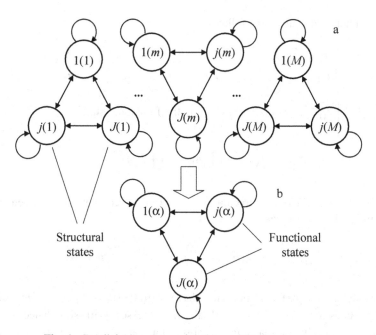

Fig. 1. Parallel (a) and complex (b) semi-Markov processes.

3 Complex semi-Markov Process

The complex semi-Markov process is shown on the Fig. 1b. This process may be defined as follows [11–13]:

$$^{M}\mu = \left\{^{M}A, ^{M}\boldsymbol{h}(t)\right\}, \tag{3}$$

where ^{M}A – is the set of states; $^{M}\boldsymbol{h}(t)$ – is the semi-Markov matrix.

Below notions «structural state» and «functional state» will be used (Fig. 1). The structural state is the abstract analogue of cyclic algorithm proper operator, so m-th cyclic algorithm has $J(m)$ states. Common number of structural states is equal to the sum:

$$N_s = \sum_{m=1}^{M} |A_m| = \sum_{m=1}^{M} J(m). \tag{4}$$

Cartesian product [14] of state sets A_m gives set of functional states

$$^{M}A = \prod_{m=1}^{M} {}^{C}A_m, \tag{5}$$

where $\prod^{C}$ – is the nomination of group Cartesian product.

Set of functional states is as follows:

$$
\begin{aligned}
^{M}A = \big\{ \alpha_{1(\alpha)}, \ldots, \alpha_{j(\alpha)}, \ldots, \alpha_{J(\alpha)} \big\} = \big\{ \big[a_{1(1)}, \ldots, a_{1(m)}, \ldots, \alpha_{1(M)} \big], \ldots, \\
\big[a_{j(1)}, \ldots, a_{j(m)}, \ldots, \alpha_{j(M)} \big], \ldots, \big[a_{J(1)}, \ldots, a_{J(m)}, \ldots, \alpha_{J(M)} \big] \big\},
\end{aligned}
\tag{6}
$$

where $\alpha_{j(\alpha)} = \big[a_{j(1)}, \ldots, a_{j(m)}, \ldots, \alpha_{j(M)} \big]$ – is the functional state;

$$
J(\alpha) = \prod_{m=1}^{M} |A_m| = \prod_{m=1}^{M} J(m).
\tag{7}
$$

To define semi-Markov matrix one should consider competition between M simplest semi-Markov processes

$$
\tilde{\mu}_m = \left\{ \{ b_{1(m)}, b_{2(m)} \}, \begin{bmatrix} 0 & f_m(t) \\ 0 & 0 \end{bmatrix} \right\}, 1 \leq m \leq M.
\tag{8}
$$

Processes (8) are not ergodic. They have starting states $b_{1(m)}$, $1 \leq m \leq M$, and absorbing states $b_{2(m)}$, $1 \leq m \leq M$. If all M processes start simultaneously, then weighted time density of reaching the absorbing state $b_{2(m)}$ by m-th semi-Markov process $\tilde{\mu}_m$ the first is as follows;

$$
h_{wm}(t) = f_m(t) \prod_{\substack{k=1, \\ k \neq m}}^{M} [1 - F_k(t)],
\tag{9}
$$

where $F_k(t) = \int_0^t f_k(\tau) d\tau$.

From (9) probability and pure time density of reaching the absorbing state $b_{2(m)}$ by m-th semi-Markov process $\tilde{\mu}_m$ may be obtained as follows [15, 16]:

$$
p_{wm} = \int_0^{\infty} f_m(t) \cdot \prod_{\substack{k=1 \\ k \neq m}}^{M} [1 - F_k(t)] dt;
\tag{10}
$$

$$
f_{wm}(t) = \frac{h_{wm}(t)}{p_{wm}}.
\tag{11}
$$

Expectation and dispersion of $f_{wm}(t)$ are as usual:

$$
T_{wm} = \int_0^{\infty} t f_{wm}(t) dt;
\tag{12}
$$

$$D_{wm} = \int\limits_{0}^{\infty} (t - T_{wm})^2 f_{wm}(t)dt, 1 \leq m \leq M. \tag{13}$$

To define the semi-Markov matrix $^M h(t)$ one should to define Cartesian product of matrices $h_m(t)$ as follows:

$$^M h(t) = \prod_{m=1}^{M} {}^C h_m(t). \tag{14}$$

Rows and columns of $^M h(t)$ should be numerated as follows:

$$\prod_{m=1}^{M} {}^C\{1(m),\ldots,j(m),\ldots,J(m)\}$$
$$= \{[1(1),\ldots,1(m),\ldots,1(M)],\ldots,[j(1),\ldots,j(m),\ldots,j(M)],\ldots, \tag{15}$$
$$[n(1),\ldots,n(m),\ldots,n(M),\ldots,[J(1),\ldots,J(m),\ldots,J(M)]]\}$$
$$= \{1(\alpha),\ldots,j(\alpha),\ldots,n(\alpha),\ldots,J(\alpha)\}$$

Cartesian product of two semi-Markov matrices may be defined as follows:

$$^2 h(t) = h_k(t) \times h_m(t) = \left[h_{j(k),n(k)}\right] \times \left[h_{j(k),n(k)}\right] = \left[h_{j(\alpha),n(\alpha)}(t)\right], \tag{16}$$

where $j(\alpha) = [j(k),j(m)], n(\alpha) = [n(k),n(m)]$ – are indices in two-dimensional space; $\times$– is the designation of Cartesian multiplication of matrices, in which $h_k(t)$ and h_m are considered as specifically ordered sets, so matrices Cartesian product result is the matrix too.

Let us consider the functional state $a_{[j(k),j(m)]}$ of complex semi-Markov process, which represented with product (16). The functional state $a_{[j(k),j(m)]}$ describes the competition between processes in structural states $a_{j(k)}$ and $a_{j(m)}$. Let the functional state becomes $a_{[n(k),n(m)]}$ after a switch. In the competition must be only one winner (probability of draw the competition is vanishingly small), so the Hamming distance between the indices $j(\alpha)$ and $n(\alpha)$ must be as follows:

$$H = \begin{cases} 0, & \text{when } j(k) = n(k), \ j(m) = n(m); \\ 2, & \text{when } j(k) \neq n(k), \ j(m) \neq n(m); \\ 1 & \text{in all other cases.} \end{cases} \tag{17}$$

Time density of residence the process $h_k(t)$ in the structural states $a_{j(k)}$ is as follows:

$$f_{j(k)}(t) = \sum_{n=1}^{J(k)} h_{j(k),n(k)}(t). \tag{18}$$

Time density of residence the process $h_m(t)$ in the structural states $a_{j(m)}$ is as follows:

$$f_{j(m)}(t) = \sum_{n=1}^{J(m)} h_{j(m),n(m)}(t).\tag{19}$$

Element of the semi-Markov matrix $^2h(t)$, placed on the intersection of the $[j(k),j(m)]$-th row and $[n(k),n(m)]$-th column determines weighed time density of switch from the functional state $a_{[j(k),j(m)]}$ to the functional state $a_{[n(k),n(m)]}$. This element with use (27) may be obtained as follows:

if $H = 0$, then

$$h_{j(\alpha),n(\alpha)}(t) = f_{j(k),j(k)}(t)\left[1 - \sum_{n(m)=1}^{J(m)} H_{j(m),n(m)}(t)\right]$$
$$+ f_{j(m),j(m)}(t)\left[1 - \sum_{n(k)=1}^{J(k)} H_{j(k),n(k)}(t)\right],\tag{20}$$

where $f_{j(k),j(k)}, f_{j(m),j(m)}$ are determined as (2);

$$H_{j(k),n(k)}(t) = \int_0^t h_{j(k),n(k)}(\tau)d\tau;$$

$$H_{j(m),n(m)}(t) = \int_0^t h_{j(m),n(m)}(\tau)d\tau;$$

if $H = 1, j(k) = n(k), j(m) \neq n(m)$, then

$$h_{j(\alpha),n(\alpha)}(t) = f_{j(m),n(m)}(t)\left[1 - \sum_{n(k)=1}^{J(k)} H_{j(k),n(k)}(t)\right],\tag{21}$$

if $H = 1, j(k) \neq n(k), j(m) = n(m)$, then

$$h_{j(\alpha),n(\alpha)}(t) = f_{j(k),n(k)}(t)\left[1 - \sum_{n(m)=1}^{J(m)} H_{j(m),n(m)}(t)\right];\tag{22}$$

if $H = 2$, then

$$h_{j(\alpha),n(\alpha)}(t) = 0.\tag{23}$$

Semi-Markov matrix of complex process may be found with use the recursive procedure:

$$^{M}\boldsymbol{h}(t) = \prod_{m=1}^{M} {}^{C}\boldsymbol{h}_m(t) = {}^{M-1}\boldsymbol{h}(t) \times \boldsymbol{h}_l(t),\tag{24}$$

where $^{M-1}\boldsymbol{h}(t)$ – is a Cartesian product of M-1 ordinary semi Markov matrices; $\boldsymbol{h}_l(t)$ – is the M-th semi-Markov matrix of ordinary process.

Permutation of factors in (16), (24) leads only to permutation in rows and in columns, and not change matrix as a whole. Also it is necessary to admit, that if all ordinary processes μ_m, $1 \le m \le M$, are the ergodic ones, then complex semi-Markov process $^{M}\mu$ is the ergodic too. Complex semi-Markov process obtained is just alike ordinary semi-Markov process with set of states and semi-Markov matrix (3). To solve the problem of evaluation time intervals of wandering through the process states, and probabilities of residence in states one can use known methods [5, 6, 11] applied directly to (3).

4 Example

As an example let us consider parallel operation of M robot onboard equipment units, which may be in one of two states, $b_{1(m)}$ and $b_{2(m)}$ (Fig. 2) [17]:

$$\mu_m^b = \left\{ \{b_{0(m)}, b_{1(m)}\}, \begin{bmatrix} 0 & ^{on}f_m(t) \\ ^{off}f_m(t) & 0 \end{bmatrix} \right\}; \ 1 \le m \le M,\tag{25}$$

where $b_{0(m)}$ – simulates the switched-off state of m-th unit; $b_{1(k)}$ – simulates the switched-on state of m-th unit; $^{off}f_m(t)$ – is the time density of m-th unit residence in the «off» state; $^{on}f_m(t)$ – is the time density of m-th unit residence in the «on» state.

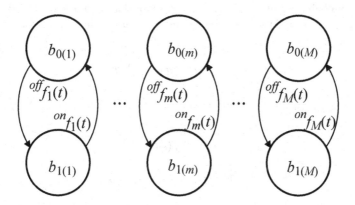

Fig. 2. Operation of M units, which may be in «on» and «off» state.

In the semi-Markov process (3) elements $b_{j(m)}$, $1 \leq m \leq M$, of the functional state $\alpha_{j(\alpha)} = [b_{j(1)}, \ldots, b_{j(m)}, \ldots, b_{j(M)}] \in {}^M A$ is an element of the alphabet $b_{j(m)} \in \{b_{0(m)}, b_{1(m)}\}$. So, the state $\alpha_{j(\alpha)}$ may be written as M-digit binary number, in which:

$$b_{j(m)} = \begin{cases} 0, \text{ when } m - \text{th unit is in state } b_{0(m)}; \\ 1, \text{ when } m - \text{th unit is in state } b_{1(m)}. \end{cases} \tag{26}$$

Switches in the system occur, in such a way, that only one binary digit of $\alpha_{j(\alpha)}$ changes from 0 to 1, or from 1 to 0. So, if semi-Markov process switches from $\alpha_{j(\alpha)}$ to $\alpha_{n(\alpha)}$, then Hamming distance between $\alpha_{j(\alpha)}$ and $\alpha_{n(\alpha)}$ is equal to 1; weighed time density of switching may be defined as follows:

$$\eta_{j(\alpha),n(\alpha)}(t) = \varphi_m(t) \prod_{\substack{k=1, \\ k \neq m}}^{M} [1 - \Phi_k(t)] \tag{27}$$

where

$$\varphi_m(t) = \begin{cases} {}^{off}f_m(t), \text{ when } b_{j(m)} = 0; \\ {}^{on}f_m(t), \text{ when } b_{j(m)} = 1; \end{cases} \tag{28}$$

$$\Phi_{\ldots}(t) = \int_0^t \varphi_{\ldots}(\tau)d\tau.$$

All other elements of $2^M \times 2^M$ semi-Markov matrix ${}^M h(t)$ $j(\alpha)$-th matrix row are equal to zeros.

For particular case, when ${}^{on}f_1(t) = \ldots = {}^{on}f_m(t)\ldots = {}^{on}f_M(t) = {}^{on}f(t)$, ${}^{off}f_1(t) = \ldots = {}^{off}f_m(t)\ldots = {}^{off}f_M(t) = {}^{off}f(t)$ (homogeneous system), may be found, f.e., distribution of probabilities of residence complex semi-Markov process in the state, when m ordinary processes (25) are in off-state, and $(M - m)$ ordinary processes are in on-state, as follows:

$$^{on}P_M^m = C_M^m(p)^m \cdot (1-p)^{M-m}. \tag{29}$$

where $C_M^m = \frac{M!}{m! \cdot (M-m)!}$ – is the m-th binomial coefficient;

$$p = \frac{\int\limits_0^\infty {}^{off}f(t)t dt}{\int\limits_0^\infty {}^{off}f(t)t dt + \int\limits_0^\infty {}^{on}f(t)t dt}. \tag{30}$$

For verification of (29) direct computer experiment was executed with use the Monte-Carlo method. Homogeneous system model under verification includes 100 units of hardware. Distribution densities of stay of every unit in one of possible states were described by exponential laws with parameters v and w. In the program m-th unit was described by the next data: B_m – is a current state ($B_m = 1$ means on-state, $B_m = 0$ means off state); v and μ are intensities of streams of "on" and "off": events, correspondingly; T_m – is random time of stay in current state. Besides global current time T, lately supervision time t and period of supervision Δt are defined.

Computer experiment was carried out as follows:

1. For all units initial state of B_m ($1 \leq m \leq M$) is accepted equal to 0, global current time T and lately supervision time t are established as $T = 0$, $t = 0$. Period Δt of system supervision is established too.
2. For all units computation of random time of residence in current state $T_m(B_m)$ as follows:

$$T_m(B_m) = \begin{cases} -\ln(1 - \xi)/v, & \text{when } B_m = 0; \\ -\ln(1 - \xi)/w, & \text{when } B_m = 1, \end{cases}$$

where $1 \leq \xi \leq 1$ is a random value.
3. The index m^* of unit with smallest time of residence in a current state, $m^* = \arg \min_{1 \leq m \leq M} \{T_m\}$, is defined.
4. For all units correction of time of residence in s current state is executed:
$T_m = T_m - T_{m^*}$.
5. The global current time T is increased on the value T_{m^*}.
6. For m^*-th unit current state B_{m^*} is changed on the inverse one and generation of the next random time interval of residence of m-th unit in current state, $T_m(B_m)$, is carried out.
7. If $(T - t) < \Delta t$, then transition to 10, otherwise transition to 8.
8. In accordance with the current distribution of unit states, quantity of units, r being in state 0, is defined. Defined number is added to the statistics of supervision.
9. Lately supervision time t is increased on Δt.
10. If global current time T is less than the end time of experiment, then transition to 3, otherwise end of computer experiment.

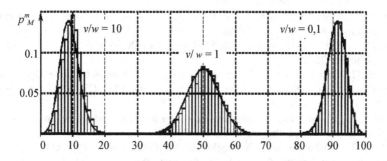

Fig. 3. Histograms obtained.

On Fig. 3 histograms of supervision of swarm for different ratios v/w are shown. Parameters of computer experiment were the next: $M = 100$, $\Delta t = 10$, $T_{end} = 100000$. Histograms rather precisely correspond to theoretical distributions (are shown by continuous line) defined by (14).

5 Conclusion

In such a way common approach to analytical description of parallel semi-Markov processes is proposed. Approach permits to control system states as a whole. After transformation M-parallel semi-Markov process into complex semi-Markov process time and probabilistic characteristics of system states can be calculated with use rather simple known methods.

Further research in this area may be directed to building up the model of mobile robot, with description of unit behavior with use of strong Markov process abstraction, and development of numerical methods of complex semi-Markov matrix parameters calculation with use numerical parameters of ordinary processes only.

Acknowledgements. The research was carried out within the state assignment of the Ministry of Education and Science of Russian Federation (No. 2.3121.2017/PCH).

References

1. Tzafestas S.G.: Introduction to Mobile Robot Control. 692 p. Elsevier (2014)
2. Kaharl S. et al.: A review of wireless technology usage for mobile robot controller. In: International Conference on System Engineering and Modeling (ICSEM 2012). International Proceedings of Computer Science and Information Technology IPCSIT, vol. 34, pp. 7–12 (2012)
3. Cook G.: Mobile Robots: Navigation, Control and Remote Sensing, 319 p. Wiley-IEEE Press (2011)
4. Siciliano, B.: Springer Handbook of Robotics, p. 1611. Springer, Heidelberg (2008). https://doi.org/10.1007/978-3-540-30301-5
5. Larkin E.V., Ivutin A.N.: Estimation of latency in embedded real-time systems. In: 3-rd Meditteranean Conference on Embedded Computing (MECO-2014), pp. 236–239 (2014). https://doi.org/10.1109/meco.2014.6862704
6. Larkin, E., Ivutin, A., Kotov, V., Privalov, A.: Semi-Markov modelling of commands execution by mobile robot. In: Ronzhin, A., Rigoll, G., Meshcheryakov, R. (eds.) ICR 2016. LNCS (LNAI), vol. 9812, pp. 189–198. Springer, Cham (2016). https://doi.org/10.1007/978-3-319-43955-6_23
7. Buttazo, G.C.: Hard Real-Time Computing Systems. Predictable Scheduling Algorithms and Applications, p. 521. Springer Science + Buseness Media. LLC, US (2011). https://doi.org/10.1007/978-1-4614-0676-1
8. Limnios, N., Swishchuk, A.: Discrete-time semi-Markov random evolutions and their applications. Adv. Appl. Probab. 45(1), 214–240 (2013)
9. Bielecki, T.R., Jakubowski, J., Niewęgłowski, M.: Conditional Markov chains: properties, construction and structured dependence. Stochast. Processes Appl. 127(4), 1125–1170 (2017)

10. Janssen, J., Manca, R.: Applied Semi-Markov Processes, p. 310. Springer, US (2005). https://doi.org/10.1007/0-387-29548-8
11. Larkin, E.V., Lutskov, Y., Ivutin, A.N., Novikov, A.S.: Simulation of concurrent process with Petri-Markov nets. Life Sci. J. **11**(11), 506–511 (2014)
12. Ivutin, A.N., Larkin, E.V.: Simulation of concurrent games. Bulletin of the South Ural State University. Ser. Math. Model. Program. Comput. Software **8**(2), 43–54 (2015)
13. Larkin, E.V., Ivutin, A.N., Kotov, V.V., Privalov, A.N.: Simulation of relay-races. Bulletin of the South Ural State University. Math. Model. Program. Comput. Softw. **9**(4), 117–128 (2016)
14. Gallied, J.: Discrete Mathematics. Elementary and Beyond. Undergraduate Texts in Mathematics, p. 453. Springer, New York (2003). https://doi.org/10.1007/b97469
15. Bauer, H.: Probability Theory, 523 p. Walter de Gruyter, Berlin (1996)
16. Shiryaev, A.N.: Probability, p. 611. Springer Science + Business Midia, Heidelberg (1996). https://doi.org/10.1007/978-1-4757-2539-1
17. Ivutin, A., Larkin, E., Kotov, V.: Established routine of swarm monitoring systems functioning. In: Tan, Y., Shi, Y., Buarque, F., Gelbukh, A., Das, S., Engelbrecht, A. (eds.) ICSI 2015. LNCS, vol. 9141, pp. 415–422. Springer, Cham (2015). https://doi.org/10.1007/978-3-319-20472-7_45

Providing Availability of the Smart Space Services by Means of Incoming Data Control Methods

Dmitriy Levonevskiy$^{(\boxtimes)}$, Irina Vatamaniuk, and Anton Saveliev

St. Petersburg Institute for Informatics and Automation of the Russian Academy
of Sciences, 14th Line V.O. 39, 199178 St. Petersburg, Russia
DLewonewski.8781@gmail.com, vatamaniuk@iias.spb.su,
antoni-fox@yandex.ru

Abstract. This paper deals with estimating and providing availability of corporate smart space services on the example of the interactive corporate television service. For this purpose, the authors explore the known methods of traffic flow filtering, propose a technique to estimate the service availability, build the mass queuing model of the service and carry out the experiments with filtering methods. The experiments show that the effect values have peaks that depend on the conditions of operating and the filtering method parameters. So, the problem of determining the filtering method parameters can be represented as an optimization problem in a multidimensional space. The changing conditions of operating may be taken into account using adaptive approaches. Further research direction include: classifying and analyzing different ways (models, scenarios, modalities) of interaction between users and service, exploring the possibility of applying non-temporal parameters to analyze request flows, building the general threat taxonomy for the corporate smart space services including threats to confidentiality, integrity and availability, considering the possibility of implementing the complex service protection taking into account threat sources, threats, risk events and effects.

Keywords: Computer security · Availability · Service-oriented architecture
Queuing models · Smart spaces

1 Introduction

Corporate information systems actively being developed nowadays correspond to the Industry 4.0 trend [5], use cloud computing technologies, multimodal interfaces, cyber-physical systems (CPS) and adopt the intelligent environment approach (Smart Space) [1, 2]. These technologies improve interactivity, functionality and efficiency of the corporate environment and human-computer interaction (HCI).

At the same time, complexity of the Industry 4.0 systems, large amount of information gathered by remote sources and processed by various consumers aggravates problems of privacy, security and trust [13]. Langeheinrich [3] describes a set of features that are specific for smart spaces and critical for security: ubiquity, invisibility, sensing and memory amplification. The problem of personal security is that it is

© Springer Nature Switzerland AG 2018
A. Ronzhin et al. (Eds.): ICR 2018, LNAI 11097, pp. 170–180, 2018.
https://doi.org/10.1007/978-3-319-99582-3_18

difficult for users to comprehend data collecting and processing techniques [4] and to be aware of the amount and nature of gathered data, and for the system to control the data transfer. Another issue is related to the corporate security: intensive use of smart spaces in the enterprise activities increases the dependence on the information infrastructure, so the enterprise should take appropriate steps to protect it from attacks and ensure fault tolerance.

Information security of a corporate smart space includes its confidentiality, integrity and availability. This is a necessary condition to achieve the admissible values of quality of service. To ensure the confidentiality, known access control models, authentication and authorization methods, cryptographic methods are used [15]. Integrity control is built on the basis of computing hashes and digital signatures, as well as doing backups [15]. Providing availability implies establishing uninterruptible power supply systems, implementing redundancy, and distributing computing power to ensure the needed throughput [6]. These techniques are extensional, their implementation causes additional costs, and in some cases they are not feasible due to limitations of communication channels and possibilities of humans to perceive information. For example, in the interactive corporate TV service, it is not possible to satisfy multiple user requests without partial loss of availability. At the same time, high availability level remains critical to implement business processes in organizations that use IT. This work takes into consideration only the factors related to the behavior of software and users under the assumption that the hardware operates correctly.

This paper considers estimating and providing availability of corporate smart space services on the example of the interactive corporate television service in MINOS [7]. Section 2 describes major factors that affect the service availability, and the protection methods. Section 3 provides the mass queuing model for a service and the method of assessing its availability. Section 4 represents the experiments with request filtering methods. The conclusion contains the final statements and outlines the further research directions.

2 Related Work

There are the following service availability threats related to the software and user behavior:

1. Targeted destructive impacts on the smart space using malicious signals. In this case, source of the threat is a user that may be either legitimate or illegitimate. Typical examples of implementation of this threat are distributed denial of service attack (DDoS), "ping of death", vulnerability exploitation.
2. Non-targeted impacts on the smart space when a lot of requests cannot be fulfilled by the service before the request relevance expires. In this case, legitimate user is the source of the threat. Typical examples of threat implementation are exhaustion of the throughput of data transfer channels at the moment of a "flash crowd".
3. Erroneous perception of incoming requests by the corporate smart space service. This threat is especially possible if multimodal interfaces are being applied and users interact with services by means of speech, gestures, etc. This threat may also

become active due to errors in client and server software. In this case, the threat source is the smart space software. If a service processes erroneously perceived data, the service availability for legitimate users will be affected negatively.

So, in order to achieve the optimal quality of service in the corporate smart space, it is necessary to develop the methods of providing service availability able to deal with characteristics of user behavior and interaction with the services.

In this paper we assume that the software is able to check the validity of requests and filter the invalid ones. Validation methods are well-known and based on formal grammars, signature analysis, regular expressions, etc. The problem is encountered when the system deals with formally valid requests that may have a negative influence on availability and are difficult to tell from safe requests using the methods mentioned above. Nevertheless, some methods are developed for this case.

In particular, the known counteraction methods are based on: mathematical statistics (methods based on statistical moment thresholds [12]; on distribution function analysis [17]), entropy [16], signature analysis, etc.

In the above approaches, the analyzed traffic characteristics are the selective statistical moments of different orders and the distribution function shape. These characteristics are determined for time intervals between requests within a single flow. Low values of statistical moments and entropy are specific for the automatically generated traffic. Such traffic may also have a nearly exponential distribution function.

Service availability under different conditions of smart space operation may be assessed using known methods of estimating the quality of service (QoS). It should be noticed that the process of interaction between users and system is a complex process subjective quality of which is determined by a lot of factors. The principal indices of fulfilling the scenarios of multimodal human-computer interaction are quality of experience (QoE) and quality of service (QoS). The first concept is more general and includes the second one as its aspect (Fig. 1).

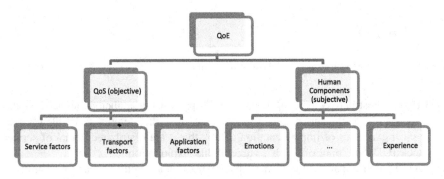

Fig. 1. QoE structure.

In the literature, the following definitions of objective and subjective QoE are proposed: the objective QoE determines the QoS delivered to the user in terms of measurable indicators of the service, network and application performance. The subjective model reflects the quality perceived by the person from the point of view of emotions, billing of services and interaction experience.

As QoS parameters, for example, the average request execution time can be used. This time is defined as the mathematical expectation of the duration between the time when the potential user requests the service to provide the necessary resource and the time when this resource is provided, expressed as the arithmetic mean of the representative number of examples.

The process of interaction between the users and the service is treated as the successive execution of user requests applying some strategy to control requests. The result of processing of every request is characterized by success and delay (waiting time). The following formula was proposed in [10] to estimate the implementation quality of a single task i:

$$E_i = \frac{T_{Fi}D_0}{T_{Pi}(D_0 + D_i)},$$ (1)

where D_0 is the delay considered to reduce the effect estimate E_i twice, D_i is the actual task delay (in case of denial, we assume that $D_i = \infty$), T_{Fi} is the actual time of the task and T_{Pi} is its planned time.

To get an integrated estimate of a certain mode of operating using task priorities, one can use the following formula:

$$E = \frac{\sum_{i=1}^{N} P_i E_i}{\sum_{i=1}^{N} P_i},$$ (2)

where P_i is the priority of the task i and N is the number of tasks.

3 Materials and Methods

A typical application area of distributed multimodal systems is corporate smart spaces that provide ubiquitous human-computer interaction between users and components of the smart space. As an example, we consider the process of interaction between users and MINOS (Multimodal Information and Navigation Cloud System) interactive digital signage service [8]. The information and navigation services of MINOS are implemented via ensemble of webcams, monitors and information screens helping visitors to navigate within the corporate environment of SPIIRAS. The webcams are involved in processes of registration, authentication and recognition of users and allows automating work of checkpoint and reception. The monitors and touchscreens help users to get required information easily.

Users generate requests by means of different modalities (speech, gestures, etc.). They can also manage the service using their mobile phones or personal computers (for administrators). Each request needs to be processed, i.e. some task needs to be performed and requires allocation of some resource (display and sound channels, user session) during some time. In case when there is only one user working with the system at a certain moment of time, every new request implies suspending any other requests if they require the same resource, so there is no conflict between them. But in case of multiple users, the system may encounter the impossibility of allocating the needed resource for all tasks. Then it is necessary to determine the optimal strategy of request managing that results in the highest possible availability metrics.

Each request is characterized by a set of properties that include the original user identifier, the session identifier, the active modality, the timestamp, and the requested resource identifier.

While analyzing requests flows, the following should be taken into account:

1. The probability of accurate perception and recognition of multimodal requests is very significant. Requests sent from mobile devices and PC's are recognized the most accurately, because a user needs to start the service application, open a session, scan the QR code of the smart space component (for mobile devices) and send a command through the application. These actions must be performed purposefully, and the probability of their accidental execution is extremely small. In case when speech recognition is applied, the probability of a mistake is higher, for gesture-based control it is even higher [9]. This issue was explored in [10] and results in selecting strategies of request processing.

2. Credibility and legitimacy of incoming requests are to be considered. Lack of credibility may take place, for example, if the request flow from a certain user does not look like a human-generated one (it can possess a very high frequency of events or be contradictory). This problem can be caused by perception inaccuracy as well as malicious activity (for example, when a bot connects to the service interface). In the latter case the requests are illegitimate. In both cases some requests are denied or assigned the lowest priority. For this purpose, filtering methods described in Sect. 2 may be used.

At the same time, formula (2) does not take into account the credibility estimate of flows. While modelling, we use the accumulated traffic patterns for legitimate requests and traffic generators for illegitimate requests, so, for each request i the estimate $C_i \in \{0; 1\}$ may be determined, where 0 stands for malicious requests and 1 denotes acceptable ones. In this case, formula (3) may be rewritten as follows:

$$E = \frac{\sum\limits_{i=1}^{N} P_i C_i E_i}{\sum\limits_{i=1}^{N} P_i}, \tag{3}$$

In more general case, any fuzzy credibility estimates $C_i \in [0; 1]$ may be applied.

4 Experiments

The conducted experiments consist in the simulation of the incoming user request flow and the process of performing the requests. For this purpose, a mass queuing model was built by means of Python (Fig. 2).

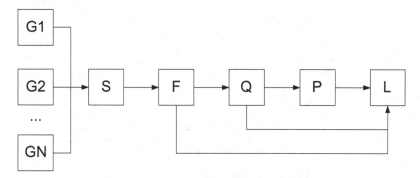

Fig. 2. Mass queuing model.

The system consists of the following blocks: flow generators (G1...GN), session manager (S), filter (F), queue controller (Q), request processor (P) and logger (L). Flow generators (G1...GN) create flow objects that simulate user sessions. They are characterized by either traffic patterns or probability distributions. Traffic patterns are used to simulate legitimate traffic, distributions are applied to generate automated flows. The session manager (S) stores the flow objects and generates requests for active flows. The filter (F) implements the protection methods considered in Sect. 2. The queue controller (Q) transfers the requests to the processor using request priorities and control strategies. In this experiment the optimal strategy determined in [10] was used. This strategy implies using the queue for low-priority tasks and cancelling the conflicting tasks in other cases. The request processor (P) simulates the corporate television display. The logger (L) accepts all the requests and stores their history.

If the request intensity is low, the probability of request conflicts is low as well, and the estimate (2) is close to 1. If the request intensity grows and no filtering is carried out, some requests will be refused due to the implementation of the control strategy. In particular, in presence of an availability threat, legitimate requests may be cancelled, and illegitimate ones fulfilled. Consequently, the estimate (3) will fall. Figure 3 presents the dependence of the effect value E on the average intensity of request flows λ_R and the intensity of flow appearance λ_S under the assumption that all requests are legitimate and, accordingly, formulas (2) and (3) are identical:

The effect value falls sharply on appearance of illegitimate request patterns with intensity λ_M (Fig. 4):

Filtering allows partly removing illegitimate requests and increase the effect value. By means of modeling we estimated the effect values using different thresholds of statistical moments and entropy. In Figs. 5, 6 and 7 the graphs that illustrate these values are given.

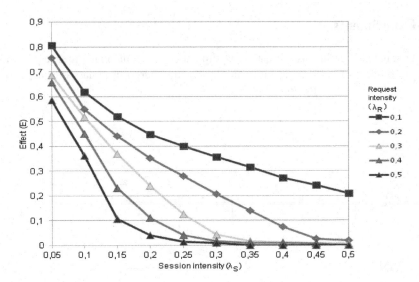

Fig. 3. Effect depending on λ_R and λ_S.

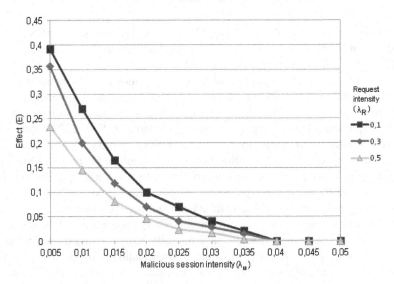

Fig. 4. Effect depending on λ_R and λ_M ($\lambda_S = 0,1$).

The experiment results show that the effect values have peaks that depend on the conditions of operating and the filtering method parameters. Too low threshold values cause a lot of alarm skips, high values result in false alarms. Thereby, the problem of determining the filtering method parameters can be represented as an optimization problem in a multidimensional space, where the set of dimensions depends on applied

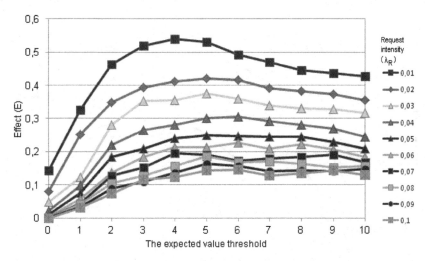

Fig. 5. Effect value depending on request intensity and the expected value threshold.

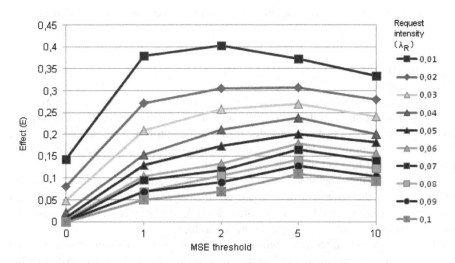

Fig. 6. Effect value depending on request intensity and the MSE threshold.

filtering methods. The changing conditions of operating may be taken into account using adaptive approaches. For example, in [16] the authors propose an approach to reconsidering protection measures in changing conditions.

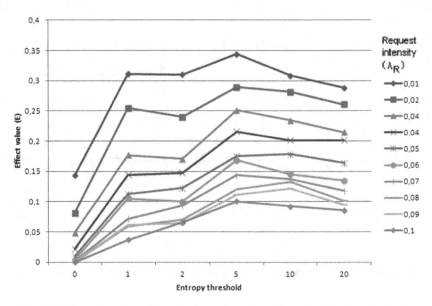

Fig. 7. Effect value depending on request intensity and entropy filtering threshold.

5   Conclusion

This paper deals with estimating and providing availability of corporate smart space services on the example of the interactive corporate television service. For this purpose, we analyze the known methods of traffic flow filtering, propose a technique to estimate the service availability, build the mass queuing model of the service and carry out the experiments with filtering methods.

The experiments show that simple filtering methods are able to remove the DDoS-like patterns in the request flows but are insufficient if the patterns have a complex structure or are distributed between separate flows. In the latter case, classifiers may be used to distinguish factual flows in the mixed traffic.

Further research direction include: classifying and analyzing different ways (models, scenarios, modalities) of interaction between users and service, exploring the possibility of applying non-temporal parameters to analyze request flows, building the general threat taxonomy for the corporate smart space services including threats to confidentiality, integrity and availability, considering the possibility of implementing the complex service protection taking into account threat sources, threats, risk events and effects.

Acknowledgements. The presented work was supported by the Russian Science Foundation (grant No. 16-19-00044).

References

1. Kopacek, T.: Development trends in robotics. In: International Federation of Automatic Control Conference Paper, pp. 36–41 (2016)
2. Toro, C., Barandiaran, I., Posada, J.: A perspective on knowledge based and intelligent systems implementation in Industrie 4.0. In: 19th International Conference on Knowledge Based and Intelligent Information and Engineering Systems (2015). Procedia Comput. Sci. **60**, 362–370
3. Langheinrich, M.: Privacy by design — principles of privacy-aware ubiquitous systems. In: Abowd, G.D., Brumitt, B., Shafer, S. (eds.) UbiComp 2001. LNCS, vol. 2201, pp. 273–291. Springer, Heidelberg (2001). https://doi.org/10.1007/3-540-45427-6_23
4. Nixon, P.A., Wagealla, W., English, C., Terzis, S.: Security, privacy and trust issues in smart environments. In: Smart Environments: Technologies, Protocols, and Applications, Chap. 11. Wiley, New York (2005)
5. Schwab, K.: Fourth Industrial Revolution. World Economic Forum (2016)
6. Paveliev, S.V.: [Metody obespechenija dostupnosti informacionnyh resursov v territorial'no-raspredelennyh avtomatizirovannyh sistemah obrabotki dannyh] Methods for ensuring the availability of information resources in geographically distributed automated data processing systems. Ph.D. thesis (2008). (in Russian)
7. Levonevskiy, D.K., Vatamaniuk, I.V., Saveliev, A.I.: Multimodal Information and Navigation Cloud System ("MINOS") for the corporate cyber-physical smart space. Programmnaya Inzheneriya **3**, 120–128 (2017). https://doi.org/10.17587/prin.8.120-128. (in Russian)
8. Vatamaniuk, I., Levonevskiy, D., Saveliev, A., Denisov, A.: Scenarios of multimodal information navigation services for users in cyberphysical environment. In: Ronzhin, A., Potapova, R., Németh, G. (eds.) SPECOM 2016. LNCS (LNAI), vol. 9811, pp. 588–595. Springer, Cham (2016). https://doi.org/10.1007/978-3-319-43958-7_71
9. Liu, H., Wang, L.: Gesture recognition for human-robot collaboration: a review. Int. J. Ind. Ergon. (2017, in Press). https://doi.org/10.1016/j.ergon.2017.02.004
10. Levonevskiy, D., Vatamaniuk, I., Saveliev, A.: Processing models for conflicting user requests in ubiquitous corporate smart spaces. In: MATEC Web Conference, vol. 161, p. 03006 (2018). https://doi.org/10.1051/matecconf/201816103006
11. Li, K., Zhou, W., Li, P., Hai, J., Liu, J.: Distinguishing DDoS attacks from flash crowds using probability metrics. In: Proceedings of the Third International Conference on Network and System Security, IEEE, pp. 9–17. IEEE Computer Society, Washington, DC (2009). https://doi.org/10.1109/nss.2009.35
12. Babenko, G.V., Belov, S.V.: Analysis of TCP/IP traffic based on the methodology of specified threshold and the deviation as a tool of detecting information security accidents. Technol. Technospheric Saf. **5**(39), 1–9 (2011)
13. Osipov, V.Yu., Vorobiev, V.I., Levonevskiy, D.K.: Problems of protection against false information in computer networks. SPIIRAS Proc. **53**(4), 97–117 (2017). https://doi.org/10.15622/sp.53.5
14. Osipov, V.Y., Nosal, I.A.: Substantiation of the period of revision of information security measures. Inf. Control Syst. **1**, 63–69 (2014)

15. Andress, J.: The Basics of Information Security: Understanding the Fundamentals of InfoSec in Theory and Practice. Syngress, Waltham (2014)
16. Bellaïche, M., Grégoire, J.-C.: SYN flooding attack detection based on entropy computing. In: GLOBECOM 2009 (2009). https://doi.org/10.1109/glocom.2009.5425454
17. Lu, W., Traore, I.: An unsupervised approach for detecting DDoS attacks based on traffic-based metrics. In: PACRIM 2005, pp. 462–465 (2005)

Automatic Synthesis Gait Scenarios for Reconfigurable Modular Robots Walking Platform Configuration

Sergey Manko and Evgeny Shestakov[✉]

Russian Technological University (MIREA), Moscow, Russia
shestakov.e.i@yandex.ru

Abstract. Reconfigurable mechatronic modular robots distinguished mainly by their ability to adapt their structure to specific tasks to be performed as well as to specific environments, are of great interest for a wide range of different applications. One of the key problems in motion control of this type of robots lies in the necessity to use original algorithms for each of the possible configurations whose variety is determined by the structure of mechatronic modules their number and the coupling option selected. Some standard configurations of mechatronic modular robots allow the possibility to develop motion control algorithms invariant to the number of modules in the kinematic structure. Yet, a promising approach to solving the problem is generally related to the development of self-learning means and methods to enable an automated synthesis of motion control algorithms for multi-unit mechatronic modular robots, taking into account the selected configuration. The present article discusses the results of exploratory research on using the apparatus of self-learning finite state machines for solving the problem of automated synthesis of gait scenarios in the walking plat-form configuration. The paper presents the results of model experiments confirming the workability and efficiency of the developed algorithms.

Keywords: Reconfigurable modular robots · Self-learning
Intelligent control systems · Finite state machine

1 Introduction

Attractiveness and functionality of modular reconfigurable robots conceptually developed by the end of the last century are wholly and totally determined by application of certain principles of modular design of complex technical systems. A combination of the mechanical structures modularity, hardware and software determines potential advantages of reconfigurable robots, such as a new class of electromechanical systems based on typical modules. Reconfigurable robots have a unique set of properties like multifunctionality, the adaptability of kinematic structure and its operational modifiability according to features of applied application and environmental conditions. Practical implementation of this similar approach related to the need for solving a number of key problems among which one of the most important are self-learning and automatic synthesis of multilink mechatronic modular robot control algorithms for its configuration synthesized based on the specifics of the current situation.

© Springer Nature Switzerland AG 2018
A. Ronzhin et al. (Eds.): ICR 2018, LNAI 11097, pp. 181–191, 2018.
https://doi.org/10.1007/978-3-319-99582-3_19

2   Features of Reconfigurable Mechatronic Modular Robot Functioning

The concept of construction mechatronic robots with adaptive kinematic structure means a presence of typical modules, combined into a single multilink structure. The typical mechatronic modules involve one or several motors with rotate joints and a simple mechanical transmissions, connectors for mechanical, electrical and information connection, controller, various sensors and autonomous power supply. Similar construction of typical modules provides their automatic docking and undocking for the operational formation of the necessary robot kinematic configuration depending on the goals and functional conditions.

Despite the diversity of the proposed variants of typical mechatronic modules, overwhelming majority of developers consider three main configurations of modular reconfigurable robots [1] for the targeted motion tasks, shown in Figs. 1 and 2:

- wheel configuration for moving on a flat surface;
- snake configuration for moving in a limited space;
- walking configuration for moving on a variable surface in complex scenes with numerous obstacles and irregularities.

Fig. 1. Examples of different configurations of modular robot PolyBot (PARK, Xerox, USA): wheel, snake and walking configuration.

Fig. 2. Examples of different configurations of modular robot CkBot (Modlab, UPenn, USA): wheel, snake and walking configuration.

It should be noted, the control of this type of robots in snake and wheel configurations can be implemented using universal algorithms providing the wave-like recurrence of module movements in common kinematic chain for its targeted motion [2].

In common case the robot transformation requirement in a walking configuration imposes by complication of environment and permeability conditions. The number of legs and a number of joints in each of them must be determined based on the analysis of the actual situation considering the size of irregularities and obstacles, weight and size parameters of robot, payload and other factors.

The a priori uncertainty and plenty of possible options of modular robot kinematic scheme in a walking configuration don't allow for development required gait scenarios and according control algorithms. Consequently obviously the control problems of reconfigurable robots in walking configuration mainly related to the self-learning organization for automatic generation of gait scenarios for reasonably selected kinematic scheme with a fixed number of legs and their joints (Fig. 3).

Fig. 3. Reconfigurable robot transformation in walking configuration because of complication of environment and permeability conditions.

3   Self-learning Methods and Technologies of in Intelligent Control Systems of Autonomous Robots

One of the key problems of construction intelligent control systems of autonomous robots and other types of complex dynamic objects operating in uncertainty conditions related to self-learning organization to acquire new knowledge about the surrounding world laws and behavior rules in certain situations.

Variety of self-learning tasks relevant to autonomous robotics [3] makes it necessary to find adequate methods of their solution. It should be noted that the theory of machine learning, as an independent subsection of artificial intelligence, has a lot of special tools and methods [4]. There are technologies based on clustering methods, reinforcement learning, evolutionary algorithms, regression analysis, Naive Bayes classifier, classification trees, particle swarm optimization, neural networks etc which are widely applied from medical and technical diagnostics to computer security and pattern recognition. The results of fundamental research in the field of intelligent control systems show some of these methods can be successfully used to solve some problems of self-learning autonomous robots [5–8]. In particular, the methods of evolutionary programming allows for automatic synthesis of algorithms for motion control of mobile platforms of various types [5, 6].

The methods of classification trees serve as an effective tool for autonomous robots self-learning, for example, to form knowledge about the patency of heterogeneous sections of the route in order to correct it quickly, taking into the minimization of the "cost" characteristics of the chosen trajectory.

Among the many well-known approaches to the self-learning organization, the specialized class of finite-state automata, the main principle of the construction and operation of which is associated with a change state depending on the current depth of its storage in memory, is of particular interest and perspective. Their peculiarity, realized in one way or another in automata of this kind, provides the solution of self-learning tasks aimed at identifying the conditions of the most effective interaction with the environment.

There is a number of characteristic representatives among of self-learning automata. One of them is Tsetlin machine (or linear tactics automata), whose state diagram is given by Fig. 4. For each action completed, the machine receives either negative or positive signals as a response from the environment.

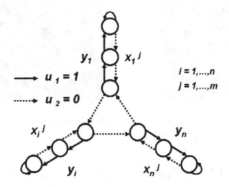

Fig. 4. Tsetlin machine state diagram.

In case of a positive response, the current state of the machine is restarted at the next higher memory level. A negative response causes a decrease in the depth of the current state storage or its cardinal change at the lowest memory level.

Thus, the finite state machine of this type can be interpreted as a dynamic system, which under the influence of some control command coming to the entrance at the time t, changes its current state x and the level j of its memory storage depth to a new one:

$$x(t), j(t) = f((x(t-1), j(t-1), u(t))$$
$$y(t) = h(x(t)), \tag{1}$$

where f, h are transition and output functions set by Table 1.

The depth of memory determines the inertial properties of the machine and allows to save the execution of the optimal action, even if there are single-piece negative responses. Herewith, it is proved that at sufficiently large values of the automata memory depth, its behavior tends to the optimum [9, 10].

Table 1. State transition table of Tsetlin machine.

Inputs\States	$x_i^j, \quad 1<j<m$	$x_i^j, \quad j=1$	$x_i^j, \quad j=m$
$u_1 = 1$	x_i^{j+1}/y_i	x_i^{j+1}/y_i	x_i^j/y_i
$u_2 = 0$	x_i^{j-1}/y_i	x_{i+1}^j/y_{i+1}	x_i^{j-1}/y_i

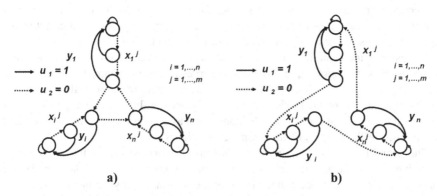

Fig. 5. Krinsky machine state diagram (a), Robbins machine state diagram (b).

Krinsky «trustful» machine is in mainly similar to the Tsetlin machine in principles of its construction and operation. As shown in Fig. 5(a), the main difference is in the current state transition of the machine to the deepest level of storage when receiving a positive response to the performed action.

As for Tsetlin machine, Krinsky and Robbins machines, whose transition and output functions are presented by Tables 2 and 3, it is strictly proved that their behavior in any stationary environment is rational.

Table 2. State transition table of Krinsky machine.

Inputs \ States	$x_i^j, \quad 1<j<m$	$x_i^j, \quad j=1$	$x_i^j, \quad j=m$
$u_1 = 1$	x_i^m/y_i	x_i^m/y_i	x_i^j/y_i
$u_2 = 0$	x_i^{j-1}/y_i	x_{i+1}^j/y_{i+1}	x_i^{j-1}/y_i

Table 3. State transition table of Robbins machine.

Inputs\States	$x_i^j, \quad 1<j<m$	$x_i^j, \quad j=1$	$x_i^j, \quad j=m$
$u_1 = 1$	x_i^m/y_i	x_i^m/y_i	x_i^j/y_i
$u_2 = 0$	x_i^{j-1}/y_i	x_{i+1}^m/y_{i+1}	x_i^{j-1}/y_i

4   Automatic Generation of a Reconfigurable Mechatronic Modular Robot Gait Scenarios in the Walking Configuration

One of the statement options of the considered problem on automatic synthesis of gait scenarios for walking configuration related with its interpretation from the point of view construction and functioning of self-learning automata. In this context, the set of interrelated states at different depths of the automata's memory is to be interpreted as a sequence of possible actions performed within a particular gait.

We assume the desired gait scenarios should be a cyclical process during which part of the legs is in motion, and the others serves as a static support. These requirements fully satisfys most simple and reliable (safe?) variant of the so-called "cautious" gait, when at each stage the motion is moved only one leg. In this case, the loss or save of the walking platform stability can be considered as criteria for selection of a suitable gait scenario in the process of its automated synthesis.

The simplification of the problem lies in its decomposition into two stages respectively, associated with the formation of a sequence of articulations for the rearrangement of a single leg and the order of the steps necessary for the robot transfer.

The use of such representations allows to totally determine the structure of automata which define the variety of gait scenarios as a set of combinations of possible actions for their implementation. A standard scenario of leg rearrangement in a new step interprets as a elementary sequence of joints rotations by value of the processed angle Δ.

Thus, the problem of automatic synthesis of scenario permutations of the leg rearrangement reduced to a combinatorial setting, allowing for the self-learning automata application to search for the necessary solutions. The general structure of a self-learning machine to search for a sequence of elementary rotations from start leg configuration to some target support state is shown in Fig. 6.

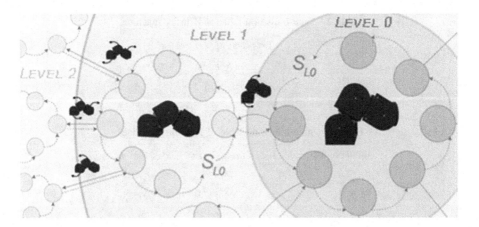

Fig. 6. General structure of self-learning machine for the scenario formation of the leg rearrangement.

Virtually this machine is divided into levels, in each of them one elementary action is generalized as leg joints angles change to the value Δ in the negative or positive direction either remain unchanged. Then the number of states S_{Li} in the i-th level to be determined by the following Eq. (2):

$$S_{Li} = \left(3^N\right)^{i+1}, \; (i = 0, 1, \ldots, L), \qquad (2)$$

where N is the number of joints in extremities; L is the number of levels calculated by the Eq. (3):

$$L = \frac{|q_{min} - q_{max}|}{\Delta}, \qquad (3)$$

where q_{min} and q_{max} are the minimum and maximum possible angles in the joint. Then, the total number of machine states does not exceed the value S_1:

$$S_1 = \sum_{i=0}^{L-1} S_{Li}. \qquad (4)$$

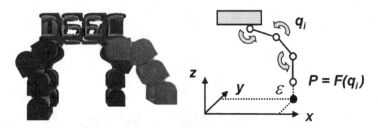

Fig. 7. Conformity assessment the current configuration of the leg to condition support.

As a criterion for desired solution selection, the condition for matching the leg joints current configuration with the support state can be used. In this case, as shown in Fig. 7, the current position of the leg P relative to the reference surface doesn't not exceed the specified level ε:

$$P \leq \varepsilon, \qquad (5)$$

- $q_i = k_i \Delta$, $(i = 1, 2, \ldots, N)$ are generalized coordinates of the leg;
- k_i is the conversion coefficient, determined by the self-learning machine in its working process;
- N is the number of joints in the leg;
- F is the transfer function between generalized and Cartesian coordinates.

Importantly the assignable elementary rotation value Δ selection and matching the current configuration to the support state ε condition essentially influence on search time of suitable scenarios, but also on the walking platform dynamics. In case of these parameters increasing should be a duration search reduction but to the dynamics impairment in the sense of amplitude vertical oscillations of robot center of mass increasing. Vice versa the elementary rotation value angle Δ and tolerance range ε decreasing should cause duration search increasing and dynamics motion improving.

The gait scenario is to regulate the rearrangement legs order of the walking platform during motion. As an example the structure of the self-learning machine, for a four-legged walking configuration is presented in Fig. 8. States S2 of this machine are determined by a set of rearrangement legs variants in accordance with the "cautious" gait concept:

$$S_2 = K!, \tag{6}$$

where K is the number of legs. To get all possible "cautious" gait variants one of the known generating permutations algorithms can be used. State transitions determinate by the self-learning automata idea with input negative or positive signals meaning loss or preservation of the robot stability. Stability assessment defines on software level by condition to entry projection of the center of platform gravity in the support area or by virtual physics simulation.

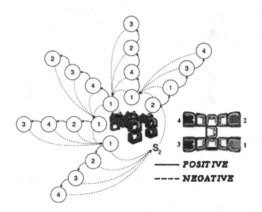

Fig. 8. General structure of self-learning machine for the sequence formation of the robot steps.

For the four-legged configuration, given for example in Fig. 9, not all cautious gait options are successful. As shown in Fig. 9 the scheme "1-2-3-4" changing the position of the center of robot gravity after first step, stability loss resulting. But the other scheme "4-3-1-2" safes the motion stability (Fig. 10).

A model experiments series convincingly testifies to possibility and efficiency of the offered approach use for automatic gait scenarios synthesis. The produced experimental results are shown in Tables 4 and 5 and Fig. 11. confirm expected and actual nature dependence of the duration search of gait scenarios and amplitude robot center of mass oscillations on the elementary rotation angle values Δ and tolerance leg position over the reference surface ε.

Fig. 9. Modeling of walking platform motion based on "cautious gait" scheme "1-2-3-4" where there is a loss of stability.

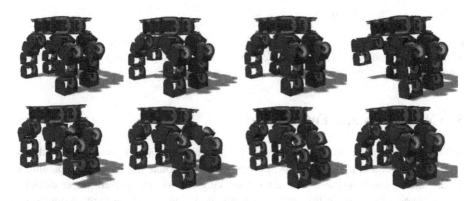

Fig. 10. Modeling of walking platform motion based on "cautious gait" scheme "4-3-2-1" where there isn't a loss of stability.

Table 4. Center of mass amplitude oscillations dependence on discretization angle and clearance.

	$\varepsilon = 2.0$ cm	$\varepsilon = 2.5$ cm	$\varepsilon = 3.0$ cm	$\varepsilon = 3.5$ cm
$\Delta = 30°$	181,38	161,76	27,7	26,6
$\Delta = 20°$	55,25	36,28	36,1	33,4

Table 5. The average learning time dependence on the angle discretization values and the clearance.

	$\varepsilon = 2.0$ cm	$\varepsilon = 2.5$ cm	$\varepsilon = 3.0$ cm	$\varepsilon = 3.5$ cm
$\Delta = 30°$	181,38	161,76	27,7	26,6
$\Delta = 20°$	55,25	36,28	36,1	33,4

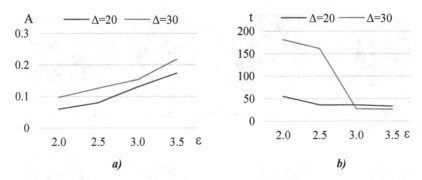

Fig. 11. Experimental results: a) dependence of the center of mass amplitude oscillations on angle of discretization and clearance b) dependence of the average learning time on the angle discretization values and the clearance.

5   Conclusions and Future Works

Self-learning opens up broad prospects for the automation of intelligent control systems synthesis and configuration, and to improve their functional and adaptive capabilities by the analysis and synthesis of the their working results. The present paper demonstrates development possibility and expediency attracting of self-learning automata for gait scenarios synthesis for modular robots in walking configuration. There are other approaches to solving this problem related, for example, to the use of genetic algorithms and evolutionary programming methods [5, 6]. Development of autonomous robot with advanced adaptive capacity including reconfigurability assumes necessity of their effective self-learning on-board equipment. In this regard, the future work related to a comparative analysis to effectiveness assessment of the genetic algorithms and self-learning automata use for automatic behavior and control algorithms generation.

References

1. Makarov, I.M., Lokhin, V.M., Manko, S.V.: Multilink mechatronic modular robots with adaptive kinematic structure. Mechatron. Autom. Control **11** (2006)
2. Makarov, I.M., Lokhin, V.M., Manko, S.V.: Motion control of mechatronic modular robots with adaptive kinematic structure. Mechatron. Autom. Control **3** (2008)
3. Lokhin, V.M., Manko, S.V., Diane, S.A.K., Panin, A.S., Alexandrova, R.I.: Mechanisms of intellectual feedbacks, knowledge processing and self-learning in control systems of autonomous robots and multiagent robotic groups. Mechatron. Autom. Control **16**(8) (2015)
4. Nikolayenko, S.N., Tulupyev, A.L.: Self-Learning Systems. MTSNMO Publ, Moscow (2009)
5. Makarov, I.M., Lokhin V.M., Manko S.V., Kadochnikov M.V., Sitnikov M.S.: Use of genetic algorithms for automatic knowledge base formation of intelligent control system for Autonomous mobile robot. Mechatron. Autom. Control **6** (2008)

6. Makarov, I.M., Lokhin, V.M., Manko, S.V., Kadochnikov, M.V., Vostrikov, G.S.: The use of genetic algorithms in the problems of automatic learning and self-organization of intelligent robotic systems. Mechatron. Autom. Control **9** (2008)
7. Makarov, I.M., Lokhin, V.M., Man'ko, S.V., Romanov, M.P.: Automation of the Synthesis and the Learning of Intelligent Control Systems. Nauka Publ, Moscow (2009)
8. Lokhin, V.M., Manko, S.V., Diane, S.A.K., Panin A.S., Aleksandrova R.I.: Self-learning mechanisms in multiagent robotic groups based on evolutionary tree forest classification. Mechatron. Autom. Control **18**(3) (2017)
9. Tsetlin, M.L.: Studies on the Theory of Automata and Modeling of Biological Systems. Science Publ, Moscow (1969)
10. Varshavsky, V.I., Pospelov, D.A.: The Orchestra Plays without a Conductor: Reflections on the Evolution and Control of Some Technical Systems. Science Publ, Moscow (1984)

Fast Frontier Detection Approach in Consecutive Grid Maps

Petr Neduchal(✉)(iD), Miroslav Flídr(iD), and Miloš Železný

Faculty of Applied Sciences, New Technologies for the Information Society,
University of West Bohemia, Univerzitní 8, 306 14 Plzeň, Czech Republic
{neduchal,flidr,zelezny}@kky.zcu.cz
http://fav.zcu.cz/en/, http://ntis.zcu.cz/en/

Abstract. This paper deals with frontiers detection in occupancy grid maps. The proposed method is based on differences between consecutive maps. Using this approach, frontiers detection is accelerated by calculating the third map which contains only new data. Thus, only new frontiers are detected and added to the list of frontiers. The main contribution of this paper is the description of the proposed approach and its open sourced implementation in Python. Moreover, several results of experiments are discussed. The proposed approach is capable to run very fast even for large maps with many frontiers.

Keywords: Autonomous robotics · Frontier detection
Localization and mapping · Image processing

1 Introduction

Mobile robotics is a highly active research area. One of the main topics that are addressed by mobile robotics is the problem of a kidnapped robot. A robot is placed in the unknown environment and it is forced to create a map of the environment and localize itself in that environment. Moreover, there is a requirement that the final map has to be complete and accurate. To solve this problem, the system containing robot perception, localization, mapping and navigation has to be used.

The important part of the autonomous robot system is a localization and mapping algorithm which is often called Simultaneous Localization And Mapping (SLAM) or Concurrent Mapping and Localization. The goal is to create a map of the environment and localize itself based on the data from attached sensors such as Light Detection And Ranging (LiDAR) or Camera. Based on the sensor choice, a different approach is performed. In this paper, 2D LiDAR-based approach creating so-called Occupancy Grid Map (see Fig. 1) is used. Grid map is matrix-like representation composed of cells which preserves probabilistic information about its occupancy. Probability 1 represents cell occupied by an obstacle. Probability zero represents free space. Values between these two represent uncertainty in the cell – i.e. unknown space.

© Springer Nature Switzerland AG 2018
A. Ronzhin et al. (Eds.): ICR 2018, LNAI 11097, pp. 192–201, 2018.
https://doi.org/10.1007/978-3-319-99582-3_20

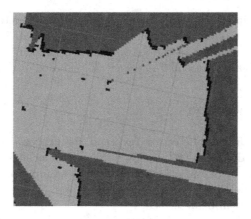

Fig. 1. Occupancy Grid Map example. Obstacles are black, free space is bright and the rest is unknown space.

The robot is supposed to map its environment completely and as quickly as possible. Thus, a path of the robot has to be calculated online based on the set of goals. The difficulty is that the complete map is not known, thus it is necessary to create set of goals online too. In this paper, the approach of setting goals based on the detection of frontier points is discussed. Frontiers are groups of cells which lay between free and unknown space on the map. The image processing methods are used to detect the frontier points.

The main goal and contribution of this paper is a description of proposed approaches to detect frontier points. It is a core part of a frontier-based exploration system which is a goal of our research.

The paper is structured as follows. In Sect. 2, related work is discussed. Proposed Frontier detection approach is described in Sect. 3. Section 4 contains experiments and discussion. Paper is summarized in conclusion at the end of the paper in Sect. 5.

2   Related Work

A lot of related research in autonomous mobile robotics were focused on localization and mapping [2,3] problem. Many systems based on various sensors were created. Two main groups of systems are based on LiDAR sensor [7,14] and on the camera sensor [1,4,12]. The later one is often called visual SLAM.

The frontier-based exploration problem was addressed in 1997 by Yamauchi [18] for the first time. The more recent implementation of frontier-based exploration on grid map is presented in paper [17]. Another approach is proposed in papers of Jadidi et al. [8,9] where frontiers are computed from the continuous occupancy map created by trained Gaussian process. Authors also propose a formula for computing frontiers from continuous occupancy map. A similar approach is proposed in this paper for discrete grid map. The developed system is described in the next section.

There are also interesting papers focusing on frontier detection algorithm. An example is Fast Frontier Detection [10], which accelerates detection process by processing only new part of the map. Similar approach is employed in this paper. Another research presented in paper [16] is based on Random Trees.

3   Frontier Detection

In this section the frontier detection task and the proposed algorithm will be described. Frontier detection task is closely related to localization and mapping task. A map created by SLAM algorithm is used as an input of frontier detection algorithm. Thus, the SLAM will be mentioned first. Then proposed frontiers detection algorithm will be described.

3.1   Simultaneous Localization and Mapping

The goal of SLAM [2,3,15] is to create the map of the environment and localize robot inside of this map. More formally it is defined as searching for joint posterior density function in the form

$$p\left(x_k, m \mid Z_{0:k}, U_{0:k}, x_0\right), \tag{1}$$

where x_k is a vehicle location and m is the map that contains landmarks. The initial pose of the vehicle x_0, a set of observation $Z_{0:k}$ and all control inputs $U_{0:k}$ are given at time step k. A vehicle location x_k and the map m together defines the state space.

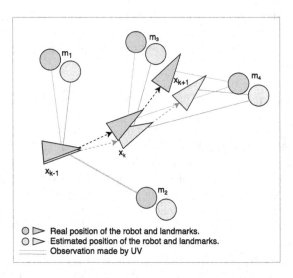

Fig. 2. Three steps of SLAM algorithm. Based on the graph from [15]

The diagram in Fig. 2 shows three steps of SLAM algorithm. Landmarks in the environment are observed by the mobile robot and their positions are estimated as well as the position of the mobile robot. The difference between real and estimated position is called the drift. The main goal of the SLAM task can be defined as a reduction of this drift in order to create the consistent map.

In this paper, the 2D LiDAR-based SLAM is assumed. There are three widely used open source implementations of LiDAR-based SLAM systems. The first one is gMapping [6] which is also used for the experiment in this paper. GMapping system is based on the particle filters and has good and consistent results. The next one is Hector SLAM [11], which is based on least square optimization. Unfortunately, this system can cause errors in the long narrow hallways. The most recent one is Google Cartographer [7] which is based on least square optimization technique too.

3.2 Proposed Approach

In this subsection, the proposed approach to the frontiers detection will be described. In theory, frontiers are points in the map on the edge between free space and an unknown space. In other words, frontier points are the points of free space which are next to the point of unknown space. Frontier points are detected in the cells of occupancy grid map. An example of grid map and detected frontier points is shown in Fig. 3. Grid map M consists of obstacles (black cells), free space (white cells) and unknown space. Free space is the space where the robot can move without danger of collision. In practice, obstacles are usually labelled by number 1, free space by number 0 and unknown space by number -1.

The proposed approach is based on the image processing methods. Particularly 2D convolution and binary operations are used. Detection algorithm of our approach consists of four steps. In the first step, 2D convolution (details in [13])

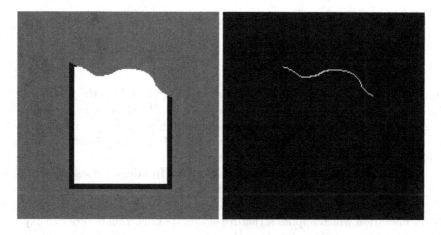

Fig. 3. Example of the map and its frontier map

is performed. Convolution is defined as follows

$$f(i,j) = h * g = \sum_m \sum_n h(i - m, j - n) g(m, n) \qquad m, n \in \rho, \qquad (2)$$

where g is an image – a map, h is the kernel, f is convolution response on the kernel and ρ is a local neighbourhood on which response is computed. Indexes m and n represents image coordinates in ρ and indexes i and j represents coordinates of the used kernel. The contribution of cells is weighted by the kernel. Thus, based on the kernel various results can be computed. Image gradient kernels – usually used for edge detection – are used in the proposed approach. Used kernels are shown in the Eq. 3.

$$h_1 = \begin{bmatrix} 0 & -1 \\ 0 & 1 \end{bmatrix}, \; h_2 = \begin{bmatrix} 0 & 0 \\ -1 & 1 \end{bmatrix}, \; h_3 = \begin{bmatrix} -1 & 0 \\ 0 & 1 \end{bmatrix}, \; h_4 = \begin{bmatrix} 0 & -1 \\ 1 & 0 \end{bmatrix}. \qquad (3)$$

It worth mentioning that kernels h_1 and h_2 are created with zeros on the left and top positions respectively. It is designed this way because of half-cell offset of the kernels of size 2×2. The result after 2D image convolution is a new image. Responses on all kernels are summed up as follows

$$D = \sum_k M * h_k \qquad k \in 1, 2, \ldots K, \qquad (4)$$

where M is grid map, h_k is k-th kernel and K is a number of kernels.

The same calculation is made on the map of obstacles M_o, which is a map created from M where obstacles are labelled by number 1 and other cells are set to 0 – i.e. grid map with no unknown space. Thus,

$$D_o = \sum_k M_o * h_k \qquad k \in 1, 2, \ldots K, \qquad (5)$$

is the sum of obstacle map M_o responses on kernels h_k. A frontiers map F is then computed using following formula

$$F = D - \beta \cdot D_o, \qquad (6)$$

where β is a parameter and its value should be set based on the used kernels. The parameter should be big enough to subtract all obstacles in D_o from the difference map D. In the case of kernels described in (3), it was found that $\beta = 2$ is minimal value in order to get accurate results. In the final frontier map only frontier points values are greater than zero.

Detected frontiers points can be connected into frontiers regions which represent individual future goals for the mobile robot. Moreover, it is possible to use morphological operation called dilation to enlarge frontiers regions. Dilation is a binary operation which applies structure element – i.e. kernel in order to expand object in the image. More details in [13]. It can connect two close neighbouring regions into one.

When the map becomes too large, the number of detected frontiers can be significant, which can slow down the whole process. Image processing technique called motion analysis can accelerate this process and reduce the number of detected frontiers in the current step. It is based on the difference between current map and the map obtained in the previous step. Simply calculated using subtraction of the maps. Only non-zero cells of this difference are relevant for the frontiers detection. In other words, the algorithm process only new frontiers which are detected in the current map. An example of this approach is shown in Fig. 4.

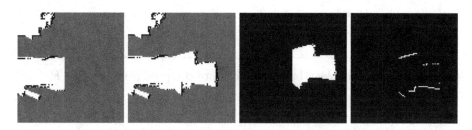

Fig. 4. Example of two consecutive maps (the first and the second image from the left), their differential map (the third one) and the frontier map (image on the right)

The difference can be computed using two approaches. The first approach is naive and it just labels all free space cells which are same on both maps as obstacles (see Algorithm 1). It is a simple solution but it has a disadvantage. If the known part of the map is not exactly the same, then there are detected false positive frontiers regions and causes problems during robot exploration.

Input: consecutive maps map_k and map_{k-1}, kernels $h_1, \ldots h_k$, β
Output: frontiers map F
begin

$\quad M = map_k[map_k \mathrel{!=} map_{k-1}]$
$\quad D = \sum_k M * h_k \qquad k \in 1, 2, \ldots K$
$\quad M_o = M[M == 1]$
$\quad D_o = \sum_k M_o * h_k \qquad k \in 1, 2, \ldots K$
$\quad F = D - \beta \cdot D_o,$

end

Algorithm 1: Naive algorithm to compute frontiers map F

A better way is to create difference map as follows (see Algorithm 2). Copy new map into difference map object. Create mask such as free space and obstacles from the previous map are labelled as number 1. Perform morphology operation dilation to enlarge mask. Apply mask to label cells in difference map as obstacles. This approach is based on kernel size parameter of dilation operation which can be computed based on the size and resolution of the map.

Input: map_k and map_{k-1}, $h_1, \ldots h_k$, structure element size S, β
Output: frontiers map F
begin
    diff_map = map_k
    mask = $(map_{k-1}$!= -1$)$
    mask = dilate(mask, S)
    diff_map[mask == 1] = 1
    M = diff_map
    $D = \sum_k M * h_k$ $k \in 1, 2, \ldots K$
    $M_o = M[M == 1]$
    $D_o = \sum_k M_o * h_k$ $k \in 1, 2, \ldots K$
    $F = D - \beta \cdot D_o,$
end

Algorithm 2: Morphology-based algorithm to compute frontiers map F

4 Experiments

In this section, results of performed experiments will be discussed. Important properties of the frontiers detection algorithm are processing time and accuracy, i.e. the algorithm detects only real frontiers and no false positives. Implementation of the detector was tested on synthetic data generated using Stage[1] simulator in Robot Operating System (ROS) [5]. In the Fig. 5, the part of map sequence called cave is shown.

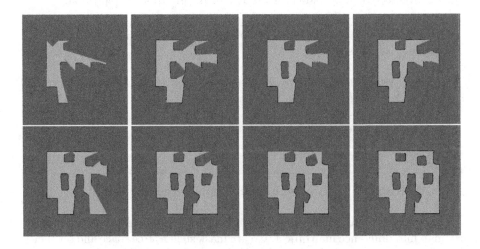

Fig. 5. Example of maps used in the experiments

---

[1]   http://wiki.ros.org/stage.

Two versions of Algorithm 1 and Algorithm 2 were tested. The first one computes the whole map at every time step. The second one computes local neighbourhood of the robot – based on sensors range – and calculates frontiers in this area. The mean processing times are summarized in the Table 1. It is clearly visible from the table that morphology-based approach is faster than naive. Moreover, the local version can run in real time which is usually not necessary because the map is generated with lower frequency. The local version of morphology-based approach has better performance than the approaches presented in paper [10].

Table 1. Results of speed test of proposed algorithms.

Approach	mean t[s]	var	local mean t[s]	local var
Naive	0.4986	0.0784	0.0138	$8.6e^{-5}$
Morphology	0.2888	0.0132	0.007	$1.4e^{-5}$

The accuracy of the algorithm was evaluated manually by a human expert. The results are based on the quality of mapping algorithm. When the changes between two consecutive maps are significant and if there is noise in the positions of walls, false positive of frontiers can be detected by the naive version of the proposed approach. In Fig. 6, the examples of naive and morphology-based results are shown.

In the example, there are visible false positives in the naive approach (first row). False positive has to be deleted which increases computational complexity. The result of the morphology-based approach is accurate – i.e. only new and real

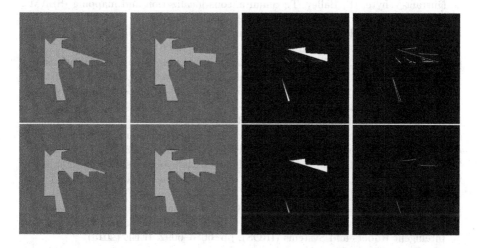

Fig. 6. Naive (first row) and Morphology (second row) based approaches. Example of two consecutive maps (the first and the second image from the left), their differential map (the third one) and the frontier map (image on the right).

frontiers are detected. Thus, this approach is a better solution for the frontier detection and as the core of the frontier-based exploration system.

5 Conclusion

Proposed algorithms are capable to detect frontiers in real time. Moreover, a morphology-based method is fast and accurate. Especially approach with the computation of local neighbourhood of the robot. Thus, it can be used as a core of the frontier-based exploration system. Am implementation of proposed approaches in python and generated data is available on GitHub in frontiers_detector[2] repository under MIT licence

There is two main research direction to improve proposed algorithms. The first way is to implemented approaches using GPU. It accelerates detection process significantly. The second way is to Dynamically change local neighbourhood of the robot in order to minimize the area for frontiers computation.

In the future research, we also want to implement ROS node on the top of proposed algorithms and use it in the frontier-based exploration system with graph structure of possible goals defined by detected frontiers regions.

Acknowledgments. This work was supported by the Ministry of Education of the Czech Republic, project No. LTARF18017. This work was supported by the Ministry of Education, Youth and Sports of the Czech Republic project No. LO1506.

References

1. Davison, A.J., Reid, I.D., Molton, N.D., Stasse, O.: MonoSLAM: real-time single camera SLAM. IEEE Trans. Pattern Anal. Mach. Intell. **29**(6), 1052–1067 (2007)
2. Durrant-Whyte, H., Bailey, T.: Simultaneous localization and mapping (SLAM): part 2. IEEE Robot. Autom. Mag. **13**(2), 99–108 (2006)
3. Durrant-Whyte, H., Bailey, T.: Simultaneous localization and mapping (SLAM): part i. IEEE Robot. Autom. Mag. **13**(2), 99–110 (2006)
4. Engel, J., Schöps, T., Cremers, D.: LSD-SLAM: large-scale direct monocular SLAM. In: Fleet, D., Pajdla, T., Schiele, B., Tuytelaars, T. (eds.) ECCV 2014. LNCS, vol. 8690, pp. 834–849. Springer, Cham (2014). https://doi.org/10.1007/978-3-319-10605-2_54
5. Garage, W.: Robot operating system (ROS) (2012)
6. Grisetti, G., Stachniss, C., Burgard, W.: Improved techniques for grid mapping with rao-blackwellized particle filters. IEEE Trans. Robot. **23**(1), 34–46 (2007)
7. Hess, W., Kohler, D., Rapp, H., Andor, D.: Real-time loop closure in 2D lidar slam. In: 2016 IEEE International Conference on Robotics and Automation (ICRA), pp. 1271–1278. IEEE (2016)
8. Jadidi, M.G., Miro, J.V., Dissanayake, G.: Mutual information-based exploration on continuous occupancy maps. In: 2015 IEEE/RSJ International Conference on Intelligent Robots and Systems (IROS), pp. 6086–6092. IEEE (2015)

---

[2] https://github.com/neduchal/frontiers_detector.

9. Jadidi, M.G., Miro, J.V., Dissanayake, G.: Gaussian processes autonomous mapping and exploration for range-sensing mobile robots. Autonom. Robots **42**(2), 273–290 (2018)
10. Keidar, M., Sadeh-Or, E., Kaminka, G.A.: Fast frontier detection for robot exploration. In: Dechesne, F., Hattori, H., ter Mors, A., Such, J.M., Weyns, D., Dignum, F. (eds.) AAMAS 2011. LNCS (LNAI), vol. 7068, pp. 281–294. Springer, Heidelberg (2012). https://doi.org/10.1007/978-3-642-27216-5_20
11. Kohlbrecher, S., Meyer, J., Graber, T., Petersen, K., Klingauf, U., von Stryk, O.: Hector Open source modules for autonomous mapping and navigation with rescue robots. In: Behnke, S., Veloso, M., Visser, A., Xiong, R. (eds.) RoboCup 2013. LNCS (LNAI), vol. 8371, pp. 624–631. Springer, Heidelberg (2014). https://doi.org/10.1007/978-3-662-44468-9_58
12. Mur-Artal, R., Montiel, J., Tardos, J.D.: ORB-SLAM: a versatile and accurate monocular SLAM system. IEEE Trans. Robot. **31**(5), 1147–1163 (2015)
13. Sonka, M., Hlavac, V., Boyle, R.: Image processing, analysis, and machine vision. Cengage Learn. (2014)
14. Steux, B., El Hamzaoui, O.: tinySLAM: A SLAM algorithm in less than 200 lines C-language program. In: 2010 11th International Conference on Control Automation Robotics & Vision (ICARCV), pp. 1975–1979. IEEE (2010)
15. Thrun, S., Burgard, W., Fox, D.: Probabilistic Robotics. MIT Press (2005). http://www.probabilistic-robotics.org/
16. Umari, H., Mukhopadhyay, S.: Autonomous robotic exploration based on multiple rapidly-exploring randomized trees. In: 2017 IEEE/RSJ International Conference on Intelligent Robots and Systems (IROS), pp. 1396–1402. IEEE (2017)
17. Uslu, E., Çakmak, F., Balcılar, M., Akıncı, A., Amasyalı, M.F., Yavuz, S.: Implementation of frontier-based exploration algorithm for an autonomous robot. In: 2015 International Symposium on Innovations in Intelligent Systems and Applications (INISTA), pp. 1–7. IEEE (2015)
18. Yamauchi, B.: A frontier-based approach for autonomous exploration. In: Proceedings of the 1997 IEEE International Symposium on Computational Intelligence in Robotics and Automation, CIRA 1997, pp. 146–151. IEEE (1997)

Design and Operation Principles of the Magnetomechanical Connector of the Module of the Mobile Autonomous Reconfigurable System

Nikita Pavliuk$^{(\boxtimes)}$ ⓘ, Konstantin Krestovnikov,
Dmitry Pykhov, and Victor Budkov ⓘ

St. Petersburg Institute for Informatics and Automation of Russian Academy
of Sciences, SPIIRAS, 39, 14 Line, St. Petersburg 199178, Russia
`antei.hasgard@gmail.com`

Abstract. The object of this research is a multifunctional modular robot that can reconfigure the nodes and operatively change their position in the process of operation depending on the current task. The purpose of work is to study and develop homogeneous groups of robots capable of moving autonomously and forming various structures by connecting separate modules to each other. The novelty consists in the design of a module for mobile autonomous reconfigurable system (MARS), which differs from the analogues by the presence of a hybrid coupling mechanism embedded into the motor-wheel module. The developed magnetomechanical connector provides for positioning of the robotic modules relative to each other at the coupling stage and the connection of blocks of complex structures. Control of the polarity of the magnetic circuit, which is part of the connector, is carried out by the supply of short-term pulses that perform the coupling and decoupling of the units. In the course of experiments, we determined the parameters of the magnetic circuit and the principles of the functioning of the combined magnetic circuit ensuring the energy efficiency of the connector. The module moves along surfaces by means of motor wheels which comprise the coupling system of the modules. This approach allows one to save space in the robotics module and efficiently use its main part for the arrangement of power supplies and control devices. Two schemes for placing sets of magneto-mechanical connectors in the basic module were proposed.

Keywords: Modular robotics · Servo drives · Connector · Magnetic circuit
Magneto-Mechanical connector

1 Introduction

Among the modern prototypes of small-sized modular robots, chain-shaped robots are the most developed. Their built-in modules are in permanent connection and do not have the possibility to move independently [1]. As a result, failure of one chain module leads to a decrease in the operability of the entire robot. The development of a fully-functional autonomous module provides flexibility and reconfigurability of the modular

© Springer Nature Switzerland AG 2018
A. Ronzhin et al. (Eds.): ICR 2018, LNAI 11097, pp. 202–212, 2018.
https://doi.org/10.1007/978-3-319-99582-3_21

robot with the ability to rebuild the structure and replace the failed modules [2]. In this work, elements and work principles of the autonomous unit of the MARS modular robot were designed using a hybrid magnetomechanical grip mechanism built into the motor-wheel of the module.

2 Review of Existing Modular Robots and Modular Connections

Now modular robotics developers solve the problems associated with movement modules speed. There is no possibility to use powerful motors because of small size of the modular units. Therefore, in addition to low speed, there is the problem of connectors synchronizing. Developed at the Massachusetts Institute of Technology (MIT) the ChainFORM robot [3] is equipped with a sensory touch control system, an angular tilt control system, and a servo drive for crawling or climbing movements. Another development of the MIT is the m-Block robot [4]. Each module of the m-Block is autonomous and can move independently using inertial movement, untwisting flywheel inside the module. The Mori robot developed by National Centre of Competence in Research (NCCR) in Robotics and École Polytechnique Fédérale de Lausanne specialists [5] is a set of triangular modules, each equipped with drives, sensors and an integrated controller. The Dtto robot is the development of the ideas of the M-TRAN project [6]. The mechanism proposed in [7] provides an effective and high-strength connection due to a non-contact drive and specially designed clamping profiles. In work [8, 9], authors attempt to simplify the comparison of modular robots prototypes by briefly studying methods of modular robots development, coupling technologies, and the hardware architectures of modular self-healing and reconfigurable robots. The light reconfigurable Evo-bot modular robot for studying long-term evolutionary processes is presented in [10]. The connector mechanism for modular robots, which provides a rigid reversible connection capable operating in three independent modes, is presented in [11]. A comprehensive review of reconfigurable modular robots that includes the origin, history, current state, key technologies, problems and applications of reconfigurable modular robots is presented in [12]. The modular robotic mechanism HexaMob in [13]. The magnetic connection of the so-called "soft" modules (Soft robotics) is described in [14]. Algorithms for coupling mobile self-repairing robots that equipped with inexpensive sensors is presented in [15]. The modular principle of constructing functional blocks of mobile robots is considered in [16]. An autonomous modular robotic system Mecabot is an example of a search and rescue operation system in urban areas [17, 18]. The problem of dynamic reconfiguration using an example of the ModRED set based on the graph theory is considered in [19]. The development of a mechanical coupling device for a heterogeneous self-reconfigurable multinodular system is presented in [20]. The modular robot capable of design reconfiguring in rough terrain is presented in [21].

It is clear from the review that in modular robotic developing useful functionality are overlooked in favour of a separately developed technology or operation algorithm. This creates problems to use resulting modular robot solutions in the future. Potential mechanism scope is not indicated for any developments described in the review.

The mobile autonomous reconfigurable system presented in this work has a magne-tomechanical connector with high energy efficiency, consuming energy only at the moment of operating mode switching.

3   Mobile Autonomous Reconfigurable System

The concept of the developed robot is based on the robot construction based on a pair of motor-wheels, a basic unit with a rotary servo, whose axis is perpendicular to the motor-wheel axes. An axial servomotor is installed inside the base module unit. Servomotor is responsible for motor wheel turning of 90 degrees away from the main motion axis. The platform in the design can deflect the driven motor-wheel axes within 180°. The standard modular robot position is illustrated in Fig. 1. This allow each individual robot block-module to move faster than analogs, unfold in place with a zero turning radius, and also change the structure organized from such blocks without disconnection. When connecting, servomotors correct themselves to the angle necessary for the precise positioning of the "key" grooves of the active and reciprocal parts of the magneto-mechanical connector on one axis.

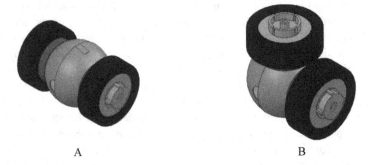

A   B

Fig. 1. A generalized model of a single block-module: A – the module standard position; B – module with a motor-wheel with a B-type connector offset around the base unit axis.

The motor-wheels servomotors are responsible for positioning the two platforms relative to each other. The basic kinematic module scheme for the offset of the motor-wheel with the B-type connector is demonstrated in Fig. 2.

This scheme consists of motor-wheel servomotors and the axial base unit servo-motor. The module number in one hitching determines the final number of freedom degrees. In the base unit, in addition to the servomotor, a computing control·unit, a battery, a wired and wireless communication interfaces are installed. Motor wheel designs for connectors A and B are different because B is a driven wheel and its design does not include massive and heavy elements to reduce the load on the axial servo while driving. The B-type connector base is a special shape steel ring for reducing the lateral shift backlash and loads coming to the magnetic circuit. This ring acts as a contact pad for the active part of the magnetic-mechanical connection. Active magnetomechanical

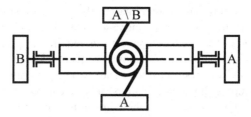

Fig. 2. Kinematic block-module scheme: A – motor-wheel servomotor; B – axis base unit servomotor.

connector, the main magnetic circuit, is located in the wheel with the A-type connector. The A-type motor-wheel is fixed relative to the base unit and does not move around the base unit servomotor axis for optimality of the kinematic circuit and control system. Two schemes for the module-module connectors, ABBB and AABB, were developed. The sign "+" in the schemes (Fig. 3) indicates the possibility of connector connecting to each other, the sign "−" indicates the impossibility of connecting one module to another in this position relative to each other.

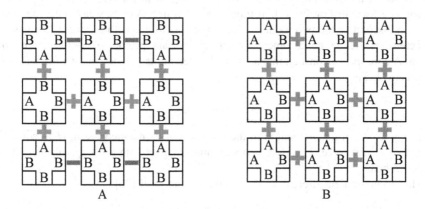

Fig. 3. Connectors schemes and their possible application in the structure: A – the ABBB connector scheme; B – AABB connector scheme.

These schemes differ from one another in the implementation features and the possibilities of forming structural entities [22–24]. The scheme (Fig. 3a) is easily applicable in the module design because it uses one active magnetic circuit and three response areas in the body of one module. This scheme is suitable for forming a linear structure of series-connected modules in steps of up to two modules away from the main scheme. Nevertheless, it is impossible to form a closed structure with the ABBB scheme. This means that the ABBB scheme does not allow to create a modules stable array for solving complex problems of moving and interacting with the environment. Such scheme is suitable for the basic mechanism formation, for example, manipulators.

The AABB scheme (Fig. 3b) is more massive because it is necessary to place two magnetic circuits side by side, which increase in module weight and power consumption. Modification of the A-type connector is required to place the base module unit in the body. However, this scheme allows the modules to assemble into a closed system, where each device is connected to at least two neighboring ones. Thereby, it is possible to form complex modular structures of different configurations and assignments using only one type of modular robots. It can be seen in Figure that the AABB scheme is preferable because it allows to create more multitasking mechanisms than in the case of the ABBB scheme.

4 Magnetomechanical Connector

The proposed connector mechanism allows the use of a control system that does not require constant monitoring and consumes power only during module connection and disconnection from each other. This significantly reduces energy costs and increases the battery life of each module. The A-type connector acts as a working member and consists of a constant magnet. This magnet serves as a base in a steel liner with a contact pad at the end face and with an electromagnet in the steel liner cavity. Electromagnet is switched on for a short time, when it is necessary to weaken the magnetic field and disconnect the two modules. Requirements to magnetomechanical connector characteristics define development of an appropriate prototype configuration and design. A appropriate constant magnet was decided on its magnetomotive force should be equal to [25]:

$$F_{MC} = H_{MC} \times l_{MC}, \tag{1}$$

where l_{MC} constant magnet length in the direction of its magnetization, H_{MC} constant magnet coercitive force. Therefore, a neodymium magnet with a 3.8 kg adhesion force is approached.

The magnetic field strength in the magnetic core steel [26]:

$$H_{ST} = \frac{B_{ST}}{\mu_0 \times \mu_{ST}}, \tag{2}$$

where μ_{ST} magnetic core steel relative permeability, a μ_0 the vacuum permeability equal to:

$$4\pi \times 10^{-7} \, \text{H/m}. \tag{3}$$

It is on this basis now it was decided to use ordinary steel grades used in industry. There is an air gap arises between the active and passive gripper parts because of the imperfect fit of the magnetic gripping parts that results in a gripper weakening.

When the small air gap width air gap section is equal to the magnetic circuit section. The magnetic field strength in the magnetic core air gap [26]:

$$H_A = \frac{B_A}{\mu_0}.$$ (4)

The Ampere's circuital theorem for the magnetic field of a magnetic core with an air gap [26]:

$$H_A \times l_A + H_{ST} \times l_{ST} = F_{MC}.$$ (5)

Based on 1, 2, 3 and 4, the magnetic induction in the air gap of the magnetic circuit is:

$$B_A = \frac{(F_{MC} - H_{ST}l_{ST})\mu}{l_A}.$$ (6)

Then, the adhesion force of the magnetic grip F can be calculated using Maxwell's formula based on an analysis of the magnetic field acting on the poles surface [25]:

$$F = \frac{B_A^2 S}{2\mu_0},$$ (7)

where S – cross-sectional area of the magnetic circuit.

The first magnetic grip prototype was realized in the two semisphere form, a constant magnet, a control electromagnet and a counterpart (Fig. 4). The constant magnet is installed between the steel semispheres forming an open circuit and the control electromagnet is located above the constant magnet at a distance 0.001 m. An active part of the magnetomechanical connector is the A-type connector.

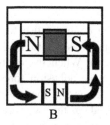

A   B

Fig. 4. The first prototype of the magnetic circuit: A – connection grip state; B – disconnection grip state.

With adhesion force equals 5 kg the force changing was less than 5 g in case when the control signal is applied to the electromagnet to switch the grip in the uncoupling state. Similar experiments with constant magnets were earlier [27, 28]. In the design, the magnetic lines of the constant magnet were supposed to be closed along the magnetic circuit through the passive grip counterpart when the control signal was applied to the electromagnet. Electromagnet current induces a magnetic field in the electromagnet core opposite to the constant magnet field (Fig. 4a). The grip passes into connection state with this a control pulse. The current of control pulse induces a magnetic flux in the electromagnet core with the direction of the magnetic constant magnet flux (Fig. 4b). The magnetic lines of the constant magnet are closed through the electromagnet core and the connector circuit goes into disconnection state. The first experiments data with the prototype showed that this configuration (Fig. 4) has no the required magnetic circuit characteristics. Based on the obtained data, the configuration and design of the magnetic circuit was revised. The new design work principle stays that way but differs in that the control electromagnet connected by the magnetic circuit with constant magnet is located on the opposite side of the passive counterpart (Fig. 5). The constant magnet is shifted toward the grip counterpart. When a control pulse is applied its current induces a magnetic flux in the electromagnet core with a directional constant magnet flux. The magnetic flux closes along the contour formed by the electromagnet core. The grip passes into disconnection state (Fig. 5b). the grip goes into the connection state with a current directed in the opposite direction (Fig. 5a). New prototype experiments showed that this configuration and connector design correspond to the required characteristics of the magnetomechanical connector.

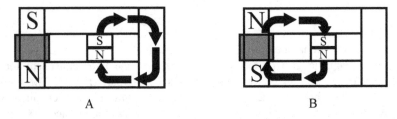

Fig. 5. The second prototype of the magnetic circuit: A – connection grip state; B– disconnection grip state.

When the control pulse was applied to transfer the grip to connection state the adhesion force was 3.7 to 7.3 kg. This is confirmed by the graph of the experiment results (Fig. 6). When the control pulse was applied to transfer the grip to disconnection state the adhesion force is less than 20 g. The adhesion force varied every experiment because of the incompletely uniform alignment of the working and counterparts. Based on the two developed magnetomechanical connector prototypes 150 experiments were executed. The obtained results were processed using interval estimation of a random variable. Based on the measurement data a statistical plot is constructed for analyzing the magnetic circuit operation (Fig. 6). An experiment series was executed with the same control pulse magnitude equal to 6 V and a current 0.17 A. It is also necessary to take into account the adhesion force applied to the grip is directed along the normal. When there are lateral, shearing forces on the magnetic grip the coupling force reduces. These effects is reduced by using the connector counterparts with a special geometric shape of the grip "key". The result processing shows the

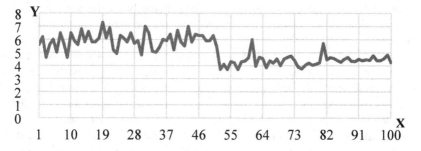

Fig. 6. Graph of the results of magnetic circuit operation with the first experiment series by the measurement number using the interval estimate of a random variable: X – number of the measurement; Y – tbreacking force for the magnetic circuit.

possible minimum and maximum breaking forces of the magnetic circuit and allows to determine its average value. Based on the results of the first experiment series the prototype design was developed providing with enough the necessary adhesion force of the magnetic circuit. Comparison of the differences between the prototype No. 1 and the prototype No. 2 is shown in Table 1.

Table 1. Comparative characteristics of the developed prototype connectors.

Prototype number	The breaking force in the connection mode, kg	The breaking force in the disconnection mode, kg	The control pulse power, v; a
№ 1	3.7	0.02	6; 0.17
№ 2	3.7	3.70	6; 0.17

That coupled with key to eliminate backlashes and loads allows one A-type connector to hold the three similar modules weight or a load with a compatible connection in the various structures formatting. For practical magnetomechanical connector use, it is advisable to use the minimum value of grip adhesion force reliable and predictable operation. The proposed magnetomechanical connector model has a high energy efficiency because it consumes a small amount of energy and only during switching operation modes.

5 Conclusion

Analysis of existing modular robotics and their compounds is presented in this work. Based on the identified advantages and disadvantages, the following results were formed:

1. A model of homogeneous modular robots, which includes a set of magnetomechanical connectors, two motor wheels and a base unit of the module, is proposed. Motor-wheels of dual purpose are intended for movement and as an auxiliary

mechanism of connection of modules among themselves. The basic module unit includes an axial servomotor, a computational unit, communication modules and batteries.

2. The model and work principle of the magnetomechanical connector based on the redirection of the constant magnet flux is proposed. A magnetomechanical connector prototype was developed. Connector provides connection between the modules by a mechanical fixing connection, a permanent magnet for connecting the modules with each other, and an electromagnet for disconnection. The proposed magnetomechanical connector model has a high energy efficiency because it consumes a small amount of energy equal to 6 V and a current 0.17 A and only at the moment of switching operating modes. Furthermore, the prototype adhesion force was 3.7 kg.

3. Two schemes for placing sets of magnetomechanical connectors are proposed. These schemes offer different possibilities for forming a plurality of modules with basic linear designs and with more complex structures of various types and purposes.

The research results will be used in the development of modular connection mechanisms for anthropomorphic robot units, in particular, for the robot Antares [29] to obtain a modular and reconfigurable design.

Acknowledgement. The research was carried out with the support of the Russian Foundation for Basic Research (No. 16-29-04101 ofi_m; № 16-37-60085).

References

1. Ivanov, A.A., Shmakov, O.A.: An algorithm for defining the inner geometry of a snakelike manipulator in case of leading link movements along the incremental trajectory. SPIIRAS Proc. **49**(6), 190–207 (2016). https://doi.org/10.15622/sp.49.10

2. Dashevskiy, V., Budkov, V., Ronzhin, A.: Survey of modular robots and developed embedded devices for constructive and computing components. In: Ronzhin, A., Rigoll, G., Meshcheryakov, R. (eds.) ICR 2017. LNCS (LNAI), vol. 10459, pp. 50–58. Springer, Cham (2017). https://doi.org/10.1007/978-3-319-66471-2_6

3. Nakagaki, K., et al.: ChainFORM: a linear integrated modular hardware system for shape changing interfaces. In: Proceedings of the 29th Annual Symposium on User Interface Software and Technology, pp. 87–96. ACM (2016). https://doi.org/10.1145/2984511.2984587

4. Romanishin, J.W., Gilpin, K., Rus, D.: M-blocks: momentum-driven, magnetic modular robots. In: IEEE International Conference on Intelligent Robots and Systems, vol. 6696971, pp. 4288–4295. IEEE (2013). https://doi.org/10.1109/iros.2013.6696971

5. Belke, C.H., Paik, J.: Mori: a modular origami robot. IEEE/ASME Trans. Mechatron. **22**(5), 2153–2164 (2017)

6. Murata, S., et al.: M-TRAN: self-reconfigurable modular robotic system. IEEE/ASME Trans. Mechatron. **7**(4), 431–441 (2002). https://doi.org/10.1109/TMECH.2002.806220

7. Saab, W., Ben-Tzvi, P.: Development of a novel coupling mechanism for modular self-reconfigurable mobile robots. In: ASME 2015 International Design Engineering Technical Conferences and Computers and Information in Engineering Conference, p. V05BT08A007 (2015). https://doi.org/10.1115/detc2015-46659

8. Chennareddy, S., Agrawal, A., Karuppiah, A.: Modular self-reconfigurable robotic systems: a survey on hardware architectures. J. Robot. (2017). https://doi.org/10.1155/2017/5013532

9. Saab, W., Ben-Tzvi, P.: A genderless coupling mechanism with six-degrees-of-freedom misalignment capability for modular self-reconfigurable robots. J. Mech. Robot. 8(6), 061014 (2016). https://doi.org/10.1115/1.4034014

10. Escalera, J.A., Mondada, F., Groß, R.: Evo-bots: a modular robotics platform with efficient energy sharing. In: Modular and Swarm Systems Workshop at IROS (2014)

11. Moubarak, P.M., Ben-Tzvi, P.: A tristate rigid reversible and non-back-drivable active docking mechanism for modular robotics. IEEE/ASME Trans. Mechatron. 19(3), 840–851 (2014). https://doi.org/10.1109/TMECH.2013.2261531

12. Liu, J., Zhang, X., Hao, G.: Survey on research and development of reconfigurable modular robots. Adv. Mech. Eng. 8(8) (2016). https://doi.org/10.1177/1687814016659597

13. Reddy, C.S.S., et al.: HexaMob — a hybrid modular robotic design for implementing biomimetic structures. Robotics 6(4), 27 (2017). https://doi.org/10.3390/robotics6040027

14. Lee, J.Y., Cho, K.J.: Development of magnet connection of modular units for soft robotics. In: 2017 14th International Conference on Ubiquitous Robots and Ambient Intelligence (URAI), pp. 65–67. IEEE (2017). https://doi.org/10.1371/journal.pone.0169179

15. Won, P., Biglarbegian, M., Melek, W.: Development of an effective docking system for modular mobile self-reconfigurable robots using extended Kalman filter and particle filter. Robotic 4(1), 25–49 (2015). https://doi.org/10.3390/robotics4010025

16. Andreev, V., Kim, V.: Control system and design of the motion module of a heterogeneous modular mobile robot. Ann. DAAAM Proc. 586–595 (2016)

17. Castillo, R.A., Gómez, D.J., Vargas, G.A.: Implementation and assembly of a robotic module for the MECABOT-3 reconfigurable system. Int. J. Appl. Eng. Res. 11(21), 10681–10684 (2016)

18. Motienko, A., Dorozhko, I., Tarasov, A., Basov, O.: Proactive robotic systems for effective rescuing sufferers. In: Ronzhin, A., Rigoll, G., Meshcheryakov, R. (eds.) ICR 2016. LNCS (LNAI), vol. 9812, pp. 172–180. Springer, Cham (2016). https://doi.org/10.1007/978-3-319-43955-6_21

19. Baca, J., et al.: Modred: Hardware design and reconfiguration planning for a high dexterity modular self-reconfigurable robot for extra-terrestrial exploration. Robot. Auton. Syst. 62(7), 1002–1015 (2014). https://doi.org/10.1016/j.robot.2013.08.008

20. Wenzel, W., Cordes, F., Kirchner, F.: A robust electro-mechanical interface for cooperating heterogeneous multi-robot teams. In: 2015 IEEE/RSJ International Conference on Intelligent Robots and Systems (IROS), pp. 1732–1737. IEEE (2015). https://doi.org/10.1109/iros.2015.7353601

21. Kumar, P., Saab, W., Ben-Tzvi, P.: Design of a multi-directional hybrid-locomotion modular robot with feedforward stability control. In: ASME 2017 International Design Engineering Technical Conferences and Computers and Information in Engineering Conference, p. V05BT08A010 (2017). https://doi.org/10.1115/detc2017-67436

22. Ronzhin, A.L., et al.: O sposobah kontaktnogo soedinenija gruppy modul"nyh robotov. Robototehnika i tehnicheskaja kibernetika 3(12), 34–41 (2016)

23. Ronzhin, A., Vatamaniuk, I., Pavluk, N.: Automatic control of robotic swarm during convex shape generation. In: Proceedings of the 2016 International Conference and Exposition on Electrical and Power Engineering, EPE 2016, vol. 9, pp. 675–680 (2016)

24. Shljahov, N.E., Vatamanjuk, I.V., Ronzhin, A.L.: Obzor metodov i algoritmov agregacii roja robotov. Mehatronika, avtomatizacija, upravlenie **18**(1), 22–29 (2017)
25. Devochkin, O.V., et al.: Jelektricheskie apparaty: ucheb. posobie dlja stud. uchrezhdenij sred. prof. obrazovanija. Electrical apparatus: training. Allowance for stud. Establishments of environments. Prof. of education, Moskva (2010)
26. Lomonosov, V., Polivanov, K.M., Mihajlov, O.P.: Jelektrotehnika. Jenergoatomizdat, Moskva (1990)
27. Flynn, C.J.: Methods for controlling the path of magnetic flux from a permanent magnet and devices incorporating the same. US Patent No: US 6,246,561 B1 (2001)
28. Flynn, J.C., et al.: Path Magnetic Technology for High Efficiency Power Generators and Motor Drives (2006). https://doi.org/10.1063/1.2169303
29. Kodyakov, A.S., et al.: Stability study of anthropomorphic robot antares under external load action. IOP Conf. Ser. J. Phys. Conf. Ser. **803**, 012074 (2017). https://doi.org/10.1088/1742-6596/803/1/012074

Trends in Development of UAV-UGV Cooperation Approaches in Precision Agriculture

Quyen Vu[1(✉)], Mirko Raković[2], Vlado Delic[2],
and Andrey Ronzhin[1,3]

[1] St. Petersburg State University of Aerospace Instrumentation,
St. Petersburg, Russia
vuquyenntk@gmail.com
[2] University of Novi Sad Faculty of Technical Sciences, Novi Sad, Serbia
[3] St. Petersburg Institute for Informatics and Automation of the Russian
Academy of Sciences, St. Petersburg, Russia

Abstract. Multiple unmanned aerial vehicle (UAV) and unmanned ground vehicle (UGV) heterogeneous cooperation provides a new breakthrough for the effective applications. UGV is generally capable of operating outdoors and over a wide variety of terrain, functioning in place of humans. Multiple UAVs can be used to cover large areas searching for targets. However, sensors on UAVs are typically limited in operating airspeed and altitude, combined with attitude uncertainty, placing a lower limit on their ability to resolve and localize ground features. UGVs on the other hand can be deployed to accurately locate ground targets, but they have the disadvantage of not being able to move rapidly or see through such obstacles as buildings or fences. Analysis of the tasks of existing UAVs in the field of agriculture is presented and main tasks of UGV in context UAV-UGV cooperation are considered.

Keywords: UAV · UGV · Heterogeneous robots · Group control
Precision agriculture

1 Introduction

Technologies involving joint activity of a group of robots and operators are nowadays actively being introduced into the agricultural sector [1]. Usually, agriculture robots are autonomous ground vehicles (tractors, combines…) that can work 24/7, and can be remotely supervised by a human sitting in one of the machines or remotely without his/her presence in the field. Among other unmanned aerial vehicles (UAVs), multicopters have the most diverse set of use cases since they do not require a runway, have a high resolution of embedded vision system and therefore have high prospects for widespread use. In addition to the on-board video camera, the multicopters can also be equipped with other sensory means, for example: a thermal imager, a thermometer, gas sensors, sonar sensors, wind speed sensors, pressure sensors, infrared and many other sensors.

© Springer Nature Switzerland AG 2018
A. Ronzhin et al. (Eds.): ICR 2018, LNAI 11097, pp. 213–221, 2018.
https://doi.org/10.1007/978-3-319-99582-3_22

A distinctive feature of agrarian robotics is the relatively stable regularity of the topology of planting of cultivated crops, in contrast to other areas of application of robots, where the objects to be managed do not have known coordinates in advance and can move in space.

The world market of agricultural robots currently has significant growth [2]. Robots are used in many stages and in various types of agriculture: field work, livestock, production and collection of food [3, 4]. The robotization of agricultural production is caused by the need to raise labor productivity, renewal of equipment and technology, the disposal of workers from physically difficult tasks.

The greatest progress in the robotization of agricultural production is now visible in the field of precise farming, the distinguishing feature of which is the local differentiation of agrotechnical influences, taking into account the spatial variability of soil and other factors of crop formation within a single agricultural field (agrocontour) [5, 6].

The goal of using a cooperative team of Unmanned Aerial Vehicles (UAVs) in monitoring missions is to minimize the elapsed time between two consecutive observations of any point in the agricultural field (AF). The techniques based on AF partitioning achieve this goal by fully utilizing capabilities of each UAV. In the literature, several approaches have been proposed to monitoring fields by using mutiple UAVs. In [7], the author considered time varying missions for each UAV. The Agent Mission Planner (AMP) has been developed to assign tasks to each UAV in the group. A novel block-sharing technique is presented in [8] to accelerate the convergence to an optimal partition. The approach developed in [9] utilizes an ambient light display (ALD) to continuously externalize the commander's monitoring performance using ambient visual cues in the peripheral field. However, non of the aforementioned works considered the joint functioning of groups of heterogeneous unmanned vehicles (UAVs and mobile unmanned ground vehicles (UGVs)).

High precision navigation is usually crucial for unmanned aerial vehicles' (UAV) fruit picking applications. The support UAVs needs to provide highly accurate location of the fruits in three-dimensional agricultural fields, otherwise the service UAVs can harm the threes or cannot pick the fruit properly. Using Global Positioning Systems (GPS) for this application may not work. Therefore, Local Navigation Systems (LNS) are generated for UAVs in several works [10–12].

Due to their three-dimensional mobility, unmanned aerial vehicles (UAVs) serve a large number of specialized roles, which often involve work in hazardous environments, carrying payloads and using sensors or cameras to survey areas [13]. A large amount of research is being carried out regarding improving the capabilities of UAVs. Pairing UAVs with UGVs in heterogeneous teams of robots is an idea that has seen recent research.

Different vehicles in a heterogeneous robot group have the ability to compensate for the weaknesses of each other. The load that aerial vehicles can carry is limited compared to ground-based vehicles. Similarly, ground-based vehicles often have limited mobility compared to aerial vehicles. In the context of an UAV-UGV team, these specific attributes could enable the pair to serve a role, where the UGV – capable of carrying heavier loads – would be used as a base vehicle. In several publications, the base vehicle is often presented as a vertical take-off and landing (VTOL) pad [13–15].

2 Analysis of the Tasks of Existing UAVs in the Field of Agriculture

At the beginning, a classification of existing UAV solutions applied in agriculture was considered. There are basically two types of UAVs available at the moment: rotary wings and fixed wings. Rotary wing UAV is able to hover and also move directly sideways. Fixed-wing UAV, by contrast, has a positive minimum velocity constraint due to stall condition, bounded maximum velocity because of thrust limitation and saturated angular velocity. As a result, although fixed wing UAVs under specific conditions can be modeled like mobile robots, their limitations are completely different. More recently, new generation of fixed wing UAVs has been introduced with the hovering property. Thus they enjoy the advantages of speed and endurance of the classic fixed-wing UAVs and hovering and vertical takeoff and landing of rotary wing UAVs, simultaneously [16].

Dominant type of the commercially available UAVs that are currently used in agricultural applications are devices designed for different imaging tasks. On the other hand, UAVs that are specifically designed for precision spraying or other tasks that involve some planned actions are still very rare. As the best representative of the first group can be considered a range of products provided by the Chinese company DJI (https://www.dji.com), which enable easy customization and mounting of different sensor equipment selected by the user. Depending on the specific application such frameworks can include different levels of automation and in some cases require visual interpretation by the human expert. Therefore, dedicated software usually aims just for the appropriate visualization (https://pix4d.com) and adequate preprocessing of the raw data intended for the later analysis. Table 1 shows the existing UAVs used in agriculture.

Table 1. Existing UAVs used in agriculture.

Name	UAV Type	Main task	Engine type	Empty/Max. takeoff weight (kg)	Flight time (min)	Max. flight range (km)
Agrofly TF1A	Rotary Wing	Spraying	Electric	10,2/22,5	9–11	1
MCA-6	Rotary Wing	Spraying	Electric	10/20	12	0,5
DJI Agras MG-1	Rotary Wing	Spraying	Electric	8.8/22.5	10–24	NA
Yamaha RMAX	Rotary Wing	Spraying	Internal combustion engine	78/94	NA	35
DJI Matrice 200	Rotary Wing	Monitoring	Electric	3.75/5.75	38	7
eBee Plus	Fixed wing	Aerial photography	Electric	1.1	59	3–8
RIEGL VUX-1UAV	Rotary Wing	Monitoring	Electric	11/14	30	550 m

(*continued*)

Table 1. (*continued*)

Name	UAV Type	Main task	Engine type	Empty/Max. takeoff weight (kg)	Flight time (min)	Max. flight range (km)
eBee SQ	Fixed wing	Aerial photography	Electric	1.1	55	3
Luftera LT-1	Rotary Wing	Cartography	Electric	5/6	120	15
MIIGAiK X4	Rotary Wing	Cartography	Electric	1/1.5	90	2
Burevestnik	Fixed wing	Monitoring	Internal combustion engine	180/250	6–10 h	290
OCA	Rotary Wing	Spraying	Electric	20/30	NA	NA
AC-32-10	Fixed wing	Monitoring	Electric	10.5/13.5	240	240
AC-32-12	Fixed wing	Monitoring	Electric	9.5/13.5	4,5 h	140
Sapsan-3000	Fixed wing	Monitoring	Electric	9/11	4–5 h	40
3 M	Fixed wing	Video monitoring	Gas	12/20	60	20
Gamma	Fixed wing	Aerial photography	Internal combustion engine	25/50	12 h	50
Delta-M	Fixed wing	Aerial photography	Electric	7.25/9	150	50
Supercam X6	Rotary Wing	Video monitoring	Electric	1.5/1.8	40	5
Geoscane 201 Agro	Fixed wing	Aerial photography	Electric	7/8.5	180	210

UAV engines include electric motors, internal combustion engines and gasoline engines. More popular are UAVs with electric motors with a payload of less than 10 kg. UAVs with internal combustion engines are used for large loads and long flight times (Burevestnik, Gamma).

Aside from the described functional role of such UAVs in the specific imaging task, their design can vary from multi-, single-rotor to fixed-wing, or hybrid, which determines their maneuverability and overall flight characteristics. Depending on the specific requirements established by the imaging sensor, environment and particular agricultural application, different designs can be preferred (www.sensefly.com, www. sentera.com/phx-uav/, www.carbonix.com.au/aerospace). Significant impact on the cost of the vehicle also has the level of flight automation and the optional mission planning capabilities. Flight trajectory is usually predetermined by the geometry of the field, sensor characteristics and the pre-specified spatial resolution of the final image or the resulting model of the scene that is derived from the measurements.

In comparison to such platforms, the second type of UAVs as the primary task has some action in the field, which can be partially planned in advance based on the detailed analysis with information from multiple sources, or can be mostly based on the real time on-board processing of the data stream from the imaging sensor that is mounted on the same flying platform. Some examples include Yamaha's single-rotor vehicles like the product labeled as RMAX (www.yamahamotorsports.com/motorsports/pages/precision-agriculture), or the DJI's solution AGRAS MG-1 (https://www.dji.com/mg-1). However, both of these platforms can potentially have an inadequate payload capacity for some large scale spraying tasks or high intensity spraying. This brings up a question of action optimization and the design of an adequate utility function for the specific agricultural task. RMAX can carry 2x13 l, while the DJI's capacity is 10 l.

Further specific tasks of the UAV in the present and future will be considered. UAVs are currently used for tasks such as spraying (Agrofly TF1A, MCA-6, DJI Agras MG-1, OCA6 Yamaha RMAX), field surveys (DJI Matrice 200), aerial photography (eBee Plus, eBee SQ, Gamma, Delta-M, Geoscane 201 Agro), monitoring (RIEGL VUX-1UAV, Burevestnik, AC-32-10, AC-32-12, Sapsan-3000), cartography (Luftera LT-1, MIIGAiK X4), video monitoring (3 M, Supercam X6), etc.

Looking further into the future, UAVs might involve fleets, or swarms, of autonomous drones that could tackle agricultural monitoring tasks collectively, as well as hybrid aerial-ground drone actors that could collect data and perform a variety of tasks, such as:

- Aerial survey of lands from drones, including multispectral survey.
- Ecological monitoring of agricultural lands.
- Creation of electronic maps of fields.
- Assessment of the scope of work and constant monitoring of their implementation.
- Determination of boundaries and areas of sites where agricultural work was carried out.
- Flying around the fields to monitor the work of hired personnel, the location and use of agricultural machinery.
- Support of land reclamation, monitoring of irrigation systems.
- Formation of maps of the relief of agricultural fields, determination of directions of water erosion.
- Inventory of crops and fields, establishment of an objective area of arable land, as well as hayfields, pastures, perennial grasses, deposits.
- Determination of the actual area of sowing, under-sowing.
- Monitoring of the introduction of seed and emergence of agricultural plants, monitoring the germination of crops, rapid determination of seedling quality and development of crops during the period of vegetation with the subsequent calculation of the normalized vegetative index.
- Determination of the need for the application of fertilizers. This makes it possible to optimize (reduce) the application of fertilizers – to fertilize and fertilize fertilizers.
- Objective area for harvesting in the context of crops, yield forecast for this area.
- Determination of areas of contamination or diseases of crops, the degree of contamination.
- Phytosanitary control.
- Spraying landings from a drone.
- Documentation of damage from natural disasters.
- Protection of harvest on the field.

3 The Main Tasks of UGV in Context UAV - UGV Cooperation

UGV should provide basic logistics and working autonomy for the UAVs, but also high level interaction with the user. Depending on the type of agricultural field and terrain characteristics it should determine the optimal position for the initial deployment of the units and their supply. Depending on the requirements it should also load-off some of the data processing on the flying units. Since UGV could be autonomous, and potentially be moving through the field, it could also be equipped with ground sensors to enhance the overall decision process.

The team strategy of the multi-robot system is the following: the UGV carries the UAV on own platform, and when it is required, the UAV takes-off, performs some tasks and lands on the UGV. The main tasks that are performed by UGV:

- Communicates with the UAV and the operator of the farm.
- Serves as a mobile docking and charging station for UAVs.
- UGV, equipped with a suitable end actuator, enters the field in cooperation with the UAV and applies precision processing.

The use of a UGV as a landing surface for a UAV is an example of physical cooperation. Autonomous takeoff is mostly a problem that involves the UAV self-stabilizing and reaching a desired altitude [17]. In reality, the problem has certain cognitive elements, such as tracking and target localization [18–20]. Increasing the robot number in the group leads to increasing the control complexity [21–23].

UAV/UGV still require human service before, after and during mission. User should usually check basic components and provide sufficient fuel/energy for the task. By this reason investigation of ergonomic user interface are continued [24–30]. In the case of multiple sensors the platform could suggest the most appropriate procedure based on the archived book of the field, which would require the user to mount appropriate equipment and perform calibration sequence. The ground platform could be multi-purpose and adaptable to different use scenarios. Since spraying chemicals can be potentially hazardous the platform should also enable storing and manipulation of such content according to currently active or planned safety standards.

4 Conclusion

An analysis of the tasks of existing UAVs in the field of agriculture is presented in this paper. The main tasks of UGV in context UAV-UGV cooperation are considered in more details.

The commercially available UAVs that are currently used in agricultural applications are devices designed for tasks such as spraying, field surveys, aerial photography, monitoring, cartography, video monitoring. The highest impact of the precision spraying by UAVs from the user's perspective should be expected in the case of high value crops such as vegetables, fruits or flowers, in the case of the widely grown crops the cost of spraying per field area could be higher than the potential gain. Such consideration should be taken into account during platform optimization stage. Therefore, it is quite possible that there will be the need for the specific agricultural expertise in order to have an estimate of the influencing parameters such as spraying frequency, required spray solution concentration, influence of the volatile weather conditions on the spraying duration and spraying time.

Unmanned ground vehicle (UGV) is generally capable of operating outdoors and over a wide variety of terrain, functioning in place of humans. Multiple UAVs can be used to cover large areas searching for targets. However, sensors on UAVs are typically limited in operating airspeed and altitude, combined with attitude uncertainty, placing a lower limit on their ability to resolve and localize ground features. UGVs on the other hand can be deployed to accurately locate ground targets, but they have the disadvantage of not being able to move rapidly or see through such obstacles as buildings or fences. Therefore, multiple UAV/UGV heterogeneous cooperation provides a new breakthrough for the effective application of UAVs and UGVs.

Acknowledgments. This work is partially supported by the Russian Foundation for Basic Research (grant № 18-58-76001_ERA.Net) in the framework of the ERA.Net Plus Project 99-HARMONIC.

References

1. Bechar, A., Vigneault, C.: Agricultural robots for field operations: Concepts and components. Biosys. Eng. **149**, 94–111 (2016)
2. Wolfert, S., Ge, L., Verdouwa, C., Bogaardt, M.J.: Big Data in smart farming – a review. Agric. Syst. **153**, 69–80 (2017)
3. Perez-Ruiz, M., Slaughter, D.C., Fathallah, F.A., Gliever, C.J., Miller, B.J.: Co-robotic intra-row weed control system. Biosys. Eng. **126**, 45–55 (2014)
4. Holloway, L., Bear, C., Wilkinson, K.: Re-capturing bovine life: Robot-cow relationships, freedom and control in dairy farming. J. Rural Stud. **33**, 131–140 (2014)
5. Afanas'ev, R.A., Ermolov, I.L.: Future of robots for precision agriculture. Mechatron. Autom. Manage. **12**, 828–833 (2016)
6. Sidorova, V.A., Zhukovsky, E.E., Lekomtsev, P.V., Yakushev, V.V.: Geostatistical analysis of soil characteristics and productivity in the field experiment on precise agriculture. Agrochemistry Fertil. Soils **8**, 879–888 (2012)
7. Sampedro, C.: A flexible and dynamic mission planning architecture for UAV swarm coordination. In: 2016 International Conference on Unmanned Aircraft Systems (ICUAS), Arlington, pp. 355–363 (2016). https://doi.org/10.1109/ICUAS.2016.7502669
8. Caraballo, L.E. et al.: The block-sharing strategy for area monitoring missions using a decentralized multi-UAV system. In: 2014 International Conference on Unmanned Aircraft Systems (ICUAS), Orlando, FL, pp. 602–610 (2014). https://doi.org/10.1109/ICUAS.2014.6842303
9. Fortmann, F., Muller, H., Ludtke, A., and Boll, S.: Expert-based design and evaluation of an ambient light display to improve monitoring performance during multi-UAV supervisory control. In: 2015 IEEE International Multi-Disciplinary Conference on Cognitive Methods in Situation Awareness and Decision, Orlando, FL, pp. 28–34 (2015)

10. Mingguo, Z., Chengdong, W., and Dongyue, C.: UAV image identification in urban region satellite image using global feature and local feature. In: 2016 Chinese Control and Decision Conference (CCDC), Yinchuan, pp. 5377–5382 (2016). https://doi.org/10.1109/CCDC.2016.7531959
11. Chen, T., Li, X., Cong, Y., Qian, S.: UAV formation visual navigation algorithm based on determination sampling type filter. In: 12th IEEE International Conference on Electronic Measurement & Instruments (ICEMI 2015), Qingdao, pp. 747–752 (2015). https://doi.org/10.1109/ICEMI.2015.7494322
12. Ziyang, Z., Qiushi, H., Chen, G., Ju, J.: Information fusion distributed navigation for UAVs formation flight. In: Proceedings of 2014 IEEE Chinese Guidance, Navigation and Control Conference, Yantai, pp. 1520–1525 (2014). https://doi.org/10.1109/cgncc.2014.7007417
13. Wargo, C.A., Church, G.C., Glaneueski, J., Strout, M.: Unmanned aircraft systems (UAS) research and future analysis. In: 2014 IEEE Aerospace Conference, 2014, pp. 1–16 (2014). https://doi.org/10.1109/AERO.2014.6836448
14. Langerwisch, M., Wittmann, T., Thamke, S., Remmersmann, T., Tiderko, A., Wagner, B.: Heterogeneous teams of unmanned ground and aerial robots for reconnaissance and surveillance - a field experiment. In: IEEE International Symposium on Safety, Security, and Rescue Robotics (SSRR 2013), pp. 1–6 (2013). https://doi.org/10.1109/SSRR.2013.6719320
15. Harik, E.H.C., Guérin, F., Guinand, F., Brethé, J.F., Pelvillain, H.: UAVUGV cooperation for objects transportation in an industrial area. In: IEEE International Conference on Industrial Technology (ICIT 2015), pp. 547–552 (2015). https://doi.org/10.1109/ICIT.2015.7125156
16. Tokekar, P., Hook, J.V., Mulla, D., and Isler, V.: Sensor planning for a symbiotic UAV and UGV system for precision agriculture, 6(32), 1498–1511 (2016). https://doi.org/10.1109/TRO.2016.2603528
17. Hui, C., Yousheng, C., Xiaokun, L., Shing, W.W.: Autonomous takeoff, tracking and landing of a UAV on a moving UGV using onboard monocular vision. In: Proceedings of the 32nd Chinese Control Conference, pp. 5895–5901 (2013)
18. Ghamry, K.A., Dong, Y., Kamel, M.A., Zhang Y.: Real-time autonomous take-off, tracking and landing of UAV on a moving UGV platform. In: 24th Mediterranean Conference on Control and Automation (MED 2016), pp. 1236–1241 (2016). https://doi.org/10.1109/MED.2016.7535886
19. Fu, M., Zhang, K., Yi, Y., and Shi, C.: Autonomous landing of a quadrotor on an UGV. In: IEEE International Conference on Mechatronics and Automation, pp. 988–993 (2016). https://doi.org/10.1109/ICMA.2016.7558697
20. Marchini, B.D.: Adaptive control techniques for transition to hover flight of fixed-wing UAVs (Master's thesis). California Polytechnic State University (2013)
21. Guzey, H.M.: Adaptive consensus-based formation control of fixed-wing MUAV's. In: Proceedings of IEEE 4th International Conference on Actual Problems of Unmanned Aerial Vehicles Developments, APUAVD 2017, pp. 184–187 (2018)
22. Andreev, V.P., Pletenev, P.F.: Method of information interaction for distributed control systems of robots with modular architecture. SPIIRAS Proc. 57(2), 134–160 (2018). https://doi.org/10.15622/sp.57.6
23. Vatamaniuk, I., Panina, G., Saveliev, A., Ronzhin, A.: Convex shape generation by robotic swarm. In: Proceedings of 2016 International Conference on Autonomous Robot Systems and CoΠmpetitions, ICARSC 2016. pp. 300–304 (2016). https://doi.org/10.1109/icarsc.2016.33

24. Jokisch, O., Huber, M.: Advances in the development of a cognitive user interface. In: 13th International Conference on Electromechanics and Robotics "Zavalishin's Readings", ER (ZR) 2018. MATEC Web of Conferences. vol. 161, paper 1003, (2018). https://doi.org/10.1051/matecconf/201816101003

25. Strutz, T., Leipnitz, A.: Adaptive colour-space selection in high efficiency video coding. In: 25th European Signal Processing Conference, EUSIPCO 2017, pp. 1534–1538 (2017)

26. Vatamaniuk, I., Levonevskiy, D., Saveliev, A., Denisov, A.: Scenarios of multimodal information navigation services for users in cyberphysical environment. In: Ronzhin, A., Potapova, R., Németh, G. (eds.) SPECOM 2016. LNCS (LNAI), vol. 9811, pp. 588–595. Springer, Cham (2016). https://doi.org/10.1007/978-3-319-43958-7_71

27. Rakhmanenko, I.A., Meshcheryakov, R.V.: Identification features analysis in speech data using GMM-UBM speaker verification system. SPIIRAS Proc. **3**(52), 32–50 (2017)

28. Levonevskiy, D., Vatamaniuk, I., Saveliev, A.: Integration of corporate electronic services into a smart space using temporal logic of actions. In: Ronzhin, A., Rigoll, G., Meshcheryakov, R. (eds.) ICR 2017. LNCS (LNAI), vol. 10459, pp. 134–143. Springer, Cham (2017). https://doi.org/10.1007/978-3-319-66471-2_15

29. Ivanko, D., et al.: Using a high-speed video camera for robust audio-visual speech recognition in acoustically noisy conditions. In: Karpov, A., Potapova, R., Mporas, I. (eds.) SPECOM 2017. LNCS (LNAI), vol. 10458, pp. 757–766. Springer, Cham (2017). https://doi.org/10.1007/978-3-319-66429-3_76

30. Pakoci, E., Popović, B., Pekar, D.J.: Improvements in Serbian speech recognition using sequence-trained deep neural networks. SPIIRAS Proc. **58**(3), 53–76 (2018). https://doi.org/10.15622/sp.58.3

Structural Analysis and Animated Simulation of Biotechnical Position-Velocity Control System of a Robot-Manipulator

Ekaterina Rostova[1,3(✉)], Nikolay Rostov[2], and Boris Sokolov[1,3]

[1] St. Petersburg Institute for Informatics and Automation of the Russian Academy of Sciences, 14th Line V.O. 39, 199178 St. Petersburg, Russia
rostovae@mail.ru, sokolov_boris@inbox.ru
[2] Peter the Great St. Petersburg Polytechnic University, Polytechnicheskaya Str. 29, 195251 St. Petersburg, Russia
rostovnv@mail.ru
[3] ITMO University, Kronverksky Pr. 49, 197101 St. Petersburg, Russia

Abstract. The comparative analysis of different types of structures of algorithms for a robot-manipulator control has been performed for the open-loop and closed-loop semi-automatic control by the gripper velocity and position vectors. Computer models have been developed for a position-velocity control system with reconfigurable structure of algorithms for a robot performing standard operations set by a human operator with a 3-degree-of-freedom handle. In the developed models an operator is represented by a vector dynamic element with dead time. Animated simulation of dynamic processes in systems with different structures of control algorithms has been performed and their precision characteristics have been evaluated. Some practical recommendations are given on the application of the achieved results for the development of training simulators for operators of robot control systems.

Keywords: Biotechnical systems · Robot-manipulator · Human operator
Semi-automatic control system · Position-velocity control
Computer simulation

1 Introduction

In biotechnical robot control systems (BRCS) a human operator (HO) performs remote control of a robot using a master manipulator or handles with multi-degree of freedom like joysticks with special calculator units. Such master-slave and semi-automatic control systems (CS), in which an operator is considered as a part of a robot CS, are widely used at space stations, in underwater vehicles, etc. [1–6]. These systems can be applied for real-time robot control and installed on training simulators for HO.

One of the theoretical problems of BRCS modeling is a description of a HO as a part of a system. There are different approaches to the description of a HO interacting with a robot-manipulator and different types of models can be used for that. One of the main weaknesses of the approaches to simulation given in works [3–5] is inadequate description of a HO functioning as a subsystem within a whole BRCS. But for the adequate

A. Ronzhin et al. (Eds.): ICR 2018, LNAI 11097, pp. 222–232, 2018.
https://doi.org/10.1007/978-3-319-99582-3_23

simulation of a HO it is necessary to consider the operation mode of a CS as well. Another important practical issue that should also be considered is the development of training simulators for HO (astronauts, surgeons, etc.) [8, 9, 13].

In semi-automatic systems different algorithms of robot motion control are implemented depending on a type of technological operations performed [4, 5]. For transportation operations that do not require high accuracy, the gripper velocity control is usually used, while for precise point-to-point and continuous-path control it is necessary to use the gripper position control. When contact operations are performed (e.g. assembling) the control of force and torque in a robot gripper is required [10].

In this paper we consider a semi-automatic CS for a robot-manipulator with reconfigurable structure in which different control algorithms are combined. Depending on operation mode, actuators of robot links are local CSs for regulation of motor speeds and position servosystems with digital PI and PID regulators. The purpose of the work is the structural analysis of different types of algorithms applied in the CS and the study of its dynamics in typical operational modes of a robot.

The main tasks of the research are the following:

1. The structural analysis of algorithms for vector open-loop and closed-loop velocity and position control of the robot gripper trajectory.
2. The design of computer models for the analysis of dynamic processes in CS under consideration in standard operational modes with the use of dynamic models of HO.
3. Animated simulation of the CS for the robot performing the following standard operations: transportation of the gripper to a specified area in the velocity control mode; precise point-to-point positioning of the gripper into the start point of a specified trajectory; the gripper movement along a trajectory in continuous-path control mode.
4. The evaluation of dynamic and contour errors that occur when moving along the trajectory in given operation modes.

For the comparative analysis of different types of structures, it is acceptable to use simplified models of the manipulator and joint actuators. Thus, for the solution of the above stated tasks we used only kinematic models of the manipulator without the consideration of its nonlinear dynamics, and the drives were represented by linear dynamical models of the 2nd and 3rd order. The animation of links of the handle and the robot was performed using functions from Robotics Toolbox [14, 15]. The simplified models can be implemented in training simulators.

2   Structural Analysis of Robot Gripper Vector Control Algorithms

2.1   The Algorithms of Robot Gripper Velocity Control

Velocity control includes the sequential solution of the following problems [7, 11, 12]:

(1)   The forward kinematics problem related to the handle position:

$$S_h = F_h(q_h) = (X_h, Y_h, Z_h)^T, \tag{1}$$

where q_h – the vector of the handle joint positions, $F_h(q_h)$ – the vector-function corresponding to the handle kinematics scheme. In this control mode the calculated coordinates X_h, Y_h, Z_h are interpreted as the velocity vector coordinates set by a HO.

(2) Scaling the programmed velocity of the robot gripper:

$$V_p = (V_{xp}, V_{yp}, V_{zp})^T = (M_{vx}X_h, M_{vy}Y_h, M_{vz}Z_h)^T. \tag{2}$$

(3) The inverse kinematics problem related to the programmed robot joint velocities:

$$\dot{q}_p = J_M^{-1}(q)V_p, \tag{3}$$

where q – the vector of the robot joint positions, $J_M^{-1}(q)$ – the matrix inversed to the Jacobi matrix of the robot-manipulator.

Figure 1 illustrates the Simulink model of the open-loop velocity CS. The model includes the following blocks: *Human-Handle Interface* calculates expressions (1) and (2); *ikine_V* calculates the programmed robot joint velocities using expression (3); *Velocity Drives* contains the models of the robot link velocity drives; *fkine_P* solves the forward kinematics problem related to the gripper position:

$$S_r = F_M(q_r) = (X_r, Y_r, Z_r)^T, \tag{4}$$

where q_r – the vector of the real robot joint positions, $F_M(q_r)$ – the vector-function corresponding to the manipulator kinematics scheme; block *fkine_V* solves the forward kinematics problem related to the gripper velocity:

$$V_r = J_M(q)\dot{q}, \tag{5}$$

where $\dot{q}$ – the vector of the robot joint velocities, $J_M(q)$ – to the Jacobi matrix of the robot-manipulator.

It is possible to simulate the system with two structures of algorithms of the open-loop velocity control using the switch unit shown in Fig. 1. For the first structure the Jacobi matrix is calculated in block *ikine_V* using the programmed robot joint positions that are obtained by integrating the programmed velocities $\dot{q}_p$. For the second structure – by the real robot joint velocities.

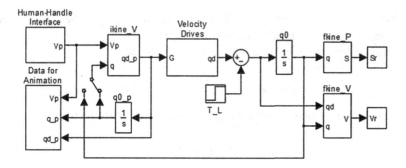

Fig. 1. The model of the open-loop velocity control system.

Figure 2 shows the Simulink model of the closed-loop velocity CS with the feedback closed through block *fkine_V*. Block *PID-V* is the vector of PID-regulators of the gripper velocity coordinates. Block *ikine_V* calculates the input actions for the robot joint velocity drives.

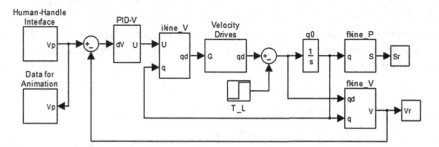

Fig. 2. The model of the closed-loop velocity control system.

Block *T_L* in the models in Figs. 1 and 2 simulates external stepwise disturbances. These disturbances imitate the influence of the load torques which decrease robot joints velocities in dynamic processes. Unlike the traditional open-loop structures (Fig. 1), the suggested closed-loop structure of the system (Fig. 2) enables greater precision of the robot operating in the velocity control mode due to coordinated multivariable control of the robot link drives.

2.2   The Algorithms of Robot Gripper Position Control

Robot gripper position control includes the sequential solution of the following problems [7, 11, 12]:

(1)   The forward kinematics problem related to the handle position:

$$S_h = F_h(q_h) = (X_h, Y_h, Z_h)^{\mathrm{T}}, \tag{6}$$

where q_h – the vector of the handle joint positions, $F_h(q_h)$ – the vector-function corresponding to the handle kinematics scheme.

(2) Scaling the programmed position of the robot gripper:

$$S_p = \left(X_p, Y_p, Z_p \right)^{\mathrm{T}} = \left(M_x, X_h, M_y Y_h, M_z Z_h \right)^{\mathrm{T}}. \tag{7}$$

(3) The inverse kinematics problem related to the programmed joint positions:

$$q_p = F_M^{-1}(S_p), \tag{8}$$

where q – the vector of the robot joint positions, $F_M^{-1}(q)$ – the vector-function inversed to the vector-function $F_M(q)$ of the manipulator.

Figure 3 illustrates the Simulink model of the open-loop position CS: block *Human-Handle Interface* calculates expressions (6) and (7); *ikine_P* calculates the programmed robot joint positions, which are the input actions for the position drives of the robot links, using expression (8); *Position Drives* contains the models of the robot link position drives; *fkine_P* solves the forward kinematics problem related to the gripper position using expression (4); *ikine_V* calculates programmed gripper velocities using expression (3) in order to compensate for velocity errors when the robot operates in continuous-path control mode.

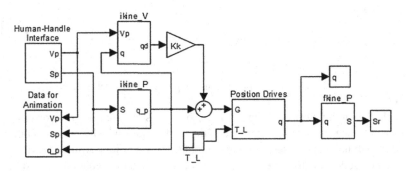

Fig. 3. The model of the open-loop position control system.

Figure 4 shows the Simulink model of the closed-loop position CS with the feedback closed through block *fkine_P*. Block *Kp* is the vector of P-regulators of the gripper position coordinates; *Kk* is the vector of compensators; *ikine_V* calculates the input actions for the robot joint velocity drives. The second block *ikine_V* is used in the vector compensator channel in order to minimize velocity errors when the robot operates in continuous-path control mode.

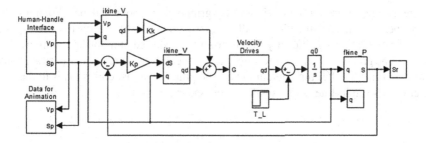

Fig. 4. The model of the closed-loop position control system.

Unlike the traditional open-loop structures (Fig. 3), the suggested closed-loop structure of the system (Fig. 4) enables greater precision of the robot operating in the position control mode due to coordinated multivariable control of the robot link drives.

2.3 Human Operator Modeling

The simplest dynamic model of a HO for digital control system simulation is the linear discrete-time model in the form of transfer function with dead time:

$$W_{op}(z) = \frac{B_{op}(z)}{A_{op}(z)} z^{-d}, \tag{9}$$

where $A_{op}(z)$ and $B_{op}(z)$ are some polynomials, d is the number of time intervals in the operator's reaction time delay $\tau_{op} = d \cdot T_o$, T_o – the interval of time discretization.

The dynamic blocks (9) with polynomials of the 2nd order are included in the blocks *Human-Handle Interface* of the developed models (Figs. 1, 2, 3 and 4). Also, nonlinear time functions are included for every coordinate of the handle position vector corresponding to the robot operation mode.

3   The Research of Dynamic Processes in the Biotechnical System of Robot Position-Velocity Control

3.1   The Analysis of Processes in the Biotechnical Velocity Control System When the Robot Performs a Transportation Operation

When the robot performs some transportation in the velocity control mode a HO quickly turns the handle keeping it in this position and then quickly returns it in the initial position. In this case the trajectories of handle links have trapezoidal shape.

The results of simulation for three structures of the system are given below: 1 – for the open-loop control with calculation of the Jacobi matrix by the programmed robot joint positions (the switch in Fig. 1 is set to the right); 2 – for the open-loop control with calculation of the Jacobi matrix by the real robot joint positions (the switch in Fig. 1 is set to the left); 3 – for the closed-loop control (Fig. 2).

Figure 5 represents the animations of the gripper and robot when the robot transports the gripper in a required direction for all three structures. The blue curve that corresponds to the first structure significantly differs from the required straight-line motion of the gripper. The green curve that corresponds to the second structure is close to straight-line motion but has a rather big contour error. The pink curve that corresponds to the third structure is straight-line with a small contour error.

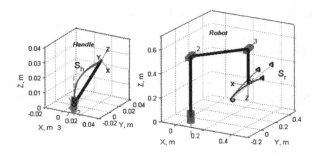

Fig. 5. The animation of the handle and the robot for three algorithms of velocity control. (Color figure online)

Figure 6 shows the curves of the gripper velocity coordinates for the third structure where the programmed coordinates are represented by the dash line (p) and the real coordinates – by the solid line (r).

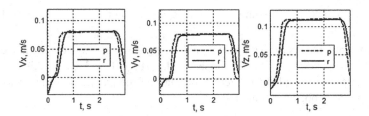

Fig. 6. The gripper velocity coordinates for the closed-loop velocity control.

The gripper velocity coordinates have rather big errors at the beginning of the motion because of the influence of external disturbances on the load torques in the drives imitated in the block T_L and, in addition, because of the HO dead time reaction. So, to decrease these errors it is recommended to switch from initial position mode to velocity control mode with the time delay $\tau > \tau_{op}$.

3.2   The Analysis of Processes in a Point-to-Point Motion of the Robot Gripper

HO smoothly turns the handle from the initial position to the required position. The handle link trajectories are calculated by the polynomials of the 5th order. The simulation results were obtained for open-loop (Fig. 3) and closed-loop (Fig. 4) position control, when the external disturbances in the drives were not taken into account.

Figure 7 shows the animations of the gripper and robot when the gripper is positioned to the required point. The blue curve corresponds to the open-loop position control and the pink curve – to the closed-loop position control.

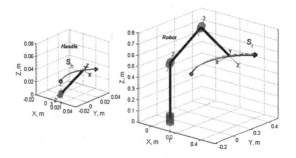

Fig. 7. The animation of the robot point-to-point motion for two algorithms of position control. (Color figure online)

Figure 8 represents the gripper position coordinates for this structure of the system where programmed coordinates are shown with the dash line (p) and the real coordinates – with the solid line (r).

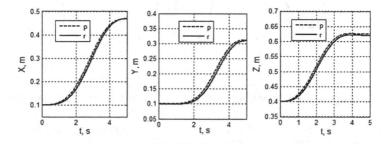

Fig. 8. The gripper position coordinates in the closed-loop system for a point-to-point motion.

The closed-loop position CS provides the gripper position with smaller dynamic errors. As it can be seen from Fig. 8 in the final position of the gripper is reached without error.

3.3   The Analysis of Processes in a Continuous-Path Motion of the Robot Gripper

In the continuous-path mode a skillful HO moves the handle along the required trajectory of a complex shape, e.g. a helical line. Figure 9 illustrates the animations of the gripper and robot when the gripper should move along the helical line for two structures of the system. The blue curve corresponds to the open-loop position control and the pink curve – to the closed-loop position control.

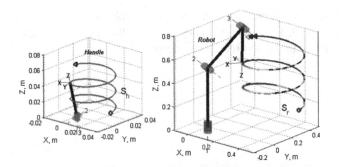

Fig. 9. The animation of the robot continuous-path motion for two algorithms of position control. (Color figure online)

Figure 10 represents the curves of the gripper position coordinates for the closed-loop structure of the system where programmed coordinates are shown with the dash line (p) and the real coordinates – with the solid line (r).

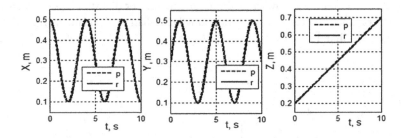

Fig. 10. The gripper position coordinates in the closed-loop system for continuous-path motion.

Figure 11 shows the curves of dynamic errors of the gripper trajectory for the open-loop and closed-loop CS calculated by the following formula:

$$E = \sqrt{\left(X_p - X_r\right)^2 + \left(Y_p - Y_r\right)^2 + \left(Z_p - Z_r\right)^2}. \tag{10}$$

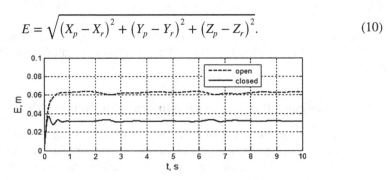

Fig. 11. The dynamic errors of the gripper trajectory of a continuous-path motion.

The curves of errors for the open-loop and closed-loop control are shown with the dash line (open) and with the solid line (closed).

The closed-loop CS gives a smaller dynamic error for the gripper trajectory. In addition, the analysis of gripper trajectories in Fig. 9 shows that the closed-loop control system enables a smaller contour (geometrical) error compared to the open-loop control system due to coordinated multivariable position control of the robot link drives.

4 Conclusion

The comparative analysis of different algorithm structures has shown that it is reasonable to build biotechnical systems with reconfigurable structures. The results of simulation have proved that closed-loop algorithms of position and velocity control enable smaller dynamic and contour errors in comparison with open-loop algorithms.

The developed computer models of the position-velocity CS allow to perform operations set by a HO in standard operation modes taking in the account the HO dynamics. In the developed models a HO is represented as a vector of dynamic elements with dead time. Since the parameters of the models were not specified for a certain robot, the error estimations obtained in the process of computer simulation are comparative.

The developed computer models can be implemented in training simulators for HOs of BRCS in real time mode. From the ergonomic point of view, the animation of both the handle and the manipulator on the control panel monitor can increase the effectiveness of HO work.

Acknowledgments. The research outlined in this paper is partially supported by the Russian Science Foundation - grant #16-19-00199 (Sects. 1 and 2 of the paper) and the state project #0073-2018-0003 (Sects. 3 and 4 of the paper).

References

1. Soares, B.F.: Master-slave servo-bilateral control of direct drive electrical manipulators. In: ABCM Symposium Series in Mechatronics, vol. 3, pp. 246–255 (2008)
2. Golovin, V.F., Arkhipov, M.V., Zhuravlev, V.V.: Ergaticheskie i biotekhnicheskie sistemy upravleniya v meditsinskoy robototekhnike. Mekhatronika Avtomatizatsiya Upravlenie **5**(12), 54–56 (2011)
3. Petukhov, I.V.: Issledovanie sensorno-motornogo vzaimodeystviya cheloveka-operatora i tekhnicheskoy sistemy. Mekhatronika Avtomatizatsiya Upravlenie **2**(12), 33–37 (2012)
4. Filaretov, V.F., Katsurin, A.A.: Method of semiautomatic combined control by manipulator using mobile telecamera. In: Proceedings on 11th International Conference on Control, Automation and Systems, pp. 649–654. KINTEX, Gyeonggi-do (2011)
5. Filaretov, V.F., Katsurin, A.A.: Method of semiautomatic position control by manipulator using telecamera which changes its orientation. Adv. Mater. Res. **717**, 573–578 (2013)
6. Wall, J., Chandra, V., Krummel, T.: Robotics in general surgery. In: Medical Robotics, pp. 491–506. InTech, Rijeka (2008)
7. Zenkevich, S.L., Yuschenko, A.S.: Osnovy upravleniya manipulyatsionnymi robotami. MSTU by name N. E. Bauman, Moscow (2005)

8. Strashnov, E.V., Torgashev, M.A.: Modelirovanie dinamiki electroprivodov virtualnykh robotov v imitatsionno-trenazhernykh kompleksakh. Mekhatronika Avtomatizatsiya Upravlenie **11**(12), 762–768 (2016)
9. Denisov, A., Budkov, V., Mikhalchenko, D.: Designing simulation model of humanoid robot to study servo control system. In: Ronzhin, A., Rigoll, G., Meshcheryakov, R. (eds.) ICR 2016. LNCS (LNAI), vol. 9812, pp. 69–78. Springer, Cham (2016). https://doi.org/10.1007/978-3-319-43955-6_10
10. Denisov, A., Budkov, V., Mikhalchenko, D.: Designing simulation model of humanoid robot to study servo control system. In: Ronzhin, A., Rigoll, G., Meshcheryakov, R. (eds.) ICR 2016. LNCS (LNAI), vol. 9812, pp. 69–78. Springer, Cham (2016). https://doi.org/10.1007/978-3-319-43955-6_10
11. Ignatova, E.I., Lopota, A.V., Rostov, N.V.: Sistemy upravleniya dvizheniem robotov. Komp'yuternoe pro'ektirovanie. Polytechnic Publishing Center, St. Petersburg (2014)
12. Yurevich, E.I.: Osnovy robototekhniki. BHV, St. Petersburg (2005)
13. Alferov, G.V., Kulakov, F.M., Chernakova, S.A.: Informatsionnye systemy virtualnoy real'nosti v mekhatronike i robototekhnike. SOLO, St. Petersburg (2006)
14. Corke, P.I.: MATLAB toolboxes: robotics and vision for students and teachers. IEEE Robot. Autom. Mag. **14**, 16–17 (2007)
15. Corke, P.I.: Robotics Toolbox 9.7 for MATLAB R4 (2012)

Proactive Localization System Concept for Users of Cyber-Physical Space

Anton Saveliev⬡, Dmitrii Malov$^{(\boxtimes)}$⬡, Alexander Edemskii⬡, and Nikita Pavliuk⬡

SPIIRAS, 14-th Line of V.O, Saint-Petersburg 199178, Russia
dmalov@iias.spb.su

Abstract. We propose proactive localization system as a part of cyber-physical-social space. The proactive localization system allows to track every mobile entity of the system: man, autonomous mobile robot, etc. It's possible to predict activity of the tracking object, using machine learning techniques. In this paper we compare different machine learning models for our system, and present the results of testing trained models.

Keywords: Proactive localization · Cyber-physical space
Time series prediction · Decentralized intellectual space

1 Introduction

1.1 Fundamental Problem

Active implementation of Internet of Things (IoT) systems contributes the creation of fully decentralized cyber-physical-social space, representing integration of digital and physical components into social structures. Physical components of this system can be represented as autonomous robotic unit. This unit can offer variety of services: navigation system, reference service, corporate TV, video conference, etc. So the number of those units are limited, that's why it's urgent to locate them more efficient, than just changing its coordinates from time to time. So, these robotic units can use information from proactive localization system, which predicts location of users. Behavior of robot, based on current and future location of users can optimize the existing resources.

The fundamental problem of proactive localization system can be formulated as multivariate time series prediction of entities in intelligent decentralized space [1–3]. This can refer to cyber-physical-social system, where decentralized connections are established [4–6].

1.2 Basic Algorithms

The multivariate form of the Box-Jenkins univariate models is sometimes called the ARMAV model, for AutoRegressive Moving Average Vector or simply vector ARMA process. The ARMAV model for a stationary multivariate time series, with a zero mean vector, represented by

A. Ronzhin et al. (Eds.): ICR 2018, LNAI 11097, pp. 233–238, 2018.
https://doi.org/10.1007/978-3-319-99582-3_24

$$x_t = (x_{1t}, x_{2t}, \ldots, x_{nt})^T, \quad -\infty < t < \infty \tag{1}$$

is of the form:

$$x_t = \phi_1 x_{t-1} + \phi_2 x_{t-2} + \cdots + \phi_p x_{t-p} + a_t - \theta_1 a_{t-1} - \theta_2 a_{t-2} - \cdots - \theta_q a_{t-q}, \tag{2}$$

where

- x_t and a_t are $n \times 1$ column vectors with a_t representing multivariate white noise,
- $\phi_k = \{\phi_{kjj}\}, k = 1, 2, \ldots, p$
  $\theta_k = \{\theta_{kjj}\}, k = 1, 2, \ldots, q$
  are $n \times n$ matrices for autoregressive and moving average parameters,
- $E[a_t] = 0$
- $E[a_t a'_{t-k}] = 0, k \neq 0$
  $E[a_t a'_{t-k}] = \sum_a, k = 0,$

where $\sum_a$ is the dispersion or covariance matrix of a_t.

Some of the machine learning models can be used for time series prediction. One of such model is neural networks. For instance, LSTM-network (Long Short-Term Memory) can be used. LSTM-network is recurrent neural network, composed of LSTM units. This architecture is often used for sequences regression problems, provided that there is large enough dataset (e.g., millions of history data points).

Random Forest is another machine learning ensemble algorithm, which allows to make predictions on non-stationary time series. Additionally, it can be applied to multidimensional datasets.

Random Forest is ensemble of Decision Trees algorithm. Decision Tree itself is good basic classifier for bagging (bootstrap aggregation). Bagging is one of the first simple type of ensembles; it's based on statistical bootstrap method, which allows to evaluate many statistics of complex distributions.

The method of bootstrap is as follows (Fig. 1). Let X is sample set of size N. We take uniformly from the X set of objects with a return. In other words, we will choose N times an arbitrary sample object (we assume, that each object is obtained with the same probability $1/N$), each time we select from all the original N objects. Note, that due to the return of obtaining objects, there will be repetitions. Denote new sample subset by X_1. In this way we generate M sample subsets $X_1, \ldots, X_M$, repeating this procedure M times. Now we have large enough number of sample subsets and we are able to evaluate different statistics of original distribution.

Describe briefly bagging algorithm (Fig. 2). Let X is training set. We generate subsets $X_1, \ldots, X_M$ from original one, using bootstrap algorithm described above. Now we train own classifier $clf_i(x)$ on each of those subsets. Final classifier averages predictions of all algorithms (in case of classification task this step is corresponded to voting):

$$clf(x) = \frac{1}{M} \sum_{i=1}^{M} clf_i(x). \tag{3}$$

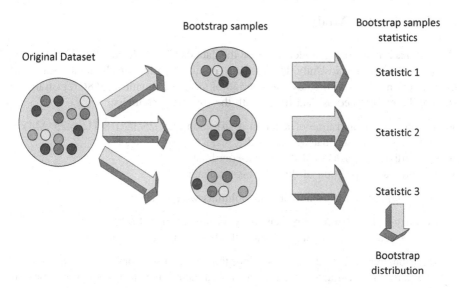

Fig. 1. Statistical bootstrap method scheme.

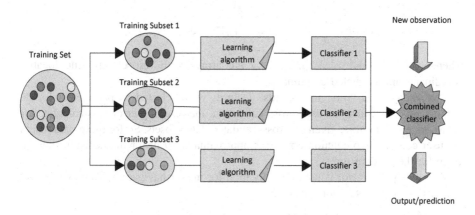

Fig. 2. Bagging method scheme.

Support Vector Machine (SVM) also can be applied to regression problem. This model is similar to logistic regression in that it's driven by a linear function $w^T x + b$. Unlike logistic regression, the SVM doesn't provide probabilities, but only outputs a class identity. One key innovation associated with SVM is the kernel trick. This kernel trick consists of observing that many machine learning algorithms can be represented exclusively of dot products between examples.

2 Training the Model

To train machine learning model, we used the data that was collected by simulating the movements of the user in Unity3D. This data contains information about the location of the user during the working day for a period of around 2 months (23686 registrations) and can be represented as data frame with the following columns:

- datetime – date and time of location registration (e.g. 25/3/2018 11:16:25 AM);
- user_id – id of user that was located;
- x_coordinate – position of the user x-coordinate;
- z_coordinate – position of the user z-coordinate.

After preprocessing, additional data columns were created:

- weekday – day of week represented by an integer from 1 to 7;
- time_in_seconds – time elapsed since the beginning of the working day.

Decision tree and random forest algorithms were used for the training process. Initially, a root mean square error was taken as a metric, but such a representation was not correct enough for this task. Therefore, we decided to use a metric that is expressed in absolute error of prediction of location in meters:

$$error = \frac{1}{n} \sqrt{\left(x_{true} - x_{predicted}\right)^2 + \left(z_{true} - z_{predicted}\right)^2}, \tag{3}$$

where x_{true}, z_{true} and $x_{predicted}$, $z_{predicted}$ are arrays with respectively true location coordinates and predicted coordinates.

"Weekday" and "time_in_seconds" features were selected as parameters for the training process. Since we used cross validation, the resulting error was calculated as the average of all errors, given on cross-validated data subsets. So for these parameters, the user coordinate prediction error was approximately 9 m for the decision tree and 10 m for the random forest.

Obviously, this error is unacceptably high for indoor navigation. Thus we decided to add more parameters for our model:

- x_previous – last registered position of the user x-coordinate;
- z_previous – last registered position of the user z-coordinate;
- time_difference – time difference between current and previous registration.

And for these parameters, the user coordinate prediction error was approximately 6 m for the decision tree and 0.4 m for the random forest.

After that, we carried out another Unity3D simulation, but with the involvement of two users (Fig. 3).

To start the training process on these data we have preprocessed it as well as in the previous case. And after training, the average error in predicting the user's coordinates was 0.7 m.

The following Table 1 shows the results of training with different parameters.

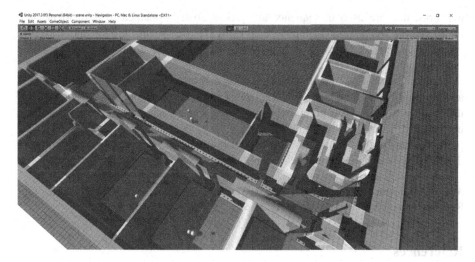

Fig. 3. Unity3D simulation interface.

Table 1. Results of training.

Method	Parameters	Number of users	Error
Decision tree	time_in_seconds weekday	1	≈9
	time_in_seconds weekday x_previous z_previous time_difference	1	≈6
Random forest	time_in_seconds weekday	1	≈10
	time_in_seconds weekday x_previous z_previous	1	≈2
	time_in_seconds weekday x_previous z_previous time_difference	1	≈0.4
		2	≈0.7

3 Conclusion

Several machine learning algorithms were tested for using in proactive localization system: support vector regression, decision trees, random forest, linear regression. As a result, random forest has shown the least error on the testing set with 0.4 m error. Further research is aimed at using artificial neural networks, like LSTM or GRU neural networks, that are used in sequence analysis. Also it is planned to implement deep reinforcement learning algorithms using Unity3D ML-Agents toolkit and Bayesian machine learning methods. It is expedient to use probabilistic methods of machine learning, namely: oriented graphs (Bayesian networks of trust) and undirected graphs (Markov networks and random fields). Bayesian networks of trust represent a directed acyclic graph, to each vertex of which there corresponds a random variable, and arcs of the graph code the ratios of probabilistic dependencies according to Bayes. Markov networks are an undirected graph in which a set of random variables has the Markov property that the conditional probability distribution of the future states of the process depends only on the current state, and not on the sequence of events that preceded it.

Acknowledgments. This research is supported by the Council for Grants of the President of the Russian Federation (project No. MK-383.2018.9).

References

1. Levonevskiy, D., Vatamaniuk, I., Saveliev, A.: Integration of corporate electronic services into a smart space using temporal logic of actions. In: Ronzhin, A., Rigoll, G., Meshcheryakov, R. (eds.) ICR 2017. LNCS (LNAI), vol. 10459, pp. 134–143. Springer, Cham (2017). https://doi.org/10.1007/978-3-319-66471-2_15
2. Lee, J., Bagheri, B., Kao, H.A.: A cyber-physical systems architecture for industry 4.0-based manufacturing systems. Manuf. Lett. **3**, 18–23 (2015)
3. Amri, M.-H., et al.: Indoor human/robot localization using robust multi-modal data fusion. In: IEEE International Conference on Robotics and Automation (ICRA). IEEE (2015)
4. Liu, Z., et al.: Cyber-physical-social systems for command and control. IEEE Intell. Syst. **26**(4), 92–96 (2011)
5. Frazzon, E.M., et al.: Towards socio-cyber-physical systems in production networks. Procedia CIRP **7**, 49–54 (2013)
6. Shi, J., et al.: A survey of cyber-physical systems. In: International Conference on Wireless Communications and Signal Processing (WCSP) 2011. IEEE (2011)

Current Control in the Drives of Dexterous Robot Grippers

Vladimir Serebrennyj, Andrey Boshlyakov,
and Alexander Ogorodnik$^{(\boxtimes)}$

BMSTU, Moscow, Russia
{vsereb, boshlyakov, alexander.ogorodnik}@bmstu.ru

Abstract. At present, the actuality of improving approaches to the creation of dexterous gripper for robots with force controls and their control algorithms is growing due to the need to develop areas of robotics related to the manipulation of fragile objects, interaction with people, prosthetics and rehabilitation robotics. The force control in the dexterous grippers of robots using an electric drive is provided by current control. Therefore, the purpose of this article is to consider various current regulators in the context of their application in dexterous grippers and manipulators with the force control. PI, adaptive, relay and relay, with adjustment of the hysteresis loop, current regulators are compared in such characteristics as transient response, accuracy, robustness, switching losses and switching frequency stability. The article proposes a new method for synthesizing hysteresis regulators with the adjustment of the hysteresis loop, which assumes the use of standard frequency synthesis of control systems with feedback. The proposed method extends such quality parameters as stability stocks, transient time, cutoff frequency to the adjustment loop. The considered hysteresis controller with the adjustment loop, in contrast to the classical hysteresis regulator, ensures the stabilization of the switching frequency and the reduction of the current pulsations in the motor driver. The article also presents the results of the two-finger gripper force control with the use of various current regulators for the chosen law of forces distribution between the drives.

Keywords: Current control · Current loop · Force control · Torque control
Dexterous gripper · Gripping · Forces distribution

1 Introduction

Currently dexterous robotic and manipulation systems are increasingly used in various technical fields. One of the important parameters determining the efficiency of such systems is the quality of force control [1, 2]. In consequence of which today there is a need to improve control algorithms dexterous handles and gripping devices of robots. The most common used actuators in robotics are electric. In these, the torque control is provided by the current regulation. Therefore, the aim of this article is to review the work of the various methods of current control from the point of view of regulation of the forces in the gripping device of the robot and algorithms for the allocation of force between the actuators.

© Springer Nature Switzerland AG 2018
A. Ronzhin et al. (Eds.): ICR 2018, LNAI 11097, pp. 239–248, 2018.
https://doi.org/10.1007/978-3-319-99582-3_25

2 Current Controllers

There are many current controllers for motors and power supplies. The most common current controllers are linear PI and non-linear hysteresis regulators [3]. PI controllers have small current ripples, stable switching frequency. This makes it possible to reduce electrical energy losses and noise, in amplifiers using such regulators. Hysteresis regulators have a shorter time of transients and better dynamic characteristics. However, at the same time they have large current ripples and a variable switching frequency of power transistors or thyristors.

For the mathematical description of electromechanical processes in a drive built based on a DC motor, will use a nonstationary model with lumped parameters [3]. Friction will be described by the Coulomb model with linearization near zero velocities [4]. Will assume that in the sensor measurement signals the noise spectrum will correspond to band-limited white noise.

2.1 PI Current Controller

The PI current controller is described by the following formula:

$$W(s) = k_1 + \frac{k_2}{s} = K\frac{Ts+1}{Ts}, \tag{1}$$

where T is the time constant.

The estimation signal of the counter EMF have been added to the current loop for increasing regulator's dynamic characteristics (Fig. 1). The computed control voltage value is applied to the motor after the PWM (block C2D in Fig. 1).

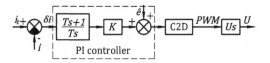

Fig. 1. PI current controller block diagram.

2.2 Adaptive Current Controller

The adaptive controller was synthesized, which during the control system sampling interval seeks to bring the value of the current to a predetermined value. The control voltage u is calculated by the formula:

$$u = \frac{di}{K_1} + K_2, \tag{2}$$

Where di is the current increment at the sampling interval end, K_1 and K_2 is the adjustable parameters, their theoretical values are calculated from the ratios: $K_1 = 1/(R + L/T_S), K_2 = Ri_0 + e$ based on the estimation of such parameters as i_0 – the current at the initial moment, e – the counter EMF, L – inductance of the armature winding of the motor, R - motor resistance and T_S is the sampling interval.

The adaptive regulator block diagram is shown in the Fig. 2. It should be noted that such regulators are rarely used, since, despite their good dynamic characteristics, because they are not robust.

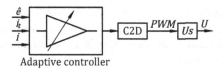

Adaptive controller

Fig. 2. Adaptive current controller block diagram.

2.3 Hysteresis Current Controller

Figure 3 shows a typical hysteresis current controller with a single hysteresis loop (a) and its structure diagram in a mathematical model (b). Owing to their good dynamic characteristics, simplicity and robustness, relay regulators have found wide application both in the field of power supplies and in the field of electric drives [2, 5–8]. Due to high dynamics of the controller, it is possible to reduce the torque pulsations and to provide more smooth control [9–12]. The regulator has disadvantages in the form of variable switching frequency and large current ripples. The maximum switching frequency and pulsation range are related by the formula:

$$f_C = \frac{u}{4L\Delta i},$$ (3)

where f_C is the switching frequency of power transistors or thyristors, and Δi is the current ripple amplitude.

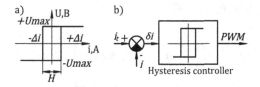

Fig. 3. The current controller's hysteresis curve (a) and its block diagram (b).

The maximum allowable switching frequency in the worst case determines the hysteresis loop's width, because current ripples Δi always will be high. In addition, due to the variable switching frequency during operation, the noise will be distributed over a wide frequency band and it will be difficult to filter.

2.4   Hysteresis Current Controller with Adjusting Loop

To reduce disadvantages of conventional hysteresis current controllers were proposed hysteresis controllers with the adjustment of the hysteresis loop width (Fig. 4). Such controllers stabilize the switching frequency and reduce current ripple by means adaptation of the hysteresis loop [13, 14]. There are individual solutions to the parameter's choice of the controller for adjusting loop [2, 13, 15, 16]. Some of these controllers may be require large computational resources [17, 18]. Controllers with fuzzy logic are also may be used to stabilize the switching frequency [19, 20]. Since the existing methods are particular solutions, there is a need to form a general approach to synthesis of the adjusting loop.

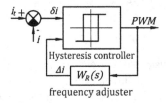

Fig. 4. Hysteresis current controller with an adjusting loop of the hysteresis.

Theoretical model. Solving the Kirchhoff's equation [3] for stationary case, we have:

$$i = \frac{u - e}{R} - \frac{u - e - Ri_0}{R} e^{-\frac{t}{L/R}}, \tag{4}$$

where e – is the counter EMF.

Then, in the first approximation, solving the boundary-value problem, the period and the switching frequency in the current window of the hysteresis regulator will be describing by the following formulas:

$$T_C = \frac{4L\Delta i}{u(1 - (e + Ri_0)^2/u^2)}. \tag{5}$$

$$f_C = \frac{u(1 - (e + Ri_0)^2/u^2)}{4L\Delta i}. \tag{6}$$

It follows from formula (6) that, the width of the hysteresis loop, which is equal to Δi, will be inversely proportional to the switching frequency.

Hysteresis controller with adjusting the hysteresis loop's width. Synthesis of the frequency stabilization loop. Let's consider the synthesis algorithm of the adjusting controller the hysteresis loop's width. Formula (6), under the condition $e + Ri_0 \ll u$, can be reduced to the form:

$$f_C \approx \frac{u}{4L\Delta i}. \tag{7}$$

From formulas (5) or (6) and the transfer function of the frequency adjuster, it is can be to form the control loop to adjust the hysteresis. It should be noted that the overall gain in the circuit will vary with the current and the counter EMF. Moreover, in the controller based of formula (5) with increasing counter EMF, the gain in the tuning loop will increase and the stability stocks will decrease. Therefore, it is rational to create loop for adjusting the hysteresis width based on formula (6), introducing feedback on the switching frequency in the motor driver to stabilize it. Thus, based on the dependence (6), we obtain the reduced model of the frequency stabilization loop. Figure 5 shows the mathematical model block diagram, where $K_F W(s)/s$ is the transfer function of the switching frequency stabilization loop.

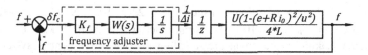

Fig. 5. Reduced model of the frequency stabilization loop.

To synthesize of the stabilization loop by classical methods, it is necessary to linearize the obtained model. Linearizing the reduced model using the dependence (7), we obtain the linear control loop of frequency stabilization, the block diagram of which is shown in Fig. 6.

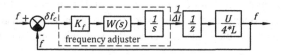

Fig. 6. Linearized model of the frequency stabilization loop.

Further, using the linear model, it is possible to use standard techniques of classical control theory to synthesis the controller $W(s)$.

In accordance with the model in Fig. 6, the controller of the form $K_F(Ts + 1)/Ts^2$ was synthesized. The transient processes for the full model with the adjusting loop in Fig. 4, the reduced model (6), Fig. 5 and the linearized model (7), Fig. 6 is shown in Fig. 7. From the Fig. 7 it can be seen that transient responses of complete and reduced model are almost identical. The linearized model, although it gives a discrepant transient response (it is due to the fact that the effect of the counter EMF and current on the switching frequency is not taken into account), but it correctly describes the stability margins. With increasing current and counter EMF in accordance with (5), the gain will

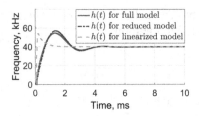

Fig. 7. Transient response for different models of frequency stabilization loop.

decrease, and the stability margins increase. Therefore, by the formulas (5) and (6) it is possible to synthesize controller, which guarantees the control system stability.

2.5 Comparison of the Current Loops Control Quality with Different Current Regulators

For the electric drive with following parameters: resistance $R = 1.85\ \Omega$, inductance $L = 0.96$ mHn, torque equation constant $C_T = 22.9 \cdot 10^{-3}$ Nm/A, counter EMF equation constant $C_E = 23 \cdot 10^{-3}$ V * s/rad, inertia $J = 9 \cdot 10^{-6}$ kg * m^2, voltage $U_{MAX} = 12$ V, taking into account the sampling interval of the control system equal 25 µs, the synthesis of controllers was performed. The following regulators were considered: PI current controller (PI controller), adaptive current controller (ACC), hysteresis current controller (HCC) and hysteresis current controller with adjusting loop (HCCA).

Figure 8(a) shows the frequency response of for transfer functions of closed-loop systems and transfer functions of error. The data were obtained from a series of measurements of the system response when the sinusoidal signal is fed to the input. The measurements were carried out at a current of 1 A, which is close to the rated motor armature current. The figure shows that at high frequencies hysteresis current controller have the lowest error. Moreover, the frequency response of the classic hysteresis controller from the hysteresis controller with adjusting the hysteresis loop's

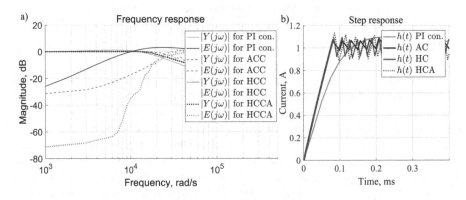

Fig. 8. Frequency response (a) and transient response (b) of current control loops.

width are not significantly different. High dynamic characteristics of such controllers allow to provide better and more accurate torque control [21] in the gripper device drivers or manipulator drives.

Figure 8(b) shows transient responses in current control loops with different controllers. It follows from the figure that hysteresis and adaptive current controllers have the best transient responses.

3   Force Control

Current controllers are the important elements in the dexterous gripper or manipulator. By means current control provides force control in the electric drives [1, 22]. Above we have discussed various current controllers, the proposed method of linearization and synthesis of hysteresis controllers with adjusting loop. Therefore next, consider application these controllers to force control in gripper device.

Modern dexterous gripper and manipulators can have many degrees of freedom (DOF) and drives, as well as have a complex construction and kinematics [23, 24]. However, next, consider the torque control on the example of a two-fingered gripper with two DOF. For a two-finger gripper the force control algorithm was implemented, which provides a predetermined force to grip the object at any deviation of the jaws (Fig. 9).

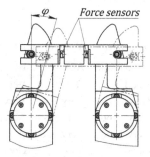

Fig. 9. The design of the stand for the investigation of a two-fingered gripping device.

Taking into account the kinematics of the gripping device, the system behavior was modeled using a solid model of the stand and drive models.

Figure 10(a) shows the resultant force and torque values at the set change for target angle with a frequency of 6 Hz. With the use of different current controllers at such a low operating frequency, all the current controllers provided the sufficiently accurate torque setting. It can be seen from the figure that it is provided a constant clamping force $N = 10$ N.

Figure 10(b) shows switching frequency diagrams of a classical hysteresis controller and hysteresis controller with the frequency stabilization loop. A hysteresis controller with frequency stabilization loop provides the stable switching frequency of 40 kHz during operation, while the switching frequency of the classical hysteresis

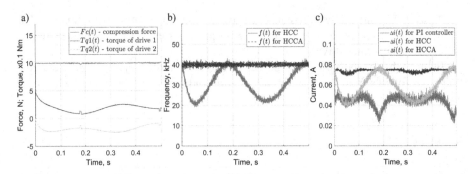

Fig. 10. Switching frequencies (a) and current ripples (b) in motor driver.

controller under the influence of counter-EMF and current can be changing in 2 times. PI and adaptive current controllers provides a stable switching frequency of 40 kHz. In addition to the stability of the switching frequency, losses and noises caused by current ripple are an important parameter. Figure 10(c) shows current ripples in motor driver for different current regulators. It can be seen that the PI controller with PWM provides the lowest current ripple. The hysteresis controller has stably large pulsations, determined by the current window. A hysteresis controller with frequency stabilization loop provides a reduction in ripples due to adaptive reduction of the current window.

Table 1 shows the comparative analysis results of the current controllers for manipulators and robot drives.

Table 1. Comparative analysis of current controllers.

Controller type	PI controller	ACC	HCC	HCCA
Accuracy	Good	Good	Very good	Very good
Response time	Good	Very good	Very good	Very good
Switching losses	Very good	Very good	Acceptable	Good
Frequency stability	Very good	Very good	Poor	Good
Robustness	Good	Poor	Good	Acceptable

4 Conclusion

Different current regulators were considered for the implementation of the force control in the dexterous gripper and manipulators based on electric drives. The method for synthesizing the hysteresis controller with frequency stabilization loop is proposed, which makes it possible to use classical approaches to the synthesis of feedback control systems for the synthesis the adjustable hysteresis loop. Such a controller has a simple structure and does not require large computing performance, in addition it can be implemented on standard digital and analog ICs. Four basic types of regulators provided the possibility of a force control according to the selected control law. The comparative analysis results of the current controllers are given in Table 1.

From the analysis of the obtained results it follows that for the realization of the current loop and its use in the force control of the gripper or robot drive, it is advisable to choose the PI current controller, as it ensures acceptable performance and control quality at the simplest implementation. In the case of increased demands for fast response or requirement of astaticism for current loop in terms of the counter EMF should be choose one of the types of hysteresis controllers. If it is necessary to provide better electromagnetic compatibility, as well as to exclude the driver switching frequency to the audible or other range, the hysteresis controller with the frequency stabilization loop should be selected. If such requirements are not imposed, it is advisable to apply the classic hysteresis current controller.

References

1. Malchikov, A., Yatsun, A., Bezmen, P., Tarasov, O.: Control features of the electromechanical system with end-effector considering the regulated torque. In: MATEC Web of Conferences. EDP Sciences, vol. 113, pp. 1–5 (2017)
2. Mesherayakov V., Voekov V., Ivashkin V.: Designing the universal vector control system with relay current regulator principle for general purpose industrial AC motor drive control. In: IEEE International Power Electronics and Motion Control Conference (PEMC), pp. 680–685 (2016)
3. Blejz, E.S., Brodovskij, V.N., Vvedenskij, V.A.: Sledyashhie privody. In: CHemodanov, B. K. (eds.) 2nd edn. Publishing house Bauman MSTU, Moscow (2003) (in Russian)
4. Marques, F., Flores, P., Claro, J.C.P., Lankarani, H.: A survey and comparison of several friction force models for dynamic analysis of multibody mechanical systems. Nonlinear Dyn. 86(3), 1407–1443 (2016)
5. Dutta, K., Puthra, P.P., Das, P.K.: Constant torque angle controlled permanent magnet synchronous motor drive using hysteresis band current controller. In: 2016 7th India International Conference on Power Electronics (IICPE), pp. 1–5. IEEE (2016)
6. Poonia, A., Dey, A.: Space phasor based improved hysteresis current controller for shunt active power filter using 3-level inverter. In: 2016 18th European Conference on Power Electronics and Applications (EPE 2016 ECCE Europe), pp. 1–10. IEEE (2016)
7. Priandana, E.R., Saputra, M., Prabowo, Y., Dahono, P.: Analysis and design of variable double-band hysteresis current controller for single-phase full-bridge bidirectional converters. In: 2014 International Symposium on Technology Management and Emerging Technologies (ISTMET), pp. 143–148. IEEE (2014)
8. Putri, A.I., Rizqiawan, A., Rozzi, F., Zakkia, N., Haroen, Y., Dahono, P.A.: A hysteresis current controller for grid-connected inverter with reduced losses. In: International Conference of Industrial, Mechanical, Electrical, and Chemical Engineering (ICIMECE), pp. 167–170. IEEE (2016)
9. Gobbi, R., Ramar, K.: Optimisation techniques for a hysteresis current controller to minimise torque ripple in switched reluctance motors. IET Electr. Power Appl. 3(5), 453–460 (2009)
10. Kurian, S., Nisha, G.K.: Torque ripple minimization of SRM using torque sharing function and hysteresis current controller. In: 2015 International Conference on Control Communication & Computing India (ICCC), pp. 149–154. IEEE (2015)
11. Muralidhar, J.E., Aranasi, P.V.: Torque ripple minimization & closed loop speed control of BLDC motor with hysteresis current controller. In: 2014 2nd International Conference on Devices, Circuits and Systems (ICDCS), pp. 1–7. IEEE (2014)

12. Shi, T., Niu, L., Li, W.: Torque-ripple minimization in switched reluctance motors using sliding mode variable structure control. In: 2010 29th Chinese Control Conference (CCC), pp. 332–337. IEEE (2010)

13. Kolokolov, Y.V., Tej, D.O.: Dinamika relejno-impul'snykh regulyatorov peremennogo toka s adaptatsiej gisterezisa. Vestnik YUgorskogo gosudarstvennogo universiteta 3(22) (2011). (in Russian)

14. Serebrennyj, V.V., Boshlyakov, A.A., Ogorodnik, A.I.: Relejnye regulyatory toka ehlektroprivodov s adaptatsiej shiriny petli gisterezisa. Desyataya vserossijskaya mul'tikonferentsiya po problemam upravleniya (MKPU-2017), pp. 177–180 (2017). (in Russian)

15. Suru, C.V., Dobriceanu, M., Subtirelu, G.E.: Direct current control by constant frequency hysteresis controller in active filtering systems. In: 2017 5th International Symposium on Electrical and Electronics Engineering (ISEEE), pp. 1–6. IEEE (2017)

16. Dudkin, M.M., Brylina, O.G., TSytovich, L.I., Tyugaev, A.V.: CHastotno-shirotnoimpul'snyj adaptivnyj regulyator peremennogo napryazheniya s integriruyushhej sistemoj upravleniya. Vestnik YUzhno-Ural'skogo gosudarstvennogo universiteta. Seriya: EHnergetika, vol. 13(2), pp. 45–52 (2013) (in Russian)

17. Panda, G., Dash, S.K., Sahoo, N.: Comparative performance analysis of Shunt Active power filter and Hybrid Active Power Filter using FPGA-based hysteresis current controller. In: 2012 IEEE 5th India International Conference on Power Electronics (IICPE), pp. 1–6. IEEE (2012)

18. Talib, M.H.N., Isa, S.N.M., Hamidon, H.E., Ibrahim, Z., Rasin, Z.: Hysteresis current control of induction motor drives using dSPACE DSP controller. In: 2016 IEEE International Conference on Power and Energy (PECon), pp. 522–527. IEEE (2016)

19. Tabatabaei, H., Fathi, S.H., Jedari, M.: A comparative study between conventional and fuzzy logic control for APFs by applying adaptive hysteresis current controller. In: 2017 Iranian Conference on Electrical Engineering (ICEE), pp. 1313–1318. IEEE (2017)

20. Uddin, M.N., Rebeiro, R.S.: Fuzzy logic based speed controller and adaptive hysteresis current controller based IPMSM drive for improved dynamic performance. In: 2011 IEEE International Electric Machines & Drives Conference (IEMDC), pp. 1–6. IEEE (2011)

21. Nakashima Y., Ando T., Kobayashi Y., Fujie M.: Gait-controlled mobility-aid robot: treadmill motor current based anteroposterior force estimation using frictional model reflects characteristics of ground reaction force. In: 2012 4th IEEE RAS & EMBS International Conference on Biomedical Robotics and Biomechatronics (BioRob), pp. 1305–1310. IEEE (2012)

22. Aghili, F.: Fault-tolerant torque control of BLDC motors. IEEE Trans. Power Electron. 26(2), 355–363 (2011)

23. Pavlyuk, N.A., Ronzhin, A.L.: Konstruktivnye resheniya nizhnih konechnostej dlya antropomorfnogo robota Antares. EHkstremal'naya robototekhnika, 1(1), 422–427 (2016). (in Russian)

24. Pavlyuk, N.A., Budkov, V.Y., Bizin, M.M., Ronzhin, A.L.: Razrabotka konstrukcii uzla nogi antropomorfnogo robota ANTARES na osnove dvuhmotornogo kolena. Izvestiya YUzhnogo federal'nogo universiteta. Tekhnicheskie nauki, 1(174), 227–239 (2016). (in Russian)

Comparing Fiducial Markers Performance for a Task of a Humanoid Robot Self-calibration of Manipulators: A Pilot Experimental Study

Ksenia Shabalina[1], Artur Sagitov[1], Mikhail Svinin[2],
and Evgeni Magid[1(✉)]

[1] Laboratory of Intelligent Robotic Systems, Kazan Federal University,
Kazan 420008, Russian Federation
{ks.shabalina,sagitov,magid}@it.kfu.ru
[2] Robot Dynamics and Control Laboratory, College of Information Science
and Engineering, Ritsumeikan University,
Noji Higashi 1-1-1, Kusatsu 525-8577, Japan
svinin@fc.ritsumei.ac.jp
http://kpfu.ru/robolab.html

Abstract. This paper presents our pilot study of experiments automation with a real robot in order to compare performance of different fiducial marker systems, which could be used in automated camera calibration process. We used Russian humanoid robot AR-601M and automated it's manipulators for performing joint rotations. This paper is an extension of our previous work on ARTag, AprilTag and CALTag marker comparison in laboratory settings with large-sized markers that had showed significant superiority of CALTag system over the competitors. This time the markers were scaled down and placed on AR-601M humanoid's palms. We automated experiments of marker rotations, analyzed the results and compared them with the previously obtained results of manual experiments with large-sized markers. The new automated pilot experiments, which were performed both in pure laboratory conditions and pseudo field environments, demonstrated significant differences with previously obtained manual experimental results: AprilTag marker system demonstrated the best performance with a success rate of 97,3% in the pseudo field environment, while ARTag was the most successful in the laboratory conditions.

Keywords: ARTag · AprilTag · CALTag · Fiducial marker systems
AR-601M · Humanoid robot · Experimental comparison

1 Introduction

Camera calibration is an important procedure that is necessary for application of any machine vision algorithms in robotics tasks, which require high precision

© Springer Nature Switzerland AG 2018
A. Ronzhin et al. (Eds.): ICR 2018, LNAI 11097, pp. 249–258, 2018.
https://doi.org/10.1007/978-3-319-99582-3_26

of manipulations that are coordinated using digital cameras as a primary sensor. Calibration produces intrinsic and extrinsic parameters of a camera, which define correspondence between 2D coordinates of an object point in the image plane and its 3D coordinates in a particular world frame, and provides distortion coefficients to alleviate cameras lens imperfections. Classical calibration methods require a human involvement in calibration process; the human holds a classical checkerboard pattern [14] and manually moves it in front of a camera.

However, there is a modern way of camera calibration that implies use of fiducial marker systems. Fiducial marker systems are popular in many application areas, including physics, medicine, and augmented reality (AR). In robotics, fiducials find their application in navigation, localization, camera pose estimation and camera calibration. Such systems have high performance under classical chessboard system due to a more specific approach of pattern recognition and detection. However, each system has strengths and drawbacks and cannot be effective in all the above-mentioned application fields. We investigate how effectively could fiducial markers perform in different environment conditions, how a size of the markers influences their recognition rate and identify possible strengths and drawbacks of each selected fiducial marker: ARTag, AprilTag and CALTag. The focus of our research was to select the most suitable marker system for a Russian humanoid robot AR-601M (Fig. 1) autonomous camera calibration. By comparing these systems (ARTag, AprilTag, CALTag) with each other we could understand strengths and drawbacks of each system. Fiducial systems have a set of criteria, which determine a performance of a marker system with regard to each criterion. In our case, we plan to place the markers on robot manipulators in order to allow autonomous calibration without a human assistance, even though it may naturally increase possibilities of marker's arbitrary occlusion.

Fig. 1. Russian humanoid robot AR-601M.

In this paper we systematically estimate performance potential of selected fiducial marker systems and further analyze how each system is applicable in various scenarios (i.e., with small sizes of the marker, limitations of it position and orientation induced by robot kinematic constraints, distance to the marker and uneven lighting conditions in field environments). Specifics of this application imposes particular requirements on a marker system, i.e., the selected system should be at least resistant to some degree of a marker overlap with other parts of the AR-601M robot.

2   Overview of Fiducials: Related Work

Each fiducial marker system is designed in a such way that its marker (or fiducial) could be automatically detected by a camera with a help of the detection algorithm. Particular design of a marker directly depends on specific application area and, in most cases, a developed for certain purposes fiducial may not be suitable for another application. However, most fiducials have general shape: an external envelope (often a square or a circle) and an interior marking (an internal image), which encodes useful information (e.g., an identification code).

One of the first fiducial marker system that was created for augmented reality applications is ARToolKit system (its first release was in 1999 [8]). ARToolKit has a simple approach in marker recognition in space. Firstly, ARToolKit system transforms an image into grayscale and uses a threshold parameter for image binarization. After this steps, the system extracts edges and corners of the image. Basing on the identified corners, the system calculates 3D coordinates of a marker and defines its position. To identify a marker, a symbol (i.e., an image) inside the marker is matched against the set of ARToolKit templates. If the system succeeds finding a match for the template, it retrieves the ID of the marker and projects a corresponding 3D virtual object (knowing the position and orientation of the marker) into a video frame. Digital interior recognition was absent in original ARToolKit system, but it was implemented in future marker systems (including ARToolKit Plus that was the next version of ARToolKit [4]).

Drawbacks of ARToolKit were listed by Mark Fiala, who later has developed a new ARTag system, which uses a digital approach in pattern recognition [4]. Digital approach is utilized in many fiducial marker systems: an internal pattern of a marker represents a grid of black and white square cells interpreting a bit sequence, which is referred as a marker ID. At the moment, a large variety of different types of fiducial markers exists: markers with a general square [2] or a circle shape, [9] markers that consist of dots, [13] of a certain picture [6].

For our investigation we had selected three marker systems: ARTag (Fig. 2, left), AprilTag (Fig. 2, center) and CALTag (Fig. 2, right). The ARTag [3] system is based on ARToolKit [8], but uses a digital approach to read an internal pattern that is a binary code (barcode) [7]. AprilTag is visually similar to ARTag (square with a binary code inside) but has a different approach to marker detection and recognition. CALTag was proposed as an alternative solution for camera calibration [1] after analysis of classical chessboard-based camera calibration and fiducial markers approach.

Fig. 2. From left to right: ARTag (ID 2), AprilTag (ID 4) and CALTag fiducials.

This work is an extension of our previous work on fiducial marker comparison under various types of occlusion and rotation (Fig. 3). In [11] we used simple experiment design and cheap web camera Genius FaceCam 1000X to investigate markers' performance when low cost video-capture equipment is used. For the experiments we printed markers on a white paper and fixed them on a flat surface of a neutral color to avoid marker's false positive effect. The experiment design consisted of systematic and arbitrary occlusion experiments. For systematic occlusion (Fig. 3 shows the example of experiments) each tag was covered with a white paper template starting from the bottom so that the template was occluding K percent of the marker's area. Occluded area K was gradually increased while taking a value from the 5-values array [0, 10, 20, 50, 70]. In the case of arbitrary occlusion, each tag was randomly overlapped with one of two different objects (i.e. metal scissors and white strip object) so that an object was entirely located within tag's area and thus the overlap percentage was always kept constant. In [12] we used AR-601M front facing camera Basler acA640-90gc (Fig. 5) in a more complicated experiment design, where we added rotations of a marker (Fig. 4).

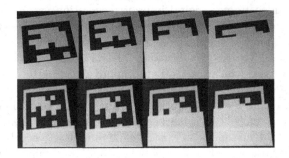

Fig. 3. ARTag ID 3 (top set of images), AprilTag ID 4 (middle) and CALTag 4x4 (bottom) occlusion for 10, 20, 50, 70 percent (from left to right) using FaceCam 1000X.

All experiments in [11,12] were conducted manually and this imposed limitations on the work: a reasonable (but small) number of trials, an accuracy of a marker rotation angles measurement during the experiments, and an amount time that was consumed by the experiments. For this reason, we continued

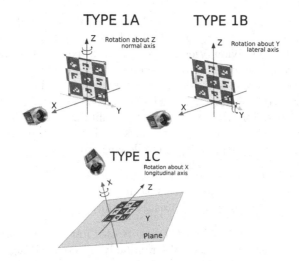

Fig. 4. Experiment design of marker rotation experiments.

Fig. 5. Rotation of ARTag (ID 34) marker regard to Z axis using Basler acA640-90gc.

our work using similar experiment design approach but partially automated the experiments with a humanoid robot as explained in the next sections.

3 Experimental Setup

For the experiments we used AR-601M humanoid robot (Fig. 1) that was developed by Russian company "Android Technics" [10]. The robot has 41 active degrees of freedom (DoF) and each of its two manipulators has 5 DoFs. Its head is equipped with two Basler AG cameras: one camera is a rear view camera (Basler acA1300-60gc) and another is a front camera (Basler acA640-90g). For this work we used only front camera and both robot's manipulators, and controlled servo drives of the neck and the head. To see robot front camera view of AR-601M, we used Pylon Viewer program to take and save images; every twentieth camera frame was stored in order to get frames with different marker and manipulator positions and orientations for further use in image processing.

Official source code of AprilTag and CALTag code were compiled and utilized for the experiments. For ARTag we used ArUco library, which also detects and recognizes various kinds of other tag families [5]. For field experiments the tags were printed on a white paper with the following sizes:

- ARTag: 5.6×5.6 cm, total area 31.36 cm^2
- AprilTag: 5.8×5.8 cm, total area 33.64 cm^2
- CALTag 4x4: 4.9×4.9 cm, total area 24.01 cm^2

Each ARTag and AprilTag marker has its own unique ID, which is encoded in the internal pattern of the tag. We randomly selected ARTag markers with IDs 2, 3, 6, and 34 and AprilTags with IDs 4, 6, 8, and 9 for all experiments (laboratory and pseudo field experiments).

The small size of all field experiments markers is explained by the size of the end-effector (the palm of AR-601M robot arm), where the tags were placed.

Fiducial systems have a set of criteria, which determine the performance of a marker system with regard to each criterion. The design of markers directly depends on their intended application area and, in most cases, a developed for certain purposes marker may not be suitable for another application. In our case, we plan to place the marker on robot manipulator end-effectors; thus, the possibility of marker's arbitrary occlusion increases. This imposes the requirement that a marker should be resistant to an overlap. We performed experimental work in order to compare ARTag, AprilTag, and CALTag markers resistance to occlusions, which is defined as a partial overlapping of the marker with other objects in the scene, potentially including other parts of the robot.

The experiments consisted of laboratory and pseudo field experiments; the technical design and light conditions were the same for both types of experiments (i.e., we carried out the experiments in daylight and switched on ceiling lamps), but they differed in the conditions under which the experiments were carried out. To conduct an experiment with fiducial markers, firstly we set desired joint angles that provide an initial pose (position and orientation) of AR-601M end-effector to allow a good visibility of a marker as well as to select initial pose for the neck and for the head of AR-601M (Fig. 6). Each marker was printed on a small white paper and fixed on the back of the palm of both AR-601M manipulators. Both manipulators performed marker rotations in order. We used AR-601M software shell to control robot systems servo drives, check joint states and manage robot configuration. After a set of rotations (with simultaneous capturing of camera frames) was completed we replaced the current marker with a new one and repeated the procedure. This way for each marker ID we obtained 14 distinct images (frames) with the marker. Finally, these images were used by detection and identification software for each corresponding fiducial marker.

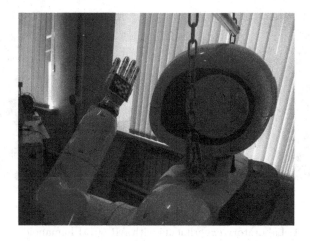

Fig. 6. Example of an experiment with AprilTag marker.

4   Experimental Results

Table 1 demonstrates results of laboratory experiments (Fig. 7). For each marker ID the robot moved its palm for 3 min, and for each marker ID 200 frames were captured with random delays of 0,1 to 2 s between the frames. Next, we randomly selected a subset F_s of 14 different frames from the set of 200 frames in the following manner: the first frame was selected completely at random and added to the set F_s, while every next frame should have a significant difference in its content (in pixels) and at least 0,5 s time difference from all frames that are already in F_s. Next, this subset F_s of 14 frames for each marker was used for marker detection and identification using the appropriate algorithms.

As a result, ARTag marker system was the most resilient in laboratory conditions and the same (best) success rate of the system was detected for markers ID2, ID3 and ID34 at the level of 92.8% (i.e., 13 recognized markers out of 14 input frames). At the same time, CALTag and AprilTag showed still satisfactory but significantly lower level of success (e.g., CALTag 4x4 recognition succeeded in 9 out of 14 frames and AprilTag succeeded in 9 to 11 out of 14 frames with varying number of successful frames for different IDs). In laboratory conditions many factors affected the recognition of a marker: a size of the marker, the manipulator pose with regard to the robot camera, and input set of images.

Table 2 presents the results of a (pseudo) field experiment (Fig. 7). For this type of experiments we used 28 frames for each marker ID, which were selected randomly. In comparison with the results of previous experiments, AprilTag showed better results with 97.3% average success rate. ARTag and CALTag success rate was significantly behind: 83% and 64.3% accordingly. We believe that the results of the field experiments strongly depended on frames selection and lighting conditions and this issue is further discussed in Sect. 5.

Fig. 7. Experiments in a laboratory (left) and a pseudo field (right) environments.

Table 1. Laboratory experiments with AR-601M humanoid robot.

Tag	Success rate (%)	Tag	Success rate (%)
AprilTag (ID 4)	71.4	ARTag (ID 2)	92.8
AprilTag (ID 6)	71.4	ARTag (ID 3)	92.8
AprilTag (ID 8)	64.3	ARTag (ID 6)	78.6
AprilTag (ID 9)	78.6	ARTag (ID 34)	92.8
CALTag 4x4	64.3		

Table 2. Pseudo field experiments with AR-601M humanoid robot.

Tag	Success rate (%)	Tag	Success rate (%)
AprilTag (ID 4)	100	ARTag (ID 2)	78.6
AprilTag (ID 6)	92.8	ARTag (ID 3)	75
AprilTag (ID 8)	96.4	ARTag (ID 6)	78.6
AprilTag (ID 9)	100	ARTag (ID 34)	100
CALTag 4x4	64.3		

5 Conclusions and Future Work

Fiducial markers are becoming a new alternative method for a camera calibration instead of using the classical method of a checkerboard pattern and its variations. In this paper we investigated CALTag, ARTag and AprilTag fiducial marker patterns in laboratory and field environment. We conducted a series of experiments to study weakness and strengths of the selected markers. Rotations and occlusions were selected as a comparative quality criteria as these are the most frequent situations that occur in real world operating; e.g., a marker could be occluded by some object between a robot and the marker or there could be various rotations of the marker with regard to the robot camera that appear due to robot locomotion within its workspace.

After series of the experiments we concluded that a marker detection and experimental identification results obtained for ideal conditions could not be directly transferred to the real world calibration tasks. According our previous work [11,12] the idealized condition experiments on marker detection and recognition demonstrated that AprilTag and ARTag have high sensitivity to edge overlapping, while CALTag, due it's design and detection algorithm, can be detected with overlapped pattern's edge up to 50% of marker's area. Moreover, while AprilTag, CALTag and ARTag all showed resistance to overlapping of their interior by small complex objects and small geometric objects, CALTag system demonstrated the best resistance to such overlapping. Overall, manual experiments with large size markers showed that the best performance among AprilTag, ARTag and CALTag markers should be expected for CALTag marker.

In the similar to the previously conducted manual experiments we were expecting similar results. Yet, the new pilot experiments in the laboratory and the (pseudo) field environments demonstrated almost the opposite results. ARTag demonstrated the highest success rate of 89.25% in average for the laboratory experiments. AprilTag demonstrated the highest success rate of 97.3% in average for the field experiments. And CALTag this time had the lowest success rate of 64.3% in average for the laboratory experiments as well as for the field experiments. We believe that the reason of the CALTag failure was its weak resistance to scaling of the marker size. Our ongoing work concentrates on extending these pilot experiments in order to confirm the obtained results within statistically significant number of laboratory and field experiments. Finally, this should lead to establishing of a new framework for self-calibration of cameras and manipulators of a humanoid robot AR-601M, that could be further extended to other types of robots.

Acknowledgements. This work was partially supported by the Russian Foundation for Basic Research (RFBR) project ID 18-58-45017. Part of the work was performed according to the Russian Government Program of Competitive Growth of Kazan Federal University.

References

1. Atcheson, B., Heide, F., Heidrich, W.: Caltag: high precision fiducial markers for camera calibration. In: VMV, vol. 10, pp. 41–48 (2010)
2. DeGol, J., Bretl, T., Hoiem, D.: ChromaTag: a colored marker and fast detection algorithm. arXiv preprint arXiv:1708.02982 (2017). https://doi.org/10.1109/iccv.2017.164
3. Fiala, M.: ARTag revision 1, a fiducial marker system using digital techniques. Natl. Res. Council Publ. **47419**, 1–47 (2004)
4. Fiala, M.: Comparing ARTag and ARToolkit Plus fiducial marker systems. In: IEEE International Workshop on Haptic Audio Visual Environments and their Applications, pp. 147–152 (2005). https://doi.org/10.1109/have.2005.1545669
5. Garrido-Jurado, S., Muñoz-Salinas, R., Madrid-Cuevas, F.J., Marín-Jiménez, M.J.: Automatic generation and detection of highly reliable fiducial markers under occlusion. Pattern Recogn. **47**(6), 2280–2292 (2014). https://doi.org/10.1016/j.patcog.2014.01.005

6. Higashino, S., Nishi, S., Sakamoto, R.: ARTTag: aesthetic fiducial markers based on circle pairs. In: ACM SIGGRAPH 2016 Posters, p. 38 (2016). https://doi.org/10.1145/2945078.2945116
7. Hirzer, M.: Marker detection for augmented reality applications. In: Seminar/Project Image Analysis Graz, pp. 1–2 (2008)
8. Kato, H., Billinghurst, M.: Marker tracking and HMD calibration for a video-based augmented reality conferencing system. In: 2nd IEEE and ACM International Workshop on Augmented Reality (IWAR), pp. 85–94 (1999). https://doi.org/10.1109/iwar.1999.803809
9. Krajnik, T., Nitsche, M., Faigl, J., Duckett, T., Mejail, M., Preucil, L.: External localization system for mobile robotics. In: 2013 16th International Conference on Advanced Robotics (ICAR), pp. 1–6. IEEE (2013). https://doi.org/10.1109/icar.2013.6766520
10. Magid, E., Sagitov, A.: Towards robot fall detection and management for Russian humanoid AR-601. In: Jezic, G., Kusek, M., Chen-Burger, Y.-H.J., Howlett, R.J., Jain, L.C. (eds.) KES-AMSTA 2017. SIST, vol. 74, pp. 200–209. Springer, Cham (2018). https://doi.org/10.1007/978-3-319-59394-4_20
11. Sagitov, A., Shabalina, K., Lavrenov, R., Magid, E.: Comparing fiducial marker systems in the presence of occlusion. In: 2017 International Conference on Mechanical, System and Control Engineering (ICMSC), pp. 377–382. IEEE (2017). https://doi.org/10.1109/icmsc.2017.7959505
12. Sagitov, A., Shabalina, K., Li, H., Magid, E.: Effects of rotation and systematic occlusion on fiducial marker recognition. In: MATEC Web of Conferences, vol. 113, p. 02006. EDP Sciences (2017). https://doi.org/10.1051/matecconf/201711302006
13. Uchiyama, H., Saito, H.: Random dot markers. In: Virtual Reality Conference (VR), pp. 35–38. IEEE (2011). https://doi.org/10.1109/vr.2011.5759433
14. Zhang, Z.: A flexible new technique for camera calibration. IEEE Trans. Pattern Anal. Mach. Intell. **22**(11), 1330–1334 (2000). https://doi.org/10.1109/34.888718

Robust Webcam-Based Hand Detection for Initialisation of Hand-Gesture Communication

Tilo Strutz[(✉)], Alexander Leipnitz, and Björn Senkel

Institute of Communications,
Leipzig University of Telecommunications (HfTL), Leipzig, Germany
{strutz,alexander.leipnitz,bjoern.senkel}@hft-leipzig.de

Abstract. The recognition of hand gestures is still a challenging task in real-life scenarios, especially when the hardware is restricted to a cheap optical camera. The first step in such systems is to find at least one hand that can be tracked in order to identify postures or gestures. We propose a robust and real-time method that is able to reliably detect the hand in various environments to initialize hand-gesture communication. It is based on an innovative combination of different sources of information (colour, motion, trajectory) and a dynamic hand-wave gesture commencing hand tracking and hand gesture recognition.

Keywords: Hand detection · Human-machine interaction
Initialisation of communication · Gesture recognition

1 Introduction

The research on human-machine interaction based on visual gestures can look on a history, which longs back to the mid-90th. The progress of research and development led even to a dedicated book [1]. Nevertheless, until today, it remains difficult to identify the hand and to decide about its actions when the illumination and the background can be arbitrary or they are even changing.

Hand detection got a push with the availability of affordable depth cameras. Depth information benefits the detection of object contours and extends the scene analysis to the third dimension. As depth cameras output infra-red light, they also can measure the distances of objects in dark environments. This advantage turns into a drawback in scenarios where the objects are exposed to bright sunlight, which contains a significant amount of infra-red radiation disturbing the camera light [2]. Another problem arises, when there are other objects (head or body) having the same distance as the hand and it cannot immediately be decided which pixels belong to the hand.

The intention of the proposed approach is to provide a reliable low-cost and real-time technology that quickly determines the position of an operating hand in an arbitrary scene. This detection is the prerequisite, for example, for the

© Springer Nature Switzerland AG 2018
A. Ronzhin et al. (Eds.): ICR 2018, LNAI 11097, pp. 259–269, 2018.
https://doi.org/10.1007/978-3-319-99582-3_27

subsequent tracking and posture or gesture classification. The performance is demonstrated under various conditions.

As soon as the position of the hand centroid can be reliably determined in each frame of an image sequence, the tracking of the hand and further processing is possible. Information from the time-line can even benefit the detection process, since it can be assumed that the hand does not arbitrarily jump from one position to another, for example.

2 Related Work and Proposal

Hand detection can be described as a segmentation problem where different features are needed for the discrimination between the object of interest and the remaining content of the image (i.e. background and other objects). These features are mainly derived from colour, texture, motion, and/or depth. While textural information is hardly used for foreground-background classification, it is typically required for the derivation of motion information. There are also attempts to find hands based on texture, as for instance in [3].

This paper focusses on hand detection based on colour and motion information. Depth information is not considered yet, because the low-cost restriction limits the required hardware to a simple web camera. The aim is to make full use of the information provided by the optical camera. However, the proposed approach does not exclude the possible integration of depth information in future set-ups.

There have been numerous attempts in the past to solve the problem of detection and tracking. The majority of them is limited to fixed conditions. A typical (and wrong) assumption is that there is something like "skin colour" and this is enough to distinguish between hand and background. This colour is mostly defined either by one or more regions in the three-dimensional colour space, or each RGB-triple is assigned a probability of belonging to skin. Videos from real-life show, however, that there can be many objects in the background also having skin-like colour, including the body (e.g. forearm or the face) of the operator. In addition, the illumination may heavily influence the appearance. Shifts in the RGB values can be observed as well as shaded areas or bright reflections in the hand region depending on the position of the light source. In [4] this had been already taken into account and a more advanced technique was proposed combining colour and motion information, while the uncertainty in finding the correct hand position was compensated using a Hidden-Markov model.

The problem of hand detection has also been addressed in a different context than tracking and gesture recognition. [5] discusses an approach that tries to find all hands in still images. Based on three methods working in parallel and utilising oriented gradients, skin colour, and face and arm detection, the hand positions and their rotated bounding boxes are determined. While showing excellent detection performance, this approaches is far too complex for real-time application.

A significant step towards reliable hand tracking including the provision of the hand shape has been presented by Stergiopoulou and his co-workers [6]. They also combine colour and motion information, while the initial colour model adapts to the actual image content. Besides of this, a background model containing the skin-like regions has been used to improve the detection. [6] also serves as a good review of earlier proposals, which cannot be discussed here again. Recent successes in image classification with convolutional neural networks (CNN) have also inspired investigations into object detection. In [7], CNNs are used to find hands in still images with high reliability, while in [8] the detection approach is part of a hand segmentation and activity recognition process. However, the high computing effort does not allow real-time applications with low-cost hardware.

This paper proposes a novel method that initially identifies the operating hand based on a probabilistic and innovative combination of colour information, motion information, and trajectory. The influence of skin-coloured background is significantly reduced by applying a background model that is updated frame by frame. Even moving objects such as other hands or faces are effectively suppressed. The overall complexity remains low so that real-time applications are possible.

3   Method

The underlying idea of the proposed detection approach is to use a hand-wave gesture. This has at least three advantages. Firstly, a wave gesture is intuitive, like "hello, here I am". It is similar to the initial voice command used in voice-controlled devices, like Amazon Echo or Apple's Siri. Secondly, this gesture does not require hand contours or other precise information and, therefore, it can be recognised based on relative simple techniques. Thirdly, the detection is robust as it combines colour, motion, and constraints on the hand-position sequence, while minimizing the chance of false detections of other skin coloured objects.

In our system, the captured images are resized down to 320 × 240 pixels ensuring a real-time processing on state-of-the-art computers. All empiric thresholds are related to this size, if not differently stated. The next subsections describe how the necessary information is derived and combined.

3.1   Colour Information

Based on the ideas of [10] a skin-colour model is established that defines for each RGB triplet a probability of belonging to a skin region. These probabilities have been learned once in an offline training phase based on annotated pictures (HGR and ECU data banks [10,11]). The probability of colour c belonging to a skin region is determined by

$$P_{\text{predef}}(skin|c) = \frac{n(c, X_{skin})}{n(c, X)}, \tag{1}$$

with $n(c, X_{skin})$ being the frequency that this colour occurred in a skin region and $n(c, X)$ being the total number of observations of this colour.

As already discussed in the introduction, such a predefined (offline trained) model might fail when the actual light conditions produce divergent colours. To overcome this problem, we implement a second colour probability model $P_{\text{adapted}}(skin|c)$ that is initialised by the predefined probabilities. If the hand-blob position could be determined with a sufficient reliability, the second colour probability model is updated frame-by-frame by increasing the number of observations for each colour according to Eq. (1). Strictly speaking, this adapted model does not represent general skin-colour probabilities but hand-colour probabilities in the actual scenario.

Fig. 1. Combination of skin and movement information: (a) original image, (b) skin-probability map (predefined); (c) skin-probability map (adapted); (d) skin-coloured background; (e) motion-vector field; (f) movement-probability map; (g) multiplicative combination of (c) and (f); (h) binarised version of (g); (i) after morphological processing

Figure 1 shows an example of an image and results of different processing steps. The pictures (b) and (c) visualise the difference between the predefined and the adapted model after 38 frames of a test sequence. In the adapted colour model, the wooden bars have a much lower probability of being part of a skin-coloured object and hand pixels now show a higher probability. However, as the update process cannot utilise the correct hand contour, also background pixels in regions that have been temporarily occluded by the moving hand could be assigned higher probabilities.

3.2 Motion Detection

Motion is the second source of information in our set-up. Based on the method of Farnebäck [12], a dense motion-vector field is generated. A vector $\mathbf{v} = (d_x, d_y)$ represents the horizontal and vertical movement of each pixel. The magnitudes of the motion vectors are converted into a movement-intensity map (Fig. 1e and f). It can be seen that, due to the camera noise, some movement is also detected for non-moving image content.

The normalisation of the vector magnitudes

$$|\mathbf{v}| = \sqrt{d_x^2 + d_y^2}, \tag{2}$$

to their maximum value transfers the intensity map into a probability map

$$P(motion|\mathbf{v}) = \frac{|\mathbf{v}|}{\max\left[10, \max_i \left(|\mathbf{v}_i|\right)\right]}, \tag{3}$$

It must be considered, however, that the motion-detection process generates vectors that are affected by noise and the maximum motion vector can be very small if there are no moving objects. To avoid these problems, the normalisation value is limited to a minimum vector length of 10 pixels.

3.3 Combination of Skin and Movement Information

The hand-detection is based on the assumption that there must be a skin-coloured object that is moving. Consequently, the probability, whether a pixel belongs to the waving hand, is the product of both single probabilities

$$P(hand) = P(motion|\mathbf{v}) \cdot P_{\mathrm{adapted}}(skin|c). \tag{4}$$

This is an effective method to eliminate non-moving objects in the background (Fig. 1g).

3.4 Determination of Hand Position

After computation of the hand probabilities the resulting map is binarised yielding the hand object and some spurious blobs. In contrast to many other approaches, we do not apply Otsu's method but determine the binarisation threshold in such a manner that the sum of the entropies of the resulting sub-sets is maximised [13], as it showed a better trade-off between missing hand parts and false detection of background pixels in our set-up. Figure 1(h) shows an example of a binarised probability map.

When the image contrast is rather low, it can happen that sufficient large motion vectors are determined only at the boundary of the moving hand, while no motion can be recognised for the inner part of the hand and the wrist. The binarisation can lead to scattered binary objects (blobs, Fig. 2c) necessitating special morphological post-processing. At first, possibly scattered small blobs have to be merged via dilatation using a circular structural element (Fig. 2d). The diameter d_s of the structural element is dependent on the size of the largest blob, roughly according to $d_s = 25 \cdot \exp(-\text{blobSize}/9000)$. Afterwards, the largest blob is newly determined and connected with surrounding blobs if (i) they have a contour point that is closer to the largest blob than the half of their own contour length and (ii) they do not have a contour point that is farther away than the doubled width or height of largest blob's bounding box. The second condition avoids connections with lengthy blobs which probably belong to structures in the background.

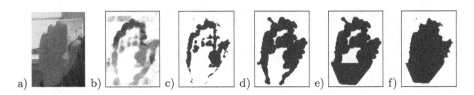

Fig. 2. (a) low contrast within hand region; (b) probability map $P(motion)$; (c) binarised $P(hand)$; (d) after dilatation and connection of blobs; (e) filled convex hull in the lower third of the blob; (f) blob after holes are filled and erosion

This results in a binarised hand probability covering only some boundary parts of the hand region (Fig. 2c), which cannot be closed by simple dilatation. After connecting the largest blob with small nearby blobs (Fig. 2d) two little blobs are spuriously connected to the main blob, however, the bottom region could correctly be extended. Nevertheless, the hand structure remains open in the wrist region. Drawing the convex hull around the entire blob would close the open parts and would surely comprise all pixels of the hand. If, however, the fingers are spread, too much background pixels would be integrated in the blob spoiling the skin-colour-adaptation process. The dilemma can be resolved by drawing the convex hull only around the lower third of the blob (Fig. 2e). This closes the blob structure in the hand-palm region while keeping the separated fingers.[1]

Finally, all holes in the resulting blob structure are filled and the blob is eroded (Fig. 2f) using the same structural element as the dilatation described above. This also removes the spurious spot, which can be seen in the top-left of Fig. 2d. This well-designed sequence of morphological operators yields a binary image in which the largest blob represents the region of the waving hand and can be used to determine the current hand position (centroid of the blob).

---

[1] During the hand-wave gesture, it can be assumed that the hand is presented with fingers pointing upwards.

3.5   Removing the Forearm

The detected moving foreground object does not only contain the hand but also the forearm if the latter is uncovered. This affects the hand-position determination and the adaptation of the skin probabilities. Hence, the forearm has to be removed. This problem had been addressed already in [9,14,15]. Typically the palm region is first identified based on a distance transform of the blob, then the wrist position is located. We follow a similar approach including some new steps that increase the reliability in difficult scenarios. The entire procedure is explained in the following with reference to Fig. 3.

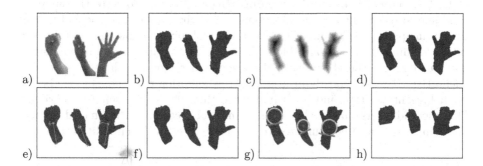

Fig. 3. Removing the forearm: (a) hands from original image; (b) hand blobs; (c) distance transformation; (d) points of largest distance and maximum inscribing circle; (e) principal component analysis; (f) shifted inscribing circles; (g) dividing lines between hand and forearm; (h) final hand blobs (Color figure online)

Palm and Orientation of the Hand. A distance transformation (Fig. 3c) of the hand blob yields a point $\mathbf{c} = (c_x, c_y)$ having a distance to the blob boundary that is equal to the radius r of the largest inscribing circle. So, ideally $\mathbf{c}$ is representing the palm (Fig. 3d). Based on a principal-component analysis, the orientation of the blob is determined (Fig. 3e, green line: main axis; blue line: orthogonal axis).

Modifying the Position of the Inscribing Circle. There are cases where the inscribing circle is not at the correct position. Figure 3(d) shows three examples where (i) the circle is almost at the top of the blob (blob of a fist), (ii) the circle is in the middle of the hand (with closed fingers), and (iii) the circle is at the wanted position (hand with spread fingers). Obviously, in some cases the position of the circle has to be corrected by shifting it towards the wrist. This is done by taking advantage of the distance d between the circle centre $\mathbf{c}$ and the top of the hand (with respect to the orientation of the hand).

In order to find the offset $\Delta\mathbf{c}$ by which the centre point of the inscribing circle has to be moved along the main hand axis, three fix points can be identified. First of all, if the palm is correctly located ($d = 3 \cdot r$), no movement is necessary.

Secondly, if the distance $d = r$ (circle touches the top of the hand), it is assumed that the hand is actually a fist and probably the circle is located right. The maximum $\Delta c = r$ is required when the circle is in the middle of the hand blob ($d = 2 \cdot r$). Between these points, a linear function is assumed to be helpful.

When the distance d is greater than $3 \cdot r$, then no correction is performed because it is most likely that r simply has been underestimated. This can happen if the blob contains only part of the entire hand.

The result of the modification can be seen in Fig. 3(f). The shifted circle represents the palm region much better than the original one.

Calculate Tangent of the Inscribing Circle. In order to correctly separate hand and forearm, the tangent of the inscribing circle that is orthogonal to the main principal axis is required, Fig. 3(g). All blob pixels below this tangent are erased yielding the final hand blob, Fig. 3(h). The entire procedure enables a fast and largely accurate forearm detection and removal with respect to the orientation. It is rotationally invariant on the condition that the hand is always in an upright position and not tilted more than 90° to the left or the right. This method offers an excellent compromise between forearm-removal ability and computational time compared to the approaches in the cited literature.

3.6   Evaluation of the Wave Gesture

If the hand-blob position can be determined for a sequence of images, it must be checked, whether the direction of movement has changed. As we assume that the hand wave is performed horizontally, only the horizontal components of the corresponding motion vectors have to be evaluated.

The entire process uses a simple state machine comprising the states: "no object found", "skin-coloured object is moving", "movement has changed its direction once", and "movement has changed its direction twice". If the last state is reached and the distance (d(wave) in Fig. 4) between the two reversing points is larger than a half of the blob's bounding box, then the hand has reliably been detected and can be tracked. The state machine is accompanied by a consistency check. The state machine is reset, when the current centroid position is not within a region that can be predicted based on the previous position and the motion vector field. Changes of motion directions are only taken into consideration if the

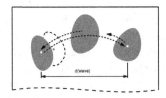

Fig. 4. Determination of direction changes

average horizontal movement exceeds a distance of three pixels.[2] In addition, the motion direction must have been consistent for the last 200 milliseconds assuming that the whole motion in one direction typically lasts about a half second.

At the reversing points, the movement is typically close to zero and the hand blob cannot be determined correctly because the probability of being part of a hand decreases for all pixels, see Eq. (4). A missing blob is tolerable for a period of about 200 milliseconds. This duration has been determined empirically. If the blob cannot be found for a longer time, the state machine is reset to its initial state.

3.7   Generation of a Skin-Colour Background Image

After the first direction change has been detected, the hand-blob position is known with certain reliability. From now on, the adapted skin-probability map is copied for each frame into a skin-colour background image excluding the region of the identified hand blob.

This background information can improve the combination of colour and motion as described in Subsect. 3.3. Equation (4) is modified to the heuristic formula

$$P(hand) = P(motion|\mathbf{v}) \cdot \max\left[0, P_{\text{adapted}}(skin|c) - b\right],$$

while $b = P_{\text{background}}(skin|c)$ is the skin-probability value of the corresponding background pixel. This technique effectively avoids the leakage of the hand blob into skin-coloured background regions and suppresses slightly moving objects like faces.

4   Results

Figure 5 shows the results directly after the second direction change of the putative hand blob has been detected. From left to right, the images contain: the original frame with a green dot indication the centroid of the detected blob, the probability map of the predefined skin-colour model, the probability map of the adapted skin-colour model, the skin-coloured background, the hand-probability image, and the final blob.

As can be seen, the original images are very diverse with respect to background colours and texture, the contrast, and the lighting conditions. The adapted skin-colour model reflects the colour of the moving hand at least as well as the offline trained model and mostly much better. In Fig. 5(b) the inner parts of the hand palm have the same colours as the wall in the background, which makes the distinction very difficult. Figure 5(c) shows challenging conditions not only with respect to the colours in the background, but also the shirt seems to be much more skin-like than the hand according to the predefined skin probability map. During the short wave gesture, the actual hand pixels are assigned higher

---

[2] Keep in mind that the vector magnitudes are often close to zero for inner hand parts.

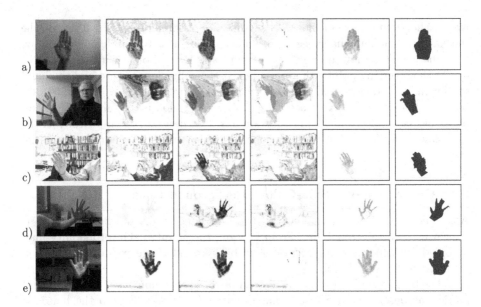

Fig. 5. Results after wave gesture has been completed for different sequences. The four pictures in the middle show the probability maps $P_{\mathrm{predef}}(skin|c)$, $P_{\mathrm{adapted}}(skin|c)$, $P_{\mathrm{background}}(skin|c)$, and $P(hand)$; the darker the pixel is, the higher is the probability. See text for more details. (Color figure online)

probabilities in the adapted model. Nevertheless, the binarisation keeps parts of the shirt leading to a blob that is too large. The hand detection is still successful as hand and forearm could be separated using the dedicated processing step. Figures 5(d) and (e) underline that the approach is able to keep finger information when the conditions are sufficiently good. It has to be mentioned that the method also works well when the camera is slightly moving.

5   Summary

We have presented a very robust method for the initial detection of a skin-coloured moving object (the hand). The probabilistic combination of colour and motion information, the inventive sequence of morphological processing steps together with a time-line observation of the position reliably finds the waving hand. The adapted skin-colour model is another key feature as the predefined skin-colour model tends to fail under realistic light conditions. The generated skin-coloured background image suppresses the influence of other skin-coloured objects, especially slightly moving faces or persons in the background. Forearms can be removed with sufficient accuracy.

The entity of the different processing steps is not required in each scenario and some steps might have no effect sometimes. However, the conditions in real-life applications vary a lot making it necessary to have a cure for each case at hand. Supporting reproducible research, all image sequences and the hand detection software can be downloaded from [16].

References

1. Premaratne, P.: Human Computer Interaction Using Hand Gestures. Springer, Singapore (2014). https://doi.org/10.1007/978-981-4585-69-9
2. Langmann, B., Hartmann, K., Loffeld, O.: Depth camera technology comparison and performance evaluation. In: Proceedings of the 1st International Conference on Pattern Recognition Applications and Methods, pp. 438–444 (2012)
3. Triesch, J., von der Malsburg, C.: Robust classification of hand postures against complex background. In: Proceedings of 2nd International Conference on Automatic Face and Gesture Recognition, pp. 14–16, October 1996
4. Chen, F.-S., Fu, C.-M., Huang, C.-L.: Hand gesture recognition using a real-time tracking method and hidden Markov models. Image Vis. Comput. **21**(8), 745–758 (2003)
5. Mittal, A., Zisserman, A., Torr, P.H.: Hand detection using multiple proposals. In: BMVC, pp. 1–11 (2011)
6. Stergiopoulou, E., Sgouropoulos, K., Nikolaou, N., Papamarkos, N., Mitianoudis, N.: Real time hand detection in a complex background. Engin. Appl. Artif. Intell. **35**, 54–70 (2014)
7. Deng, X., Zhang, Y., Yang, S., Tan, P., Chang, L., Yuan, Y., Wang, H.: Joint hand detection and rotation estimation using CNN. IEEE Trans. Image Process. **27**(4), 1888–1900 (2018)
8. Bambach, S., Lee, S., Crandall, D.J., Yu, C.: Lending a hand: detecting hands and recognizing activities in complex egocentric interactions. In: IEEE International Conference on Computer Vision (ICCV), pp. 1949–1957, December 2015
9. Palacios, J.M., Sagüs, C., Montijano, E., Llorente, S.: Human-computer interaction based on hand gestures using RGB-D sensors. Sensors **13**(9), 11842–11860 (2013)
10. Kawulok, M., Nalepa, J., Kawulok, J.: Skin detection and segmentation in color images. In: Celebi, M.E., Smolka, B. (eds.) Advances in Low-Level Color Image Processing. LNCVB, vol. 11, pp. 329–366. Springer, Dordrecht (2014). https://doi.org/10.1007/978-94-007-7584-8_11
11. Phung, S.L., Bouzerdoum, A., Chai, D.: Skin segmentation using color pixel classification: analysis and comparison. IEEE Trans. Pattern Anal. Mach. Intell. **27**(1), 148–154 (2005)
12. Farnebäck, G.: Two-frame motion estimation based on polynomial expansion. In: Bigun, J., Gustavsson, T. (eds.) SCIA 2003. LNCS, vol. 2749, pp. 363–370. Springer, Heidelberg (2003). https://doi.org/10.1007/3-540-45103-X_50
13. Kapur, J.N., Sahoo, P.K., Wong, A.K.: A new method for gray-level picture thresholding using the entropy of the histogram. Comput. Vis. Grap. Image Process. **29**(3), 273–285 (1985)
14. Wang, B., Xu, J.: Accurate and fast hand-forearm segmentation algorithm based on silhouette. In: 2012 IEEE 2nd International Conference on Cloud Computing and Intelligent Systems (CCIS), vol. 2. IEEE (2012)
15. Chai, X., Fang, Y., Wang, K.: Robust hand gesture analysis and application in gallery browsing. In: IEEE International Conference on Multimedia and Expo, ICME 2009, pp. 938–941. IEEE (2009)
16. http://www1.hft-leipzig.de/strutz/Papers/RoHaDe-resources/ . Accessed 13 June 2018

Multi-agent Robotic Systems in Collaborative Robotics

Sergey Vorotnikov[✉], Konstantin Ermishin, Anaid Nazarova, and Arkady Yuschenko

Robotic Center of Education and Research, Bauman Moscow State Technical University,
Izmaylovskaya Sq., 7, 105007 Moscow, Russian Federation
vorotn@bmstu.ru

Abstract. This paper describes the principles of control of multi-agent robotic systems. It is a new area of robotics oriented for introduction of robotic not only into industry but into life of human. The main principles of collaborative robotics are the safety of human and easiness of robot control. The problem is how to control not a single robot but a group of robots working together. It is most important for such tasks as rescue operations, environment monitoring etc. Some approaches to solve the task of human control of a group of robots are presented in the paper.

Keywords: Collaborative control · Multi-agent system · Decentralized systems
Dialog mode · Collaborative robots · Engineering education

1 Introduction

Collaborative robotics is a new stage in the development of the technogenic human environment. The basic requirements towards a collaborative robotic system (CRS) are the safety of the robot operating in a working area where a human being is also present, as well as the robot's easiness in handling, not requiring any special operator training. In our opinion, the term "collaborative robotics" is much broader than the frequently used "service robotics", because it is associated not only with the facilitation of human activities and the provision of certain services. CRS applied in various fields use groups of robots jointly solving common tasks. Two related problems arise here. The first is the need to provide for well-coordinated functioning of the individual robots that interact with each other and form the actual multi-agent robotic system (MARS). The second is the use of MARS in interaction with the person who manages the system, bearing in mind that the system agents might find themselves in an area where other people are also present. That said, management should remain simple enough for the operator, and the functioning of the robotic agents should be completely safe for the people and the technical equipment located in the MARS envelope area. We should point out that the application range of such systems is far beyond the examples mentioned above, as it is not limited solely to use in extreme environments. These can be health care systems in hospitals, involving the use of groups of robots for various purposes, and robots designed for training in schools and universities.

© Springer Nature Switzerland AG 2018
A. Ronzhin et al. (Eds.): ICR 2018, LNAI 11097, pp. 270–279, 2018.
https://doi.org/10.1007/978-3-319-99582-3_28

It is apparent that the use of groups of robots puts forward new requirements both towards the structure of the navigation and control system, and towards the organization of interaction with the operator, as well as towards the very methods of controlling the individual robotic agents. In this case, we can refer to a new class of robotic systems, that is, the collaborative MARS.

2   The Structure of Multi-agent Collaborative RS

The "collaborativeness" concept significantly expands the opportunities of the group management of robots, both for manipulative and mobile robotics. As is known, the group management systems belong to the multi-agent systems type, and two basic approaches are used in their management: the centralized and the decentralized approach. The first is intended for cases where similar agents perform similar tasks. The second is effective if agents have diversified structures and are able to perform various tasks.

A collaborative mobile robot is an intellectual agent functioning in an environment that is not completely deterministic, and its task is not clear. An example of such a task is the patrolling of some large crowded space, say, airport, railway station, hypermarket, etc. The unified robotic system, including both fixed and mobile observation stations, has to identify potential offenders at transportation facilities.

The priority task is to design a hardware and software package that includes a computer vision system and a group of mobile robots, in order to detect, track and accompany people whose appearance and behavior is deviant, and to convey the information about such persons to the operator's post. It should be pointed out that the group has a common goal, according to the general task. The goal is further divided into local targets of individual robotic agents, with each agent having its own route. The agents' algorithms are not completely formalized, due to the fact that the actions of the surveillance object cannot be known in advance. For instance, the surveillance object can move into another robot's patrolling area, or another object may attract the agent's attention. The robot perceives the movements of people in its patrol zone as non-deterministic. Thus, the agents have to modify their preset algorithms, such as their routes, agreeing them among themselves and with the operator. Preliminary analysis has shown that the solution of complex problems under conditions of uncertainty primarily requires a distributed system of a hybrid type, combining the centralized and decentralized systems. Here, team management is performed by way of the agents' exchanging information. The managing center sets up tasks and deals with the processing of the current information.

Thus, a hybrid MARS unit includes a control center, a team of robotic agents with different "specialization" and auxiliary equipment. The human operator's functions include system monitoring and taking decisions in complex or difficult situations. The control center performs team management as a whole, giving appropriate commands, and processes the information received by the robots during the performance of their tasks. Depending on their functional abilities, the robots may perform surveillance, search or technological tasks. According to the tasks received from the control center, the robots exchange messages, join into groups and distribute tasks among themselves according to the specified optimality criteria.

The modular [1] structure of the MARS hierarchical control system includes four levels. The control center is the first level of the control system. It contains the instruction control unit which is responsible for the instruction sequence generation and for passing those instructions along to the robots; there is also a data processing unit which receives information from the robotic agents and from the auxiliary gauges and information tools. The second level is responsible for the overall planning of the MARS actions. It breaks down the tasks to be solved by MARS into simpler tasks and distributes them among the robots. Using the appropriate algorithms, target point coordinates for each robot are determined.

The third level provides the robots' movement trajectories via the local planning algorithms which are based on a method similar to the method of potentials. Generation of the motion trajectories requires knowledge of the robots' current coordinates in the workspace; this task is solved by the combined navigation system.

The fourth, executive, level performs the direct interaction between all MARS elements and the outer environment. It is responsible for the creation of control signals for the robots' drives, navigation sensors, special and auxiliary equipment, and it also supports the sensor system operation.

3   Scheduling

The implementation of both centralized and multi-agent (distributed) control methods requires solving of the global planning tasks. That is, a bigger task is to be broken down into smaller-scale tasks and distributed among the individual agents according to the general (global) task facing the group. In case of centralized management, the control center distributes the tasks among the team of robots according to the established optimality criteria. Usually, the task time serves as such criterion. The easiest way to solve tasks of **centralized control** is the direct search method. However, in most instances it is impractical because it takes too long. Evolution methods (genetic algorithms) also require considerable time due to their computational complexity. Due to this, a simpler weighted algorithm [1] has been worked out, tested and introduced. It allows managing a team of robots in real-time mode. The tasks to be solved by a group of agents are perceived as known. As it has been already said, all robots are similar and each task can be solved by several robots. For each robotic agent, the control center forms an array of weights $\{c_{ij}\}$, where $i = 1,2,\ldots,n$ stands for the robot number, and $j = 1,2,\ldots,m$ stands for the task number. This array contains the proposed tasks of a robot, for instance, the time or energy required to solve each task. The control center has to distribute tasks among the group of robots. so that to minimize the appropriate graphs of weights (Fig. 1a). For instance, for the first task a robot with the number "i" is selected and provided with $min_i c_{i1}$.

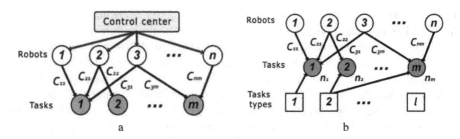

Fig. 1. Group task distribution patterns: centralized (a) and multi-agent (b).

When there are many robots in a group, centralized control appears to be somewhat inexpedient. Among its drawbacks, there will be low reliability of the system, heavy workload on communication channels and high consumption of computing resources of the control center. Besides, centralized approach will be ineffective for working areas with rapidly changing parameters.

The second pattern of task distribution among robots is devoid of these drawbacks. It is **multi-agent (distributed) control task** setting where agents themselves distribute their tasks to build the collaboration basis on the specified optimality criteria (Fig. 1b).

This task distribution is optimally achieved through "auction" type negotiation pattern which is based on information exchange between individual agents. At the auction, resources are announced which are required for the agents to achieve their goals; that is, they are, so to speak, "set up for sale". Resources are limited, and so the agents compete in the "bidding" process. When tasks are distributed among the robot team, tasks themselves serve as resources. The expediency of the "purchase", that is, assignment of specified tasks to each robot, is estimated by the set criterion of optimality [2]. On each stage of the auction, robot agents form their own weight arrays, and one of them becomes leader. From the responding agents, the leader chooses those who offer the lowest weight loss and sends them a command to carry out the task. At the next stage, another agent currently on standby will become leader. The auction is held until all tasks are distributed. Thus, multi-agent management pattern ensures self-organization of the system and increases its operational reliability. Comparison of the multi-agent patterns has shown that the task distribution algorithm based on the "auction" communication model, is much simpler from the computational point of view ($0.12 * n$ times, $n \gg 8$) compared to another well-known multi-agent method of collective plan improvement [3].

For multi-agent task distribution, each robot agent has to be able to exchange information with all the other robots that make up the team. This problem can be solved by dividing of the team of robots into smaller groups, each having its leader agent who will be able to exchange data with the rest of the agent forming the group. The number of such leaders should be kept minimal. As a result, the robot team is broken down into smaller groups each having a leader. After that, within each formed group it will be possible to use the previously considered multi-agent task distribution algorithm.

The easiest task is uniform distribution of robots in the working area. A more meaningful task is to move robots to specified target points and to perform operations at these points. In the latter case, the control system has to provide robots with appropriate routes, that is, to solve local planning tasks. The appropriate algorithms are implemented on the third level of the control system (Fig. 2). They are basic for the trajectory formation unit. The kinematic analog of the well-known "method of potentials" can be used as the basic algorithm for trajectory formation. The implementation of this method ensures uniform distribution of robots in the work area when it is examined for emergencies. It also ensures the transfer of the robots to the required target points for the performance of technological operations. In both cases, this method enables the robots to avoid collisions with fixed and moving obstacles, including other robots. In particular, the considered method of multi-agent management was effectively used for mapping of terrain exposed to radioactive contamination [1]. The robots collecting data are evenly distributed across the work area and the required parameters are measured. The measurement results are fed into the control center database and plotted on the special-purpose local map.

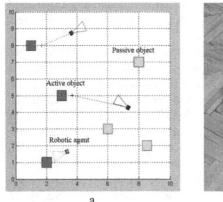

a   b

Fig. 2. Graphic model (a), mock-up specimen of robots (b).

4   Dialog Control of Multi-agent Robotic Systems

Management of autonomous mobile robots on the operator's part takes form of setting the tasks and the dialogue accompanying the performance of those tasks. This management requires "natural", from the human point of view, space-time relations [4] which greatly facilitate the task of controlling the robot. The description of a robot's outer world includes both the description of objects relevant for the performance of the set task, and the spatial relations between the objects of the world, including the robot itself. Extensional and intentional fuzzy relations are used to describe the spatial relations between the objects of the working scene [4]. The first include the relationship of position and orientation of objects. For instance, "object $a1$ is far away, ahead and to the right of object $a2$". Intentional relations include such relations as "to contact"; "to be inside"; "to be out"; "to be in the center", etc. Using formal rules of conjunction and disjunction, from elementary spatial binary relations it is possible to obtain other relations encountered in practice.

The current situation embracing M objects, including a controlled robot, is described by a binary frame system (<object m>, <relationship>, <object n>), $m, n = 1,2,...,M$. If the fuzzy binary relations between all objects that can be observed by the robot in the course of movement are set in advance, then we will get a fuzzy semantic network, or a fuzzy map. Using this map, it is possible, in particular, to navigate the robot along the observable benchmarks, i.e. the objects whose position was known in advance [5]. The image of the current situation may include other fuzzy features besides the spatial ones. [6].

Since the outer world is continuously changing both due to the movement of the objects under surveillance and due to the movement of the robot itself, the description of the situation will also vary with time. This circumstance requires taking into general consideration not only spatial but also temporary relations in the outside world, such as "to coincide", "to take place earlier", or "to follow". Such relations have to be used, in particular, for control of mobile robots moving around areas that contain other moving objects [7]. They make it possible to provide for automatic accompaniment of mobile objects, or to avoid collision with them.

Having described the current situation in the language of linguistic variables and fuzzy relations, one can specify the behavior of an autonomous robot in an external, not completely defined environment using fuzzy rules of the production type. These behavioral stereotypes have the form of production rules: "*if the situation is S_i, then the tactics is T_i*". Typical situations can be input in the robot's fuzzy knowledge base in advance, using the experience of the human operator. Using this database, a set of behavioral rules (tactics) can be drawn up that correspond to the pursuit of a new object, exit to a specific point shown on the electronic map, etc. The tactics themselves can be included into the robot's knowledge base by way of teaching a neural fuzzy system on which the fuzzy controller is based [8].

Operator can only inform the robot of the final goal of its movement in a space with a partially known structure. In this case, there arises the problem of autonomous traffic planning, which requires special consideration [9]. The planning is accompanied by a dialogue with the operator. The organization of the interactive control system involves the formation of a speech interface that includes a recognition module and a linguistic analyzer. The first module is a device for converting speech signals and interpreting them as separate words or phrases. The linguistic analyzer performs syntactic and semantic analysis of the statement, making it possible to fill-in the frame slots used for the description of actions [10].

5 Mobile Robotic Agent in Collaborative Robotic System

The control system of a mobile service robot is a two-tier architecture which consists of a base unit and an extension unit [11]. The base unit of a control system is responsible for controlling the movement of the mobile robot. It collects and analyzes sensory information, draws up a map of the working area, localizes the robot and its surrounding objects, schedules the route and manages the movements of the robot, including manipulation of objects.

The extension unit of the control system provides a mechanism for collaborative interaction of the robot with the human companion in the natural language. They interact through a dialogue block, with the help of which the human companion forms a sequence of tasks for the robot. When a task is formed in a natural language, its description is related to the working area topography, geometric coordinates indcated on the room plan, or is linked to certain objects or interaction with them.

Multimodal representation of the surrounding space in the form of a multi-layered map of the robot's working area provides for the mobile service robot's safe movement and effective interaction with its human companion.

A robot designed by Applied Robotics Ltd can be considered as an example of a mobile collaborative robot. It is a multifunctional robotic complex intended for various service and educational tasks. It consists of a differential type mobile chassis, anthropomorphic torso with two movable manipulator hands having five grades of mobility, and a head with two grades of mobility. The height of the robot is 130 cm. The load-carrying capacity of the manipulator arm is 0.75 kg, the battery life is 8 h.

The control system of the mobile collaborative robot is based on a combined modular hardware and software complex. The hardware complex includes navigational, onboard and multimedia controllers. Navigational controller processes the sensory device readings, builds a map of the surrounding space, detects the position of the robot and the objects around it, arranges the robot's routes and controls its movement. The onboard controller is the key element of the robot's control system. It is intended for the implementation of the basic robot control programs and for the management of functioning of the robot's systems. The multimedia controller is intended for the implementation of the of the robot's human-machine interfaces, such as remote telepresence system, speech dialogue system and graphic information visualization system. The robot functions in cooperation with a human companion, who manages the robot through natural language speech commands.

Besides interaction with the human companion, the robot can interact with people around it, when it encounters them on its route. In this case, the robot has to plan its further route so that to ensure traffic safety. Since the robot is operated under restricted conditions, i.e. among people who are constantly near and who move in close proximity, the robot control system is designed so that it would be able to assess the environment it is interacting with.

The robot's onboard sensor systems represent the surrounding space as an aggregate of a topographic plan, security areas, traffic control areas and a local map. The topographic plan is a geometric plan of the room divided into zones which are further subdivided into traffic control zones and zones associated with the job performance. The surrounding environment is clarified by way of compiling the information from a variety of different local maps obtained from the onboard sensor systems. For instance, the map received from the laser-beam scanning range meter will be used for the robot's localization on a topographic plan, and the map taken from the array of sonars located around the robot's perimeter will show the presence of objects around the robot during its movement. As a result, the assessment of the working area alteration, together with the task posed, allows to form a sequence of safe robot maneuvers for movement in rapidly changing constrained conditions.

6   Educational Complex for Studying the Methods of the Collaborative Robotic System Management

To test the various group behavior scenarios of robotic agents and to prevent possible collisions, the Center for Education and Research "Robotics" of the Bauman Moscow State Technical University has designed a software model for decentralized control of a group of mobile wheeled robots in the Matlab[1] environment (Fig. 2a) and their large-scale models (Fig. 2b).

The simulation was performed to solve the tasks of planning the robotic agent's actions in the group and the actions of the group as a whole. The simulation also provided for a possibility of obstacles (passive objects) hindering the movement of an individual robot along its route, which the robot had to bypass in automatic mode. When were present in the working area, one of the tasks of the robotic agents was to select the tracking object automatically taking into account the distance and the orientation of the appropriate robotic agent. At the same time, it was possible to automatically engage another robotic agent in tracking of the object. In turn, it required redistribution of escort objects among the robotic agents.

The studies have shown that the centralized group planning system is too complex from the computational point of view, because it depends on the number of agents in the group. Besides, it significantly complicates information exchange between the robots and the operator. Therefore, for the model development we used a method that we called "method of distributed action planning". In this case, each robot of the group independently solves the task of planning its actions in the current situation. A robotic agent which is a member of the group can change its actions solely on the basis of information concerning the current state of the environment, current situation and actions of other robots of the group, for a certain time interval. A desired action of a robot in the current situation is an action that contributes the most towards the achievement of the common (group) goal, i.e. gives the maximum possible increment of the target functional.

The modeling assumed that the "effect" of R_j robot achieving the goal $X_i \in \{X\}$ was determined by the meaning of a certain a priori efficiency assessment $d_{ji} = F(S_j, X_i, K_i)$, where K_i is the priority of the target X_i. Then, the task of target allocation within the group of robots will boil down to the need to distribute robots R_j ($j = \overline{1,n}$) among the subjects X_i ($i = \overline{1,m}$) so that to obtain the maximal cumulative effect

$$Y = \sum_{j=1}^{n} d_{ji_j},$$

where i_j is the number of target X_i selected by robot R_j.

The formation of the functional took into account that the number of the robots in the group n_i sent to the same target X_i at the same time should not exceed a certain $n_i^{\max}$, $i = 1,2,\dots m$, which is selected based on the required group behavior strategy, and

---

[1] The mathematical and software models were developed by V.G. Ponomaryov.

depends on the target priority, or on the correlation between the number of the robots and the targets.

Agent's control system includes two levels. The upper level (the action planning module) is intended for constructing of the robot's route and for setting the task to the lower level (the route module) that forms the control of the robot drives.

The action planning module of a robotic agent implements an iterative procedure for optimizing the collective solution in accordance with a given efficiency criterion, say, minimization of the total distance covered by the robots. The central part of this module's pattern is PU processor node PU, implemented as a finite automaton. The PU input unit receives information about the ID of the object, vector E denoting the environmental situation, vector S denoting the robot's condition, vector K denoting coefficient, and S_M vector denoting the route module condition. At the output, the elements of the action vector $A = (T, S)$ and the vector of the robot condition CS are formed.

For full-scale testing of the decentralized collective management model, prototype robot mock-ups were made featuring a traditional three-wheel scheme with two driving wheels and a two-level control system. The upper layer is implemented on the basis of Odroid controller with installed ROS (robot operating system) and ultrasonic range-finders. It is intended for dealing with the navigation issues (routing, obstacle avoidance, etc.), escorting of objects and communication with the operator and other robots through Wi-Fi. The lower layer implements the route module and uses the Arduino UNO processor which performs the function of the drive controller with PI regulator of the speed of the driving wheels.

A functioning action planning module was subjected to analysis, within the framework of the robotic system modeling. It required two series of ten experiments where robots and targets were placed randomly in the working area. The findings showed that the iterative procedure of the group decision optimization allowed to distribute robots according to their goals in a short time. By the third step of the iteration, more than 60% of the robots have made the final selection of the target.

The developed complex makes it possible to conduct comparative studies of various methods of managing a group of robots under the control of a human operator. Its use has shown its effectiveness as a tool for researching and developing new methods for collective robot management in collaborative robotic systems.

7 Conclusion

The development of robotics enters a new phase, when remote control of mobile and manipulative robotic devices gives way to collaborative control where the robot becomes an equal partner of the human operator, fully participating in the task solving process. The operator's task is substantially simplified, and specialized training is no longer needed. However, the robotic system in itself becomes more complex; now it possesses a high degree of autonomy and has capabilities that are usually referred to as artificial intelligence. Today, the problems are posed, primarily, by the capabilities of computer technology which has to assess the current situation and to manage mobile robots in real-time mode, taking into account sufficiently high speeds of movement.

Another source of the problem is the psycho-physiological capabilities of the human operator who manages autonomous activities of mobile robots in the outside world.

References

1. Nazarova, A.V., Rizhova, T.P.: Technology and algorithms of multi-agent control of robotic system. Vestnik BMSTU, Priborostroenie **6**, 93–105 (2012)
2. Jennings, N., Paratin, P., Jonson, M.: Using intelligent agents to manage business processes. In: The Practical Application of Intelligent Agents and Multi-Agent Technology: Proceedings of the First International Conference, London (UK), pp. 345–376 (1996)
3. Kapustyan, S.G.: Algorithm of collective improvement of planning of the tasks distribution in a group of robots. Schtuchny Intllect **3**, 463–474 (2005)
4. Kandrashina, E.Yu., Litvinceva, L.V., Pospelov, D.A.: Kowledge Representation of Time and Space in Intelligence Systems. Nauka, Moscow (1989)
5. Yuschenko, A.S.: Mobile robot route planning in undetermined situation. Mechatron. Autom. Control **1**, 31–38 (2004)
6. Yuschenko, A.S., Tachkov, A.A.: An integrated control system of a fire reconnaissance robot. Vestnik BMSTU Priborostroenie **6**, 106–111 (2012)
7. Vorotnikov, S.A., Ermishin, K.V.: Intelligent control system of a service mobile robot. Vestnik BMSTU Priborostroenie **6**, 285–289 (2012). Special issue «Robotic Systems»
8. Yushchenko, A.S.: Dialogue mode of robot control on the base of fuzzy logic. In: Transaction of the Conference «Extreme Robotics», S-Pb. "Politechnika service", pp. 143–146 (2015)
9. Yuschenko, A.S.: Intelligence task planning of robot work. Mechatron. Autom. Control **3**, 5–18 (2005)
10. Zhonin, A.A.: Training algorithm of dialogue manager for a dialogue speech control system of robot. In: Proceedings of International Conference "Integrated Models and Soft Computing in Artificial Intelligence" Moscow, FizMatLit, pp. 395–406 (2011)
11. Yuschenko, A., Vorotnikov, S., Konyshev, D., Zhonin, A.: Mimic recognition and reproduction in bilateral human-robot speech communication. In: Ronzhin, A., Rigoll, G., Meshcheryakov, R. (eds.) ICR 2016. LNCS (LNAI), vol. 9812, pp. 133–142. Springer, Cham (2016). https://doi.org/10.1007/978-3-319-43955-6_17

Hybrid Force/Position Control of a Collaborative Parallel Robot Using Adaptive Neural Network

Seyedhassan Zabihifar$^{(\boxtimes)}$ and Arkadi Yuschenko

Bauman Moscow State Technical University (BMSTU), Moscow, Russia
zabihifar@student.bmstu.ru

Abstract. In this paper, a new stable adaptive neural network control scheme has been presented for hybrid position and force control of the Delta parallel robot. Force control is an important technique in programming and safety for collaborative robots. The hybrid control scheme is introduced to tackle the interaction problem between the robot and its environment such that the robot follows the position trajectory and desired force, which is applied in a certain position. The goal of the control is applying desired force trajectory in a certain position in which there is a constraint for movement. Fewer parameter settings, adaptive algorithm, and efficient control input signals are the advantages of the proposed controller.

Keywords: Adaptive neural network · Collaborative robot · Delta robot
Force control

1 Introduction

Recent progress dealing with physical Human-Robot Interaction have covered in an integrated way mechanical, actuation, sensing, planning, and control issues, with the goal of increasing safety and dependability of robotic systems [1]. When a collaborative robot manipulator performs a task in contact with its environment and humans, the position and force control is highly required because of the constraints imposed by the environmental conditions. Also, it is important to the requirements of safety standards for collaborative robots. In such contact tasks of the manipulator, the impedance control method is one of the most effective methods to control a manipulator in contact with its environments. This approach can realize the desired dynamic properties of the end-effector by the appropriate impedance parameters with the desired trajectory. In general, however, it would be difficult to design them based on the tasks and their environments including nonlinear or time-varying factors [2].

The dynamics of a Delta parallel robot is governed by a highly nonlinear coupled, time-varying system with many uncertainties such as load variation, friction and external disturbances [3]. In high-speed applications, the traditional PID controller cannot satisfy the requirement of accurate trajectory tracking. As a result, the computed-torque based controller is proposed to meet this need. So artificial intelligence methods are presented, such as neural network, fuzzy PID control, adaptive

© Springer Nature Switzerland AG 2018
A. Ronzhin et al. (Eds.): ICR 2018, LNAI 11097, pp. 280–290, 2018.
https://doi.org/10.1007/978-3-319-99582-3_29

control, etc. for this problem. During the last decade, neural network technology has gained popularity among control community due to its versatile features such as parallel-distributed structure and learning capability. The main idea behind adaptive neural network based control is to learn unknown nonlinear dynamics and compensate the existing uncertainties in the dynamic model without requiring any preliminary offline training [3–6].

Due to the complexity of the dynamic model, it is very difficult to design an integrated control system for variable conditions, which the robot is faced with. In the current research, an Adaptive Neural Network (ANN) controller was developed for a parallel robot as a MIMO system to simultaneously control three actuators, which are corresponding to the dynamics of the robot in different situations. In fact, the controller has been designed to eliminate some common problems like inverse dynamic and un-modeled dynamics. The proposed method can estimate the dynamic model and make a position control of the end-effector by producing an efficient control signal.

The proposed method improves the previous works by introducing a simple integrated hybrid control system. The supposed system is the key to improve the efficiency of the controller through reducing the chattering and position errors while the rising time is going to be decreased.

The next goal of the current presentation is to control the force when the robot's end-effector moves perpendicular to the force direction. In addition, to estimate the dynamic model of the robot, optimizing the effects of the force error in robot actuator's command has also been taken as an incentive to present the current research. The remarkable point is that the goal is to apply desired force at a certain position at which there is a limitation of movement.

Analysis and simulations are used to evaluate the controller's ability to carry out trajectories using feedback from a force sensor and position sensors found in the robot joints. The results show that the proposed approach has been successful enough to achieve stable and accurate control of force and position trajectories for a variety of test conditions.

2 Delta Robot Dynamics

In [7, 8] the dynamic model of the Delta parallel robot has been described as follows:

$$T = M\ddot{q} + C(q.\,\dot{q}) + G_{gr}, \tag{1}$$

where T is the vector of torques that have to be applied to the motors, $q = [\theta_1, \theta_2, \theta_3]^T$ is the vector of joint angles, M is the mass matrix of the robot, $C(q, \dot{q})$ is the Coriolis and centrifugal contributions and G_{gr} is the gravity part. The Eq. (1) can be written as:

$$\ddot{q} = F(x) + G(x)T, \tag{2}$$

where $F(x) = -M^{-1}(C(q.\dot{q}) + G_{gr})$, $G(x) = M^{-1}$.

The dynamics of a robot manipulator is governed by a highly nonlinear coupled, time-varying system with many uncertainties such as friction and external disturbances. High coupling and nonlinear properties of the dynamic model is so explicit that it becomes a major impediment to develop a model-based controller like computed-torque controller. In this paper, the Delta Robot has been modeled by Solidworks and is imported to Simulink for simulation.

3 Problem Statement

The Delta robot dynamic model is the nonlinear time-varying system described by one differential equation from (2) with the following structure:

$$\ddot{Y} = F(x) + G(x)U \tag{3}$$

where $x = \left[y_1 \dot{y}_1 y_2 \dot{y}_2, \ldots, \dot{y}_p\right]^T$ is the output which is assumed available for measurement, $u = [u_1 \ldots u_p]^T$ is the input vector, $y = [y_1 \ldots y_p]^T$ is the output vector and $F(X)$ and $G(X)$ are smooth nonlinear functions.

Assumption 1: The desired output trajectory $Y_d(t)$ and its first derivative are smooth and bounded.

Assumption 2: The gain $G(X)$ is bounded, positive definite and slowly time-varying.

Let's define the tracking error as:

$$e(t) = Y_d(t) - Y(t) \tag{4}$$

and the filtered tracking errors by:

$$S = \dot{e} + \lambda(t)e, \tag{5}$$

where $S = [s_1 \ldots s_p]^T$ and $\lambda(t) \in \Re^{p \times p})0$ is a diagonal matrix. From (5) we deduce that the convergence of S to zero implies convergence of the tracking error and its derivative to zero [9]. So, the objective of control is summarized in the synthesis of a control law that allows the filtered error to converge to zero. The filtered error first-time derivative is given by:

$$\dot{S} = \upsilon - F(x) - G(x)U, \tag{6}$$

where $\upsilon = \ddot{Y}_d + \lambda(t)\dot{e} + \dot{\lambda}(t)e$. The ideal sliding mode control (SMC) which guarantees the closed loop system performances may be given by:

$$U^* = U_{eq}^* + U_{cor}^*, \tag{7}$$

where U_{eq}^* is the ideal equivalent control and U_{cor}^* is the ideal corrective control introduced as follows:

$$U_e q^* = G^{(-1)}(v - F);$$ (8)

$$U_c or^* = k^* sat(\frac{s^*}{\varphi}),$$ (9)

where k^* presents the sliding gain optimal value and s^* is the sliding surface with the ideal slope $\lambda^*(t)$. Using $sat(s/\varphi)$ helps us to make a bound for filtered error to decrease the chattering phenomenon [9].

Substituting (7), (8) and (9) in (6), filtered error dynamics becomes:

$$\dot{S} = -Gk^* sat(\frac{s^*}{\varphi}),$$ (10)

which implies that $s \to 0$ and therefore $e, \dot{e} \to 0 \ \& \ j = 1 : r_1 - 1, i = 1 : p$. However, the implementation of the control law which is defined in Eq. (7) is quite difficult.

Therefore, our goal is to use an adaptive neural network to solve the problems encountered by the classical sliding mode technique, but the problem is to design an integrated control approach to control the force and position. Although the second part of this paper considered the hybrid force and position control. Therefore, in this paper, a novel approach is presented to solve these problems and it has been compared with PID force control.

4 Adaptive Neural Network Controller Design

In this section, Single Hidden Layer (SHL) Networks will perform the approximation of the corresponding command. According to universal approximation theory, the neural network of the SHL type can estimate any nonlinear, continuous, and unknown function [10]. Now, according to the universal approximation property of NN, there is a Two-layer NN such that:

$$G^{-1}(v - F(x)) = f(x) = W^T \sigma(V^T x) + \varepsilon,$$ (11)

where V, W are the NN weights, x is the input vector of the neural network, σ is a sigmoid activation function. moreover, the approximation error ε bounded on a compact set by $\|\varepsilon\| \langle \varepsilon_N$.

Thus, the proposed control law is given by the following expression:

$$U_{eq} = \hat{W}^T \sigma(\hat{V}^T x) + k_v s. U_{cor} = -k_s sat(\frac{s}{\varphi});$$

$$U = \hat{W}^T \sigma(\hat{V}^T x) + k_v s - k_s sat(\frac{s}{\varphi}),$$ (12)

where $\hat{V}, \hat{W}$ are the matrices of input and output neural network weights respectively, which should be specified given the tuning algorithms. Note that $\hat{V}, \hat{W}$ are estimates of the ideal weight values. $x'_i = \left[e_i, \dot{e}_i, \theta_{id}, \dot{\theta}_{id}, \ddot{\theta}_{id}\right]$ is the input vector of each neuron where $e_i = \theta_{id} - \theta_i, i = 1, 2, 3$ and k_v, k_s are the constants and U_{cor} provides robustness in the face of higher-order terms in the Taylor series, but it can produce some chatters in the output. The structure of the controller is shown in Fig. 1.

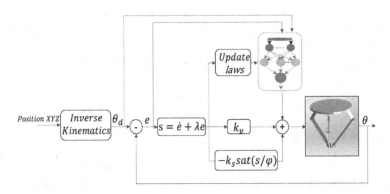

Fig. 1. Structure of position controller scheme.

Assumption: $\|W\| \le W_m, \|V\| \le V_m, \|\varphi\| < \delta$, where W_m, V_m, δ are unknown positive constants and the weight deviations or weight estimation errors are defined as $\tilde{V} = V - \hat{V}, \tilde{W} = W - \hat{W}$.

E-modification technique usually used in robust adaptive control, which is applied for improving the robustness of the controller in the presence of the NN approximation error [11]. Hence the weight adaptation laws based on e-modification technique has been provided by [12]:

$$\begin{aligned}
\dot{\hat{W}} &= F_w\big(\hat{\sigma}s^T - k\|s\|\hat{W}\big); \\
\dot{\hat{V}} &= F_v\big(xs^T\hat{W}^T\hat{\sigma}' - k\|s\|\hat{V}\big),
\end{aligned} \tag{13}$$

with any constant positive definite design matrices F_w, F_v and k is a positive constant. Then the tracking error $s(t)$ approaches to zero with t and the weight estimates of $\hat{V}, \hat{W}$ are bounded.

4.1   Error System Dynamics

Define the hidden layer output error for a given x as:

$$\tilde{\sigma} = \sigma - \hat{\sigma} = \sigma\big(V^T x\big) - \sigma(\hat{V}^T x). \tag{14}$$

The Taylor series expansion of $\sigma(x)$ for a given x may written as:

$$\sigma(V^T x) = \sigma(\hat{V}^T x) + \sigma'(\hat{V}^T x) \tilde{V}^T x + O(\tilde{V}^T x)^2. \tag{15}$$

The Jacobian matrix and $O(z)^2$ denotes terms of order two. Denoting $\hat{\sigma}' = \sigma'(\hat{V}^T x)$, we have [12]:

$$\tilde{\sigma} = \sigma'(\hat{V}^T x) \tilde{V}^T x + O(\tilde{V}^T x)^2 = \hat{\sigma}' \tilde{V}^T x + O(\tilde{V}^T x)^2. \tag{16}$$

Using the control law (12) and (6), (11) the closed–loop filtered error dynamics becomes

$$
\begin{aligned}
\dot{s} &= \upsilon - F(x) - G(x)\left(\hat{W}^T \hat{\sigma} + k_v s - k_s sat\left(\frac{s}{\varphi}\right)\right); \\
G^{-1}\dot{s} &= G^{-1}(\upsilon - F(x)) - \hat{W}^T \hat{\sigma} - k_v s + k_s sat\left(\frac{s}{\varphi}\right); \\
G^{-1}\dot{s} &= W^T \sigma - \hat{W}^T \hat{\sigma} - k_v s + k_s sat\left(\frac{s}{\varphi}\right) + \varepsilon.
\end{aligned}
\tag{17}
$$

Adding and subtracting $W^T \hat{\sigma}$, $\hat{W}^T \tilde{\sigma}$ yields

$$G^{-1}\dot{s} = \hat{W}^T \tilde{\sigma} + \tilde{W}^T \hat{\sigma} - k_v s + k_s sat\left(\frac{s}{\varphi}\right) + \tilde{W}^T \tilde{\sigma} + \varepsilon \tag{18}$$

and from (16) yields

$$G^{-1}\dot{s} = \hat{W}^T \hat{\sigma}' \tilde{V}^T x + \tilde{W}^T \hat{\sigma} - k_v s + k_s sat\left(\frac{s}{\varphi}\right) + W_1, \tag{19}$$

where $w_1 = \hat{W}^T O(\tilde{V}^T x)^2 + \tilde{W}^T \tilde{\sigma} + \varepsilon$. Suppose the disturbance term $w_1(t)$ in (19) is equal to zero.

Proof. Define the Lyapunov function candidate

$$L = \frac{1}{2} s G^{-1} s + \frac{1}{2} tr\{\tilde{W}^T F_w^{-1} \tilde{W}\} + \frac{1}{2} tr\{\tilde{V}^T F_v^{-1} \tilde{V}\}. \tag{20}$$

Differentiating yields

$$\dot{L} = s G^{-1} \dot{s} + tr\{\tilde{W}^T F_w^{-1} \dot{\tilde{W}}\} + tr\{\tilde{V}^T F_v^{-1} \dot{\tilde{V}}\}. \tag{21}$$

Whence substitution from (19) (with $w_1 = 0$) yields

$$\dot{L} = -k_v s^2 + s k_s sat\left(\frac{s}{\phi}\right) + tr\{\tilde{W}^T (F_w^{-1} \dot{\tilde{W}} + s\hat{\sigma})\} + tr\{\tilde{V}^T (F_v^{-1} \dot{\tilde{V}} + \hat{W}^T \hat{\sigma}' xs)\}. \tag{22}$$

Since $\hat{W} = W - \tilde{W}$, the W is constant, so $d\frac{\tilde{W}}{dt} = -d\frac{\hat{w}}{dt}$ and $d\frac{\tilde{V}}{dt} = -d\frac{\hat{V}}{dt}$. The tuning rules from (13) yield

$$\dot{L} = -k_v s^2 + sk_s sat\left(\frac{s}{\phi}\right) + kstr\{\tilde{W}^T(W - \tilde{W})\} + kstr\{\tilde{V}^T(V - \tilde{V})\}. \qquad (23)$$

Define the matrix of all the NN weights as:

$$Z = \begin{bmatrix} W & 0 \\ 0 & V \end{bmatrix}. \qquad (24)$$

Assumption: On any compact subset of $\Re^n$, the ideal NN weights are bounded so that $\|Z\|_F \le Z_B$ with Z_B known and $\|\cdot\|_F$ the Frobenius norm. Then

$$\dot{L} = -k_v s^2 + sk_s sat\left(\frac{s}{\phi}\right) + k\|s\|tr\{\tilde{z}^T(z - \tilde{z})\}. \qquad (25)$$

Since $tr\{\tilde{z}^T(z - \tilde{z})\} \le \|\tilde{z}\|_f \|z\|_f - \|\tilde{z}\|_f^2$ there results [12]:

$$\dot{L} \le -\|s\|k_v\|s\| + sk_s sat\left(\frac{s}{\phi}\right) - k\|s\| \cdot \left(\|\tilde{z}\|_f - D\right)^2 + k\|s\|D^2;$$
$$\dot{L} \le -sk_s sat\left(\frac{s}{\phi}\right) - \|s\|(k_v\|s\| + k.\left(\|\tilde{z}\|_f - D\right)^2 - kD^2), \qquad (26)$$

where $D = \frac{Z_B}{2}$. Suppose that $K_s < 0$, $K_v > 0$; then we prove that the Lyapunov first-time derivative becomes negative if: $\|s\| > \frac{kD^2}{k_v} = b_r$ or $\|\tilde{Z}\| > 2D$, where b_r is a positive constant. Then $\dot{L} \le 0$ which guarantees the stability of closed-loop system [4, 12].

5 Hybrid Force and Position Controller

The presentation of a new approach to control the force and position of a Delta robot is the main topic of the following. Here a new approach has been designed and investigated to highlight the performances. In general, the force error is applied only on the filtered tracking error and effects on the online adaptive learning algorithm to track the force command. To highlight the performance of this approach, it is compared with a popular approach like PID controller. Therefore, there is ANN controller for position control and another PID controller for force, but in the presented approach, there is only one integrated ANN controller, which is able to control the force and position together.

5.1 New Approach

In this approach, the influence of force is considered just to redesign the filtered tracking error, and the weights are updated according to the new s_f, which is defined by

$$s_{f_i} = \dot{e}_i + \dot{e}_f + \lambda(t)(e_i + e_f) \text{ for } i = 1, 2, 3,$$ (27)

where $e_f = F_d - F$. The control law is defined by

$$U_f = \hat{W}^T \sigma(\hat{V}^T x) + k_v s_f - k_s sat\left(\frac{s_f}{\varphi}\right)$$ (28)

and the adaptation laws has been provided by

$$\dot{\hat{W}} = F_w\left(\hat{\sigma} s_f^T - ks_f \hat{W}\right);$$
$$\dot{\hat{V}} = F_v\left(x s_f^T \hat{W}^T \hat{\sigma}' - ks_f \hat{V}\right).$$ (29)

Then the filtered error first-time derivative is given by:

$$\dot{s}_f = v - F(x) - G(x)U,$$ (30)

where

$$v = \ddot{Y}_d + \ddot{e}_d + \lambda(t)(\dot{e} + \dot{e}_f) + \dot{\lambda}(t)(e + e_f).$$ (31)

Here the neural network consists of three neurons in the output layer, and three neurons in the input layer as well, and the filtered error has been changed by adding the force error, which is introduced in (20). The stability of the closed-loop system can be proved by the Lyapunov function, which is introduced in (20).

6 Simulation Results

In the following section, the proposed control scheme is applied to a Delta robot. At first, the simulation of movement without any force is presented. Then, the simulation with force has been presented to show the hybrid position-force control system. The new approach which is presented, have been implemented and compared with PID

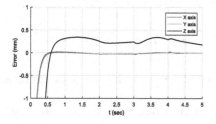

Fig. 2. The magnified tracking error of the position of the end effector.

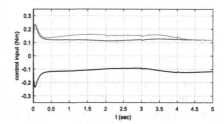

Fig. 3. The control input signals for three actuators.

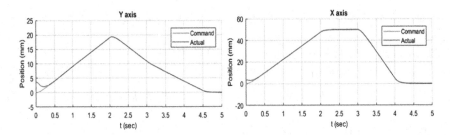

Fig. 4. The command and actual value of the end effector position in axes X, Y.

controller to highlight the efficiency of that. The simulation results for 0.2 kg payload have been shown in Figs. 2, 3 and 4.

Table 1. Controller parameters.

$F_w = 20$	$k_p = 3$	$\lambda = 10$	$W(0) = 0$	$k = 4$	$k_s = 0.1$
$F_y = 10$	$k_i = 1.5$	$k_v = 0.5$	$V(0) = 0$	$k_d = 1$	

The parameters of the controller are chosen in Table 1 where k_p, k_i, k_d are the PID controller coefficients.

Here, the simulation of proposed algorithm has been shown for hybrid force and position control problem. The force trajectory is shown in Fig. 5 with the final point of 0.5 N as a force command. The force is applied when the end effector of the robot is stable at the −240 mm of the height position in Z axis and robot is moving in the x-y plane. The force tracking error and control inputs are shown in Figs. 6, 7 and 8.

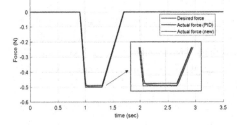

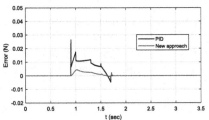

Fig. 5. The desired and actual value of force.   **Fig. 6.** Tracking error of the force.

Figures 9 and 10 show the trajectory tracking of the robot while the force has been applied in a certain position.

As it is demonstrated in Figs. 9 and 10, it is obvious that these new approaches are able to control the position and follow the force trajectory simultaneously. Control input changes are occurred in Figs. 7 and 8 due to changes the direction of the movement in x, y, z axes and changes in the force trajectory.

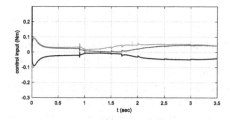

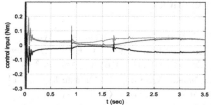

Fig. 7. The control input signals for PID approach.

Fig. 8. The control input signals for the presented approach.

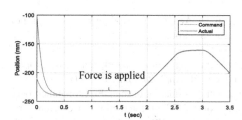

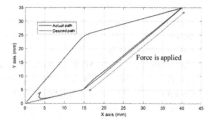

Fig. 9. The command and actual value of the end-effector position in the Z axis.

Fig. 10. The x-y path of the movement during force application

In the proposed approach, the force tracking error has been decreased significantly, and it is illustrated in Fig. 6 while the position trajectory also has been tracked well. To verify the efficiency of them, the variance of the force error has been calculated and it shows 88% improvement of the new approach in compared with the PID controller.

7   Conclusion

A new hybrid force-position controller using the adaptive neural network is proposed in this paper to control the motion of the robot in 3-dimensional axes and also follow the force trajectory in situations where there is a movement restriction for the robot. The new algorithm has been proposed to achieve the hybrid force-position controller when force trajectory tracking is needed. The controller was derived from the universal approximation property of neural networks, and weight adaptation laws were designed. The simulation results show clearly the efficiency of the proposed control law for a Delta parallel robot. The proposed controller simultaneously stabilizes the position of the robot as well as the force trajectory tracking.

References

1. Magrini, E., De Luca, A.: Hybrid force/velocity control for physical human-robot collaboration tasks. In: EEE/RSJ International Conference on Intelligent Robots and Systems (IROS 2016), pp. 857–863. IEEE (2016)
2. Tanaka, Y., Tsuji, T.: On-line learning of robot arm impedance using neural networks. In: IEEE International Conference on Robotics and Biomimetics, pp. 941–946 (2004)
3. Singh, H.P., Sukavanam, N., Panwar, V.: Neural network based compensator for robustness to the robot manipulators with uncertainties. In: Proceedings of the International Conference on Mechanical and Electrical Technology, ICMET 2010, pp. 444–448 (2010)
4. Moreno-Valenzuela, J., Aguilar-Avelar, C.S., Puga-Guzman, A., Santibanez, V.: Adaptive neural network control for the trajectory tracking of the Furuta pendulum. IEEE Trans. Cybern. **46**(12), 3439–3452 (2016)
5. Khazaee, M., Markazi, A.H.D., Rizi, S.T., Seyfi, B.: Adaptive fuzzy sliding mode control of input-delayed uncertain nonlinear systems through output-feedback. Nonlinear Dyn. **87**(3), 1943–1956 (2017)
6. Van Cuong, P., Nan, W.Y.: Adaptive trajectory tracking neural network control with robust compensator for robot manipulators. Neural Comput. Appl. **27**(2), 525–536 (2016)
7. Codourey, A.: Dynamic modelling and mass matrix evaluation of the DELTA parallel robot for axes decoupling control. In: Proceedings of IEEE/RSJ International Conference on Intelligent Robots and Systems (IROS 1996), vol. 3, pp. 1211–1218 (1996)
8. Du, J., Lou, Y.: Simplified dynamic model for real-time control of the delta parallel robot. In: IEEE International Conference on Information and Automation (ICIA 2016), pp. 1647–1652. IEEE (2016)
9. Slotin, E.: Applied Nonlinear Control. Prentice Hall, New Jersey (1991)
10. Hana Boudjedir, N.R., Yacef, F., Bouhali, O.: Dual neural network for adaptive sliding mode control of quadrotor helicopter stabilization. Int. J. Inf. Sci. Tech. **2**(4), 101–115 (2012)
11. Ge, S.S., Hang, C.C., Lee, T.H., Zhang, T.: Stable Adaptive Neural Network Control. ASIS, vol. 13. Springer, New York (2002). https://doi.org/10.1007/978-1-4757-6577-9
12. Lewis, F.L., Jaganathan, S., Yesildirek A.: Neural network control of robot manipulators and nonlinear systems (1999)

Swarm Robotics: Remarks on Terminology and Classification

Aufar Zakiev⑩, Tatyana Tsoy⑩, and Evgeni Magid$^{(\boxtimes)}$⑩

Laboratory of Intelligent Robotic Systems,
Kazan Federal University, Kazan 420008, Russian Federation
{zaufar,tt,magid}@it.kfu.ru
http://kpfu.ru/robolab.html

Abstract. Swarm robotics is a fast-growing field of research in recent years. As studies count increases, the terminology requires a revision in order to provide a proper level of unification and precision - even a unique "swarm robotics" term needs to be established. Since there are multiple types of collective robotics approaches and corresponding methodology, swarm robotics field terminology must be explicitly distinguished from others. In this paper, we attempt to compare and refine definitions that had been proposed in previous researches. We demonstrate relations between swarm robotics and concepts of adjacent fields including multi-agent systems, multi-robot systems and sensor networks.

Keywords: Swarm robotics · Sensor network · Robotic group
Multi-agent system · Multi-robot system

1 Introduction

Swarm robotics is one of multiple forms of robotic groups. Terms like a "multi-robot system", a "multi-agent system" and a "sensor network" are frequently used in researches that are dedicated to robotic groups. These terms are often perceived as synonyms although there are some important differences between them. As the field is still establishing itself, the basic terms of swarm robotics vary from one paper to another and this must be carefully considered. For example, groups of multiple robots are denoted in various recent studies as:

- Multi-Robot System (MRS) [3,12,16,30]
- Multi-Agent System (MAS) [9,13,20,25,29]
- Swarm Robotics System (SRS) or Robotic Swarm (RS) [4,10,14,15,21,22]

There are a few other terms used to express similar, yet not the same, meaning in robotic field studies. Researchers often use terms like "collaborative robots" [1], "sensor network" [23] to denote groups of mobile robots or/and mobile sensors. In addition, there is very special "weak robot" term [6,8] that was used primarily in the early beginning of the 21-st century. It mostly disappeared

ⓒ Springer Nature Switzerland AG 2018
A. Ronzhin et al. (Eds.): ICR 2018, LNAI 11097, pp. 291–300, 2018.
https://doi.org/10.1007/978-3-319-99582-3_30

in recent studies; yet, it should be mentioned since weak robots have a lot of similarities with swarming robots and the results of weak robots researches could be applied in swarming robotic systems development. This paper is dedicated to an attempt of defining a unique "swarm robotics" terminology and distinguishing it from other terms being used in the field of robotic groups. Furthermore, we structure and compare the previously proposed definitions and terminology of the field.

One of the first studies that mentioned swarm robotics as a distinct term was a paper by Gregory Dudek et al. [7] published in 1993. This study was one of the major triggers for multiple researches, which targeted for analyzing and classifying multi-agent systems. However, "swarm" definition and classification that were proposed by Dudek et al. were not globally accepted by subsequent authors. For instance, Sigihara et al. [26] and Suzuki et al. [27] used such terms as "many mobile robots" and "distributed anonymous mobile robots" in order to define robotic group capabilities as accurate as possible. Other attempts to identify "swarm robotics" term were made by Beni [1] and Sahin [23] in 2004. These studies distinguished robotic swarms between other forms of group robotics and proposed sets of properties to identify swarm robotics. These properties mostly remain constant until recent studies of swarm robotics done by Tan et al. [28] and Navarro et al. [19] in 2013.

2   On "Swarm Robotics" Term

As it was mentioned in the previous section, Dudek et al. first defined "swarm" term in a context of robotics in "A taxonomy for swarm robots" research paper. They referred to Beni's paper [2] that had been published in 1989 as to the origin, which had suggested to use a word "swarm" for a robotic group type. Dudek et al. proposed swarms classification that was based on multiple properties such as swarm size, inter-robots communication range, control topology, swarm homo- or heterogeneity. "Swarm" was defined as "a large number of smaller, simpler robots". However, the paper included multiple cases of using "swarm" term as a synonym to terms "multi-robot system" and "multi-agent system". It shows that swarm robotics concept was not yet established uniquely by that time. However, Dudek et al. proposed a reasonable taxonomy of MRS, which is still actual: this taxonomy was even used after two decades by Navarro et al. to separate swarm robotics from other types of MRS.

Next major attempt to define swarm robotics and classify it was made by Beni in 2004. He mentioned swarm robotics as a distinct field of robotics research and defined swarms through a set of the following requirements to be met in order to call a group of mobile robots "a swarm" [1]:

1. A swarm has a scalable architecture: there is no strict requirements for a swarm to include a large number of members
2. Inter-robot communications and sensing are limited to be only local
3. Scalability requirement determines distributed control topologies usage
4. Members of a swarm must be simple and quasi-identical

All these properties still remain in recent swarm robotics definitions and have only additions and refinements.

Sahin [23] made his research on swarm robotics terminology at the same time with Beni and specified a robotic swarm more precisely, excluding some types of collective robotics terminology from swarm terminology. In addition to all properties of Beni some new clarifications were proposed. Swarm members "simplicity" property was replaced by a "relative incapability" property; this definition is more precise because term "simple" is vague and it is hard to conclude unambiguously, for instance, if a particular type of quadcopters (that are often employed in swarm related researches) is simple or not. The quadcopters' capabilities may be significantly limited relatively to a task size, but even these capabilities may require complex hardware and software to operate in synergy. Next, Beni required swarm members be autonomous in a such way that they should be able to perceive information from an environment and interact with the environment autonomously. For instance, this requirement excludes sensor networks from swarm robotics. This is reasonable because of sensor networks dissimilarity with natural swarms, which inspire robotic swarms. Table 1 presents main properties of different definitions in an easy for their simultaneous comparison form.

Table 1. Swarm robotics properties according to previous researches

Dudek et al., 1993	Beni, 2004	Sahin, 2004
large number of members	scalable	aim for scalability
simple and small	simple	relatively incapable
inter-robot communication	local interactions	local sensing and communication
	decentralized	distributed
	quasi-identical members	a few homogeneous members
		autonomous

Tan et al., 2013	Navarro et al., 2013
large number of members	large number of members or scalable
mostly simple	incapable or inefficient
local sensing and communication	local sensing and communication
decentralized	distributed
homogeneous	mostly homogeneous
autonomous	autonomous
	cooperative
	knowledge aware
	strongly coordinated

A number of researchers provide similar to Sahin [23] concepts of swarm robotics (e.g., [19,28]) that specify the following properties:

- Scalability. Swarm architecture must be designed to be applicable with both small and large numbers of robots. This is essential for robotic swarms which are, theoretically, could have an unlimited count of members.
- Members simplicity. A single member of a swarm is incapable to perform a common swarm goal alone or/and multiple robots usage should significantly increase efficiency of a task performance. Therefore, achievement of the goal becomes dependent on the inter-swarm (i.e., inter-robot) communication quality and effectiveness.
- Local interactions. All sensing and communications are only local. This property is directly inherited and transferred into robotics from natural swarms: insects, fishes and birds are not capable to perform global measurements. Local interactions usage is a key to an easy scalability of a swarm; this increases the swarm robustness and flexibility.
- Control topology is distributed. Centralization limits scalability, therefore, all decisions should be made by swarm members independently.
- A swarm consists of a number of homogeneous robots. The swarm must easily overcome a loss of any of its members. The only way to provide such robustness is to make all swarm members as similar to each other as it is possible. This similarity gives both functional robustness and economical effect when a swarm cost decreases because of standardization.
- Autonomy: robots must be capable to perceive data from environment and interact with it. This property may seem obvious and redundant, however, it explicitly excludes sensor networks from swarm robotics.

In addition, Navarro et al. reference to MRS classification by Iocchi et al. [11] declaring that a swarm is a cooperative, knowledge aware and coordinated MRS and thus should feature the following properties:

- Cooperation. A situation in which several robots operate together to perform some global task that either cannot be achieved by a single robot, or whose execution can be improved by using more than a single robot, thus obtaining higher performance.
- Awareness. The property of a robot that reflects its knowledge about the existence of the other members of the MRS.
- Coordination. A sort of cooperation where particular actions that are performed by each separate robotic agent (viewed locally) take into an account the actions, which are executed by the other robotic agents in such a way that the MRS activity (viewed globally) ends up being a coherent and high-performance operation.

These properties need to be analyzed separately. Declaration of awareness is too strict for robotic swarms: as it is shown in [17,24], a swarm may have all the above mentioned properties, yet members of the swarm may perform tasks without knowledge about other members' existence. Moreover, a partial or complete unawareness cannot stop coordination processes [24], and robots of the swarm just react on other swarm members, as if the later were static or dynamic obstacles of the environment. A particular example in [17] demonstrated that even without inter-swarm coordination it is possible to perform a task of environment exploration. At the expense of optimality, the simplest robots could show swarming behavior. It is worth to note that swarm coordination is not always observed even in nature, for instance, insects in a case of high risk could act like distinct members, ignoring other swarm members and trying to stay alive even at the expense of other swarm members. Therefore, it seems unnecessary for swarming behavior to be coordinated and knowledge aware.

Nevertheless, the cooperation is very important to define swarm robotics properly. This property effectively excludes (from the swarm definition) such groups of robots that are not united to achieve the common goal. For example, a sequence of manipulators on a conveyor are not a type of a robotic swarm.

3   Swarm Robotics Relations with Other Collective Robotics Terms

This section explores the differences between various terms that are frequently used by researchers to denote groups of mobile robots and robotic swarms. Each subsection includes a clarification, which is related to some terms and a scheme in Fig. 1 combines our findings into a single structure.

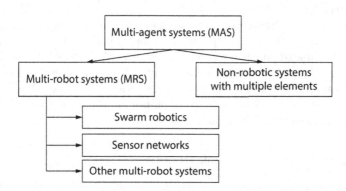

Fig. 1. Proposed relations scheme between MAS, MRS, sensor networks and robotic swarms.

3.1   Swarm Robotics Vs. Multi-robot Systems and Sensor Networks

Dudek et al. [7] use the three terms - robotic swarm, Multi-Robot Systems (MRS), Multi-Agent Systems (MAS) - as synonyms. Therefore, their pioneering approach was rather far from a modern understanding of swarm robotics definition, which, as we have described in the previous section, became very precise and well-defined with time.

First, we explore the differences between MRS and swarm robotics. Iocchi et al. [11] studied specifically MRS and proposed a very comprehensive MRS taxonomy. After more than a decade this taxonomy was used by Navarro et al. [19] to set the place of swarm robotics among other MRS. MRS in this context is a system containing multiple robots. This definition includes a very wide range of robots; for example, it includes both teams on the robotic soccer match as whole or sequential industrial manipulators on conveyor line. The provided examples are only multi-robot systems, they do not have any of the collaborative or swarm robotics properties that we have mentioned in the previous section. Swarm robotics studies multiple robots; therefore, it is worth concluding that any robotic swarm is a multi-robot system but not vice versa. Beni [1] also proposed to consider swarm robotics to be included into multi-robot systems as a subset. Such inclusion seems logically correct and, in our opinion, remains true.

Sahin [23] suggested a next clarification, explicitly excluding sensor networks from swarm robotics. This was made by adding the autonomy requirement to the definition of a swarm. Sensor networks members cannot interact with environment, and therefore, they are not autonomous in terms of Sahin. However, sensor networks are still a subset of multi-robot systems.

3.2   Swarm Robotics vs. Multi-agent Systems

A term "multi-agent systems" is not a purely robotics term, but is very broad and includes various non-robotic groups as well. It may be used to describe biological structures like insects colonies (ant, bees, termites, etc.), mammals societies, subjects of interest in psychological studies (people crowds, worker teams), economic theories participants and more others. In robotic studies, this term is used primarily in cases when a system is analyzed through ideal models of robotic members. Concerning robotic agents, they may have zero size, instant connection capabilities or very simplified kinematics. These models are quite far from practical usage, but there is an essential need in them when even theoretical feasibility of a particular task is in a doubt.

3.3   Swarm Robotics vs. Weak Robots

There is one more term similar to robotic swarms - "weak robots". This term was used a decade ago in studies dedicated to fully theoretical researches of multiple mobile robots possibilities. Robots denoted by this term have very special characteristics [5,6], which are described as follows:

- The robots are anonymous. The members have no identity and no way to distinguish them from each other.
- The robots are autonomous. There is no any central control unit or scheduler to control robots' behavior.
- The robots are disoriented. Robots do not have any common coordinate system(s) nor a common sense of direction. In particular cases even coordinate systems handedness (or chirality) are not common [8].

- The robots are homogeneous. All robots must follow the same program.
- The robots are oblivious. Robots do not have a memory storage to store results of previous computations or observations.
- The robots are have no communication. Robots do not have any direct ways to communicate with each other.
- The robots are able to observe all other robots. All robots have the ability to observe any other robot position at any moment of time.

Such requirements are far from practical usage: it is practically impossible to have a computational unit without memory storage device (at least, RAM) or positioning system with a capability to observe multiple robots positions accurately. This model was useful for theoretical estimation of robots possibilities in such strong limitations. However, due to the problems with practical implementations a concept of weak robots is not popular. While collecting the material for this paper, we noticed that this term was not used in new robotic studies for more than five years.

4 Discussion

The terms that were reviewed in the previous sections are easy to confuse with each other and they should be used carefully. Therefore, researchers pay a lot of attention to terminology used and there are multiple examples of proper terms usage.

Multi-agent systems term - is the most conservative way to denote a group of robots without a risk to identify a studied system type incorrectly. In addition, the principles that are designed for multi-agent systems generally could be used for non-robotic systems. For example, methods that were proposed for formation tracking [13], formation producing [9], formation control [29], and multi-agent tasks reviews - they stay actual for any system with multiple entities with desired properties (sensing and communication capabilities, kinematics, etc.). Such definition includes groups of people, flocks of birds and animal packs. Therefore, the more generic is the model being used, the higher is a chance for the system to be referred as a multi-agent. This determines MAS term usage in mostly theoretical studies, e.g., [9,20].

Multi-robot systems term is a narrower term, which is used in more practical cases, when proposed methods or algorithms are designed especially for using with robotic system, considering real robot limitations and properties, for example, a robot size, sensors' noise and reliability, communication bandwidth and instability, etc. Typically, they are tested in experiments to practically prove particular advantages of proposed methods. Experiment results in such cases become the most important part of the study, allowing to understand the significance of the research: an accuracy reached [16], an observed failure rate [15] and other properties. Swarm robotics is only a part of multi-robot systems and it is easy to distinguish between them, using definitions that we have given above. Therefore, using the definitions, it is easy to verify, that a system studied in [18] is a multi-robot system, but is not a swarm, as it was explicitly denoted in the research: robots used in the study are not identical and anonymous, there is a leader to follow and every robot can distinguish its neighbors from each other.

Swarm robotics has a very narrow and precise definition; therefore, researchers should pay attention to its usage. For example, a swarm that was proposed in [21] cannot be referred as a swarm because it uses specially selected "seed robots" for creating a coordinate system. In addition, there is a subtle difference with sensor networks, as it is shown in the example of [14], where a robotic swarm changes its form sensor network after deployment within an operating site. Additional examples of robotic swarms could be found in multiple forms: methods that include complex interactions [12], or on the opposite very simple stochastic systems [17] and bioinspired systems that directly transfer natural behavior onto robotic systems [10].

5   Conclusions

Swarm robotics is a fast-growing area of robotics. Researchers around the world propose new methods to increase localization accuracy, movement control stability, collaboration effectiveness etc. All the previously constructed foundation is used to find solutions of complicated tasks, including effective environment exploration, formation control, data transmission, while practical solutions are developing at the same time. As studies count increases, the terminology requires a revision in order to provide a proper level of unification and precision - even a unique "swarm robotics" term needs to be established. Since there are multiple types of collective robotics approaches and corresponding methodology, swarm robotics field terminology must be explicitly distinguished from others.

In this paper, we reviewed and refined definitions that had been proposed in previous researches of robotics field. We demonstrated relations between swarm robotics and concepts of adjacent fields including multi-agent systems, multi-robot systems and sensor networks. We believe that our attempt to contribute toward unification of swarm robotics terminology and classification succeeded to clarify distinctions between the terms that are often mistakenly used as pure synonyms.

Acknowledgements. This work was performed according to the Russian Government Program of Competitive Growth of Kazan Federal University.

References

1. Beni, G.: From swarm intelligence to swarm robotics. In: Şahin, E., Spears, W.M. (eds.) SR 2004. LNCS, vol. 3342, pp. 1–9. Springer, Heidelberg (2005). https://doi.org/10.1007/978-3-540-30552-1_1
2. Beni, G., Wang, J.: Swarm intelligence in cellular robotic systems. In: Dario, P., Sandini, G., Aebischer, P. (eds.) Robots and Biological Systems: Towards a New Bionics? NATO ASI Series (Series F: Computer and Systems Sciences), pp. 703–712. Springer, Heidelberg (1993). https://doi.org/10.1007/978-3-642-58069-7_38

3. Cornejo, A., Nagpal, R.: Distributed range-based relative localization of robot swarms. In: Akin, H.L., Amato, N.M., Isler, V., van der Stappen, A.F. (eds.) Algorithmic Foundations of Robotics XI. STAR, vol. 107, pp. 91–107. Springer, Cham (2015). https://doi.org/10.1007/978-3-319-16595-0_6

4. Dang, V.L., Le, B.S., Bui, T.T., Huynh, H.T., Pham, C.K.: A decentralized localization scheme for swarm robotics based on coordinate geometry and distributed gradient descent. In: MATEC Web of Conferences. vol. 54. EDP Sciences (2016). https://doi.org/10.1051/matecconf/20165402002

5. Dieudonné, Y., Labbani-Igbida, O., Petit, F.: Circle formation of weak mobile robots. ACM Trans. Autonom. Adapt. Syst. (TAAS) 3(4), 16 (2008). https://doi.org/10.1145/1452001.1452006

6. Dieudonné, Y., Petit, F.: Squaring the circle with weak mobile robots. In: Hong, S.-H., Nagamochi, H., Fukunaga, T. (eds.) ISAAC 2008. LNCS, vol. 5369, pp. 354–365. Springer, Heidelberg (2008). https://doi.org/10.1007/978-3-540-92182-0_33

7. Dudek, G., Jenkin, M., Milios, E., Wilkes, D.: A taxonomy for swarm robots. In: Proceedings of the 1993 IEEE/RSJ International Conference on Intelligent Robots and Systems, IROS 1993, vol. 1, pp. 441–447. IEEE (1993). https://doi.org/10.1109/IROS.1993.583135

8. Flocchini, P., Prencipe, G., Santoro, N., Widmayer, P.: Hard tasks for weak robots: the role of common knowledge in pattern formation by autonomous mobile robots. ISAAC 1999. LNCS, vol. 1741, pp. 93–102. Springer, Heidelberg (1999). https://doi.org/10.1007/3-540-46632-0_10

9. Ge, X., Han, Q.L.: Distributed formation control of networked multi-agent systems using a dynamic event-triggered communication mechanism. IEEE Trans. Ind. Electron. 64(10), 8118–8127 (2017). https://doi.org/10.1109/tie.2017.2701778

10. Hecker, J.P., Moses, M.E.: Beyond pheromones: evolving error-tolerant, flexible, and scalable ant-inspired robot swarms. Swarm Intell. 9(1), 43–70 (2015). https://doi.org/10.1007/s11721-015-0104-z

11. Iocchi, L., Nardi, D., Salerno, M.: Reactivity and deliberation: a survey on multi-robot systems. BRSDMAS 2000. LNCS (LNAI), vol. 2103, pp. 9–32. Springer, Heidelberg (2001). https://doi.org/10.1007/3-540-44568-4_2

12. Jiang, S., Cao, J., Wang, J., Stojmenovic, M., Bourgeois, J.: Uniform circle formation by asynchronous robots: A fully-distributed approach. In: 2017 26th International Conference on Computer Communication and Networks (ICCCN), pp. 1–9. IEEE (2017). https://doi.org/10.1109/icccn.2017.8038468

13. Kang, S.M., Ahn, H.S.: Design and realization of distributed adaptive formation control law for multi-agent systems with moving leader. IEEE Trans. Ind. Electron. 63(2), 1268–1279 (2016). https://doi.org/10.1109/tie.2015.2504041

14. Kim, J.H., Kwon, J.W., Seo, J.: Mapping and path planning using communication graph of unlocalized and randomly deployed robotic swarm. In: 2016 16th International Conference on Control, Automation and Systems (ICCAS), pp. 865–868. IEEE (2016). https://doi.org/10.1109/iccas.2016.7832414

15. Kohlbacher, A., Eliasson, J., Acres, K., Chung, H., Barca, J.C.: A low cost omni-directional relative localization sensor for swarm applications. In: Wf-IoT 2018 (2018)

16. Krajník, T., Nitsche, M., Faigl, J., Vaněk, P., Saska, M., Přeučil, L., Duckett, T., Mejail, M.: A practical multirobot localization system. J. Intell. Robot. Syst. 76(3–4), 539–562 (2014). https://doi.org/10.1007/s10846-014-0041-x

17. Li, H., Feng, C., Ehrhard, H., Shen, Y., Cobos, B., Zhang, F., Elamvazhuthi, K., Berman, S., Haberland, M., Bertozzi, A.L.: Decentralized stochastic control of robotic swarm density: Theory, simulation, and experiment. In: Intelligent Robots and Systems (IROS) (2017). https://doi.org/10.1109/iros.2017.8206299
18. Maeda, R., Endo, T., Matsuno, F.: Decentralized navigation for heterogeneous swarm robots with limited field of view. IEEE Robot. Autom. Lett. **2**(2), 904–911 (2017). https://doi.org/10.1109/lra.2017.2654549
19. Navarro, I., Matía, F.: An introduction to swarm robotics. ISRN Robot. 2013 (2012). https://doi.org/10.5402/2013/608164
20. Oh, K.K., Park, M.C., Ahn, H.S.: A survey of multi-agent formation control. Automatica **53**, 424–440 (2015). https://doi.org/10.1016/j.automatica.2014.10.022
21. Rubenstein, M., Cornejo, A., Nagpal, R.: Programmable self-assembly in a thousand-robot swarm. Science **345**(6198), 795–799 (2014). https://doi.org/10.1126/science.1254295
22. de Sá, A.O., Nedjah, N., de Macedo Mourelle, L.: Distributed and resilient localization algorithm for swarm robotic systems. Appl. Soft Comput. **57**, 738–750 (2017). https://doi.org/10.1016/j.asoc.2016.07.049
23. Şahin, E.: Swarm robotics: from sources of inspiration to domains of application. In: Şahin, E., Spears, W.M. (eds.) SR 2004. LNCS, vol. 3342, pp. 10–20. Springer, Heidelberg (2005). https://doi.org/10.1007/978-3-540-30552-1_2
24. Sakai, D., Fukushima, H., Matsuno, F.: Flocking for multirobots without distinguishing robots and obstacles. IEEE Trans. Control Syst. Technol. **25**(3), 1019–1027 (2017). https://doi.org/10.1109/tcst.2016.2581148
25. Sakai, D., Fukushima, H., Matsuno, F.: Leader-follower navigation in obstacle environments while preserving connectivity without data transmission. IEEE Trans. Control Syst. Technol. (2017). https://doi.org/10.1109/tcst.2017.2705121
26. Sugihara, K., Suzuki, I.: Distributed algorithms for formation of geometric patterns with many mobile robots. J. Robot. Syst. **13**(3), 127–139 (1996). https://doi.org/10.1002/(sici)1097-4563(199603)13:3⟨127::aid-rob1⟩3.0.co;2-u
27. Suzuki, I., Yamashita, M.: Distributed anonymous mobile robots: Formation of geometric patterns. SIAM J. Comput. **28**(4), 1347–1363 (1999). https://doi.org/10.1137/s009753979628292x
28. Tan, Y., Zheng, Z.y.: Research advance in swarm robotics. Defence Technol. **9**(1), 18–39 (2013). https://doi.org/10.1016/j.dt.2013.03.001
29. Xia, Y., Na, X., Sun, Z., Chen, J.: Formation control and collision avoidance for multi-agent systems based on position estimation. ISA Trans. **61**, 287–296 (2016). https://doi.org/10.1016/j.isatra.2015.12.010
30. Xin, L., Daqi, Z., Yangyang, C., Qingqin, L.: Formation tracking and transformation control of nonholonomic auvs based on improved SOM method. In: 2017 29th Chinese Control And Decision Conference (CCDC), pp. 500–505. IEEE (2017). https://doi.org/10.1109/ccdc.2017.7978146

Author Index

Printed in the United States
By Bookmasters